UNEVEN
DEVELOPMENTS

WOMEN IN CULTURE AND SOCIETY
A Series Edited by Catharine R. Stimpson

UNEVEN DEVELOPMENTS

*The Ideological
Work of
Gender in
Mid-Victorian
England*

MARY POOVEY

The University of Chicago Press

The University of Chicago Press, Chicago 60637
Virago Press Limited, London
©1988 by The University of Chicago
All rights reserved. Published 1988
Printed in the United States of America

97 96 95 94 93   543

Library of Congress Cataloging-in-Publication Data

Poovey, Mary.
      Uneven developments.

      (Women in culture and society)
      Bibliography: p.
      Includes index.
      1. Sex role—England—History—19th century.
2. Anesthesia in obstetrics—History—19th century.
3. Divorce—England—History—19th century. 4. Women
authors—England—Social conditions. 5. Governesses—
England—Social conditions. 6. Nurses—England—Social
conditions. 7. Sex role in literature. I. Title.
II. Series.
HQ1075.5.G7P66 1988   305.3'0942   88—4783
ISBN 0—226—67529—7
      0—226—67530—0 (pbk.)

For Jane Widseth

Contents

Foreword

Virginia Woolf's last novel, *Between the Acts* (1941), famously imagines a performance of that sweet but silly genre, the village pageant about Merry England's history. "The Victorians," muses Lucy, an older spectator, born during Victoria's reign, "I don't believe . . . there ever were such people. Only you and me and William dressed differently."

To which William retorts, "You don't believe in history."

This exchange reflects the distances between a visionary old woman, who has endured a whole life, and a nervous young man, with only a half-life to call his own. Helping to divide them are competing pictures of time that the late twentieth century has inherited. Lucy sees a deep unity of past and present. Prehistoric man, in swampy England, heard the same birdsongs as she does near her lily pond. William severs past from present. The past looms back there, a solid and self-sufficient block, different in fact and name.

Mary Poovey's new book, *Uneven Developments,* concerns Victorian history, especially the first third of the queenship that went on and on from 1837 to 1901. Its vision of the past mediates and questions the notions of both a William and a Lucy. Obviously, the past lives on in the present. Poovey shows how the religious discourse of the eighteenth century was entangled with the secular, scientific discourse of the nineteenth. However, unlike Lucy, *Uneven Developments* does not interpret "human nature" or "humanity" as a universal, constant entity or force. "Human nature" is an empty concept that various historical periods define, fill up—if and as they will.

Establishing such definitions is the ideological task of any culture. Poovey urges us to look at the beginnings of the Victorian period as an interaction among structures, processes, and human agency. If those structures and processes shape human actors, in turn the actors shape them. Poovey does not forget that people hurt, get hurt; have too much food, go hungry. Parliament, the courts, and an angry Lady Caroline Norton collide and collude. Once established, ideology is to organize these interactions morally, legally, and cognitively; to make sense of everything. A bundle of interpretative strategies and paradigms, explanatory narratives, and legitimizing stories, ideology is, in effect, the magnet of meaning.

The effort to understand the past, then, demands the sensitivities and skills of both the literary critic and the historian. Having such skills in abundance, Poovey warns us that the smooth surface of Victorian ideology, like that of an unhappy family keeping up appearances, is artificial and deceptive. Actually, ideology was "fissured," self-contradictory, contested. In brief, it developed unevenly.

A powerful and precise intellect, a supple and incisive reader, Poovey foregrounds the ways in which the Victorians constructed gender. Using the reductive, double categories of a binary opposition, they wrote up sexual differences as ontological polarity. Men and women were two radically different beings who inhabited "separate spheres." Women were redemptively maternal; the female body a "socially undifferentiated" womb. However, in part because of the persistence of the narrative of wicked Eve, Victorians quarreled over whether that flesh was decorous and controllable or devilishly wild and uncontrollable. Moreover, they could not reconcile an ideology that gave all women one maternal identity with the actualities of class, which obviously divided women materially. Encounters with racially different peoples, with the racial Other, which imperial adventures made inevitable, even further fragmented the unity that gender identity imposed on women.

In a series of chapters, at once systematic acts of historical interpretation and vivid case studies, Poovey examines the ideology of gender at work, and working against itself, in five major institutions: medicine, particularly its use of anesthesia; law, especially its codification of marriage and property; literature, newly professionalized, producing the narratives of modern subjectivity; education and work, which the figure of the governess brought together; and, finally, nursing. Representations of the nurse married, here with marvelous efficiency, two gendered narratives: that of the domestic, welfaring woman, and that of the public, warfaring man, whom she would tend when battles (including those for the Empire) got too bloody. Franchising this representation for an eager mass audience, Florence Nightingale simultaneously marketed a misrepresentation of herself as superefficient cosmic balm and healer.

To a degree, William is "right." The Victorians are history. However, their organization of gender is with us still. In a tautly argued conclusion, which examines our own discourse, Poovey shows the complex self-contradictions of contemporary feminist theory, which both erases Victorian ideology and reinscribes a universal picture of "woman" that ideology invented. An account of the modern genealogies of difference, *Uneven Developments* summons us to greater self-consciousness about our own acts. Nineteen years old when Queen Victoria died, Virginia Woolf, I believe, would have praised Poovey's rethinking of Lucy and William's England.

Catharine R. Stimpson

Acknowledgments

WORK ON THIS PROJECT WAS sponsored by research grants from the American Council of Learned Societies, the National Endowment for the Humanities, and the Swarthmore College Faculty Research Fund. In addition, both Swarthmore College and Rutgers University generously funded release time for me to write this book. Without the support of these institutions, I could not have completed this work. I also thank the staffs of the following libraries, where I conducted most of my research: the Beinecke Rare Book Library at Yale University, the Bodleian Library, the British Museum Library, Cambridge University Library, the Fawcett Library, the Greater London Records Office, the New York Public Library, the Philadelphia College of Physicians, McCabe Library at Swarthmore College, and the Wellcome Institute. A version of chapter 2 appeared in *Representations* 14 (Spring 1986).

I could not have imagined this book without the emotional support and intellectual challenge my friends have given me during the last few years. In particular, I thank Abbe Blum, Julia Epstein, Catherine Gallagher, Elaine Hansen, Ludmilla Jordanova, Leslie Katz, Judy Newton, Charles Russell, Carroll Smith-Rosenberg, Susan Snyder, Barbara Taylor, Martha Vicinus, Judith Walkowitz, and Carolyn Williams. My students at Swarthmore and Rutgers deserve special thanks for their forbearance while I was developing my ideas, and the numerous audiences on whom I have tested parts of this book have earned my heartfelt gratitude. Finally, my warmest thanks to Jane Caplan and Margie Ferguson, who, in their different ways, consistently pushed me to ask difficult questions while providing me the support I needed to find answers that would suffice.

CHAPTER ONE

The Ideological Work of Gender

In 1862, in an Essay entitled "Why Are Women Redundant?" the liberal manufacturer W. R. Greg addressed what he saw as one of the most pressing issues of his age. For Greg, the problem

> resolve[d] itself into this: that there is an enormous and increasing number of single women in the nation, a number quite disproportionate and quite abnormal. . . . There are hundreds of thousands of women—not to speak more largely still—scattered through all ranks, but proportionally most numerous in the middle and upper classes,—who have to earn their own living, instead of spending and husbanding the earnings of men; who, not having the natural duties and labours of wives and mothers, have to carve out artificial and painfully sought occupations for themselves; who, in place of completing, sweetening, and embellishing the existence of others, are compelled to lead an independent and incomplete existence of their own.[1]

Greg identified unmarried working women as a "problem" because he assumed that women normally "complet[ed], sweeten[ed], and embellish[ed] the existence of others" as wives and mothers. To Greg, women's natural role was indisputable—or, more precisely, if it *were* disputed, an arbiter was close at hand. "Now what does Nature say in reference to the case before us?" he asks, by way of definitively silencing skeptics.

> By dividing and proportioning the sexes, by the instincts which lie deepest, strongest, and most unanimously in the heart of humanity at large in all times and amid all people, by the sentiments which belong to all healthy and unsophisticated organisations even in our own complicated civilization, marriage, the union of one man with one woman, is unmistakably indicated as the despotic law of life. This is *the* rule. . . . [Those]

I

who remain unmarried constitute the problem to be solved, the evil
and anomaly to be cured.[2]

The central project of this book is to challenge Greg's assertion that certain instincts, however they are defined, "lie . . . unanimously in the hearts of humanity . . . in all times and amid all people." Instead of accepting the notion that "instincts" and a "natural" difference between the sexes delineate social roles, my project is to mark the historical specificity of this concept of nature, to point out the place it occupied in the assumptions by which the Victorian middle classes governed their lives, and to describe some of the material effects that this conceptualization of sexual difference facilitated in mid-Victorian England. In contrast to Greg, I assume that the representation of biological sexuality, the definition of sexual difference, and the social organization of sexual relations are social, not natural, phenomena.[3] In this book I argue that the construction and deployment of these images performed critical ideological work at midcentury, that they were intimately involved in the development of England's characteristic social institutions, the organization of its most basic economic and legal relations, and in the rationalization of its imperial ambitions. When Greg argues that unmarried women constitute *"the problem to be solved,"* he not only mobilizes assumptions about women; he also alludes to an entire social organization that depends upon naturalizing monogamous marriage, a sexual division of labor, and a specific economic relation between the sexes, in which men earn and women "spend" and "husband" the earnings of men.

The title of my book is intended to underscore the active role played by this complex interaction of images and social institutions in mid-Victorian society. I give the phrase *ideological work* two different emphases. In one sense, it means "the work of ideology": representations of gender at midcentury were part of the system of interdependent images in which various ideologies became accessible to individual men and women. In another sense, however, the phrase means "the work of making ideology": representations of gender constituted one of the sites on which ideological systems were simultaneously constructed and contested; as such, the representations of gender I discuss were themselves contested images, the sites at which struggles for authority occurred, as well as the locus of assumptions used to underwrite the very authority that authorized these struggles.

Both emphases are critical to the project of this book, for only when taken together do they convey the two guises of what I am calling ideology—its apparent coherence and authenticity, on the one hand, and its internal instability and artificiality, on the other. As I am using the term, an ideology is a set of beliefs—the "imaginary relationship of individuals to their real conditions of existence," as Althusser phrases it.[4] Ideologies exist not only as ideas, however. Instead, they are given concrete form in the practices and social institutions that govern people's social relations and that, in so doing, constitute both the experience *of* social relations and the nature of subjectivity.[5]

To describe an ideology as a "set" of beliefs or a "system" of institutions and practices conveys the impression of something that is internally organized, coherent, and complete, and in this introductory chapter I initially emphasize this guise of mid-Victorian ideology for the purpose of clarity. Yet it is one of the tasks of the rest of this book to reveal the other face of this ideology—the extent to which what may look coherent and complete in retrospect was actually fissured by competing emphases and interests. One of my central conclusions from this study is that the middle-class ideology we most often associate with the Victorian period was both contested and always under construction; because it was always in the making, it was always open to revision, dispute, and the emergence of oppositional formulations.

The system of ideas and institutions I examine here, in other words, was uneven, and it developed unevenly. This is the sense I want to convey by the main title of this book. This ideological formulation was uneven both in the sense of being experienced differently by individuals who were positioned differently within the social formation (by sex, class, or race, for example) and in the sense of being articulated differently by the different institutions, discourses, and practices that it both constituted and was constituted by. For some groups of people some of the time, an ideological formulation of, for example, maternal nature might have seemed so accurate as to be true; for others, it probably felt less like a description than a goal or even a judgment—a description, that is, of what the individual should and has failed to be. For some institutions or, for that matter, for some individuals or groups within institutions, an ideological formulation received one emphasis or was put to one use; while for other institutions, individuals, or groups, the same ideological formulation received a different emphasis and was used for another—even competing—goal. For these reasons, this ideology was also uneven in the degree to which it could manage or symbolically resolve the contradictions it necessarily contained.

Another way to formulate the subject of this book, then, is to say that it is about the unevenness within the construction and deployment of mid-Victorian representations of gender, and representations of women in particular. This unevenness not only characterizes the conservative ideological work of these representations, but it also allowed for the emergence in the 1850s of a genuinely—although incompletely articulated—oppositional voice. Each of the five chapters that follow focuses on a controversy that developed during the 1840s and 1850s; these controversies provide glimpses of the specific ways in which gender was simultaneously constructed, deployed, and contested—and the extent to which it was, as an effect and a cause of this ideological work, uneven. Despite concentrating primarily on only two decades, one country, one class, and one race, then, this book is about the conditions that facilitated change. It is about the specific instabilities of one ideological formulation and the sites at which that formulation was contested and its instabilities revealed.

I

Despite Greg's confident appeal to nature's "golden rule," the very fact that there were so many unmarried women at midcentury caused contemporaries to worry that all women could not—or would not—perform those tasks nature and their instincts assigned them. The scope of the "problem" had been widely publicized by the 1851 Census, which calculated that 42 percent of the women between the ages of twenty and forty were unmarried and that two million out of Britain's six million women were self-supporting.[6] Some contemporaries, like Barbara Bodichon and Harriet Martineau, addressed this problem by arguing for better educational and occupational opportunities for women.[7] For Greg, such solutions only compounded the "evil" society faced. "To endeavour to make women independent of men," he asserted, "to multiply and facilitate their employments; to enable them to earn a separate and ample subsistence by competing with the hardier sex. . . . Few more radical or more fatal errors, we are satisfied, philanthropy has ever made."[8]

If Greg viewed competing for work with men as the "evil" that "redundant women" inflicted on England's economy, then the "evil" with which they threatened the moral order posed just as serious a problem. This evil, which Greg only alludes to here, was epitomized in prostitution, a subject Greg had explored in an essay published in 1850. In his essay on redundant women, he merely reiterates the point he drove home in that earlier essay: if the disproportionate number of women could be diminished and their "value thereby increased, men [would] not be able to obtain women's companionship and women's care so cheaply on illicit terms. . . . IF men were necessitated either to marry or be chaste . . . so far from there being too many women for the work that must be done, . . . there would be too few."[9]

Greg's plan to "remov[e] five hundred thousand women from the mother country . . . to the colonies" is therefore related to his scheme to criminalize "the propagation of syphillis" (although *not* prostitution): both would solve the problems attendant upon expressions of sexuality that exceeded monogamous marriage. Greg consistently assigns responsibility for the moral laxity that perpetuates such sexual license to men, but the solutions he devises always address the supply side of the economic balance, not the sexual demand; that is, Greg always imagines removing or sequestering the women, not regulating male sexual appetite. The reason he imagines controlling women and not men is that, according to Greg, women are not dominated by the irrepressible drive that governs the sexual lives of men. Women's sexual desire is not a problem, in other words; men's sexual desire is, and it lies behind the problem redundant women have become. To underscore his point, Greg argues that even prostitutes do not fall because of sexual desire. "Women's *desires* scarcely ever lead to their fall," he asserts,

> for . . . the desire scarcely exists in a definite and conscious form, till they *have* fallen. In this point there is a radical and essential difference between the sexes. . . . In men, in general, the sexual desire is inherent and spontaneous, and belongs to the condition of puberty. In the other sex, the desire is dormant, if not non-existent, till excited; always till excited by undue familiarities; almost always till excited by actual intercourse.[10]

While Greg laments the sexual double standard, he accepts it (and prostitution) as inevitable. "We do not argue for the application to [men]," he concedes, "of a sterner code than, in the present state of human progress, could be borne."[11] The solution to the problem redundant women pose, then, is to get them out of harm's way, to send them to the colonies, where there are so few women that men will be forced "to marry or be chaste."

Greg's conceptualization of sexual desire in terms of sexual difference, not similarity, was accepted by most of his middle-class contemporaries.[12] This is only one formulation of what I take to be the characteristic feature of the mid-Victorian symbolic economy: the articulation of difference upon sex and in the form of a binary opposition rather than a hierarchically ordered range of similarities.[13] The message that the natural difference between "manly" men and "womanly" women dictated social roles permeated mid-Victorian culture in sermons, conduct material, and popular literature with such power and in such a way as to produce the norm that Greg invokes and to define whatever did not conform to that paradigm as an "anomaly" and therefore a "problem."[14]

The mid-Victorian phase of state formation and social organization was characterized by skirmishes among various secular and religious institutions for the authority to legislate social behavior. In chapters 2 and 3 I discuss two of the contests by which the medical and legal institutions began to wrest authority away from religious jurisdiction. But while I devote some attention to these contests, in the book as a whole I am more interested in the shared assumptions that underwrote these struggles than in the investments that divided contestants. Whatever their differences, I suggest, almost all of the participants in the mid-nineteenth-century battles for social authority assumed and reinforced this binary model of difference articulated upon sex.

The conceptualization of difference as a binary organization of sex had as an increasingly persuasive basis during these decades a new scientific representation of the body. According to Thomas Laqueur, ancient and Renaissance accounts of the body retained the Galenic model of an exact physiological homology between male and female reproductive organs that positioned men and women hierarchically on a spectrum of "heat."[15] By contrast, late eighteenth- and early nineteenth-century medical men began to represent the differences between male and female bodies and functions as a series of binary oppositions. Emphasizing the incommensurability of male and female bodies entailed foregrounding the role of the reproductive system, so that this difference was seen as more important than any similarities between men and women; it also entailed effacing other kinds of differences among members of the same sex, so that the similarity of women's childbearing capacity became more important than whatever other features distinguished them.

In 1843, when Theodor Bischoff observed spontaneous ovulation in a mammal for the first time, he was merely providing a scientific explanation for the principle most nineteenth-century medical men had already come to accept: the female of the species, woman included, was dominated by the involuntary periodicity of the reproductive system. The principles contemporary medical men linked to Bischoff's observation were far-reaching: not only could sexual difference apparently be proved incontestably by scientific means, but female pleasure was obviously irrelevant to reproduction.[16] If this model of periodic and involuntary ovulation marginalized the importance of women's affective participation in sexual intercourse, however, it increased the importance of another womanly feeling—maternal love. In fact, the model of spontaneous ovulation, along with other somewhat less well-documented biological "facts," was enlisted to provide a scientific explanation for what rapidly came to be considered woman's definitive characteristic—maternal instinct. In this, women even excelled over the females of other species. "The generative organs," W. Tyler Smith asserted, "reach their greatest state of development in the human species, and consist of parts adapted to coitus, ovulation, menstruation, impregnation, utero-gestation, parturition, and lactation—functions which are placed in relation to the highest affection and parental love."[17]

That maternal "instinct" was increasingly invoked by contemporaries to define woman's nature suggests that by the 1830s naturalistic explanations of difference were posing a serious challenge to scriptural explanations of the same thing. This instinct, theoretically, accounted for the remarkable fact that women were not self-interested and aggressive like men, but self-sacrificing and tender. Here, for example, is Peter Gaskell, writing in 1833.

> Love of helpless infancy—attention to its wants, its sufferings, and its unintelligible happiness, seem to form the very wellspring of a woman's heart—fertilizing, softening, and enriching all her grosser passions and appetites. It is truly an instinct in the strictest acceptation of the word. A woman, if removed from all intercourse, all knowledge of her sex and its attributes, from the very hour of her birth, would, should she herself become a mother in the wilderness, lavish as much tenderness upon her babe, cherish it as fondly . . . sacrifice her personal comfort, with as much ardour, as much devotedness, as the most refined, fastidious, and intellectual mother, placed in the very centre of civilized society.[18]

Maternal instinct was credited not only with making women nurture their children, but also with conferring upon them extraordinary power over men. Women may have been considered physically unfit to vote or compete for work, but, according to this representation, the power of their moral influence amply compensated them for whatever disadvantages they suffered. Here is Gaskell again, explaining the power of women's moral influence:

> The moral influence of woman upon man's character and domestic happiness, is mainly attributable to her natural and instinctive habits. Her love, her tenderness, her affectionate solicitude for his comfort and enjoyment, her devotedness, her unwearying care, her maternal fondness, her conjugal attractions, exercise a most ennobling impression upon his nature, and do more towards making him a good husband, a good father, and a useful citizen, than all the dogmas of political economy.[19]

The image of woman that Gaskell sketches here was further idealized by Coventry Patmore in the mid-1850s in the character of Honoria, the "Angel in the House." "Naturally" self-sacrificing and self-regulating, this domestic deity radiated morality because her "substance" was love, not self-interest or ambition. Claiming that love is woman's "special crown," Patmore draws her as the opposite and necessary counterpart to man, whose crown he calls "truth," a virtue that he characterizes as restless and self-conscious.

> For love is substance, truth the form;
>   Truth without love were less than
>   nought;
> But blindest love is sweet and warm,
>   And full of truth not shaped by thought;
> And therefore in herself she stands
>   Adorn'd with undeficient grace,
> Her happy virtues taking hands,
>   Each smiling in another's face.
> So dancing round the Tree of Life,
>   They make an Eden in her breast,
> While his, disjointed and at strife,
>   Proud-thoughted, do not bring him rest.[20]

The model of a binary opposition between the sexes, which was socially realized in separate but supposedly equal "spheres," underwrote an entire system of institutional practices and conventions at midcentury, ranging from a sexual division of labor to a sexual division of economic and political rights. In the chapters that follow, I describe some of the discourses in which this model was constructed at midcentury and the way the model was deployed to authorize these practices. In chapters 2 and 4, I discuss the different ways the idealized image of domestic woman was mobilized in arguments supporting the professionalization of medicine and writing. In chapters 3 and 4, I suggest that this representation of woman constituted the basis both for the oppositional economy that seemed to (but did not) rest on a binary opposition and for the fundamental model of male identity in capitalist society. On the one hand, this man was structurally suited to the alienated labor of the capitalist economy; on the other hand, his internal alienation (what Patmore calls his "strife") was translated into a narrative of personal development, which one woman inaugurated and another rewarded. Throughout the book, I argue that this image of woman was also critical to the image of the English national character, which helped legitimize both England's sense of moral superiority and the imperial ambitions this superiority underwrote. Finally, I demonstrate throughout how these deployments of the domestic ideal helped depoliticize class relations at midcentury, partly by translating class difference into psychological or moral difference, partly by setting limits to competition, and partly by helping subsume individuals of different classes into a representative Englishman, with whom everyone could identify, even if one's interests were thereby obliterated and not served.

Despite repeated invocations of the domestic ideal, despite the extensive ideological work this image performed, and despite the epistemological centrality of woman's self-consistency to the oppositional structure of Victorian ideas, the representation of woman was also a site of cultural contestation during the middle of the nineteenth century. These contests reveal, on the one hand, the extent to which any image that is important to a culture constitutes an arena of ideological construction rather than simple consolidation. On the other hand, however, the specific nature of the contests that mid-nineteenth-century texts disclose reflects the persistence in the domestic ideal of a historically specific and apparently antithetical image of woman. This is the representation of woman as Eve, "Mother of our Miseries." As late as the 1740s, woman was consistently represented as the site of willful sexuality and bodily appetite: whether figured as that *part* of man responsible for the Fall, as was characteristic of sixteenth- and seventeenth-century texts, or represented as man's foil, as in eighteenth-century texts like Swift's and Pope's poems, women were associated with flesh, desire, and unsocialized,

hence susceptible, impulses and passions.[21] For reasons that lie beyond the scope of this study, the eighteenth century witnessed the
gradual transformation of this sexualized image of woman as willful
flesh into the domestic ideal I have been describing. In the process,
woman became not some errant part of man, but his opposite, his
moral hope and spiritual guide.

   This transformation proceeded alongside—and was an integral
part of—the consolidation of bourgeois power and the redefinition
and relocation of the idea of virtue. Instead of being articulated
upon inherited class position in the form of noblesse oblige, virtue
was increasingly articulated upon gender in the late eighteenth and
early nineteenth centuries. As the liberal discourse of rights and
contracts began to dominate representations of social, economic,
and political relations, in other words, virtue was depoliticized, moralized, and associated with the domestic sphere, which was being
abstracted at the same time—both rhetorically and, to a certain
extent, materially—from the so-called public sphere of competition,
self-interest, and economic aggression. As superintendents of the
domestic sphere, (middle-class) women were represented as protecting and, increasingly, incarnating virtue.[22] Despite the fact that
women contributed materially to the consolidation of bourgeois
wealth and political power, their economic support tended to be
translated into a language of morality and affection; their most
important work was increasingly represented as the emotional labor
motivated (and guaranteed) by maternal instinct.[23] The domestic
ideal I have described, then, was a crucial component in a series of
representations that supported both the middle class's economic
power and its legitimation of this position.

   The rhetorical separation of spheres and the image of domesticated, feminized morality were crucial to the consolidation of bourgeois power partly because linking morality to a figure (rhetorically)
immune to the self-interest and competition integral to economic
success preserved virtue without inhibiting productivity. In producing a distinction between kinds of labor (paid versus unpaid,
mandatory versus voluntary, productive versus reproductive, alienated versus self-fulfilling), the segregation of the domestic ideal created the illusion of an alternative to competition; this alternative,
moreover, was the prize that inspired hard work, for a prosperous
family was the goal represented as desirable and available to every
man. Locating difference between men and women also helped set
limits to the groups that actually had access to liberalism's promise
of universal economic opportunities. If Samuel Smiles' cheerful for-

mulation of the effectiveness of "self-help" had been true in practice, after all, there would have been no limit to competition and no insurance that the power so recently consolidated by middle-class men would remain proof against the claims of other groups—not only women, but, more problematically, working-class men. Women helped set those structural limits, not only because they were represented as the group in opposition to which legal and economic subjects defined themselves, but also because of the more complex interplay I discuss in chapters 3 and 4. This process included generalizing the morality attributed to middle-class women to all women, translating the discrepancy between what one now has and what one could acquire into a psychological narrative of personal development, and subsuming the economic rewards capitalism seemed to promise into the emotional rewards that seemed available to every man in the castle of his home.

The place women occupied in liberal, bourgeois ideology also helps account for the persistence in the domestic ideal of the earlier image of woman as sexualized, susceptible, and fallen. The representation of woman not only as dependent but as needing the control that was the other face of protection was integral to the separation of spheres and everything that followed from it, because this image provided a defensible explanation for inequality. If women were governed not by reason (like men), but by something else, then they could hardly be expected (or allowed) to participate in the economic and political fray. Increasingly, from the late eighteenth century, the medical model of reproductive difference was invoked to define this something: when it was given one emphasis, woman's reproductive capacity equaled her maternal instinct; when given another, it equaled her sexuality.

The contradiction between a sexless, moralized angel and an aggressive, carnal magdalen was therefore written into the domestic ideal as one of its constitutive characteristics. Even though this contradiction was sometimes symbolically resolved by being articulated upon class or moral "type," it never completely disappeared from the mid-Victorian representation of woman.[24] In the chapters that follow, I identify some of the cultural debates that exposed the persistence—and effects—of this constitutive contradiction. In chapter 2, I turn to a medical discussion about childbirth—the controversy over whether to administer chloroform to women in labor—to show how conceptualizing women's reproductive capacity as *the* basis of femininity inevitably (if inadvertently) foregrounded women's sexuality alongside their moralized maternal nature. In chapter

3, I turn to a legal case, Caroline Norton's complaint that separated women could not keep their own earnings, to show how legal provisions to "protect" women also functioned to protect men against the aggression they feared women harbored. Chapter 4 highlights the symbolic work necessary to manage such anxieties about women's aggressiveness; through a series of substitutions, Charles Dickens neutralizes the sexuality he associates with some women, only to betray its imaginative persistence by the very labor with which he writes it out. In Chapter 5, I suggest that representations of governesses also alluded to women's sexual aggression, but I also show how feminists could rewrite this aggression as women's "capability" in order to argue for expanding the employment opportunities open to women. And in chapter 6, I show how women could use the contradictory nature of the domestic ideal to authorize ambitions that, in the case of Florence Nightingale at least, took them not only out of the domestic sphere, but away from mother England as well.

I call the issues I focus on here "border cases" because each of them had the potential to expose the artificiality of the binary logic that governed the Victorian symbolic economy. While it is arguable that all issues are potentially problematic for oppositional thinking because every case lies on the border between two defining alternatives, I suggest that those issues that are constituted as "problems" at any given moment are particularly important because they mark the limits of ideological certainty.[25] These issues were the site of such intensive debates, in other words, because they threatened to challenge *the* opposition upon which all the other oppositions claimed to be based—the opposition between men and women. Each of the issues I examine threatened to relocate difference—either to move it from the sexual to some other, cultural division (such as class) or to uncover it *in* woman, the very subject upon whose self-consistency the ideology rested. Either of these moves had the potential to challenge the social arrangement of separate spheres and everything that went with it: the sexual division of labor, the model of moral influence, the notion that there was some boundary to the alienation of market relations.

The discovery of the anesthesiological properties of chloroform constituted childbearing as a border case because, in making childbirth pain medically treatable, the anodyne opened the possibility that this most "natural" of all activities might be defined as "unnatural" in order to authorize medical treatment. That this occurred at a particularly critical moment in the professionalization of medicine also meant that the contradiction inherent in representations of the female body was exposed, as competing groups of medical men emphasized *either* woman's innate morality *or* her sexuality in order to authorize their own particular practice.

Divorce was constituted as a border case partly by the strain that the factory system, urban overcrowding, and the ostensible breakup of the family economic unit placed on the working-class family; partly, divorce acquired this position as a result of legal reformers' desire to rationalize the inefficient and often overlapping branches of the legal system. But divorce was not a problem in the same sense that childbearing pain became; whereas the latter was pushed from the category of the norm (health) into the category of the abnormal (illness), the former was pushed out of the category of the legal impossibility (except under very special conditions) into the category of the legally permissible (under certain carefully delimited conditions). In this sense, divorce became a solution rather than a problem; the problem it symbolically "solved" was presented by the Married Women's Property Bill, for that legislation would have constituted married women as identical to (not different from) men in relation to property, and *that*, as I argue in chapter 3, would have imperiled the symbolic economy that depended on and institutionalized binary oppositions.

The literary man (and I use that noun advisedly) came to occupy the position of a border case as a result of two sets of antithetical factors. On the one hand, technological developments in printing and papermaking made it possible for the publishing industry to feed and keep up with accelerating consumer demand; along with changes in publication practices that dramatically lowered the price even of new fiction, this increase in supply and demand positioned the literary man and literary labor at the heart of the mushrooming capitalist economy. But on the other hand, because of received (and recently elaborated) associations between writing and the expression of wisdom or even "genius," the literary man seemed immune to market relations; telling universal truths, he was— or should have been—superior to fluctuations in taste or price. The literary man—and the representation of writing, in particular— therefore became the site at which the alienation endemic to all kinds of labor under capitalism simultaneously surfaced and was erased. As I argue in chapter 4, the construction of literary labor as the exception that mitigated the rule of alienated labor had as one of its critical components the reinforcement and appropriation of another representation of nonalienated labor—the image of women's domestic labor as a nonalienated expression of a selfless self.

The 1851 Census was instrumental in the two dialectically related processes by which the unmarried woman was constituted as a social problem. On the one hand, in designating an "entire house" as the desire of "every Englishman," the Census simultaneously represented the middle-class domestic living arrangement as the norm and defined that norm as entailing both a particular (noncommercial) relation among the inmates of a house and a particular kind of house (one that was a "shrine" because it focused on "family and hearth").[26] On the other hand, however, in revealing that the proportion of women to men within the marriageable age-group of fifteen to forty-nine years was 107 percent, the Census demonstrated that this ideal was not even available to every woman.[27] In chapter 5 I argue that the governess was the prime example of what Greg called the "redundant woman" and that, as a consequence, she constituted the border between the normative (working) man and the normative (nonworking) woman. Not a mother, the governess nevertheless performed the mother's tasks; not a prostitute, she was nevertheless suspiciously close to other sexualized women; not a lunatic, she was nevertheless deviant simply because she was a middle-class woman who had to work and because she was always in danger of losing her middle-class status and her "natural" morality.

As Florence Nightingale represented and defined her, the nurse also occupied the border between the "normal" (domestic) and the "abnormal" (working) woman. But because of the particular ideological and professional contests I discuss in chapter 6, the Nightingale nurse represented a compromise between a series of normative oppositions rather than a destabilizing problem. Not a member of a religious sect, she was able to take up her "calling" without arousing religious controversy. Not a "strong-minded woman" like the would-be lady doctor, she was able to engage in health-care work without antagonizing medical men. Neither a mother nor a professional, she was able to nurture her wards and to supervise sanitary conditions; she was, in short, able to make the hospital a home and, in so doing, to enhance the reputation of an activity that had been degraded because it was traditionally women's work.

In these chapters, I discuss both the reason these cases were potentially destabilizing and some of the rhetorical and practical strategies advanced to manage the anxieties they generated or even to resolve their destabilizing potential. My argument here is that these border cases obey no inherent logic, nor do they accommodate or accomplish only one kind of symbolic work. The "problem" of female aggression, for example, could be conceptualized as female sexuality; in this form it submitted (rhetorically, at least) to medical definition, treatment, and (more or less effective) "cure." By contrast, however, it could also be represented as female "capability"; in this incarnation, it could be mobilized to "explain" women's success in such "feminine" activities as teaching or domestic nursing, but it could also be used to authorize expanding women's employment beyond the sphere that was supposedly home to women's nature. By the same token, the "problem" of female aggression was addressed and "resolved" by a variety of practical and rhetorical strategies, ranging from Greg's suggestion that "redundant women" be removed to the colonies (lest they become prostitutes in England) to Henry Mayhew's "explanation" that some (lower-class) women *did* experience sexual desire; for Mayhew, this sexuality was also a problem that had to be contained, for he saw it as the driving force behind all crime, poverty, and social disorder.[28]

Because the domestic ideal of female nature that I have been describing was both internally contradictory and unevenly deployed, it was open to a variety of readings that could be mobilized in contradictory practices. In the chapters that follow, this unevenness and these contradictory practices enable us to see both why this representation proved so resilient and how its artificiality began to become visible at last.

II

This may seem an odd book for a literary critic to have written. Very few of the primary texts I treat here are canonical literary texts, and I do not respect the boundaries of the texts I do examine, as formalist critics of all persuasions do. My strategy derives, in the first instance, from the fact that I have taken up a different object of study from the one literary critics usually analyze. The object of my study is neither the individual text (of whatever kind) nor literary history, but something extrapolated from texts and reconstructed as the conditions of possibility for those texts—what I have called the symbolic economy or, more generally, the internal structure of ideology. To identify this set of assumptions so as to delimit its internal organizing structure and its principles of operation, I have assimilated various texts, ranging from the official records of parliamentary debates to privately printed personal vindications, from *David Cop-*

perfield to medical lectures on female reproduction, from feminist analyses of work to defenses of domesticity culled from the pages of the *Saturday Review.* But while the primary documents I have analyzed vary widely in terms of their modes of publication and address, their position on the spectrum from entertainment to instruction, their audience and their politics, they have in common a middle-class authorship and, largely, a middle-class readership. In fact, in the sense that these texts articulate bourgeois values and, equally importantly, the structure of middle-class assumptions, they can be said to position their readers as middle-class individuals, even when a reader's actual class affiliation might not have been bourgeois.

My training as a literary critic shows up most explicitly in the methodology I use to interpret these texts. This methodology draws on the techniques and vocabularies of three contemporary interpretive paradigms, but the assumptions with which I approach texts significantly affect how and how much I take from each. The three paradigms that inform my work are post-structuralist versions of formalism, Marxism, and psychoanalysis. What links these three methods is their shared assumption that signification is not a singular process; signifying practices always produce meanings in excess of what seems to be the text's explicit design. This assumption underwrites my readings of the texts' implicit participation in the production and interrogation of the mid-Victorian symbolic order. It also helps explain why I discuss the multiple effects that texts produce rather than attributing to each of them some single, ahistorical meaning.

I share with formalists of all persuasions my reliance on close textual analysis. In the first instance at least, I focus on the local features and structural paradigms by which texts are semantically articulated and syntactically organized: these include both specific images and such organizational features as the patterns of repetition and the variations or transformations that derive from and alter these patterns.[29] In chapter 4, I argue that these patterns determine the reading of a text—not in the sense that they dictate a particular interpretation but in the sense that they construct the reader as a certain kind of reader and position this reader in a particular relation to the system of connotations to which a text gives specific form and in which it therefore participates. I am arguing, in other words, that the language and organization of any text make reading constitutive of the reader as well as of meaning. This constitutive process consists of a number of operations: establishing identification (which is governed by such formal features as point of view, mode of address, range of allusion and vocabulary); reproducing values and the symbolic economy that underwrites them (which is regulated by both connotation and the repetition of the structural principle by which the symbolic economy is governed); and providing various narrative paradigms that make the reading experience repeat, so as to affirm, the structure of the reading subject's identity (through such features as thematic closure, the consistency of characters, and both psychological and circumstantial realism).[30]

To discuss the ways in which a text constitutes its reader, however, is already to have transgressed the textual boundaries most formalists (including post-structuralists) set for themselves. In the chapters that follow, I deconstruct texts to reveal their internal contradictions and the artificiality of the "truths" they purport to tell. Nevertheless, unlike most deconstructive literary critics, I do not argue that there is nothing outside the text or that analyzing discrete texts is sufficient. Like critics such as Michel Foucault, Etienne Balibar, Pierre Macherey, and Fredric Jameson, I maintain that every text *works;* as an ensemble of specific discursive practices and as the outgrowth of a determinate mode of production, every text participates in a complex social activity.[31] Part of the work that texts perform is the reproduction of ideology; texts give the values and structures of values that constitute ideology body—that is, they embody them for and in the subjects who read. In this sense, reading— or more precisely, interpretation—is a historically and culturally specific activity; it is part of a public institution. As Gerald Bruns has pointed out in relation to the law, one does not have to read a set of specific texts to be bound by the conditions by which they were produced and given authority. Because texts "belong to traditions of understanding," which are effects of the social and cultural relationships that obtain at the moment of production, the conditions that govern the production of texts are reproduced in the texts themselves as the condition of possibility for meaning.[32]

This paradigm of interdependent and mutually constructive relation is crucial to both my conceptualization of causation and my organizational strategy in the chapters that follow. Despite my assumption that the conditions that produce both texts and (partly through them) individual subjects are material in the ever elusive last instance, I also maintain that this famous last instance *is* ever elusive—precisely because the material and economic relations of production can only make themselves known through representations.[33] The interdependence of material conditions and representations (as well as the interdependence *of* representations) means that causation is never unidirectional; as a consequence, the kind of linear narrative that many literary critics and historians employ necessarily obscures the critical complexity of social relations. Despite the fact that I recognize this, I sometimes provide such narratives in the chapters that follow. I do so partly because it has seemed to me necessary to remind readers of the sequences of events in which the individual texts I interpret were written and of the context in which they worked. Partly, such histories answer my own desire for narrative coherence. But I want to make it clear that I am aware of the artificiality of these histories and of the ideological work they perform in my own narrative. Ideally, an analysis of the social construction of meanings and the texts that participate in this process would contain no such unselfconscious, linear narratives, for the conventions that make these narratives meaningful are also socially constructed; they too are determined in the last instance by the material conditions I have been discussing here. Such an ideal is not attainable, however, partly because one of the effects of any ideology is to obscure the conditions of its own production, and partly because my readers and I can only communicate through the conventions of signification we share. I return in a moment to the compromise I have tried to strike in my organization of each chapter, but the effect of the self-consciousness I voice here will have to carry over into the rest of the book, where I occasionally represent the "real" as if it were a linear development that could shed both textualization and the quotation marks that signify that it is always a social construction.

My emphasis on interdependence also signals my primary departure from post-structuralist Marxists—my attitude toward class. I agree that class position is a crucial determinant of one's experience and consciousness and that class is one of the fundamental categories by which individuals are positioned within social relations and discursive practices. But I do not think that class position is always or at all times more important than other constitutive categories, such as gender, race, or national identity. In the chapters that follow I argue that in the late 1840s and early 1850s in particular, gender issues often displaced the more politically volatile issue of class so as to address and manage it symbolically, but I also point out that by the mid and late 1850s, the issue of national identity had assumed greater prominence in relation to both gender and class. My object here has been to examine the relationships among such categories. It seems to me that plotting the changing interaction of these determinants within a culture and within individual texts is more important than relentlessly subordinating any combination of these factors to an ahistorical master category.

The third methodology from which I both borrow and depart is psychoanalysis. My debt to psychoanalysis is clear in the language of the following chapters, for I use a vocabulary derived from Freud's conceptualization of the dreamwork to discuss the signifying operations of individual texts and the assimilated social text. The tropes of displacement, condensation, working through, repression, and symbolic action seem appropriate to the transmigrations and transvaluations of the images and themes I identify in these texts, and the idea of association (which is anything but free) is crucial both to the features I interpret and to my own interpretive practice. When I read a text or group of texts, my first move is to identify clusters of associated themes and images—whether the associations among these images are based on likeness (metaphor) or contiguity (metonymy). The clusters of associated images that reappear or occupy strategic positions in the text constitute my basic units of interpretation; I describe the text's operations in terms of how these units are broken up and redistributed in the text, the ways in which they combine or exchange terms with other associated clusters of images, and the extent to which they provide the vehicle in which thematic issues can be worked through by means of the symbolic resolution of contradictions or the management of destabilizing tensions. This is a *structural* psychoanalytic methodology in the sense that I interpret the organizational principles governing the production of meaning and not individual characters or writers. Unlike some psychoanalytic critics, moreover, I do not respect the boundaries of characters or texts. Just as a character is only one semantic unit in a text—the effect generated by associating a set of characteristics with a proper name—so too is the individual text only one semantic unit in a cultural field, the effect of certain conventions of authorship and closure.

The primary sense in which I differ from most psychoanalytic critics, in other words, is that I do not attribute signifying acts exclusively to individuals (whether individual characters, real historical individuals, or individual texts). Indeed, in general, I am less interested in the origin of discrete signifying acts than in their internal dynamics and interrelations with other signifying acts. If texts are parts of complex cultural economies, as I am arguing they are, then no individual can originate meaning nor can he or she contain or foresee the effects the text will produce. If even the unconscious and language (by which I mean conventions of signification) are cultural constructs, as I am arguing they are, then it is more important to examine the production and effects of meaning than its origin; it is more important to look at the structure and deployment of signifying practices than their "originality." Because I look at texts as participants in a cultural economy, my two extended analyses of literary texts in chapters 4 and 5 do not aspire to be "comprehensive" readings; instead, one of these readings intersects, and the other is intersected by, analyses of the cultural debates in which they participated.

This brings me to one of the most problematic aspects of my study: the problem of the individual. The concept of the individual is problematic for me in ways that it was not for the nineteenth-century writers I examine. In fact, for most of the writers whose works I analyze, individualism was a solution, not a problem. But one of my underlying points here is that the ego-centered subject is a historical construct, and I devote considerable attention in the following chapters to the ways in which this ideological image was produced, maintained, and deployed as a symbolic solution to problems it could not actually solve.

In chapters 4 and 6, I discuss the importance that the idea of the individualized subject held for midcentury Victorians, and in chapters 3 and 4 I discuss the contradictory structure of the individual in class society. But even though one of the projects of this book is to historicize the idea of the individual, I remain at least partly within the narrative paradigms underwritten by individualism. In conceptualizing the issues I address, I have found myself torn between focusing on individuals as if they were the agents of change and dispensing altogether with individual life stories in order to create the impression that individuals are merely points at which competing cultural forces intersect. The compromise I have reached may well be unsatisfying at both extremes: for some readers, no doubt, I rely too heavily on the biography of Caroline Norton, for example, to organize my discussion of the law; other readers will be frustrated when my discussion of the Married Women's Property Bill interrupts the narrative of Norton's life so as to question her status as agent. What I have tried to provide in each of the following chapters and in the book as a whole is closer to a fabric than a line of narration. I have tried to tell enough of each story to give the reader something to follow at the same time that I have woven several stories together in defiance of the integrity of individual stories, lives, and texts. The result, I hope, is an organization that reproduces the interrelation and process of mutual construction that I describe; in the book as a whole I have tried to describe the structural conditions in which certain changes occurred, without invoking a teleology, attributing causation to any single individual, or representing "history" as completely random or impervious to human intentions.

Thus, for example, one of the subjects I treat in this book is the emergence of an organized movement to improve women's social and economic position, and one of my aims has been to describe the ideological (and, to a lesser extent, material) conditions in which such a movement developed. Yet this book is not simply the story of that development; nor, having introduced that story, can I trace its origin directly or exclusively to the individuals who self-consciously affiliated themselves with it. As just one example of the complexity of causation, consider the role Caroline Norton played in this development. Norton was reviled by self-proclaimed advocates of women's rights like Harriet Martineau, and Norton herself explicitly denounced the "wild and stupid theories" that women should have rights equal to men's.[34] Yet, as I show in chapter 3, Norton's support for the Matrimonial Causes Bill indirectly provoked Barbara Bodichon and Bessie Parkes to organize the "ladies of Langham Place" because the passage of this bill forestalled legislative consideration of the more radical Married Women's Property Bill. One might even argue that Norton's pamphlets in favor of the divorce law did more for the development of feminist consciousness (although *not* for women's economic independence) than did the more explicitly polemical works of Mary Wollstonecraft or even John Stuart Mill. If changing women's position in society has entailed both making women of all classes conscious of their situation *and* winning concrete economic and political rights, then Norton has been as important a figure in the complex history of feminism as have more obvious protagonists like Barbara Bodichon or Elizabeth Blackwell.[35]

III

This example not only illuminates the complexity of causation; it also suggests how difficult it is to access women's participation in the developments I discuss in the following chapters. One of the most important debates among contemporary feminists has involved the ways in which women contributed to the construction and application of the domestic ideal, or, conversely, the extent to which we have participated in our own oppression. One reading of this history stresses women's ability to capitalize on and enhance the kinds of power that the nineteenth-century moralization of women and the feminization of virtue generated; another emphasizes the restrictions women suffered as a consequence of being idealized.[36] Both of these emphases perform important political work for late twentieth-century readers. The first can alert us to contributions women have made to state formation and economic development, because it urges us to reconceptualize power and to question the separation of the public from the private sphere. The second can combat complacency because it refuses to accept as straightforward triumphs women's participation in reproducing the dominant culture. Each position also has its political limitations, of course. The first *can* lead either to the idealization of women's separatism that a critique of separate spheres should undermine or else to the elimination of the possibility for *any* genuinely oppositional stance. The second can generate a sense of victimization among women readers that also defeats our desire to inaugurate change.

This is a vexed and complex debate, to which this book will inevitably make a contribution. In the chapters that follow, I do not focus exclusively on the advantages men have obtained by idealizing women, because I do not subscribe to the reading of history that casts women as helpless victims; but neither do I devote exclusive attention to the ways that women have used these representations for their own advantage, because I do not believe that "advantages" can be measured any more absolutely than causation can be traced. I have tried to highlight various forms of institutional and ideological work that these representations performed at midcentury without always analyzing exactly who benefited from this work. When I have highlighted the benefits women enjoyed—as, for example, in the opening of nursing as a respectable occupation for women—I have also suggested the other side of this gain—the extent to which benefits for middle-class women often translated into liabilities for working-class women and hence as a barrier to women's recognition of *either* the similarities of their gendered position *or* the extent to which class remained a factor dividing women into competing groups.

My argument is that both men and women were subject at midcentury to the constraints imposed by the binary organization of difference and the foregrounding of sexual nature. Sometimes, in fact, as in the professionalization of medicine, some men profited at the expense of other men as much as at the expense of women. In this, as in the other examples I explore, men were too thoroughly ensnared in the contradictions that characterized this ideology to be charged with being simple oppressors. Despite my assertion that all individuals are subject to ideological constraints, however, I do not want to lose sight of the fact that, as long as difference was articulated on gender, men and women were subject to different *kinds* of ideological constraint. Because they were positioned as nonexistent, women at midcentury did not have institutionally recognized power, no matter how much moral influence they could wield. When I emphasize early feminists' ability to reconceptualize the contradiction written into the domestic ideal or Florence Nightingale's ability to deploy this reconceptualization in the service of ennobling (some) women's work, I therefore do so in the context of reminding my readers that women's control over the terms of representation remained limited by the way in which the female sex was defined and positioned.

To argue that knowledge is socially constructed, as I do in this book, is necessarily to admit that one's own interpretations are part of larger social constructs and, as a necessary corollary, that they are ideological. To the extent that one can self consciously excavate one's own assumptions and narrative paradigms, ideology may be dignified with the name of politics, but there is no escaping the fact of investment; to adopt the position I have adopted is to renounce even the pretense of objectivity. This is not, however, to slide over into complete relativism; at any given moment, every conceivable interpretation and choice of materials is neither equal nor available, because one's own position within determinant institutional, cultural, and historical conditions dictates criteria of sufficiency, coherence, and validity that delimit (but do not exclude) personal taste. More concretely, this means that my choice of gender, instead of one of the other determinants I have discussed as a focus for analysis, is a function not of the absolute and ahistorical importance of gender, but of the coincidence between the importance this opposition held for mid-Victorian Britains and my own position as a white feminist within the Anglo-American academic establishment.

My self-consciously feminist argument here is that analyzing the history of gender is significant political work because it challenges the kind of truisms that W. R. Greg formulated in the 1860s and that other social critics reformulate now. While I acknowledge that my desire to question such commonplaces may have unforeseen effects that, in the long run of history, will be seen as reinforcing the status quo, I maintain that any challenge is important because it is an intervention—an intervention that may well disrupt processes already underway and that certainly will become part of the cultural contest by which new meanings are produced.

CHAPTER TWO

Scenes of an Indelicate Character: The Medical Treatment of Victorian Women

I

ON THE EVENING OF 4 NOVEMBER 1847, Dr. James Young Simpson, professor of midwifery at Edinburgh University, administered to himself and two colleagues yet another in the series of distillates, volatile fluids, and vapors he had been experimenting with throughout the summer and autumn of that year. Simpson was in search of the perfect anesthesia, an agent that could induce in patients the soporific state brought on by ether without ether's undesirable side effects. The vapor Simpson inhaled that night was chloroform, and its impact literally realized Simpson's ambition to "turn the world upside down" when it laid the three doctors under the table. As one of his contemporaries tells the story, Simpson awoke to find himself "prostrate on the floor," Dr. Duncan "beneath a chair . . . snoring in a most determined and alarming manner," and Dr. Keith's "feet and legs, making valorous efforts to overturn the supper table, or more probably to annihilate everything that was on it."[1]

Simpson lost no time in spreading news of his discovery to the medical community. On 8 November he first used chloroform in an obstetrical case; two days later he lectured on the subject to the Medico-Chirurgical Society; on 15 November he held the first public test of chloroform in the Edinburgh Infirmary and published a pamphlet on the subject, which sold fifteen hundred copies in less than two weeks. By the end of November he was using the anodyne constantly in his midwifery practice and urging all other medical men to follow his lead. But others were neither as enthusiastic nor as precipitate as Simpson. What he was later to call "the march of knowledge and science" was slowed by a debate that raged in the London medical journal the *Lancet* and in a flurry of pamphlets published between 1847 and the mid-1850s. The discussion abated somewhat after 1853, when Queen Victoria was administered chloroform for the birth of her eighth child, but it was still sufficiently vigorous in 1863 for the Royal Medical and Chirurgical Society of London to appoint a committee to study chloroform's physiological effects. The problem was that by that date, 123 fatalities had been positively assigned to chloroform—and this figure almost certainly fell far short of the actual number of deaths.[2] It had become apparent that no one actually understood how anesthesia worked, and by 1863 the medical community was sufficiently united to investigate the dangers apparently associated with both chloroform and ether.

The anesthesia debate is an important episode for my analysis of the ideological work of gender because the debate focused on childbearing—the capacity that most decisively signaled the physiological difference between men and women. By the mid-nineteenth century, women's social dependence on men was increasingly justified by reference not to woman's fallen nature, but to this biological difference, even though reproductive physiology had been formulated in terms of difference only since the late eighteenth century.[3] One thing we see in the chloroform debate, then, is the way in which the Church's traditional authority to assign individuals social positions—and to maintain the social subordination of women in particular— was being challenged by another institution at midcentury.[4] But what interests me most about this debate is not so much the contest it represents between spokesmen for religious and medical institutions, but the way in which the terms of religious discourse persisted in the new medical explanations in such a way as to limit the authority the newly professionalizing medical establishment was able to claim for itself. In this chapter I argue that the division among medical men about whether woman's nature—and therefore her difference from man—would be formulated primarily in terms of morality or physiology constituted an important impediment to the professionalization of medicine at the same time that it exposed the contradiction written into the Victorian image of woman. I return in the sixth chapter of this book to the form in which women were able to enter the medical profession, but in this chapter I do not address how nineteenth-century women perceived themselves or medicine—except, of course, in so far as what was represented as public opinion shows up in the medical men's representations of themselves. The texts for my analysis consist primarily of articles published between 1846 and 1856 in the period's major medical journal, the *Lancet,* the pamphlets either derived from or addressed to these articles, and a series of textbooks and medical manuals about women's physical and mental disorders written by medical men and published in or near this decade.

The debate about anesthesia first grew stormy in late 1847, when Dr. Simpson triumphantly announced in the *Lancet* that chloroform could produce what ether could not: deep anesthesia without an initial prolonged period of excitation.[5] At least some of Simpson's claims were soon corroborated by other medical men: because chloroform was more powerful than ether, less was necessary to produce the desired sleep; its odor and effects were more pleasant; it was less expensive, more portable, and required no special inhaler for application.[6] All of these properties made chloroform immediately attractive to surgeons in particular; like ether, chloroform helped transform surgery from a craft requiring speed and brute strength to a conservative practice in which careful dissection could preserve tissue that would otherwise be destroyed.[7]

By contrast to its rapid adoption in surgery, chloroform encountered vehement opposition in midwifery, and practitioners remained divided over the advisability of its use.[8] Instead of the physiological explanations a twentieth-century obstetrician might offer for employing or rejecting the anodyne, mid-nineteenth-century medical men implicitly or explicitly formulated their positions in relation to two issues that had less to do with the scientific properties of the anodyne than with the ontological nature of woman and medicine's proper relation to her.[9] The first of these issues was whether the woman in labor came under God's jurisdiction or man's.[10] This issue, as well as the fact that both clergymen and medical practitioners entered the debate, suggests the extent to which discussions of chloroform were part of the contest between medical and religious discourses for the authority to adjudicate women's social role. Both proponents and opponents of chloroform borrowed religious terminology at times, although all medical men were careful to infuse religious language with more naturalistic connotations. Opponents of the anodyne, for example, echoed clergymen's insistence that, because God's curse on Eve fixed women's labor in the no-man's land of "nature," anyone who interfered with childbirth threatened to "harden" society by attenuating this crucial link between man and God.[11] Doctors who held this position tended to emphasize the physiological dimension of nature rather than its relation to God, but their biblical imagery makes it clear that they sought their authority at least partly in the affinity of the two discourses. "To be in natural labour is the culminating point of the female somatic forces," argued the American Dr. Meigs. "There is, in natural labour, no element of disease. . . . I should feel disposed to clothe me in sackcloth, and cast ashes on my head for the remainder of my days [if a patient were to die from such] meddlesome midwifery."[12]

Meigs linked his complaint about "meddlesome midwifery" to the second issue raised in the chloroform debate—the epistemological and practical question of how a doctor could read, so as to master, a woman's body, which was so different from his own. If one conceptualized childbearing as "natural," then the doctor could assume, as Meigs did, that the woman's body would interpret its own condition more truthfully than could a doctor's medical expertise. When Meigs argued that the patient's responses to the question Does it hurt you? "are worth a thousand dogmas and precepts," he was simply adhering to the then traditional relation between a doctor and his patient, which privileged the patient's own experience of the body over any abstract theories the doctor might possess.[13] At the same time, of course, he was also implicitly blurring the line between the religious conceptualization of childbearing, which linked woman's pain to Eve's sin, and the medical conceptualization, which mandated that a medical man monitor, but not interfere with, the pain that was essentially a physiological effect of childbearing.

Simpson's response to such arguments also linked religious issues to what amounts to a theory of interpretation, but the way in which he engaged religious precepts suggests a more directly confrontational relation between spiritual and secular authorities. Written in December, one month after his discovery of chloroform, Simpson's "Answer to Religious Objections" offered seven counterarguments to those medical men who borrowed—rather than contesting—the authority of religion to dictate the terms of the debate. Simpson's answers ranged from an (inaccurate) etymological argument (he claimed that the Hebrew word for *sorrow* means muscular effort, not the sensation of pain), to a refutation of medicine's implicit double standard (if we take the Bible literally, he suggested, God's curse on Adam's labor should make the steam engine sacrilege), to an assertion that God's *real* intention was to empower men to relieve women's pain ("The very fact that we have the power by human means to relieve the maternal sufferings, is in itself a sufficient criterion that God would rather that these sufferings be relieved and removed"), to a reference to what Simpson called "the first surgical operation ever performed on man," which, of course, showed God employing anesthesia ("And the Lord God caused a deep sleep to fall upon Adam; and he slept; and he took one of his ribs, and closed up the flesh instead thereof").[14] Each of these arguments assumed

that women, like men, came under medical rather than simply religious jurisdiction because the complexities of the human organism
mandated the exercise of the most complex capacities God has given
man. As he gradually shifted the grounds of the debate from theological to medical terminology, Simpson revealed the critical place
that he assigned chloroform in rationalizing the doctor's intervention
in the woman's labor. This argument hinged upon Simpson's representation of pain.

Addressing Meigs directly, Simpson argued that the pain of
childbirth was not a simple side effect of physical stress—much less
a punishment for Eve's transgression. Instead of simply blurring the
boundary between physiological and religious categories by using
the term *natural,* Simpson conceptualized labor pain as a psychological product of the patient's mind; as such, pain could obstruct
the delivery of a child, because the "anxiety and dread" its anticipation provoked and fears about the "exhaustion and nervous
depression" that followed a painful delivery could inhibit the woman's ability to assist in the delivery. Because chloroform severed the
connection between the woman's consciousness and her body, the
anodyne could eliminate anxiety and ward off "those secondary
vascular excitements" labor indirectly caused.[15] What chloroform actually does, Simpson argued, is to split pain into two separable
components: the "severe muscular *efforts* and *struggles*" that the woman's body undergoes and the "*feelings* or *sensations* of pain" that her
mind would otherwise experience.[16] In recommending chloroform,
therefore, Simpson was recommending that medical men take control of the former, purely physical process by laying to rest the faculty
that suffered not only pain but, presumably, the guilt that was the
proper concern of religion. In the process of claiming childbirth for
medical expertise, Simpson's representation transferred to the doctor
the *knowledge* of pain by reducing the woman to a body; even if she
retained consciousness, then, the doctor could read this body more
accurately than she or any clergyman could.[17]

Beyond wresting childbearing from the jurisdiction and discourse of religion, Simpson's argument also had both practical and
epistemological implications for medical men. Practically, representing pain as separable from the patient's consciousness enabled
Simpson to represent the female body as a more passive object for
the accoucheur. As Simpson describes the patient, he rhetorically
constructs her as a child-bearing apparatus, a system of maternal
"passages" and "structures" open to the investigation and almost
mechanistic intervention of the medical expert. The "quiet and

unresisting body" he describes does not shrink from "the introduction of the hand into the maternal passages"; "this state of relaxation and dilatability" therefore renders "the artificial extraction of the infant through those passages alike more easy for the practitioner, less dangerous for the child, and more safe for the structures of the mother."[18] Epistemologically, representing woman as an "unresisting body" removed the grounds for any objections actual women might pose to the doctor's interpretation, just as representing pain as a two-part phenomenon divided the territory of childbearing neatly between the clergyman's (marginal) domain and the doctor's (essential) property. Chloroform, therefore, enabled Simpson simultaneously to claim the most important labor for medical men, to conceptualize the doctor's necessarily intimate physical contact with a woman in abstract and euphemistic terms, and to replace what Simpson described as the doctor's incapacitating vicarious suffering with a powerful feeling of having earned the thanks with which women rewarded his efforts.[19] Additional letters, collected by Simpson and printed in one of his pamphlets, fairly exult in the power with which chloroform could "lay the most restless or ungovernable patient quiet on her pillow."[20] "Screams . . . audible across the street" are silenced, an unsuspecting patient is put under "in spite of herself," and even the most recalcitrant women express "sincere gratitude" "for saving them from their agonies."[21]

It is important to recognize that, despite Simpson's physiological terminology, in none of these arguments was he arguing as a scientist. While concern for the patient's safety appears repeatedly in the controversy over chloroform and was no doubt paramount in practitioners' minds, neither Simpson's nor other doctors' arguments are based on anything remotely resembling what twentieth-century researchers would consider adequate or controlled experimentation. Some laboratory experiments were conducted, especially in England, but even those considered by opponents of chloroform to be authoritative—such as Thomas Wakley's one hundred experiments on animals—contained so many variables as to produce completely inconclusive results.[22] Even when experimental results were available, in fact, doctors were quick to interpret—or dismiss—them according to the practitioner's convenience, rather than to base their practice on these laboratory tests. Thus Dr. John Snow, who was certainly the most careful experimenter of all the practitioners who wrote about anesthesia, continued to use chloroform himself even though he thought ether safer because of the former's "ready applicability."[23] It was not unusual for correspondents to the *Lancet* to argue for or against the safety of chloroform on the basis of one application to a parturient woman.[24]

The point is that whether they borrowed or contested the theological terms in which woman's nature had traditionally been formulated, nineteenth-century medical men constructed their arguments about anesthesia on the same contradictory assumptions about female nature that dominated religious discourse. That these assumptions preceded rather than followed from physiological evidence can be seen in another issue that surfaced repeatedly in the chloroform debates. One version of this issue appears in a report Simpson delivered to the Medico-Chirurgical Society in July 1848, nine months after his enthusiastic adoption of chloroform. In this report, Simpson attributed the failure of English practitioners to achieve the same kind of success that Scottish doctors had achieved to a misreading of the anesthetized body. "Immediately before the chloroform produced anaesthesia," Simpson is reported as saying,

> more especially if there was any noise or disturbance, it not unfrequently excited the patient, who would talk incoherently for a moment or two, beg the inhalation to be suspended, perhaps struggle to get free of it, and have his [*sic*] arms and legs thrown into a state of strong clonic spasms. . . . In the English Journals such cases have been repeatedly and gravely recorded as instances of delirium, and spasms, and convulsions, and failure. They are not more anxious, or deserving of attention, than the same symptoms would be in a case of hysteria, and are quite transient if the inhalation is only persevered in.[25]

Simpson's passing reference to hysteria is telling, for what English journals repeatedly reported were not simply random "instances of delirium, and spasms, and convulsions," but specifically female displays of *sexual* excitation. Those few spasms that were reported in males were universally described as signs of fighting.[26] These reports had been appearing ever since the first successful inhalation of anesthesia, for ether, chloroform's immediate predecessor, had an even greater tendency than chloroform to stimulate motor and verbal responses. In an article published in 1847 and entitled "On the Utility and Safety of the Inhalation of Ether in Obstetrical Practice," W. Tyler Smith, a young practitioner from Bristol who was to become one of the founders of the Obstetrical Society, cited this excitation as a decisive barrier to ether's use. Smith claims to judge ether on a "physiological and pathological basis," but when he comes to "the occasional incitement of the sexual passion," it becomes clear that this, not physiology, is the heart of his objection.

> In one of the cases observed by Baron Dubois, the woman drew an attendant towards her to kiss, as she was lapsing into insensibility, and this woman afterwards confessed to dreaming of coitus with her husband while she lay etherized. In ungravid women, rendered insensible for the performance of surgical operations, erotic gesticulations have occasionally been observed, and in one case, in which enlarged nymphae were removed, the woman went unconsciously through the movements attendant on the sexual orgasm, in the presence of numerous bystanders. . . . Viewed apart from the moral considerations involved, there is not, in the whole of the wonders related of this extraordinary agent, anything more wonderful than this exchange of the smarting of the knife and the throes of parturition, not for mere oblivion, but for sensations of an opposite kind, pain, in fact, being metamorphosed into its antithesis. Still, I may venture to say, that to the women of this country the bare possibility of having feelings of such a kind excited and manifested in outward uncontrollable actions, would be more shocking even to anticipate, than the endurance of the last extremity of physical pain.[27]

As Smith continues, his interpretation of such displays becomes more elaborate. "In many of the lower animals, we know that an erotic condition of the ovaria is present during parturition, and that sexual congress and conception may take place immediately upon delivery. It was, however, reserved for the phenomenon of etherization to show that, as regards sexual emotion, the human female may possibly exchange the pangs of travail for the sensations of coitus, and so approach to the level of the brute creation." In an article written a year later, Smith would argue, like Meigs, that labor pains are beneficial, and, in offering a physiological explanation for this argument, he moves the concept of nature away from its moralistic context. Screaming, he wrote in 1848, opens a woman's glottis and thus "relieves the uterus of all extra-uterine pressure."[28] In this 1847 lecture, however, it is clear that what would soon become a physiological argument had its roots in an argument about propriety, the territory traditionally ruled by religious discourse. "May it not be," Smith writes in this early lecture, "that in woman the physical pain neutralizes the sexual emotions, which would otherwise probably, be present, but which would tend very much to alter our estimation of the modesty and retiredness proper to the sex, and which are never more prominent or more admirable than on these occasions?"

Implicit in Smith's description is the fear that, under ether, women would regress to brute animals, a state in which they would be beyond the doctor's control. It was to counter this possibility that Smith offered his paradoxical theory of a propriety "naturally" induced by pain—a theory, not incidentally, that ensured the doctor's ability to know what the woman really felt even when she "prominently" displayed its opposite: "admirable" modesty and retiredness. In this argument, Smith has moved a step beyond Meigs, for seeing sexuality where Meigs only saw pain prompts Smith to protect the doctor against being implicated in what he says the patient feels. Once more, Smith attributed this protectiveness to the "naturally" compliant woman: "chastity of feeling, and, above all, emotional self-control, at a time when women are receiving such assistance as the accoucheur can render, are of far more importance than insensibility to pain. They would scarcely submit to the possibility of a sexual act in which their unborn offspring should take the part of excitor; and as the erotic condition has been chiefly observed in patients undergoing operations on the sexual organs, we must assign as the exciting cause, either the manipulations of the attendant or the passage of the child."[29]

Paradoxically, Smith is representing woman as both an innately sexual creature and a being whose natural modesty and emotional self-control prevent her sexuality from obtruding on the medical men. One source of the confusion here is whether—or to what extent—physiology, which is indisputably the medical man's terrain, is the natural basis for morality, the domain that has previously been claimed by clergymen. Another is what definition of woman will prevail *whoever* acquires the authority to govern her: Is woman primarily a sexual or a moral creature? Is she man's temptress or his moral guide? These contradictory representations of female nature were inherited from the eighteenth century; they marked the contest between an earlier representation of woman as sexual and the domestic ideal that gradually displaced this image in the course of the century in a variety of discourses ranging from sermons to conduct books to novels.[30] The causes of this domestication, which was extremely important for both men and women, lie beyond the scope of this book, but what is important to my argument is the way in which the seventeenth-century representation of woman as essentially sexual was precipitated back out of the domestic ideal in the medical debates I am discussing. I explore in a moment the reasons why the chloroform debate returned this repressed figure, but for now I want to show the form in which the sexualized woman returned and the anxieties she aroused. The key to the latter is Smith's last phrase. If women are primarily reproductive, hence sexual, animals, then childbearing itself might be a sexually exciting experience in which no man is necessary at all. Smith's objection to anesthesia was that it would remove from female sexuality the only check to which it would submit, the "modesty and retiredness proper to her sex," but whether this "check" was "natural" or "proper" remains unclear and therefore problematic for Smith's argument.

Smith's concern reappears repeatedly in the chloroform debate. Dr. G. T. Gream, physician-accoucheur to Queen Charlotte's Lying-in Hospital and one of the most fashionable obstetricians in London's West End, was particularly outspoken on this point, but he was certainly not alone. One of his lengthy complaints before the Westminster Medical Society in 1849 prompted a fellow medical man, Dr. Tanner, to cite an operation "in King's College Hospital on the vagina of a prostitute, in which ether produced lascivious dreams."[31] So clamorous was the response that both John Snow and James Simpson rose to counter this charge. Snow simply pointed out that all "unpleasantness" could be avoided if a specialist administered chloroform; Simpson flatly denied that such scenes could exist.[32] "He had never seen, nor had he ever heard of any other person having seen, any manifestation of sexual excitement result from the exhibition of chloroform," he is reported to have said. "The excitement, he was inclined to think, existed not in the individuals anaesthetized, but was the result of impressions harboured in the minds of the practitioners." Collapsing Dr. Tanner's report with that of Baron Dubois, Simpson remarks that the experience of one "Parisian prostitute" with "lascivious dreams" should not be generalized to all women. "Surely it was," he retorted, "to say the least, very unbecoming to say that most English ladies should have sexual dreams (like one French prostitute) when under the influence of chloroform."[33]

In this exchange, Simpson was enlisting his listeners' assumptions about class and national character to bolster what he presented as a physiological argument: surely whatever "lascivious dreams" anesthetized patients might report were confined to those lower-class French women who dreamed such things anyway. But Simpson was unwilling to abandon the notion that, in childbirth at least, all women were more alike than different or to risk the success of his discovery to his claim that English ladies would display no compromising reactions. Instead of pursuing the argument about class (as some practitioners did), Simpson recommended a "large, over-whelming dose" of the anodyne as a precaution against the excitation that was so unpredictable and so easily misconstrued. By 1855, Dr. James Arnott had the temerity to suggest that Simpson's putatively scientific mode of application—the so-called Edinburgh method—had been developed not for the patient's safety, but precisely to protect the practitioner from such " 'involuntary confidences' and emotions" as light anesthesia was apt to produce.[34] Whether Arnott was correct or not, his charge points out the extent to which Simpson and Smith actually agreed about one essential fact: such "scenes of an indelicate character" were undesirable and possibly dangerous for the patient, the practitioner, and the medical profession as a whole.[35] I suggest that this shared preoccupation with propriety reveals that, in at least one important sense, the chloroform debate was not really a debate at all. Or—more precisely—it *was* a debate but *not* about the issues it purported to address. Instead of disputing the nature or position of woman with each other or with religious authorities, obstetricians on both sides agreed that woman was a reproductive creature who was, by nature, socially dependent on man but somehow morally superior to him. From this perspective, medical arguments can be seen as elaborations of the theological position, which refined—and provided a new language for—social practices that remained essentially unchanged. Nevertheless, the dis-agreement among medical men was fiercely argued because impor-tant issues were at stake: these included both the authority of individual medical men within the profession and the social status of all medical men. The real issue under dispute, then, was tactics: doctors argued about what treatment of women would consolidate the obstetricians' position within the profession and in society as a whole. I turn now to the model of the female body that both sides assumed, to show how it could ground not only both sides of the chloroform debate but also the professional dispute of which this debate was only a part. In the process, we see how the contradictory representation of woman that medical men inherited continued to pervade—and undermine the authority of—the territorial campaign they waged.

II

W. Tyler Smith's 1847–48 lecture series on obstetrics was the basis for his *Manual of Obstetrics,* one of the most popular and influential nineteenth-century textbooks on midwifery.[36] Written at a time when

Smith could have had little practical experience in obstetrics, these lectures nevertheless lamented—and set out to correct—the current poverty of knowledge Smith attributed to other medical men about the female body, and especially about parturition. "I venture without fear of contradiction," Smith states in the third lecture, "to assert, that nothing like a correct analysis or synthesis of the different forms of uterine motor action, no examination of the order in which the various uterine and extra-uterine actions of labour take place, or of the reasons why they follow each other in a certain definite and regular order, will be found in any of the works of British or Foreign writers on obstetricy." The subject deserves more attention, Smith claims, because "the uterus is to the Race what the heart is to the Individual: it is the organ of circulation to the species." As Smith continues, individual women dissolve into one enormous, universal uterus—a disembodied, faintly threatening womb, continuously generating offspring who seem dwarfed and short-lived in contrast to their great original. "Ages are the channels in which created beings circulate; and man passes continually from the womb of his mother onwards to the womb of time. . . . Parturition is the systole of the uterus, the unimpregnated state its diastole, and the living beings which flow on in countless numbers are as inconsiderable in the great stream of life as the myriads of globules revealed by the microscope are in the circulation of the blood."[37]

Smith's vision of a heartlike uterus had its counterpart in his assertion that, in any individual woman, this organ is "the largest, and perhaps the most important, muscle of the female economy."[38] Connected to all "distant parts of the economy . . . through the medium of the spinal marrow and its special incident excitor and reflex motor nerves," the uterus governs the entire female organism whether a woman is pregnant or not, and in spite of her mind, emotions, or will. "The uterus is altogether removed from the direct influence of Voluntary motion," Smith comments.[39] To quote another medical man, it is "as if the Almighty, in creating the female sex, had taken the uterus and built up a woman around it."[40]

The prominence of the uterus in representations of the female body points to the assumption held by almost all medical men that women, more than men, were governed and defined by their reproductive capacity. "The character and position" of women—indeed, their "value"—were all conceptualized as direct consequences of their procreative function. "No life seems so valuable as that of a woman in childbirth," Smith asserted.[41] Most frequently, this conclusion was reached by reasoning from the visible influences of the female reproductive organs, but it was so resilient that it could also be reached the other way around. As Thomas Laycock remarked, the "influence which the generative organs must exert over the whole animal economy, may be easily inferred from the general fact, that the final cause of all vital action is the reproduction of the species."[42] Even if a woman did not bear children, her capacity to do so dictated her health—or rather, her lack of health; in the absence of reproduction, "some other demand for the unemployed functions must be established. Accumulated force must find an outlet, or disturbance first and weakness ultimately results."[43]

The physiological mechanism on which Smith based the influence and centrality of the uterus is what he and other medical men referred to as "reflex action." The model of the human body implicit in this physiology is that of a closed system containing a fixed quantity of energy; if stimulation or expenditure occurred in one part of the system, corresponding depletion or excitation had to occur in another. For men, this theory anchored the so-called spermatic economy; for women, it grounded an economy that was perceived to be continuously internally unstable.[44] This instability was considered a function of what medical men denominated female "periodicity," a state inaugurated by puberty, signaled by menstruation, and epitomized in childbearing. Theoretically, this periodicity had no counterpart in the male; in the female it was considered so decisive because it was held to be so pervasive—even though the "periods" doctors described tended to dwindle into smaller and less visible units.[45] Thomas Laycock stated, for example, that menstruation "is only a multiple of the hebdomadal period. . . . Changes occurring every three-and-a-half and every seven days, as well as every two, three, or four weeks, come under this head." Some moments in this ceaselessly changing organism were thought to be particularly critical to its stability: "the fourth day, and the seventh, eleventh, and fourteen are critical days, and connect the doctrine of crisis with the menstrual period."[46]

The "doctrine of crisis" to which Laycock referred had to do with the recurrence in women of various nervous disorders, especially hysteria. Given a unified, self-regulating system subject to constant internal variation, the slightest irritation of any part of the system was imagined to upset the balance. The likelihood of disorder was further enhanced by the greater delicacy and sensitivity thought to characterize female nerves.[47] Given the "universal consent" that "the nervous system of the human female is . . . sooner affected by all stimuli, whether corporeal or mental, than that of the male," it hardly seems surprising that doctors thought women were subject to a bewildering array of physical and emotional disorders.[48]

This set of assumptions—that woman's reproductive function defined her character, position, and value, that this function was only one sign of an innate periodicity, and that this biological periodicity influenced and was influenced by an array of nervous disorders—constructed the woman as essentially different from man and, because of the quasi-pathological nature of this difference, as a creature who needed constant and expert superintendence by medical men. This set of assumptions was also the physiological basis offered for what was generally held to be woman's greater emotional volatility and for her artfulness or cunning.[49] Paradoxically, then, one facet of authorizing medical practice consisted of representing both menstruation and childbirth—the most "natural" of all female functions—as disorders. Parturition, Smith asserted, like menstruation, stands "at the boundary between physiology and pathology, being attended by more pain, and being liable to a greater number of accidents, than any other physiological act of the economy."[50] It is not far from this statement to Dr. W. C. Taylor's notion that "these monthly returns [are] periods of ill health" or even to the idea that woman is, by definition, disease or disorder.[51] Even doctors who did not equate periodicity and disease argued for a causal connection. Smith, for example, states unequivocally that "a great part of the pathology of hysteria consists in interruptions of the catemenial [menstrual] cycle."[52]

In 1866, Dr. Isaac Ray made explicit what was by then accepted as a medical "fact": "With women, it is but a step from extreme nervous susceptibility to downright hysteria, and from that to overt insanity. In the sexual evolution, in pregnancy, in the parturient period, in lactation, strange thoughts, extraordinary feelings, unseasonable appetites, criminal impulses, may haunt a mind at other times innocent and pure."[53] Seen in this way, hysteria was simultaneously the norm of the female body taken to its logical extreme and a medical category that effectively defined this norm as inherently abnormal.

The conceptual emergence of hysteria from childbearing, like the putative emergence of sexuality under anesthesia, reveals the contradictory implications of this representation of women. On the one hand, representing woman as an inherently unstable female body authorized ceaseless medical monitoring and control. But on the other hand, this representation of woman as always requiring control *produced* an image that always already exceeded the control that medicine could exercise. Before turning to the instabilities inherent in the medical representation of woman, I return for a moment to the chloroform debate. By showing how the model of woman invoked in this debate anchored a series of intraprofessional disputes, I can begin to suggest why this model produced uncertainty precisely where it should have fixed female nature.

III

When W. Tyler Smith addressed the issue of anesthesia directly in his ninth lecture on obstetrics, he embroiled himself in what turns out to be a characteristically circular logic. Once again, he was concerned about propriety and about whether "ordinary" women were "inferior animal[s]" or moral examples for men. Smith begins,

> My own observation convinces me . . . that sexual excitement is sometimes apparent during or after labour in a very high degree; indeed cases of this kind may pass into erotomania after parturition. . . . We should be bound to speak the truth in any case; but it would be most offensive to all the best feelings of our nature to suppose sexual excitement present during ordinary cases of labour, and it would certainly interfere very much with the confidence now placed in the obstetric practitioner. But no such suspicion need be entertained. Happily, human emotions are very much under moral control, and in women, almost universally, the utmost retiredness is preserved in everything which relates to childbearing and the puerperal state. . . . On a former occasion I pointed out that, in women, to whom ether-vapour had been administered during parturition, the sexual orgasm had been substituted for their natural pains—an exchange which women of modesty would more shrink from, than the liveliest agony. Under the chloroform, too, I have been informed of instances in which the lying-in room has been defiled by the most painful and obscene conversation. There appears, therefore, apart from considerations of safety, to be a moral objection to the administration of the anaesthetic agents now in use—one which should unite against them all men who desire to uphold the respectability of the obstetric department of medicine; for most assuredly, the present kind of attendance could not continue if the facts were understood by parents and husbands.[54]

A brief news item that appeared in the *Lancet* in 1854 underscored Smith's last concern. Entitled "Care in the Use of Chloroform," it warned British doctors about the unforeseen side effects of chloroform—or, more precisely, about the temptation the anesthetized patient might present: "An American practitioner at Philadelphia was lately tried and found guilty of violating a young lady while under chloroform. The jury recommended the prisoner to mercy, as it seemed probable the young lady was labouring under mental hallucinations from the chloroform. The case has created a great sensation in the hospitals and schools at the opposite side of the Atlantic, and suggests a word of caution to practitioners at home."[55]

The professional problem implicit in this scenario had stalked male midwives ever since they had entered lying-in chambers. It stemmed from the charge, set out at midcentury at great length by Samuel and George Gregory, that encounters between medical men and female patients were inevitably sexual. "Husbands have told me that they had no children," Samuel Gregory declared, "and wished to have none, if they must have a doctor to bring them into the world." Gregory turned to the French naturalist Count Buffon to explain this fear. "In the submission of women to the unnecessary examinations of physicians," Buffon writes, "exposing the secrets of nature, it is forgotten that every indecency of this kind is a violent attack against chastity; that every situation that produces an internal blush is a real prostitution." "An imposition upon the credulity of women, and upon the fears of their husbands," the introduction of accoucheurs therefore set up a dangerous situation midway between rape and solicitation. "Some women are attended by a half a dozen different doctors," Gregory moans, "—how much 'affection' is left for the poor husband?"[56]

To allow such doubts to enter the minds of husbands, Smith suggests, would be to jeopardize obstetrics. More specifically, it would cost obstetricians ground in their continuing struggle not only against clergymen for the right to claim moral authority, but also against female midwives for the right to dominate obstetric practice. "It should be the steady aim of every man engaged in obstetric practice," Smith declared, "to discourage midwife practice. This department of the profession will never take its true rank until this reform has been effected."[57] Despite Smith's claim, then, that "in Great Britain attendance by midwives is the exception," the vehemence of his attack on them suggests that he feared midwives to be more numerous and threatening than he admitted.[58] The threat was partly to doctors' knowledge: midwives, he says, too often hold posts in lying-in hospitals, where important advances in obstetric technique could otherwise be made. Such charity wards were nec-

essary to medicine's claims to scientific authority because only in
hospitals were lower-class patients available in sufficient numbers
and controlled circumstances to allow for any kind of applied research.[59] The threat midwives posed was partly to doctors' prestige:
the mere fact that a women's practice gave "birth" to modern obstetrics was sufficiently damaging to the reputation of obstetrics that
it prompted Smith to rewrite obstetric history in terms of an exclusively male genealogy.[60] The magnitude of the threat midwives were
thought to pose can also be measured by the fact that both proponents and opponents of anesthesia formulated part of their arguments as direct responses to midwives. Simpson, for example,
based his argument for anesthesia partly on the idea that it belonged
to the technology that distinguished "scientific" obstetricians from
untrained women, and Smith, like Meigs, formulated his objection
to anesthesia on the basis that it smacked of "meddlesome midwifery," the charge most often levied against women practitioners.
Simpson and Smith agreed that obstetrics should ground itself in
"principles" rather than empiricism or what they called "practice"
because practical experience was the area in which midwives justly
claimed superiority.[61]

From one perspective, then, the entire anesthesia debate can
be seen as displacing—although not completely containing—this
older and more virulent debate; from this, we can see that one reason
medical men retained moralistic terminology was to distance their
work from the concrete work of midwives. By the same token,
doctors' erudite arguments about nature and (pseudo)physiology
can be seen as attempts on the part of all obstetricians to distinguish
between themselves and midwives by moving the entire discussion
of obstetrical practice onto spiritual, philosophical, and scientific
terrain—terrain that women, equipped only with practical experience, could not enter.

From another perspective, however, when Smith linked the
elimination of midwives to the "rank" of obstetrics, he reveals that
this contest was itself displacing another struggle, that between obstetricians and other members of the medical profession for status
and the concomitant right to dictate the grounds of medicine's social
authority. This struggle raged partly because of the general level of
ignorance within the medical community about physiology and natural science; partly, it reflects the competing investments of various
groups of medical men that flourished in this vacuum.[62] The problem
was that even at midcentury, doctors still could not agree among
themselves about how, and on what basis, the medical profession

should be internally organized: Should individual medical men operate in a free market economy, competing for the custom of patients
on the basis of their medical expertise? Should they derive their
status from traditional social rank? Or should they claim the right
to a monopoly on the basis of some regularized training program
required to enter the profession? One sign of this internal disarray
was that in 1850 there were nineteen medical licensing bodies in
Great Britain with competing territories and qualifications and without sufficient power to enforce what sanctions they held.[63] Another
was the fact that between 1840 and 1858, seventeen bills were introduced in Parliament in attempts to reorganize medical education
and licensing; all but one of these bills failed.[64]

The crux of this professional dispute was that by midcentury
the traditional tripartite structure of the medical profession no longer
accurately represented the way medicine was practiced in England.
Legally, medicine was still divided into three branches: physicians,
who were trained in the liberal arts as well as medicine and governed
by the Royal College of Physicians; surgeons, who were descended
from the old barber-surgeons and governed by the Royal College
of Surgeons; and apothecaries, who were descended from shop-
keeping druggists and governed by the Apothecaries' Society. Despite this legal organization, however, as early as 1830 it was generally
agreed that very few "pure" physicians or surgeons remained. The
vast majority of medical men practiced physic and surgery, regardless
of which license they held, and most doctors dealt in midwifery and
pharmacy as well. Those who practiced all these branches of medicine were increasingly denominated "general practitioners"; by 1848
they were estimated to number between fourteen and fifteen thousand. Over half of these general practitioners held licenses from both
the Royal College of Surgeons and the Apothecaries' Society, but,
because of restrictions that were fiercely defended, none of these
men were allowed to sit on the powerful governing councils of the
Royal Colleges.[65]

These councils were largely run by the so-called consultants,
physicians and surgeons who held appointments to the charity and
special hospitals that had begun to proliferate in London in the
eighteenth and nineteenth centuries. These elite consultants were at
the top of the profession in terms of status, power, and income;
their substantial earnings were assured not only by teaching and
lucrative supervisory work, but also by the patronage of the wealthy
lay members of the hospitals' governing boards. These consultants,
whether physicians or surgeons, had an enormous investment in

preserving the traditional tripartite structure of the medical profession and the power of the Royal Colleges, for they wanted to protect their own privileged position by excluding from power all general practitioners, whose number was growing every day.[66]

The situation at midcentury, then, was that the majority of medical men, who carried out the vast majority of medical work, had no representation in the organizations by which medicine was officially governed, no access to research facilities, and no guaranteed income or social rank. In an interesting way, this inequity was both maintained and challenged by the ways that the two sides represented—and treated—women. Practically, the difference between the two sides is clear: whereas general practitioners almost always practiced midwifery and frequently built their practices on it, consultants almost never did.[67] The political ramification was that the Royal Colleges used the criterion of midwifery, along with that of pharmacy, as a principle of exclusion from their governing councils. The consultants' professed objection to midwifery was that it was manual labor, but their acceptance of surgery, along with such comments as that the practice of midwifery was "dishonourable" because it involved the "humiliating events of parturition," reveals that the objection was not to manual labor, but to this particular *kind* of labor.[68]

Consulting physicians and surgeons did not disdain the treatment of all female disorders, however. In fact, the nervous disorders I have discussed were the province par excellence of such expensive consultants. To authorize this treatment and not midwifery, consultants emphasized not the physiological aspect of the female body but woman's delicacy and modesty, which needed to be protected if her moral influence were to prevail. So, for example, when Dr. George Burrows, president and senior censor of the College of Physicians, testified in 1847 before the parliamentary committee that had been appointed to adjudicate this quarrel, he argued that the reason for maintaining the tripartite structure was that only such a hierarchy could protect the public by singling out an elite body of doctors who could exercise "the highest honour and utmost fidelity" to those "secrets of families" that they were required to hear.[69] For this office, medical expertise was less important than discretion—or at least the respect gentlemen accorded to men of their own class and to all ladies.

Denied all the resources that accompanied hospital posts, general practitioners' only hope for reform was to challenge the traditional criteria of status and to argue that medical expertise, not social rank, should be the basis of medicine's social authority. To accomplish this, they too invoked women. Because their investment was in midwifery, however, they emphasized not women's modesty, but the value of their reproductive capacity. Here is W. Tyler Smith again, addressing the relationship between the status of obstetrics, the status of women, and England's "standard of civilization." Notice what happens to the status of women.

> The excellence of obstetric medicine is one of the most emphatic expressions of that high regard and estimation in which women are always held by civilized races. The state of the obstetric art in any country may be taken as a measure of the respect and value of its people for the female sex; and this, in turn, may be taken as a tolerably true indication of the standard of its civilization. It may be declared as a truism, that obstetric science must flourish most in countries where the marriage tie is most respected—where women are held in the highest esteem.
>
> Long ago the philosophic Denman pointed out the influence which Christianity exerted on obstetric practice, by abolishing polygamy and enforcing a strict observance of the marriage tie—reforms which gave increased value and consequence to every means that science or art could devise for promoting the health and safety of individual women.[70]

Smith's claim that obstetrics *has* prestige is actually a plea *for* that status, and the key to that status is elevating the symbolic position of woman while fixing real women in their proper place— in relation to medical men in general and to obstetricians in particular. As he represents it, woman's proper place is in a monogamous marriage; as the legal state necessary to make children legitimate, the transfer of property patrilinear, and female sexuality controllable, marriage is the source of women's "respect and value" and therefore both the index to England's civilization and the cornerstone of its national identity.

Woman could be both the basis of obstetric prestige and its effect, in other words, because Smith *assumed* that female sexuality could be contained within monogamous marriage, which institutionalized both women's dependence and patriarchal property relations. But Smith's ability to assume that marriage was the norm for women in England and that patriarchal social relations were natural partly depended on his representing women instead of letting them represent themselves. Even more than with other subjects, the right to write about the body belonged to men at midcentury and to the medical expert in particular; partly for this reason and partly because medical practice itself was effectively closed to women, women, and especially female patients, were almost completely excluded from this debate. In the discussions of anesthesia published by and for the medical community (the primary site of these discussions), women were only quoted when their words supported a medical man's position, and even then these passages emphasized primarily the difference between women's unsophisticated attitude toward what they call "the stuff" and the doctor's scientific understanding.[71] This controlling representation also appears in medical men's tendency to define deliveries as "successful" even when the child was delivered "putrid" or, more graphically, in pieces, and it supported and was supported by a set of related truisms—that women's biology dictates their proper social role and that the maternal instinct is physiologically linked to women's reproductive capacity.[72]

It is important to recognize that the reproductive and silenced female body that results from medical discussions such as Smith's constitutes the basis for all of the debates I have set out—about the propriety of chloroform, the relative status of consultants and general practitioners, and the nature of medical authority. Reducing all women to a socially undifferentiated, reproductive body foregrounded the biological difference between man and woman in such a way as to authorize male-dominated medical expertise at the same time that this representation opened a space in which the contradictory meanings inherent in the domestic ideal could proliferate. Thus, consultants anxious to justify their moral superintendence could argue that woman is innately modest, yet dangerously susceptible to the advances of unscrupulous men and to smoldering, internal fires.[73] The general practitioner cum obstetrician let the emphasis fall on woman's reproductive, hence sexual, body, which periodically (but regularly) devolves to pathology; his role was also to protect her, but he did so with his instruments and by warding off "meddling" women. For obstetricians who opposed anesthesia, woman's body required constant monitoring, lest its inherent sexuality should overthrow modesty. For obstetricians who advocated chloroform, this sexuality had to be neutralized so that the body would display "structures" rather than desires.

The debates provoked by chloroform, then, constituted part of an intraprofessional dispute in which each side capitalized on the contradiction inherent (but generally repressed) in the Victorian representation of woman in order to authorize a particular medical practice. The problem with this strategy, however, was that the very duality authorizing these practices also produced at the site of the female body an undecidability that potentially undermined the authority of the profession as a whole. The threat posed to the profession by practitioners' own representations of woman took three related forms. The first was a nightmare version of laissez-faire market relations. If the female body would accommodate such contradictory definitions, there was no ground to limit competition among the various factions within the profession. Consultants might define woman as innately modest as a means of excluding from power any man who treated her as a reproductive animal, but in so doing they inadvertently aligned themselves both with clergymen, whose claims to authority also rested on emphasizing morality, and with gentlemanly "quacks," who, as even Burrows had to admit, often obtained the patronage of the wealthy without bothering to purchase a license.[74] General practitioners might define woman as a reproductive creature and argue that empirical knowledge of her body—and not moral or class superiority—should be the basis of medical authority, but as soon as they did so, they risked both foregrounding women's problematic sexuality and eradicating the distinction between themselves and midwives, many of whom had not only experience of a female body no man could have but also years of informal apprenticeship as well. Both definitions constructed woman in such a way as to authorize medical control, but the two definitions were inherently problematic and they implied very different roles for medical men.

If the contradiction written into the image of woman exacerbated competition among groups of medical men, it also mobilized an ambiguity that was potentially ruinous to the entire medical community's claims to expertise. One version of this problem emerges in representations of hysteria—a disorder that occupies a critical place in this discussion because of the kind of difficulty it posed, even for specialists.[75] The source of this problem, as F. C. Skey pointed out, lay in the peculiar nature of hysteria. As a disease whose symptoms could be feigned and whose organic origins were ambiguous at best, hysteria occupied the problematic border between somatic and psychosomatic disorders. Arguing that a doctor's first task is "to discriminate actual disease from no disease at all," Skey goes on to categorize hysteria as a disorder that, by definition, defies the available diagnostic categories.

> You would imagine this task an easy one, but it is not so.
> Diseases are feigned both wilfully and unconsciously; the first
> are generally detectable by a discriminating judgment; the sec-

ond are imitated by the hand of Nature herself, and are not so
readily detected. This factitious condition of the body, that
mocks the reality of truth,—that not only invades the localities,
but imitates the symptoms of real diseases in all the diversity
of its forms, deluding the judgment and discrimination of men
of even considerable experience in their profession,—is known
under the term *hysteria*.[76]

The problem here seems to be the body's capacity to mock itself,
but another way of phrasing the dilemma is to say that the medical
profession lacked a theory that could either establish a boundary
between the physiological and the moral or create some third arena
that lay between them. Given this lack (which a psychoanalytic
theory of the unconscious would soon be advanced to "solve"),
hysteria lay at the heart of the medical profession's double bind. The
inherent duplicity of hysteria, in other words, mandated retaining
moral categories at the same time that its physiological symptoms
both solicited and defied medical expertise. The impasse this caused
for doctors often provoked hostility, especially because the duplicity
frequently exposed the contradictory images written into the domestic ideal in a form that could not be contained or cured. When
Jules Falret, for example, alienist at the Salpêtrière, railed savagely
about the tendency of even genuine hysterics to "malinger" and
deceive, his fury was directed against the way hysterics hid their
sexual wantonness in ostentatious spiritual displays. "These patients
are veritable actresses," Falret complained; "they do not know of a
greater pleasure than to deceive. . . . In one word, the life of the
hysteric is nothing but one perpetual falsehood; they affect the airs
of piety and devotion and let themselves be taken for saints while
at the same time secretly abandoning themselves to the most shameful actions."[77] Falret's hostility is given another turn by Oliver Wendell Holmes's statement that "an hysterical girl is . . . a vampire who
sucks the blood of the healthy people around her"—a phrase repeated by S. Weir Mitchell, well-known American specialist on nervous diseases.[78]

One of these beset "healthy people" was, of course, the hysteric's attending medical man. The threat the hysteric posed in this
sense was a threat to the doctor's authority—his authority to define
the disease, to establish the course of treatment, to pronounce a
"cure" when symptoms could so easily be feigned. The version of
this threat that surfaces in the chloroform debate is suggested by
medical men's anxiety that women who had received the "impreg-

nation" of chloroform would become such "zealous missionaries" for the anodyne that they would override the doctor's judgment about whether chloroform was safe or advisable.[79] Simpson's pamphlets repeatedly refer to patients "eagerly," "insistently," "urgently" demanding "the stuff," and he even relates the story of one woman who, in the midst of labor, "secreted the handkerchief" so as to have control over her access to chloroform.[80]

Simpson and other pro-anesthesia obstetricians were reluctant to insist on medical authority in such cases because they wanted to enlist the enthusiasm of patients to help advertise chloroform; the argument that patients and doctors were simply obeying the logic of a free market economy could be so used in this period because neither the relationship between empirical practice and scientific theory nor the reliability of scientific knowledge had yet been institutionalized or generally accepted. Even the manner in which scientific lecture-experiments were sometimes conducted encouraged lay participation and suspended medical research somewhere between science and circus entertainment. In 1848, for example, a lecture on ether and chloroform held at the Royal Institute "attracted a very large audience, amongst whom were not a few ladies." At the end of his lecture, Mr. Brande administered chloroform to a guinea pig, which—to the lecturer's dismay and the horror of the audience—promptly died. In reporting this incident, the correspondent to the *Lancet* lamented the publicity of this debacle when he asked rhetorically: "Who among that large assembly, if the inhalation of chloroform should be at any time proposed to them,—who would not remember the fate of that animal, and dread its application to themselves[?]"[81]

As this incident suggests, entrusting the adoption of anesthesia to the enthusiasm of the public was frought with perils because, in the absence of any undisputed authority, the situation was too likely to get out of control. For opponents of chloroform, the very enthusiasm of the female public constituted a danger for exactly this reason; obstetricians might well be "dragooned" into accepting this or any other technology just because "conceited or ignorant women of fashion [made] a pastime of this as of other quackeries."[82] Even Simpson suggested this danger when he warned that "medical men may oppose, for a time, the superinduction of anaesthesia in parturition, but they will oppose it in vain; for certainly our patients themselves will force the use of it upon the profession."[83] In 1853, Dr. Robert Lee, who opposed chloroform, insisted that, by appealing to the public, the medical community had let the entire issue get out of its hands. The debate, he said, "had become almost an

extra-professional question," in which "appeals were made to the
natural timidity of women" alongside "a systematic concealment of
truth by physicians." Lee explicitly pointed to the twofold consequence of Simpson's deference to consumers: "the cause of science
and humanity [has been] placed in the hands of the most presump-
tuous and frivolous part of the community," he said, "while young
and inexperienced mothers [are] decoyed to their destruction."[84]

The third danger follows closely from the image of consumer
desire implicit in these depictions. This danger is suggested by Jules
Falret's reference to the hysterics' "shameful actions" and by the
metaphorical reference to the application of chloroform as "impregnation." One extreme version of the anxiety that underwrote
this danger appears in Robert Brudenell Carter's objection to the
speculum, "which he believed was avidly sought by women of all
ages and situations as a means of sexual gratification."[85] The problem
implicit in all these statements is the fact that medical practitioners,
in foregrounding female sexuality, were inadvertently—but inevitably—setting up a situation in which they were liable to be ensnared
by their own fantasies about sexual appetite. Partly because they
lacked the spiritual authority of clergymen, partly because their work
exposed them to direct physical contact with women's bodies, and
partly because their own self-authorizations capitalized on worries
about the conflict between sexuality and morality, medical men were
constantly exposed to their own and others' anxieties about sex. As
we have seen, medical men consistently tried to defuse the problematic aspects of sexuality rhetorically—whether through the kind
of spatial displacement by which Tyler Smith transformed the disembodied uterus into a heart, or through the consultants' relegation
of all inappropriate female assertiveness to the category of a quasi-
physiological disorder. But such attempts were doomed to failure
because the very condition of medical authority was the foregrounding of the physiological—read, sexual—nature of the human animal.
The anxieties this provoked lie behind the concern repeatedly expressed about medical men attending women in labor. "Let it be
known that [a woman] is accessible to the physician, and who that
pays the least regard for virtue would notice her?"[86] The representations implicit in this statement are mirror images of each other.
From one perspective, woman is a creature absolutely receptive,
hence infinitely susceptible to any man's influence; the corresponding representation of man is of a creature absolutely sexual, unbound
by social restraints, and desirous even of a woman in labor. Seen
another way, however, woman incarnates unfettered, insatiable sex-

ual appetite; before this creature, the attending physician stands impotent, deprived of professional authority and sexual power alike. That woman appears to these doctors to be sexually voracious at the moment at which she is most a woman—in the act of child-bearing—makes her sexuality that much more dangerous, for if the mother is sexual, monogamous marriage and all that follows from it can hardly be trusted to remain.

What medical men identified as sexuality in women is obviously as much a projection of what they feared or felt in themselves as it was what real women actually experienced.[87] Externalizing the problematic aspects of sexuality was, theoretically, one way of controlling fears about it. But in making anxieties about themselves dependent on their own definition and control, doctors set up an inherently unstable situation in which they had to regulate both feelings and fears that were externalized because they could not regulate them when they were parts of themselves. This is why doctors' representations of women always included representations of themselves as victims: the consultant was made complicitous by the secrets he had to guard; the obstetrician became the guilty partner in the woman's sexual display. Without even the underpinning of scriptural authority to explain, much less control, what they defined as women's sexuality, medical men found the very conditions of their labor enmeshed in the sphere of the sexual, which remained problematically suspended between physiological and moral governance.

As the dynamics of such projection suggest, foregrounding female sexuality as the basis for medical practice also threatened to collapse the very difference upon which the Victorian social order rested and which medical experts claimed to define more "scientifically" than clergymen could: the "natural" difference between the sexes. No one disputed the physiological difference between the sexes, of course; the issue was what this difference meant, in social and moral terms. If women were not simply moral but also sexual creatures, that is, or if the morality considered "proper" to the female was rendered problematic by the same kind of sexual desires that men represented as natural in themselves, then difference could less easily be *fixed* between men and women. If the socially operative difference was not *between* the sexes but *within* each individual, then women's self-regulation could less confidently be trusted to mitigate the effects of the aggression men assumed essential to their own nature, and women's social subordination could less easily be defended against those women (and men) who questioned the inequality of political and economic rights and the social division of labor.

To the extent that the contradiction written into the Victorian image of woman was exposed by the chloroform debate, this conflict implicitly called into question the natural difference between the sexes, upon which so much depended. As a man-made technology that made visible both the female organism's excitability and its susceptibility, anesthesia did not control women or adjudicate decisively between physiological and religious categories so much as it disclosed any body's problematic capacity to produce meanings other than and in excess of what the "exhibiters" of the technology intended. The debate about chloroform displays the extent to which medical men who used the technology were implicated in the "knowledge" it produced—for anesthesia generated at the site of the female body the possibility that the definitive female act could be accompanied by what looked like sexual desire—but which could be defined *as* sexual only by the men who controlled the technology. In so doing, anesthesia constituted childbirth as a problem—both in the sense that it was territory to be contested among medical men and between them and other social authorities, and in the sense that this most womanly of all acts revealed women to be more like men than medical science proclaimed.

The implicit challenge to the physiological definition of difference was partly the function of the competition among the discourses that sought to define female nature and, by so doing, to consolidate their own social authority at midcentury. To justify particular medical practices or account for physiologically unaccountable disorders medical doctors retained the moralistic categories traditionally employed by clergymen, and thus they mobilized a definition of woman that already had a history of contradictory meanings. The challenge I am describing here was therefore also partly a function of the contradiction so mobilized—the contradiction between the image of woman as a sexual creature that flourished in the seventeenth century and the domestic, idealized woman that gradually repressed this image in the eighteenth century. By foregrounding sexual difference as *the* decisive difference, medical men returned the earlier image of woman to prominence for reasons of their own. This prominence remained problematic, however, and therefore mandated the kind of ideological work I describe in this book, both because it continued to be at odds with the moral role Victorian women were expected to play and because differentiating between male and female sexual desire proved difficult as long as men retained a monopoly over the definition and government of what counted as sexual desire.

CHAPTER THREE

Covered but Not Bound:
Caroline Norton and the 1857 Matrimonial
Causes Act

WHEN LORD CHANCELLOR CRANWORTH INTRODUCED the Divorce and Matrimonial Causes Bill in the House of Lords in June 1854, he was carrying out the wishes not of women or the population at large, but of those reformers like Lord Brougham who wanted to eliminate the contradictions in England's matrimonial laws and divorce procedures. But despite nearly universal agreement that the procedures for obtaining a divorce needed reform, the bill was tabled and not introduced again until after the Aberdeen Coalition's incompetent handling of the Crimean War toppled the government and a new ministry took office in 1855. Under Palmerston, who served as prime minister until 1865 (except for a brief interregnum), sustained debate over the divorce bill was finally pursued in 1856 in the House of Lords, only to go to the Commons too late in the session to be passed. The bill was introduced again for a second reading in the Lords on 19 May 1857; there it was debated for four weeks before being sent to the Commons. After six weeks of heated debate and the passage of thirteen "material changes," the bill went back for the Lords to consider the Commons's amendments. There, proponents of the bill staved off a last-minute attempt to defeat it and the bill finally won the approval of the Lords. The first Matrimonial Causes Act received the royal assent on 28 August 1857 and became law on 1 January 1858.

The 1857 Matrimonial Causes Act and the debates that preceded its passage are important to this study for two reasons. In the first place, this act was the first major piece of British legislation to focus attention on the anomalous position of married women under the law. This anomaly was inherent in the common-law principle of coverture, which dictated that married women were legally represented or "covered" by their husbands because the interests of husband and wife were assumed to be the same; as a consequence, married women were not "bound" as individual subjects by contracts, debts, or some criminal laws. In addressing the issues of marital discord, separation, and divorce, debates about the Matrimonial Causes Bill called the public's attention to the paradoxical fact that in Britain, when a woman became what she was destined to be (a wife), she became "nonexistent" in the eyes of the law. In focusing attention on this paradox, the debates therefore raised the possibility that married women's anomalous position would be questioned and even changed. That this did not happen suggests how reluctant lawmakers were to examine their assumptions about women, the relationship between the sexes, and the gender bias of British law.

The second reason these debates constitute an important episode in this study is that, in acknowledging the fact of marital unhappiness, they inevitably exposed the limitations of the domestic ideal. More specifically, in publicizing the economic underpinnings of many marital disputes, the parliamentary debates threatened to reveal the artificiality of separate spheres, which was the foundation for the middle class's image of itself and its economic consolidation. During the first decades of the nineteenth century, partly because of the rudimentary nature of the British banking system and credit arrangements and partly because of the flexibility and fluidity of middle-class property, the personal reputation of a middle-class man became critical to his ability to obtain credit. For both symbolic and material reasons, the domestic ideal was crucial to establishing this reputation; as Leonore Davidoff and Catherine Hall have argued, a nonworking wife came to be considered "one of the fixed points of middle-class status," just as the right wife constituted an important source of personal connections and capital.[1] The ideology of separate spheres, then, both generated and depended on an arrangement of social and property relations that positioned women as moral superiors *and* economic dependents; indeed, for reasons I address in the next chapter, women's moral superiority was inextricably bound to their economic dependency. The naturalization of these relations during the first half of the nineteenth century involved both the articulation of difference in biological terms, as I have already suggested, and the representation of the domestic sphere as a protected territory, in which women's naturally self-sacrificing—because maternal—nature could achieve its fullest expression and influence. As the divorce debates raised the specter of marital discord, and as they uncovered in particular the vulnerability that could accompany women's economic dependence, they threatened to destabilize the ideal on which so much depended. As the victim and publicist of precisely this kind of marital distress, Caroline Norton occupies a crucial position in my analysis of the debates—even though, as we will see, her political position was as attenuated as was her legal relation to the money she earned and the children she bore.

Certain difficulties, which confront anyone attempting to analyze the making of British law, have shaped my methodology in this chapter. Because British law includes the three discrete, overlapping, and sometimes competing systems of common law, statute law, and case law, it cannot be discussed as if it were a unified system of principles and prohibitions.[2] Indeed, sometimes no single principle emerges from the various judgments levied in its name. Thus, for example, statute law, in so far as it took the form of protective legislation at midcentury, implicitly embodied the assumption that women were by nature passive; case law, on the other hand, as articulated in courtroom procedures and judicial decisions concerning rape, vagrancy, and prostitution, implied that female sexuality was an aggressive force requiring regulation and control.[3] We see in this discrepancy the same contradiction that medical practitioners exposed in their discussions of the female body. Moreover, just as the medical practices I have described functioned partly to control the effects of the contradiction written into the image of women, so too did protective legislation, which simultaneously acknowledged women's vulnerability and effectively limited their activities. Although I return to the issue of protection, such complexities generally lie beyond the scope of this book. Instead of addressing the internal contradictions of the enforcement of matrimonial and other sex-related laws, I discuss only the process by which the 1857 Matrimonial Causes Act was passed. I am interested in particular in the implicit assumptions about woman's nature and social role that set limits to the kinds of questions that could be asked in this debate and the solutions that could be adopted. To locate these, I generally treat the 1854, 1856, and 1857 parliamentary debates about divorce— and the 1857 debates about married women's property—as parts of one discussion, even though the timing and politics of a discussion are occasionally as important as its explicit content. The assumptions about gender and class that emerge in these debates were maintained to different degrees by different men and articulated in different ways, but they nevertheless reappear within discussions that otherwise ranged widely across the spectrum of political opinions and class interests. Against the background of war and international negotiations, as governments rose and fell and women like Caroline Norton complained about the law's neglect, the discussions about marriage and divorce continued, repeatedly returning to the same issues, repeatedly turning away from the possibility that men and women could be equal under the law.

I

Divorce was brought to Parliament's attention at midcentury by a number of social and economic factors, one of the most important of which was the strain placed on the working-class family unit by the factory system of labor. The rapid population growth and urbanization of the first half of the century compounded this strain, and, as overcrowding and competition for work intensified, working-class couples were subjected to increasingly complex external pressures for which domestic relationships could not possibly compensate and which they often could not survive. As one response to these problems, the pressure for family law reform mounted among radical groups like the Owenite socialists and Chartists and Utilitarians as well as reformers like Jeremy Bentham and John Stuart Mill. These groups did not always want the same things, but they generally agreed that cumbersome and contradictory legal machinery prevented the state from addressing social injustice and the problems of industrialization. The Law Amendment Society, founded by Lord Brougham in 1844, had the express design of accelerating the rationalization of the entire legal system, one aspect of which involved ending the Church's jurisdiction over matrimonial causes. Parliament had already taken up the subject of divorce in 1830, but Dr. Phillimore's motion to create a Royal Commission on Ecclesiastical Courts had been defeated. In 1850, partly because of pressure from the LAS, Prime Minister Lord Russell finally appointed a Royal Commission on the Law of Divorce, which he charged with considering what kinds of divorce or separation should be allowed, what courts should adjudicate matrimonial causes, and what grounds should justify divorce or separation. Its report, issued in 1853, provided the basis for the Matrimonial Causes Bill introduced in the Lords by Lord Cranworth in 1854.[4]

Throughout the debates about the divorce bill in both houses of Parliament, one idea united advocates and opponents: the laws governing divorce should be made consistent. Given the laws at midcentury, this would necessitate resolving three related anomalies: the procedural discrepancy between the methods for obtaining a divorce *a mensa et thoro,* on the one hand, and a divorce *a vinculo* on the other; the class inequity that resulted from the expense of both of these procedures; and the national differences between the laws governing divorce in Scotland and the more rigid laws of England.

The procedural anomaly was the legacy of England's complex religious history, for it marked the lingering coexistence of Roman Catholic practices with those that dated from the Reformation. Divorce *a mensa et thoro*—literally divorce from bed and board, which we would call legal separation—was the remnant of the Church's express desire to discourage conjugal delinquency. Divorce *a mensa* was initiated by petition from either husband or wife to the ecclesiastical courts, which had jurisdiction over these cases under canon law. Three grounds were recognized—adultery, sodomy, and (physical) cruelty; the procedure cost from £300 to £500 (when uncontested); and, if granted, the divorce relieved the two parties from the obligation to cohabit but forbade remarriage by either party. Divorce *a mensa* did not end the husband's rights to his wife's property.[5] During the late seventeenth century, as a result of the power Parliament had acquired during the Reformation, another form of divorce was developed to sidestep the Church's ban on remarriage and, more specifically, to make adequate provisions to protect property. Divorce *a vinculo* ensured that aristocrats would have legitimate heirs, even when they had unfaithful wives, by means of a private parliamentary bill—a procedure more regular and less visibly corrupt than the late sixteenth-century practice of the Catholic church's selling papal dispensations for absolute divorce in order to raise revenue.[6] The procedure that had developed for obtaining an absolute divorce was more complex than the action for divorce *a mensa*. Assuming that an aggrieved husband desired divorce because of his wife's adultery (the usual case), this procedure generally involved three steps, which were gradually regularized during the course of the eighteenth century. First, the man had to petition the ecclesiastical courts successfully for a divorce *a mensa*. Second, he had to bring suit in an ecclesiastical court or a common-law court for monetary damages against a correspondant in his wife's adultery. (The wife, whose alleged adultery was made public by the charge of "criminal conversation," was not represented in this trial.) Third, the husband presented a private bill by counsel to the House of Lords. The same bill then went to the Commons, and if all these actions were successful, the monarch would give the royal assent and the plaintiff would be free to marry again. Divorce *a vinculo* ended both the husband's property rights over his wife and his responsibility for her debts. When Mr. Justice Maule explained these procedures in 1845 in a widely publicized bigamy trial, he estimated the expense of a divorce *a vinculo* to be £1,000.[7] The prisoner's mournful reply—"Ah my Lord, I never was worth a thousand pence in all my life"—aptly points to the class bias of the procedure: under the current state of law, absolute divorce (or "relief") was effectively beyond the reach of all but the wealthiest English men.[8]

The third structural anomaly, the discrepancies between Scottish and English law, seemed as "monstrous" to most legislators as the blatant class inequity of "one law for the poor, and another for the rich." Lord Lyndhurst, who opposed the government's bill in the Lords in 1856 because it did not afford enough protection for women, stated the common opinion when he said, "What greatly strikes the minds of people is, that all law should be equal." "How monstrous is it, then," he continued, "that the law on a subject of so much importance, coming home, as it were, to every one's fireside, should be so different in different parts of the United Kingdom."[9] The two primary differences between the Scottish and English laws were that in Scotland, divorce was much simpler and less costly than in England, and in Scotland, men and women alike could petition for divorce on the grounds of a spouse's infidelity. In advocating Scottish over English laws, Lyndhurst appealed primarily to the practical consequences of the Scottish law. Citing testimony presented to the 1850 Royal Commission on Divorce, Lyndhurst argued that no greater licentiousness, no greater "inconvenience," and no more divorces occurred in Scotland than in England because women and the poor were entitled there to the same remedy as wealthy men.

The "inconvenience" to which Lord Lyndhurst referred was simultaneously practical and moral. Under current English law, the number of divorce bills remained low, not only because the expense of the procedures limited divorce to the wealthiest classes, but also because, for all practical purposes, only wealthy *men* could take advantage of this legal remedy. Women could petition for divorce *a vinculo,* but only on the grounds of aggravated adultery (which most typically involved incest). Even then, the social ostracism a divorced or separated woman inevitably faced made legal recourse an unattractive alternative for the vast majority of women; only four women had successfully petitioned Parliament for divorce before 1857. Many legislators feared that a more liberal divorce law would reverse this pattern, precipitate a run on the courts, and undermine the informal constraints that shored up marriage. While they were ready to address the procedural anomaly, therefore, they were reluctant to tamper with anything that might imperil the social institution of marriage, involve the law too intimately in commonplace marital disputes, or, in general, threaten the domestic ideal. As the divorce debates continued in Parliament, it became evident that most legislators assumed that a complex set of class and gender relations would have to be secured if the courts and marriage were to survive a more rationalized divorce procedure.

Legislators' assumptions about the relationship between domesticity, gender, and class emerge in a particularly interesting form in one of the discussions about the discrepancies between English and Scottish laws. Here, Lord Brougham is responding to Lyndhurst's argument that no "inconvenience" would attend aligning the laws of the two countries. Brougham intends to support Lyndhurst, but his support gets waylaid by this example of the unfortunate consequences of the current legal situation. "Suppose an English duke of the age of fourteen went to Scotland," Brougham says, "and fell into the hands of a prostitute, aged perhaps twenty-four, who wheedled him into love-making and then into a marriage according to the Scotch law, simply by acknowledging before witnesses that she was his wife—all the estates and honours of that unhappy young duke would be affected by that marriage, without the possibility of a remedy" (5/20/56, 423). Brougham acknowledges that the legislation under consideration—which is about divorce, not marriage—has nothing to do with this particular injustice, and thus it is not immediately clear why he introduces this example. On the surface of things, the objection to there being two different sets of laws for the two countries hinged on the fact that, under such a system, a man, simply by crossing the border, would enter into a different legal status—for example, being legally divorced and remarried in Scotland, he could return to England to find himself a bigamist and in violation of the law. In other words, such a legal contradiction within the same "united kingdom" pointed up the contradictions in the union or the law or marriage or all three; one way legislators' attempts to regularize the laws of the two countries can be seen is as an attempt to consolidate the two national identities that currently threatened to disrupt the "union" so critical to Britain's status as a kingdom. Subsequent debates about the discrepancy between Scottish and English laws suggest, however, that the danger Brougham and others perceived in Lyndhurst's particular suggestion for strengthening the union was that if the Scottish law governing divorce were extended to England, the Scottish laws about marriage might come too—and, given the wiles of twenty-four-year-old prostitutes, such laws would jeopardize naive, lusty, and propertied English lads. To legislators like Viscount Palmerston, addressing the same issue in the Commons in 1857, the possible violation of propertied English males by lower-class women was so heinous that it admitted of only one solution: Parliament must rectify the legal contradiction, he insisted, not by making English law more liberal, but by making Scottish law more restrictive.[10]

In such objections to Scottish law, concerns about class and gender seem to play equal roles. But when the issue of class comes up specifically in the debates, it becomes clear that assumptions about gender were more intractable—or at least more defensible—than were assumptions about class. The very fact that legislators explicitly addressed the issue of class inequity and not the sexual double standard suggests that, while the social and economic unrest of the 1840s had forced legislators to conceptualize class relations as a problem that needed attention, the social relation between the sexes was not yet open to the same kind of scrutiny. But the relationship between assumptions about class and gender was more complex than this formulation suggests; even if class relations could be questioned while gender relations remained largely unassailed, the way arguments about the latter were played off against the former reveals that assumptions about gender and domesticity in particular could be used at midcentury to waylay legislation that would have tampered with class hierarchy. On 26 June and again on 3 July, for example, during the second reading debate of 1856 in the Lords, Samuel Wilberforce, the bishop of Oxford, announced that in principle he was opposed to having one law for the rich and another for the poor; he was in favor of extending the right to petition for divorce to the poor—"if it could be done without incurring greater evils" (7/3/56, 232). As the bishop elaborated his position, however, it becomes clear that these "greater evils" could not be offset because granting the poor the facilities for absolute divorce "would be the opening of the floodgates of licence upon the hitherto blessed purity of English life." At the heart of his argument, the bishop reveals why he holds this opinion.

> How constantly it [has] happened that the evil which [has] resulted in a direful tragedy [has] had its commencement in the lightest cause—some difference of temper, some little alienation of affection, exposing the wife to the arts and approaches of another. But if the woman were guarded by the sure conviction that no more happiness in married life was possible, the

temptation might altogether fail. Among the lower classes, who [give] no indication of any wish for relaxation of the law, it [is] perfectly well known that a legal divorce [is] an impossibility, and to that circumstance might be traced the sacredness of the marriage tie among the lower orders of the English people which [is] so remarkable—because, even women who [have] fallen before marriage, and not attributed to that fall any great degree of moral criminality, [consider] themselves utterly abandoned if after marriage they [can] be justly charged with any infidelity whatever. That remarkable fact [has] grown up very much under the influence of the feeling that marriage with any other person [is] impossible, and the removal of that check would have the effect of unsettling altogether the present estimate which the masses [form] of the sacredness of holy matrimony. (6/26/56, 1982)

The trivia of domestic comedy, the bishop suggests, will not become "a direful tragedy" as long as women continue to believe the "remarkable fact" that the marriage vow confers two different meanings upon equivalent sexual acts. If marriage should lose its hold on women, he fears, "the whole family and social life of the community" would begin to decay, because the poor would no longer embrace monogamy, nor inculcate the middle-class virtues of domesticity, discipline, and thrift. While Wilberforce acknowledges that the "approach" comes from a man—and implies that the "difference of opinion" involves the husband—he assumes that responsibility for self-control falls solely on the woman. *She* suffers the temptation; *hers* are the feelings that must be restrained. The bishop's solution was to legislate fidelity among the women of the lower classes by making divorce unavailable to everyone, rich and poor alike. He saw such legislation as a necessary barrier against a genuinely subversive challenge to class society, which turns out to be one of the things he is most anxious to preserve. You "might depend upon it," Wilberforce warned his colleagues, "that that which [is] permitted to the rich by reason of their being able to incur great expense, would be claimed as a matter of right by the poor" (5/25/57, 825).

The bishop's fear that allowing anyone to petition for divorce would imperil the social order suggests his anxiety that the divorce legislation would extend those political rights partially granted by the 1832 Reform Bill and demanded again by the People's Charter of 1838 into the moral realm—a realm traditionally presided over by the Church but, as we have seen, increasingly being claimed by secular institutions. One way to construe the debate about the di-

vorce bill is as an elaboration of the bishop's anxiety—as a contest
about whether the established Church or secular authorities should
regulate morality, the domestic sphere, and, by implication, the stability of class relations.[11] Without denying the importance of this
interpretation, however, I suggest that the similarities between the
Church and secular positions reveal the extent to which the contest
for authority, like the debates in parliament, took place within a field
of shared assumptions about gender that contained assumptions
about class. In Wilberforce's argument, gender is simultaneously
marginal and central, and it provides the ground on which discussions of class could occur; class distinctions could be scrutinized, in
other words, as long as middle-class morality was assumed to govern
working-class women in such a way as to keep them in their proper
place—within a monogamous marriage that imitated but did not
materially challenge the middle-class ideal. The basis of class stability,
according to this representation, was morality—specifically, the morality of women and the integrity of the domestic sphere that that
morality both depended on and reproduced. "All experience show[s],"
Wilberforce stated in 1857, "that the purity of civilized society depend[s] more upon the absolute chastity of the woman rather than
the principle of the man" (6/9/57, 1417). The dispute about whether
the Church or the state would regulate morality and ameliorate class
relations, then, turned on deciding what measures would ensure
"the absolute chastity of the woman" and, more basically, what
relation existed between chastity and women's natures, their desires,
and their social position.

The one anomaly that legislators were by and large unwilling
to rectify or even consider, in other words, was the sexual double
standard—and this unwillingness stood at the crux of their difficulty
in redressing all of the legal contradictions I have set out. The problem was not that extending more rights to women lay beyond the
imagination of these legislators; if anything, it lay too close at hand,
as we see from the long wrangle about sexual equality in the Commons in July and August of 1857. But this debate shows that the
issue of equality for all classes could be safely discussed precisely—
and only—because the naturalness of the sexual double standard was
a foregone conclusion.

This Commons debate of 1857 was provoked by the attorney
general's claim that the bill currently before the Commons proposed
new legal machinery but no substantive changes in the current law;
in response, the opposition insisted that material changes were afoot
and that the government was trying to disguise the radical social

implications of the bill. On 7 August, the discussion took a new turn when a member of the opposition proposed an amendment that would have enabled men and women to petition for divorce on equal grounds. In a very long speech, Gladstone, the leader of the opposition, supported this amendment by referring to divine authority: "if it be assumed that the indissolubility of marriage has been the result of the operation of the Christian religion on earth," he says, "still more emphatically . . . it may be assumed that the principle of the equality of the sexes has been the consequence of that religion" (8/7/57, 1272). But Gladstone affixed his stand *for* sexual equality to the argument that, because the sexes are equal, neither women nor men should be able to petition for divorce. In other words, Gladstone's argument repeats the turn taken by other opponents of more liberal divorce: the argument *for* equality is part of an argument *against* divorce.

Equally important as the content of Gladstone's argument is the fact that this entire discussion of the double standard was primarily designed to stall passage of any divorce legislation whatsoever. The one subject guaranteed to provoke the government's supporters to change sides, in other words, the one subject guaranteed to produce endless discussion and countless objections was the suggestion that women should stand on an equal footing with men in relation to marriage. Initially, Gladstone would no more admit that he and his colleagues were engaged in a filibuster designed to block the bill than the attorney general would concede that his claim not to be changing the substance of the law was intended to railroad its passage, but Gladstone was eventually provoked to acknowledge that his opposition to divorce under any conditions underwrote his long speeches for sexual equality (8/14/57, 1638). If Gladstone's tactic had succeeded, not only would the bill have been tabled until the next session, but the opposition might have provoked a vote of no confidence in the Palmerston ministry. As it was, Palmerston forced Parliament to sit for marathon sessions through one of the hottest summers in years until the legislation was passed, despite weary members' complaints that they had neither sufficient energy nor wit to endure the heat and long hours. Palmerston's lack of interest in other domestic legislation suggests that holding Parliament to this issue was as much a power play as an expression of the government's dedication to marriage law reform—despite the fact that both sides in the Commons repeatedly congratulated themselves on transcending politics in their discussions of this issue.

The debate in the Commons, in other words, did not address

the issue of the sexual double standard so much as it invoked it. It is testimony to the importance of this assumption that merely raising the possibility of sexual equality could waylay discussion of the government's legislation and almost foreclose all legislative reform. Most legislators did not even acknowledge the position the double standard occupied in their arguments; in the rare cases that they did, the justification they offered for it seemed to need no elaboration. But the common argument that only a woman's infidelity could produce "spurious offspring" and so jeopardize the legitimate transmission of a man's property was profoundly one-sided. As Lyndhurst pointed out, in focusing exclusively on the woman's indiscretion, this argument overlooked the fact that the profligate man also introduces spurious offspring into another man's family.[12] Few men bothered to respond to this objection, however, and those who did dismissed it as making sexual profligacy what it should be—"a matter between man and man—not between man and woman."[13] Given the investment male legislators shared in the sexual double standard, it is not surprising that the most extensive elaboration of its attendant injustices was written by a woman. I turn now to Caroline Norton, the woman whose complaint influenced both Lyndhurst and Brougham and whose criticisms of Cranworth's bill constituted the basis of some of the most important amendments the bill finally received.[14]

II

Upper-middle-class Caroline Sheridan, the beautiful granddaughter of the Whig playwright Richard Brinsley Sheridan, was married in 1826 to George Norton, a Tory aristocratic younger son whose fortune was supposed to compensate for the fact that the couple barely knew each other when they married.[15] Caroline's mother had been misled about George Norton's finances, however, and the young couple soon found themselves almost completely dependent financially on Caroline's literary earnings and her family's Whig connections. In 1829, Caroline began to publish her poetry, and, in 1830, when George lost his seat in Parliament, she persuaded her old Whig friend Lord Melbourne, then home secretary, to appoint George justice of a magistrate's court at £1,000 per year.

The Nortons' private affairs were stormy from the beginning; they became the stuff of scandal in 1836, however, when George Norton removed their three children from their London home to retaliate for at least two wifely insurrections: Caroline refused to let

George raise money against a trust settled upon her at the time of their marriage, and she repeatedly turned to her family for protection against his physical and emotional brutality. The domestic quarrel, which was fully covered by gossip columns in London and abroad, culminated in June of that year in a lawsuit brought by George Norton against Lord Melbourne for criminal conversation—one of the necessary first steps toward George's obtaining a divorce. Melbourne was by that time prime minister; Norton demanded £10,000 in damages, and rumors spread that Norton had undertaken the suit not only in hopes of extricating himself from marital and financial difficulties, but also in response to Tory desires to bring down the Whig government, an outcome that might well have followed such outrageous domestic conduct on the part of the elderly counselor to the young Queen Victoria. So ludicrous was the evidence that Norton presented, however, that the jury returned a verdict against him without calling a single witness or leaving the box. The trial left Melbourne completely vindicated and more firmly established than ever as Victoria's mentor; Caroline, by contrast, found herself still (and now irrevocably) married to a man she loathed, deprived of her reputation, and without any legal claim to her children.

In 1854, after more than a decade of wrangling over custody of the children and the allowance George had agreed to provide her, Caroline, who was by then a renowned poet and novelist, found her dirty laundry being aired in public again. Once more the squabble was about money. When Caroline's mother died in 1851, she left her daughter an inheritance of £480 per annum. Even though he inherited from the estate the life interest of Caroline's portion from her father, George summarily reduced the £500 allowance he had agreed to pay Caroline in a deed of separation the couple had signed in 1848. George had originally agreed to this allowance in exchange for Caroline's willingness to exonerate him from responsibility for her debts and to allow George to raise money against her trust. Caroline had signed the agreement, even though its ten-year retroactive clause was considered humiliating, because she thought the contract was binding and would thus ensure her a regular income. But when Mrs. Sheridan died, George claimed that Caroline no longer needed the allowance and that he could no longer afford to pay it; he also pointed out that he was not legally bound to keep his word because a man could not contract with the wife who was legally part of him. Enraged, Caroline then turned the letter of the law back upon George. If he was not bound to give her an allowance, she reasoned, then she was not bound to pay her own debts. In an attempt to force George to agree to more advantageous terms, Caroline therefore allowed a carriage repairman to sue George for nonpayment of a bill. This action resulted in a trial held in Westminster Court on 18 August 1853, in which George, furious over the financial difficulties in which his wife continued to involve him, used the fact that Lord Melbourne had left a legacy to Caroline to insinuate once more that her conduct with the elderly statesman two decades before had been less than discreet. When the jury found for George on a technicality, Caroline resorted to the press, publishing first in the *Times,* then in two pamphlets on divorce, the litany of false accusations she had endured.

Caroline used Lord Cranworth's Matrimonial Causes Bill, which had been introduced and then tabled in June 1854, as the pretext for publishing her complaints. The first of the two pamphlets, *English Laws for Women in the Nineteenth Century,* was printed privately in 1854; the second, her *Letter to the Queen on Lord Chancellor Cranworth's Marriage and Divorce Bill,* received much wider circulation on its publication in 1855. In both of these tracts, Norton argued that what neither Cranworth's bill nor most of the legislators who debated it would acknowledge was that men's legal and economic tyranny over women lay at the heart of their idealization of the domestic sphere and the partial solutions reformers proposed. Systematically, in the *Letter to the Queen,* Caroline Norton rehearses the laws governing married women so as to call attention to their central contradiction—

> the grotesque anomaly which ordains that married women shall be "non-existent" in a country governed by a female Sovereign. . . . As *her husband,* he has a right to all that is hers: as *his wife,* she has no right to anything that is his. As her husband, he may divorce her (if truth or false swearing can do it): as his wife, the utmost "divorce" she could obtain, is permission to reside alone,—married to his name. The marriage ceremony is a civil bond for him,—and an indissoluble sacrament for her; and the rights of mutual property which that ceremony is ignorantly supposed to confer, are made absolute for him, and null for her.[16]

Norton was able to identify these injustices because she had personally endured them, but being able to voice them in such explicitly political terms required transforming herself from the silent sufferer of private wrongs into an articulate spokesperson in the public sphere. To the extent that she was able to do so, Norton's self-authorization, as she narrated it in *English Laws for Women,* implicitly challenged the entire ideological order that the legal and sexual double standards supported.

The marginal status of Norton's complaint helps account for the indirection of some of the rhetorical strategies of her self-presentation. Initially, for example, Norton justifies publicizing her private story by rhetorically splitting herself into two persons: the long-suffering victim of social injustice and the vindicating polemical writer. From the positions these persons occupy in her introduction to *English Laws,* implicitly the former is female and the latter male. As woman-victim, Norton explicitly identifies with the assassinated wife of a French nobleman, the daughter of Watt Tyler, and the "virgin girl of Rome," whose father slaughtered her rather than permit her "degradation."[17] As publicist of social injustice, Norton aligns herself with "example[s] of resistance"—men like the Good Samaritan, the prison reformer Howard, Sir Samuel Romilly, and Lord Brougham (p. 4). Despite the fact that she initially invokes this traditional gender division, however, in the course of her impassioned introduction, Norton rewrites the division as one between powerless groups—the "helpless classes"—and powerful, "earnest individuals." The helpless classes include not only women but also pauper children, insane patients, untried prisoners, and slaves; the individualized "benefactors" are, by contrast, all men but one (Harriet Beecher Stowe). The point that Norton makes indirectly is that women's legal incapacities are a function of their social *position,* not of natural, biological inferiority. Beyond this, the rhetorical achievement of her argument is to transfer her allegiance from the silent, helpless classes to the articulate individuals who inspire social change. In doing so, she elevates her personal complaint to a political critique of existing laws; she collapses the boundary between the private sphere, where injustice goes unchecked, and the public domain, where laws are made and enforced by men.

The principle by which Norton organizes her narrative repeats this pattern and generates the same subversive conclusion. Supposedly for the sake of clarity, Norton divides her story into three segments or "outlines": the Nortons' financial affairs; the treatment she suffered as a wife; and "Lord Melbourne's opinion of the affairs in which his name was involved" (p. 21). The result of this division is anything but clarity, however. Separating the economic material from the domestic narrative obscures the relationship between the two and makes it difficult for the reader to reconstruct the sequence of events or the connection between, for example, Caroline's refusing George the right to raise money against her trust and his abducting the children. What this narrative division does accomplish, however, is a separation between the more public domain of economic negotiation and the more private domain of domestic squabbles and cruelties. Like the introduction's division between men-benefactors and women-victims, this narrative separation of spheres collapses in the third story, when Norton quotes Melbourne's personal letters to prove that men's political interests exacerbated her domestic wrongs.

The climactic moment of Norton's narrative is the episode in which the domestic quarrel is bought into a court of law; this is also the moment at which the long-suffering, long-silenced woman becomes a self-conscious, articulate subject, determined to speak and write. The transformation begins when George Norton calls his wife to the witness stand and forces her to see herself as he sees her: "I felt, as I looked for an instant towards him, that he saw in me neither a woman to be spared public insult, nor a mother to be spared shameful sorrow,—but simply a claimant to be non-suited; a creditor to be evaded; a pecuniary incumbrance he was determined to be rid of" (pp. 81–82). Stripped of her status as a (middle-class) woman and mother, Norton momentarily loses her bearings. Her first response to this degradation and unsexing is to vacillate wildly between a man's "angry loudness" and a woman's frustrated speechlessness. Only when she applies Lord Melbourne's words to George can she establish an identity that allows her to speak.

> I felt giddy; the faces of the people grew indistinct; my sentences became a confused alternation of angry loudness, and husky attempts to speak. I saw nothing—but the husband of whose mercenary nature Lord Melbourne himself had warned me I judged too leniently; nothing but *the Gnome,*—proceeding *again* to dig away, for the sake of money, what remnant of peace, happiness, and reputation, might have rested on the future years of my life. Turning up as he dug—dead sorrows, and buried shames, and miserable recollections—and careless who was hurt by them, as long as he evaded payment of a disputed annuity, and stamped his own signature as worthless! (Pp. 85–86)

What Caroline Norton is doing here is reappropriating the identity of a wronged woman by casting herself as the victim in a familiar Victorian genre, the melodrama.[18] The roles in the melodramatic script were as conventional as the values underwritten by this genre.

The trio of an innocent lady-in-distress, a gnomelike, aristocratic villain, and a selfless avenger appears repeatedly in both stage melodramas and Norton's pamphlet, as, for example, when she depicts Anne Boleyn suffering the brutalities of Henry VIII, only to have her reputation vindicated (posthumously) by the poet Wyatt.[19] But if George is the villain here, and Caroline is the lady-in-distress, who, now that Melbourne is dead, is to be the lady's defender? In the current, lamentable state of society, there is no one else to play that role but Caroline Norton herself. The melodramatic plot provides the terms, her identification with other (male) defenders provides the means, and, in a dramatic moment, Caroline Norton becomes not just innocence personified, but also judge, jury, and executioner all at once:

> On that day, when in cold blood, for the sake of money, Mr Norton repeated that which he knew to be false . . . in that little court where I stood apparently helpless, mortified, and degraded—in that bitterest of many bitter hours in my life,— I judged and sentenced him. I annulled the skill of his Tory lawyer's suggestion to a Tory judge. I over-ruled the decision of Lord Abinger in that obscure and forgotten cause, which upheld him against justice. I sentenced Mr Norton to be *known*.
> (P. 136)

To appreciate the subversive implications of Norton's rhetorical vindication, it is necessary to understand the basis on which she "sentences" George. The evidence that convicts George Norton consists primarily of a series of letters in his own hand, which Caroline refers to as the "Greenacre" letters. Composed by George during 1837, after the unsuccessful criminal conversation action against Melbourne, these letters pleaded for a reconciliation and playfully entreated Caroline to meet George in an empty house to discuss terms. The signature that George appended to these letters, Caroline tells us, undercut their teasing tone because Greenacre was the name of a notorious murderer convicted of killing his fiancée in an empty house in the 1830s. These letters had been in Caroline's possession since 1837, and she had wanted to publish them in 1838 in conjunction with another trial for debt. This is the "obscure and forgotten cause" to which Caroline refers in *English Laws*. In that 1838 trial, one of Caroline's creditors had subpoenaed Sir John Bayley to testify about George's character. Bayley was never called to the witness stand, however, because Sir Fitzroy Kelly, George's lawyer, advised Lord Abinger, the judge in the case, not to accept Bayley's testimony for fear that Bayley would use the Greenacre letters to impugn George's reputation. This conspiracy of Tory silence, Caroline now charges, was mounted to protect George so that he would not reveal that a Tory plot had motivated his earlier suit against Melbourne. In other words, Caroline's reputation had twice been hostage, not simply to George's perfidy, but also to political intrigues. When the verdict in the 1838 trial was announced *for* George, Caroline determined, by publishing her account of the case, to expose her husband's lies and the way Lord Abinger had misused his judicial power. At that time, however, she was stopped by Lord Melbourne, who, as prime minister to a young queen, dreaded scandal more than anything else. "It so happened that this petty cause," Caroline now bitterly complains, "in which nothing more important than a woman's fame and a woman's interest were at stake,—was tried at the exact moment (June 1838), when, in the first year of a young Queen's reign, the Whig government was overwhelmed with business." Amid such political machinations and affairs of state, Norton's grievance was simply buried, as it had been after the 1836 trial, when Caroline also could not publicly defend her innocence. "What could my passionate printed justification be?" she asks rhetorically in 1854, "but a plague and an embarrassment to *him,* already justified, and at the pinnacle of fortune?" (p. 134).

This is the history to which Norton repeatedly returns in her 1854 defense. Once repressed by that "double chance" of Whig and Tory politics, Norton's anger now returns to punish the men who would not let her speak. By publishing not only the details of George's brutality but also Melbourne's private letters, Caroline avenges herself against both men for all their crimes—against George for hurting her, for denying her her children, for murdering her reputation; against Melbourne for smothering her domestic injuries with his political concerns. Once she acknowledges the abuses she suffered as a helpless woman, Norton the avenger can formulate the social injustices that have authorized these private wrongs. In the last chapter of *English Laws for Women* and in the bulk of *A Letter to the Queen,* Norton sets out the inequities of the current marriage laws, calling attention to their class and gender bias and pointing to the masculine investment that inhibits reform. "Property," she asserts, "not morality, [is] the thing held sacred" (p. 152); because mercenary self-interest motivates all men (as it motivated George Norton), women become "'non-existent,' except for the purpose of suffering" (p. 160).

As long as Norton occupies the position of the avenger in the melodramatic plot, she is authorized to spell out the injustice both of the individual villain and the laws that refuse her justice. But her "sentencing" is limited precisely because she also retains the domestic ideal in which she can only cast herself as the suffering lady-in-distress. This limitation emerges clearly in the solution Norton proposes for women's plight. She does not ask for equal rights for women or even for equalization of the grounds for divorce. Instead, she asks for protection. "What I write," she assures her readers in the introduction to *English Laws,* "is written in no spirit of rebellion; it is simply an appeal for protection" (p. 2). Over 150 pages later, she explains more fully her vision of the relationship between rights and protection:

> Petitioning does not imply assertion of equality. The wild and stupid theories advanced by a few women, of "equal rights" and "equal intelligence" are not the opinions of their sex. I, for one (I, with millions more), believe in the natural superiority of man, as I do in the existence of a God. . . . Masculine superiority is incontestable; and with the superiority should come protection. To refuse it because some women exist, who talk of "women's rights," of "women's equality," is to say that . . . the Chartist and Rebecca riots in Wales, or Swing fires in the rural districts of England, would have been a sound and sufficient reason for refusing justice to all the Queen's subjects in the United Kingdom. The rebellion of a group, against legitimate authority, is not to deprive the general subject-party of general protection. Women have one *right* (perhaps only that one). They have a right—founded on nature, equity, and religion—to the protection of man. *Power* is on the side of men—power of body, power of mind, power of position. With that power should come, not only the fact, but the *instinct* of protection. (P. 165)

Like the melodramatic script that underwrites her speech, Norton explicitly endorses the existence of a natural difference between men and women and the natural difference of "rights" that follows from this: because men are physically and socially more powerful, they have political rights within the public sphere, and women, the weaker sex, have the right to protection from the stresses of that sphere; women have the right, that is, to remain within the nonpolitical and nonmercenary sphere of the home. The problem is that Norton's usurpation of the defender's role, her revelation of the role politics and money have played in her domestic woes, and her entry into political discourse have already collapsed the very differences she seems to support. It is this peculiar combination of reticence

and audacity that simultaneously enabled Norton to influence legislators like Lord Lyndhurst and prevented her from formulating
the more radical analysis that a few of her contemporaries did advance. But the implications of even Norton's limited demands were
more subversive than she acknowledged. To appreciate the challenge
Norton's pamphlets implicitly posed—and to expose the limits of
the divorce debates—I turn away from Caroline Norton for a moment to examine another piece of legislation that Parliament considered alongside Cranworth's divorce bill. This piece of legislation
is the Married Women's Property Bill.

III

Neither Caroline Norton's complaint nor the parliamentary debates
about divorce can be considered apart from the issue of married
women's property. Every episode of the Nortons' dispute involved
a contest over property; one of Caroline's most adamant complaints
against Lord Cranworth's bill was that it did not allow separated
women like herself to keep whatever money they earned. And it was
the publication of Norton's *Letter to the Queen* that helped Barbara
Bodichon convince the Law Amendment Society to take up the
issue of married women's property. That Norton's complaints about
these laws were common can be seen from the more than seventy
petitions presented to the Commons in 1856 about women and property; one of these was signed by three thousand women, among
whom were many eminent writers; another was signed by twenty-
six thousand men and women.[20] In 1856, backed by the LAS, Sir
Erskine Perry introduced into the House of Commons a resolution
for debate about married women's property. His explicit design was
not to "assert a new principle of woman's social position," but to
"correct a practical grievance" overlooked by the government's divorce bill, which was then under debate in the Lords.[21] The intricate
exchange by which the divorce legislation was amended to incor-
porate some provisions of this property bill and then used to foreclose serious consideration of its inherent principle reveals the
persistent influence of a set of assumptions about gender, domesticity, property, and the law.[22]

When legislation about married women's property was finally
brought to the attention of both houses of Parliament in 1857, the
laws governing this important issue constituted a prime example of
the legal anomalies law reformers were anxious to resolve. At midcentury, married women's property was governed by two different

sets of judge-made law, the common law and equity. Under the common law of coverture, most of a woman's property became her husband's absolutely when she married, whether she brought that property into the marriage or acquired it subsequently. While the rights of the husband varied according to the nature of the property in question, the effect of the common law was to place a married woman in an indirect relation to property and to all transactions concerning it. All of a married woman's income belonged to her husband; she could not bind herself to a contract; her testamentary capacity was extremely limited and could be exercised only by the consent of her husband. According to Blackstone, who codified these principles in 1765, the common law's treatment of married women constituted a form of protection. "Even the disabilities which the wife lies under, are for the most part intended for her protection and benefit. So great a favourite is the female sex of the laws of England."[23]

Whereas common law was considered sufficient protection for the majority of English women, men wealthy enough to afford additional protection for their daughters and property could engage another kind of law. By the early nineteenth century, the Court of Chancery had established by precedent a provision that enabled a married woman to possess property (both land and chattels) separately from her husband. This principle maintained that even a person who could not legally own property might have it held for her by a trustee. Under this equity law, a man (most usually the father) would settle property upon a woman (most usually his daughter) in the form of a trust. The agent who oversaw this trust (who was frequently a male relative or the woman's husband) could raise money upon the property, sell or rent the title, and make contracts upon the property. Such trusts became increasingly common during the first half of the nineteenth century because, since trusts made available income generated from women's property that was protected from liability, they were an important source of the liquid capital so essential to the success of middle-class men.[24] But while equity could give the married woman the right to own property, her relation to that property continued to be both indirect and limited. This limitation took four forms. First, by a clause known as the restraint on anticipation, a woman could be prevented from selling her property or charging it with her debts as long as she was married. This clause, which was normally (but not always) a part of settlements, extended the "protection" over a woman's property in such a way as to anticipate—and control—both her susceptibility to her husband's influence and his interest in her property. Second, a married woman lacked testamentary capacity in respect to any property acquired after the settlement was drawn up; that is, her testamentary capacity did not represent the woman but only whatever property had been settled upon her. Third, a married woman could not bind herself by contract beyond the value of her separate property. And fourth, the provisions of the trust could set additional restrictions on a woman's rights, such as depriving her of the property if she married again or specifying the ways in which she could use or dispose of the property.[25]

The principle of separate property, then, did not function to extend women's rights but to protect the property rights of a man, initially the father, but, according to the terms of the trust, whatever man was designated trustee. Indeed, in trusts characterized by a restraint-on-anticipation clause, we can see the extent to which marriage could be considered a contest between two men over property; the woman was merely the representative or carrier of property, in this sense, and even her love for her husband imperiled her father's goods. This clause, like the other restrictions that characterized trusts, underscores the fact that a woman was economically dependent on whoever controlled "her" money.[26]

By the mid-nineteenth century, there were at least two reasons why these legal provisions might have come to seem obsolete. In the first place, the entry of increasing numbers of women into waged labor called into question the justice of there being one law for middle-class women and another for the poor—especially when working-class women had no legal protection under common law against their husbands' appropriating their earnings and spending them as they liked. In the second place, for ambitious middle-class men, the provision of separate property could hold the potential resource of "female capital" hostage to cumbersome legal machinery, unless they had been appointed trustee. From one perspective, then, it could be argued that it was in the economic interest of working-class women and middle-class men to change laws governing married women's property—either by extending the protection of equity to all women or by eliminating altogether the category of separate property.

In response to the growing popular agitation for property reform, Lord Brougham introduced a Married Women's Property Bill into the Lords in February 1857; debate on this measure was almost immediately adjourned, however, and it was permanently ended by the resignation of the government over a vote on Palmerston's foreign policy. After the general election in May, a different bill was introduced in the Commons by Sir Erskine Perry. This bill took a middle course in its proposal for reform: it did not abolish marriage settlements in equity, but it did provide that women married without such settlements would be *femes sole* in regard to property.[27] Although the bill had considerable support (most notably from Richard Monckton Milnes, Florence Nightingale's suitor), most legislators took exception to the proposal. For my purposes, what is most interesting about legislators' objections is how frequently they invoked the specter also disparaged by Caroline Norton: the "wild and stupid theories" of "strong-minded women." When Sir Richard Bethell, the attorney general, responded to Sir Erskine Perry's bill, for example, he claimed that such legislation tended "to the placing of the women of England in a 'strong-minded and independent position,' which so few [choose] for themselves, and which position . . . consist[s] in the rendering them accountable for everything that they might do or say. Now he (the Attorney General), for one, [does] not think that [is] a position which the best and most amiable of the women of England [are] anxious to occupy" (5/14/57, 275). The Conservative member for Maidstone, Alexander James Beresford-Hope, reinforced this hobgoblin when he worried aloud that the "extravagant demands of the large and manly body of 'strong-minded women' " would not be answered by Perry's bill; for pamphleteering advocates of "abstract women's rights," he claimed, no legislation would be sufficient until men and women occupied the same status under the law. What seems to have been at stake for Beresford-Hope and others was the vision of English domesticity that by midcentury had come to be equated with the very identity of an Englishman. "Let them amend the law," he graciously conceded, "but at the same time steadfastly resist the breaking down of the distinguishing characteristics of Englishmen—the love of home, the purity of husband and wife, and the union of one family" (5/14/57, 278, 280).

The second reading of the Married Women's Bill in the Commons elicited further admonitory exempla of "strong-minded women." Sir John Butler, for example, imagined a case in which a woman's domestic instincts would couple with her new rights to bring about her husband's ruin. "There were very few mothers of families," he surmised, "having the control of property which they ought to devote to the benefit of the whole of their children alike, who would have nerve and composure enough to refuse to grant pecuniary aid to any one of their children—say their first-born—who might stand in need of such assistance." From familial solicitude to foolish profligacy seems merely a small step, as his next example suggests. "She might, with the best intentions, lay [her property] out, without consulting her husband, in some worthless railway shares or in some unsound speculation, and the husband might find that the whole of that property, to which he had looked, perhaps, for the maintenance of himself during his lifetime, and for the benefit of his children afterwards, had been swept away" (7/15/57, 1515). When J. D. Fitzgerald took up the lament, the dramatized husband suffers not only financial loss but emotional damage as well. "The Bill would enable a married woman to contract what debts she pleased," he complained, "to bind herself personally; to enter into litigation; to sue and be sued, without the knowledge or control of a husband or trustee; and the consequence might be, that a gentleman who was strongly attached to an extravagant wife might find her arrested at his dinner-table in respect of transactions of which he had no cognizance whatever" (7/15/57, 1522). It is not clear whether Fitzgerald considered the most lamentable aspect of this case to be the wife's independence, the husband's ignorance, or the fact that the husband was weak enough to be "strongly attached" where there was no protection against extravagance; nevertheless, it is clear that the victim of this dining room tragedy is the husband and that the culprit is a woman's independent will.

Nowhere in these discussions are the cases of men's unwise investments raised; no one worried aloud about the much more likely case of a wife who, ignorant of her husband's transactions, found herself faced with bailiffs at the dinner table. Throughout, the assumption persisted that where property is concerned there must be one owner and that one must be the man. To extend equity's provision of a wife's separate property throughout all classes of society, legislators like Sir John Butler suggested, would be to give the wife the means with which to resist her husband's interests and therefore the wedge with which to splinter the domestic sphere: "There was no greater source of dissension in married life," Butler argued, "than the existence of separate property" (7/15/57, 1515). So bound up are property and the unity of the family in these arguments that sometimes it is difficult to tell which of the two members of Parliament wanted most to protect. The provisions of the Married Women's Property Bill, Mr. Massey argued, "might disturb the whole of the relations of married life, and revolutionize all the principles which applied to the rights of property in this country" (7/15/57, 1518).

What was at stake in these objections—and what legislators were anxious to defend—was the existence of the legal opposition between men and (married) women in relation to property.[28] To understand why legislators were so intent on defending this opposition—in spite of the proliferation of petitions and pamphlets decrying its injustice—it is important to identify the place that this legal dichotomy occupied in relation to an entire series of ideological oppositions that implicitly organized propertied men's conceptions of themselves and society. When these legal, economic, and social oppositions were aligned in parallel with each other—as they seemed to be at midcentury—they set limits to the kinds of questions and solutions that could be advanced that accorded with the natural opposition of sexual difference endorsed by both religion and science. But because there was no stability in the internal structure of each pair, in the relationships among them, or between these oppositions and either nature or the material relations of production, the delicate edifice constructed on sexual difference was always a contested site, vulnerable to challenge and to change.

Among the discourses that helped construct these oppositions, law and science occupied mutually supportive and privileged places in mid-nineteenth-century Britain. Just as science claimed the right to define one's natural identity, so law claimed jurisdiction over one's social identity. But civil law not only delineated individual rights; it also codified, and therefore marked the extent and limits of, the state's jurisdiction—especially in the period before the development of a strong, centralized bureaucracy in England. The most basic opposition established by civil and property law in nineteenth-century Britain, and therefore the opposition both protected by and crucial to the developing state, was the opposition between subjects—those people considered able to determine and act on their own interests, hence capable of binding themselves by contract—and nonsubjects, who were not considered responsible and therefore not so bound. To the latter—children, orphans under guardianship, lunatics, and married women—the law (and increasingly the state) extended its protection in lieu of awarding rights.[29]

In mid-Victorian Britain, the legal distinction between responsible subjects and individuals who needed protection codified another, underlying opposition: that between property owners, on the one hand, and representatives of property, on the other. After the abolition of slavery in 1833, women became the paradigmatic case of human property in Britain, a fact underscored by the official curtailment in that same year of the customary rights of dower.[30] Women's "passive" or metonymic relation to property was also signaled by the property restrictions I have already discussed and by the increasing popularity of life assurance and annuities as sources of women's income, because all of these symbolized and materially extended women's financial dependence.[31] Beyond this, the existence of so-called protective legislation equated women's services with property that belonged to a man, even if these services could not always be used or exchanged exactly like other forms of property. Such legislation included the law that gave a father an "interest in respect of his daughter's chastity" and the action for criminal conversation.[32]

Even though the opposition between owners and representatives of property anchored both property laws and social practice, it actually masked a crucial fact about the way the law constructed all of its subjects. In nineteenth-century Britain, the fundamental criterion of subject status—the individual's capacity to recognize and act on his own interests—was underwritten by another capacity—the ability to possess himself. Locke formulated this notion of the proprietary self in his statement that "every man has a property in his own person."[33] Structurally, this amounted to every individual being constituted as a divided subject: this internal difference was the basis for the "free" exchange of labor and therefore the production of surplus value, but it was also the basis for the alienation every man experienced in the market economy. Because his labor could be expropriated (or alienated) for someone else's profit and because a man's gain was subject to both the dictates of other people and the vicissitudes of the economy, the individual could experience himself as hostage to incomprehensible forces and frustrating restraints.

In mid-Victorian England, there were several mechanisms for symbolically resolving the alienation written into the proprietary self. As I argue in the next chapter, one of these mechanisms was the representation of internal difference as the necessary condition for personal development because it was the basis of exchange and circulation; if the individual was an economy always exchanging his own labor and potential for some achievement, then his emotional and spiritual growth simply replicated and augmented the progress of the national economy, where goods and capital passed productively from one man to another.[34] Here, however, I focus on the role that representations of gender played in making alienation tolerable. Essentially, this involved emphasizing not the difference written into the proprietary subject, but the difference *between* that subject and another figure who was not so divided. This figure was woman.

In the nineteenth century, the opposition between property owners and representatives of property was legitimized and explained by what seemed to be its physiological basis—the difference between the sexes. This difference, which privileged biological reproduction, was taken to dictate human nature and social roles: female nature, which was governed by maternal instinct, was supposedly noncompetitive, nonaggressive, and self-sacrificing—that is, internally consistent and not alienated; male nature, the counterpart, was competitive, aggressive, and acquisitive. This apparently fixed difference was then taken to anchor not only the kind of labor men and women performed, but also the opposition between the public sphere, where alienation was visible and inescapable, and the home, where there seemed to be no alienation at all.

One of the functions of the opposition between the private, feminized sphere and the masculine sphere of work outside the home was to mitigate the effects of the alienation of market relations. In the home, through his relationship with his family, a man of any class was promised economic and social dominance, as well as both sexual gratification and spiritual reinforcement. Peter Gaskell's 1833 celebration of home demonstrates how even a man's internal alienation could be transformed into "communion with himself" in the sanctity of the domestic sphere.

> Home ever has been and ever will be the school for moral education. It is here alone that man can develop in their full beauty those affections of the heart which are destined to be, through life, the haven to which he may retire when driven about and persecuted by the storms of fortune. It is here alone he can find refuge; it is here, that he may have about him if his condition is not supereminently wretched, feelings and emotions of the most holy and sacred influence; it is here that he may hold communion with himself; and it is here and here, alone, that he will be enabled to retain his pride of self, his personal respectability.[35]

The unarticulated assumptions about gender implicit in such a statement hold the key to the ideological—and social—functions of this idea. Just as the bishop of Oxford's notion of a nonconfrontational class society depended on women "naturally" taking responsibility for self and sexual control, so the effectiveness of this idea of home depended on representing women as naturally self-sacrificing.[36] The illusion that freedom and autonomy existed for the man within the home therefore depended on the illusion that within the home no one was alienated—and this depended on believing that the woman desired to be only what the man wanted her to be—that her reproductive capacity dictated her "maternal nature" and that this nature was not sexually aggressive but selfless and domestic. Only as long as women remained in the home and did not claim a sexuality more aggressive or other than maternal love could this form of (apparent) nonalienation seem to eminate from womanly nature. Only as long as her domestic labor was rhetorically distinguished from paid labor could the illusion persist that there *were* separate spheres, that there *was* an antidote to the alienation of the marketplace, and that men *were* fundamentally different from women. The ground of this circular logic, in other words, was the definition of female nature as self-consistent and self-sacrificing, but this definition assumed exactly what it was invoked to prove—that social behavior *reflected* nature, not constituted it.

As we have already seen in the chloroform debate, the representation of woman as naturally passive and self-denying might be imperiled by the very act in which her maternity was realized; if chloroform did reveal childbearing to be sexually exciting, then the laboring woman was exhibiting feelings in excess of the marital bond and she might not be exclusively a model of modesty and self-control. The same possibility also arose, from a very different quarter, in midcentury discussions of "redundant women" and women's paid labor; just as the affinity between maternal nature and sexuality jeopardized representations of womanly self-denial, so the likeness between middle-class domestic work and such forms of paid labor as governessing threatened to erode the supposedly fixed boundary between the private and public spheres.

The instability that these cases reveal in the deep structure of ideological relations helps explain why the Married Women's Property Bill was considered so "evil" a piece of legislation, why arguments about the sexual double standard held sway for so long, and why Caroline Norton's pamphlets were simultaneously potentially subversive and susceptible to appropriation by male legislators.[37] Because it proposed giving all married women rights over property, the Married Women's Property Bill of 1857 would have pointed out the artificial nature of the alignment between sex and economic privilege. The challenge to the *equation* between the two oppositions (owner/property, on the one hand, and male/female on the other) was potentially subversive to the entire social order because it threatened to reveal what was, in fact, the case: that the opposition between owner and property was specious. Moreover, the possibility that women could also be divided subjects—proprietary selves—undermined the naturalness of their putative indivisibility. If the universality of this self-contradictory structure of the individual were to have become visible, it might also have become possible to think what was equally inconceivable—that one's reproductive nature did not necessarily dictate the social position of every man and woman—that, in other words, other differences might hold sway, and men and women could therefore be equal under the law, in social responsibilities and privileges, in relation to property and sexuality, and even in terms of political rights.

These subversive possibilities remained invisible to the vast majority of men and women at midcentury, not only because of the apparently unassailable "fact" of anatomical difference and the material and conceptual importance of separate spheres, but also because of the tenacity of the sexual double standard that was bound up in these social arrangements. Even though part of the explanation for the power of the sexual double standard was, as legislators claimed, that only a woman's infidelity could inflict "spurious offspring" on a man, this consideration *assumed* that only a man should own property. Suggesting that the sexual double standard was actually neither natural nor necessary would have been subversive because it would have called attention to the artificiality of the equation of sex and social privilege that the Married Women's Property Bill also threatened to expose.

Beyond this is another more abstract but equally important consideration. The hierarchy explicit in the sexual double standard (but often masked in the other oppositions by a rhetoric of separate but equal spheres) was actually a rewriting of the complex epistemological hierarchy that underwrote all of the oppositions I have discussed. Despite the fact that real (middle-class) men exercised civil and political rights that real women did not enjoy, the epistemological category "woman" was actually not subordinate to or derived from the category "man" but the basis of that category. This is the paradox of the economy of the same, which is—but does not seem to be—the basis of liberal, individualist rhetoric. In this symbolic economy, the reification of difference as fixed and oppositional is a function of deemphasizing the importance of all but a single difference, which seems to be constitutive of identity. The paradox in this symbolic economy consists in the fact that the "primary" term remains primary only so long as the derived term remains in the secondary position. The "derived" term, in other words, is structurally the more important of the two. Man's identity as a subject with rights, then, depended on both establishing a stable identity for woman and keeping real women in the inferior position of nonsubjects or representatives of property. In the mid-nineteenth century, one strategy for stabilizing woman's identity was rhetorically to subordinate all other differences among women (such as, for example, their class position) to the single fact of their common reproductive nature. This reduction therefore "authorized" the social inferiority of all women, even though women positioned differently in the social hierarchy experienced this likeness differently. Given this system, a woman's sexual infidelity challenged not only the security of the paternal relation and the man's exclusive right to property, but also the illusion that women were "fixed" as reproductive (not sexually autonomous) beings, as dependent (not socially autonomous) subjects, and as uniformly "other" to man (not distinguished by their class positions). Because of the place that woman occupied in the symbolic order, she was the guarantor of truth, legitimacy, property, and male identity. The ideological centrality of woman helps account for the importance that the idealized domestic sphere played during this period; it also helps account for the anxiety men might feel toward themselves and her. This is the tangle of material, ideological, and emotional issues that J. W. Kaye identified in his 1855 review of Caroline Norton's pamphlet. "There is no confusion," Kaye reminds his reader, "as regards the woman's knowledge of the true and false. Whether her offspring be legitimate or illegitimate, she knows it to be her own. But a man, in this the tenderest relation which humanity recognises, may be the prey of a miserable delusion all his life. The victim of injustice himself, he may unconsciously be unjust to others, and hereditary honours and property, or wealth acquired by years of self-denying industry, may be transmitted to the offspring of a wanton and the living evidence of his disgrace."[38]

IV

The epistemological term *woman* could guarantee men's identity only if difference was fixed—only if, that is, the binary opposition between the sexes was more important than any other kinds of difference that real women might experience. And this depended, among other things, on limiting women's right to define or describe themselves. This is the context in which to understand the peculiar place of Caroline Norton in the history of nineteenth-century family

law reform. To the extent that she insisted on articulating her own
desires independent of her husband's will, and to the extent that her
history exposed the nexus of economic, social, and ideological factors
in the laws concerning married women, Caroline Norton also threatened to subvert the conceptual oppositions crucial to the middle-
class ideology of separate spheres. But to the extent that she formulated her complaint in terms derived from the prevailing ideology,
her challenge actually reinforced the idealized domesticity she seemed
to undermine.

The threat Norton posed was threefold. In the first place, in
claiming the right to represent herself in this form, Caroline Norton
violated the separation of spheres within representation. This separation engendered discourses at the same time that it unofficially
discriminated who could publish in various forms and genres. By
this engendering of genres, women were granted the authority to
write and publish literature, which had become "feminized" by midcentury, but they were largely denied access to "masculine" discourses like medicine, law, and theology.[39] In articulating her
emotional plea in legal rhetoric and in levying political charges to
defend her cause, Norton therefore collapsed both sets of distinctions: she mixed emotions and legal rhetoric in a defense that collapsed political and personal wrongs, and she spoke as a woman in
a genre in which men were the primary authors.[40] In the second
place, in exposing the extent to which politics and money matters
always underwrote and undercut her domestic life with George,
Norton exploded the supposedly stable barrier between the public
and private spheres. Her life history made absolutely clear what her
writing made legible: that women were not necessarily protected in
exchange for their dependence and that women were always alienated—both outside the home and within it—from their economic
productivity, their sexuality and desires, and even the children they
bore.

The third sense in which Norton threatened the binary opposition of separate spheres involved the specific nature of her quarrel with George. The issues of voluntary separation agreements and
independent contracts were hardly neutral in British legal history.
In fact, these were the issues in relation to which married women
had been granted some of the property rights of a *feme sole* during
the late seventeenth and early eighteenth centuries. In a series of
precedent-setting cases dating from 1682 and 1695, British courts
identified wives who lived apart from their husbands with separate
maintenance allowances as one group of women to which the law

was willing to grant property rights. This principle was spelled out in 1744, when Justice Strange declared that, where there was a voluntary separation agreement,

> and there has been an allowance of a sufficient maintenance to the wife, recent determinations have not merely held the husband discharged from the obligation of contracts entered into by her, but have regarded her as being *sui juris* with regard to matters of property, in the same manner as she is by the civil law. They have considered her therefore as being so far emancipated by the agreement from the incapacities incident to coverture, as to be capable of contracting not only for necessaries, but for every other thing which can be made the subject matter of agreement, and consequently as being liable to be sued in the Courts of Common Law as if she were a feme sole.[41]

In the late eighteenth century, whether temporal courts could decree and enforce separate maintenance agreements was fiercely debated, and in 1800 the case of *Marshall* v. *Mary Rutton* decisively overturned the seventeenth-century precedent, with the judge upholding coverture by deciding that "two parties, who . . . being in law but one person, are on that account unable to contract with each other."[42] In light of this decision, it would not have been surprising if the courts had held George Norton responsible for his wife's debts in 1853—especially since George had invoked coverture in declaring their separate maintenance agreement invalid. But the point here is less whether precedent had established grounds for Caroline's position than the fact that, because wives had once been declared autonomous persons, the argument that coverture reflected "nature" had become a site for potential contests. When the Norton dispute raised exactly the same issues that had once been used to grant married women some property rights, it threatened to expose the instability and artificiality of the dichotomy that established married women's dependence in the mid-nineteenth century. And because the property that was disputed in the Norton case was exactly the kind of property most problematic for the principle of coverture—that is, because it consisted of liquid capital that included Caroline's own earnings—the Nortons' dispute threatened to destabilize, or at least question, the principle of women's dependence in relation to property. It is precisely because this material dependence was so critical to the symbolic economy I have described that the Norton case was potentially so disruptive; it is precisely because this binary economy *could* be contested that the dispute achieved the prominence it did.

The economic and political interests that cut across the supposedly neutral territory of the private sphere were actually evident to nearly everyone in everyday practice, of course, just as the injustices of coverture were visible to thousands of working women. In this sense, Caroline Norton's story told nothing new. But the situation whereby individual cases might be explained away and tolerated as exceptions to a general rule remained bearable as long as such cases were not exposed as integral to the social fabric itself—as long, that is, as they were not represented in any discourse except literature, which rendered such marital discord a fiction that could be culturally marginalized or dismissed, or textually contained within a happy ending. When Caroline Norton dramatized her history in the form of a melodrama, she capitalized on the greater latitude granted literature to explore these matters and she sought to enlist her readers' sympathies by appealing to the investment they shared in domesticity and an image of female dependence and vulnerability. But Norton also recognized that to remain within literary discourse was to be excluded from the political realm where legislation that could define and punish the transgressions that disrupted domesticity was formulated. This accounts for both Norton's melodramatic self-representation and her refusal to take up her detractors' suggestion that she confine her complaint to novels and poetry. "*My* history *is real*," she exclaims at the end of *English Laws*. "Let that thought haunt you, through the music of your Somnambulas and Desdemonas, and be with you in your readings of histories and romances. . . . I *really* wept. . . . I *really* suffered. . . . I *really* have gone through much, that, if it were invented, would move you" (pp. 166–67).

Despite all the subversive components of Norton's complaint, however, as long as she retained the melodramatic script by which she represented her case, she remained within the terms of the ideology whose discursive rules she violated. For its characters and its plot, melodrama assumes both the naturalness of female dependence and the sexual double standard; if male sexuality were not aggressive and predatory, after all, and if females were not innocent, vulnerable, and valuable precisely in this vulnerable innocence, villainy would assume a different guise and plots would not tell of innocence persecuted and then saved. While melodrama provided Norton with terms in which to conceptualize her own suffering, it was also part of the ideology of separate spheres that set limits to the remedy she could imagine. As the lady-in-distress in search of a champion, Norton could ask only for protection, which, because it had to be enforced by male legislators and magistrates, left power just where it had always been.[43]

Caroline Norton could influence Parliament because much of what she said was what lawmakers expected and wanted to hear: that the home should be kept separate from commercial and political relations, that the sexual double standard was both natural and just, that protection was a woman's definitive right.[44] She was also influential because she provided a specific contrast to the three thousand women whose signatures on the Married Women's Property petition gave names if not faces to the army of "strong-minded women" legislators feared. In contrast to their demand for female autonomy, Norton's plea that separated women be granted protection did not violate the principle of female dependence. When the House of Lords amended the divorce legislation to address the injustice Caroline Norton represented—that of the separated woman forbidden to keep her own earnings—it foreclosed discussion of the much more subversive issue of married women's autonomy in relation to property. Even though the Married Women's Property Bill passed its second reading in the Commons, when the divorce bill came up nine days later (with the amendment Norton had inspired affixed) the property bill simply disappeared from parliamentary discussion and the subject was not addressed again until 1868.

The Matrimonial Causes Act that Parliament adopted in 1857 did not disturb either women's relation to property or the sexual double standard. It did not give all married women equity rights over property, but instead addressed only the most egregious injustice, the case of the separated wife who had no defense under common law. The act treated her as a temporarily anomalous case: as long as she remained separated from her husband she became legally a *feme sole*; if she returned to him or accepted him back, however, the "normal" relations were automatically restored.[45] The act also reinforced the sexual double standard by preserving the inequality of grounds by which men and women could sue for absolute divorce: a man could sue for simple adultery, but the woman was allowed to petition for divorce only on the grounds of "aggravated" adultery—a transgression that combined adultery with incest, bigamy, desertion, or cruelty (these last two being categories that Parliament was long loathe to define).[46] Finally, although it abolished the action of criminal conversation per se, the 1857 Matrimonial

Causes Act retained a provision whereby a man could sue a corre-spondent for damages after the divorce was granted. Lawmakers thereby legislated against any conceptualization of woman that was not based on her reproductive physiology at the same time that they retained the equation between women and property that the legal distinction between men and (married) women simultaneously dis-guised and preserved.

By allowing them to obtain legal protection against the hus-bands from whom they were separated, the divorce law undoubtedly benefited thousands of working-class women who otherwise would not have been able to protect their earnings. But this provision soon proved inadequate to the problem, partly because the law protected *only* deserted women and partly because the woman whose property had been confiscated by her husband still had to institute a suit against him—a remedy that was useless if the woman was penniless and the man was gone.[47] One could also argue that the requirement that an aggrieved wife present her case to the local police court ensured that working-class domestic relations would be more regular and accessible to state surveillance than when more informal ar-rangements compensated for the legal separations that were virtually impossible to obtain. The 1857 Matrimonial Causes Act made sig-nificant contributions to legal reform; it put an end to the Church's participation in law, for example, and rationalized overlapping legal procedures. Nevertheless, it did not actually remedy the anomalies it set out to address. Absolute divorce was still prohibitively expen-sive; the procedures in Scotland and England still differed; and men and women still received different treatments under the law. Most importantly, because the divorce legislation foreclosed debate about the legal autonomy of women and ratified the assumption on which middle-class identity was based—the assumption that sexual differ-ence was both fixed and paramount—the precarious equilibrium that held legal, economic, social, and sexual oppositions in alignment remained in place throughout the middle decades of the century. Not until 1882, when a substantive Married Women's Property Bill was passed, was this alignment fundamentally disturbed.[48]

V

The complexities of Caroline Norton's place in the ideology of sep-arate spheres become clearer if we read them against a story that occupied a prominent place in Norton's conceptualization of her own history. This is the true story of Hannah Brown, celebrated victim of the Greenacre murder. According to Caroline Norton, her husband, George, initiated the jest that equated her with Hannah Brown, but the analogy had such resonance for Caroline that she referred to it repeatedly in the forty years following George's cruel joke.[49] When she alluded to George's 1836 Greenacre letters in her 1854 divorce pamphlet, Caroline Norton clearly expected that the story would still be so familiar to her readers that George's bad taste would convict him as a villain.[50] So prominent a role did Norton assume this crime to play in the public imagination that she did not feel compelled to detail its grisly particulars until 1874. In that year, in the appendix to a privately printed pamphlet entitled *Taxation, by an Irresponsible Taxpayer,* Norton set out the story of Hannah Brown in a version that clarifies the melodramatic terms in which she continued to see her own life.

Early in 1836, James Greenacre exacted a promise of marriage from the widow Hannah Brown by claiming to own a thousand-acre farm. The couple told neighbors they were planning to marry at Christmas, but when Christmas came and the widow Brown had disappeared, Greenacre explained that the wedding had been given up. A few days later, however, on a side path near Edgware Road, a workman came across the "trunk of a female body, without head or legs, in a sack which had been tied at the mouth." One week later, the lockkeeper of Regent's Canal, investigating an impediment to the lock's gates, "dragged up by its long hair the *head* of a woman." A workman in Coldharbour Lane completed the puzzle on 2 February when he "found a sack among the bushes. There was a hole in the rotting old sack, and through the hole he saw part of the *knee* of a human being. The sack was opened, and found to contain the *legs* of a woman."[51]

The police determined that the body was Hannah Brown's. Summarizing the police report, Norton offers this gruesome description of the woman's murder: police decided that "a heavy blow given to the miserable creature's head during life, had burst her eye, fractured her skull, and broken her jaw, several of the teeth of the upper jaw being forced out and the tongue crushed between them; that her head had been sawn off while life yet lingered—though, from the blow which ruptured the eye, she was then probably in a state of temporary insensibility" (p. 31). The relationship between this story and Caroline Norton's complaint about taxation is not immediately apparent. Her primary argument in the pamphlet is that a married woman should not be obliged to pay taxes if she has no legal existence; here as elsewhere, however, her real complaint is that the husband who should protect her is protected from her financial claims on him by the law that denies her existence. "The tyranny may not be 'tremendous' which compels a female house-holder to pay taxes," she acknowledges. "But it assumes that shape when the compulsion which can be exercised *against* her, leaves no corresponding power as a balance-weight to be exercised *for* her. Lightly enough would those taxes sit, with many other expenses, if the person who *should* support this family could be proceeded against" (p. 27).

The implication of Norton's appending this story to this com-plaint is that George Norton, the ex-magistrate, is aided by the laws of his country in the brutal (if metaphoric) "assassination" of his wife. This analogy, however, is only one part of an entire set of relationships, characters, and plots: for Norton, the dismembered woman's body, its tongue crushed, its head sawed off while the body was still alive, is a precise image of the woman who is denied protection; she is inno-cence silenced; she is helplessness and vulnerability victimized by man's predatory nature. That Norton repeatedly identified herself with Han-nah Brown suggests the stark polarities of Norton's self-conceptual-ization as well as the extent to which she continued to define herself in terms derived from domestic ideology: the gratuitous brutality of Brown's murder bespeaks a world where male violence preys on fe-male helplessness and where the only imaginable remedy is giving women not political rights or economic autonomy but legal protec-tion within the separate sphere of the home.

I want to make two points about Caroline Norton's persistent identification with Hannah Brown. The first is the way in which the melodramatic story by which Norton read and wrote her own history provided a language bristling with metaphorical violence that allowed her to express her outrage against all of her oppressors— the brutal husband, the preoccupied politician, the indifferent leg-islators. Indeed, in one sense, the fact that Norton, as a married woman, could use such highly personal and hyperbolic language instead of the more abstract and euphemistic terms to which male legislators were "bound" enabled her to say things they could not say—at least on the floor of Parliament.[52] The relative freedom that came from Norton's marginal political position also enabled her to expose—whether intentionally or not—the price extracted from all subjects by the alienation that constituted the very grounds of in-dividualism. The figure of Hannah Brown's dismembered corpse not only epitomizes the violated domestic ideal; it also constitutes a trace of the alienation inherent in the proprietary self, an alienation that was most visible where it was theoretically least felt—in the woman who should have been safe and protected at home.

By contrast, my second point about Norton's identification with Hannah Brown is how it marks the limitations of Norton's complaint. Even though the woman who spoke melodramatically of domestic wrongs articulated the effects of the contradiction she lived in such a way as to mobilize her contemporaries' sympathies and fears, she did not thereby escape the situation that set the terms for her vulnerability in the first place. The language of melodrama and the idealization of domesticity that underwrote it worked against both a genuine recognition of the interests women shared, especially across class lines, and the entry of women as a group into the "public" sphere of politics and business. In a very important sense, Caroline Norton was able to tell the story of Hannah Brown's dismemberment because she did *not* identify with this working-class woman; whatever periodic brutality George might express in the privacy of the home, Norton, like most middle-class women, imagined herself to be immune to the pervasive and random violence that working-class women feared to be a condition of their daily lives. This is the sense in which class is operative in Caroline Norton's story—not as a factor Norton overcame in constructing a female alliance, but as a buffer against overidentification and therefore as the necessary condition for self-representation itself.[53] If the respect and protection (middle-class) women claimed as their right depended on keeping the sexual spheres rhetorically separate, then this symbolic separation also worked against middle-class women seeing working-class women as anything other than characters—and this, in turn, worked against all women achieving the economic and political rights that would have undermined the dependency and isolation they collectively experienced.[54]

CHAPTER FOUR

The Man-of-Letters Hero
David Copperfield and the
Professional Writer

IF THE NINETEENTH-CENTURY SUBJECT was inscribed in and partially constituted by the discourses of medicine and law, then that subject was also less formally—but no less effectively—constructed by another cultural discourse—literature. The historical emergence of "literature" as a distinct body of culturally valued texts belongs to the late eighteenth and early nineteenth centuries;[1] its social and ideological functions during this formative period were extremely complex, as were its relations to other emergent social institutions, such as literacy, the daily press, and public education.[2] In this chapter, I address only one facet of the ideological work literature performed in nineteenth-century England: I focus primarily on the way in which one writer, Charles Dickens, translated the deep structural relations I have been discussing into a psychological narrative of individual development, which both provided individual readers with an imaginative image of what identity was and created a subject position that reproduced this kind of identity in the individual reader. My implicit argument here is that one effect of the "literary" in this period was the textual construction of an individualist psychology; my explicit argument is that this process was part of the legitimation and depoliticization of capitalist market and class relations, that the definition (and defense) of the English writer's social role was intimately involved in both, and that stabilizing and mobilizing a particular image of woman, the domestic sphere, and woman's work were critical to all three.

The reading I offer here of Dickens's *David Copperfield* is not an interpretation that a nineteenth-century audience would have been likely to devise—not least because the definitions and functions of "interpretation" have undergone such changes in the last one hundred years. Instead of attempting to reproduce whatever *meaning* the text might have held for its first readers, I am describing a set of structural patterns and transformations that are written into the novel as the very conditions of its intelligibility. I am arguing, in other words, that in so far as these substitutions and transformations constitute the terms of the novel's narrative development, they define the operations by which the text produces meanings; in so far as these operations organize the reading of *David Copperfield,* they construct the reader as a particular kind of subject—a psychologized, classed, developmental individual—even if the reader is not conscious of this pattern and even if the reader interprets the meaning of the novel differently from other readers or not at all. Because the kind of subject the novel constructs and describes enjoys as one of its definitive characteristics the illusion of universality, the twentieth-century reader seems simply to replicate the Victorian reader. One of the things I argue in this chapter is that, even though the kind of subject we see being constructed here *is* the modern subject and therefore seems "like us," this subject is *not* universal but historically specific. Our apparent likeness to this subject is, in fact, the effect of the very ideological operations I describe here, and this appearance of likeness has helped keep this subject's internal contradictions invisible. I also argue, however, that the contradictions inherent in this subject constitute the basis for the distance readers *can* achieve from it and for the post-structuralist interpretive techniques by which the historicity of this subject is becoming visible to an increasing number of readers.[3]

I

The kind of subject described and reproduced by *David Copperfield* is individualized, psychologized, and ahistorical; it is also gendered. In fact, (masculine) gender is the constitutive feature of this subject; identity here takes the form of a physical and emotional development in which the male subject tempers his sexual and emotional desires by the possibilities of the social world. This conceptualization of the subject, then, also entails a specific model of desire. This desire is insatiable and potentially transgressive; it begins in the home as the condition of the individual's individuation and growth; it motivates his quest for self-realization; and, ideally, it is stabilized and its transgressive potential neutralized in the safe harbor of marriage.[4]

Structurally, this model of desire depends on difference being a constitutive part of the self, for without some difference within the individual, there would be no impetus for movement and no basis for change. In the last chapter, I argued that this internal difference was the basis for both the "free" exchange of labor and goods and the alienation contemporaries associated with the market economy. Here I extend that argument by suggesting that, by the mid-nineteenth century, the economic and political components of this internal difference—and, indeed, of this entire model of desire— had been masked by a vocabulary of emotional needs and sexual drives. Whereas in one vocabulary, the insatiable nature of this desire might be said to fuel the apparently limitless expandability of the market economy, in the other, the insatiable nature of desire might be said to motivate a search for the partner of one's dreams. And whereas in one vocabulary, transgression might be figured as class conflict, in the other it might take the form of falling in love with an inappropriate person.

By the end of this chapter, I will have set out the traces of this displaced system of class and economic issues, but for now I focus on the terms the novel foregrounds the terms of personal attach- ment, psychological development, and romantic love. The figure who is critical to David's development, in these terms, is David's mother, Clara Copperfield. Clara plays two, apparently contradic- tory, roles in David's quest to become the "hero" of his own story. On the one hand, she incarnates what seems to the boy and, retro- spectively, to the man to be perfect love. When, as narrator, David looks back "into the blank of [his] infancy," Clara's image is there alongside David's first "experience of [him]self." The effect of this narration is to tie the boy's sense of himself inextricably to his sense of Clara so as to make the mother the ground of the boy's identity. "We are playing in the winter twilight," writes David, as he re-creates his childhood self, "dancing about the parlour. When my mother is out of breath and rests herself in an elbow-chair, I watch her winding her bright curls round her fingers, and straightening her waist, and nobody knows better than I do that she likes to look so well, and is proud of being so pretty."[5]

On the other hand, Clara's prettiness and her vanity make her susceptible to the admiration of others beyond her young son. In so doing, Clara undermines David's vision of union and perfect love, for she soon brings home Mr. Murdstone, the "pa" who decisively ends David's childhood happiness. David's trip to the Peggottys' and his terms at Mr. Creakle's school are therefore indirect effects of his mother's vanity, and when Clara dies and David is exiled to the bottling warehouse, the full significance of her self-absorption becomes clear. In Murdstone's "crazy old house," David is no longer a special child, valued for who he is, but just another cog in the laboring unit "boys," the subordinate member of a crew in which everyone is simply an instance of the lowest common denominator, labor: "All this work was my work," he writes of this "degradation," "and of the boys employed upon it I was one" (p. 143).

Clara Copperfield's contradictory roles are critical to the novel for two reasons. In the first place, the imaginary plenitude she seems to embody constitutes the ideal that David will strive to re-create throughout the novel, even though—or, rather, precisely because—it is the discrepancy between what Clara seems to offer and what she indirectly causes that provokes David to run away in search of the love and station he "deserves." Only the fact that Clara is not (just) what she seems to David to be, in other words, allows for his separation from her and for that gap within himself between the experiences and infatuations he suffers and the perfect love he imagines is "evermore about to be."[6] In the second place, that the union with Clara is so obviously a retrospective construction by the adult narrator points to the symbolic reworking necessary to transform woman into the idealized mother. If his mother is not (only) the ideal David imagines and desires, then she must be transformed into this figure—for only then can she orient and domesticate his desire, just as only separation from her can inaugurate it. Even though the difference within the woman constitutes the condition of possibility for the difference *of* and *in* David, this difference must be repressed for the idealized unity to exist at all. In *David Copperfield*, then, we see the construction of the ideal of unity at the site of the mother; this takes the form of a series of substitutions that exposes and punishes the mother's guilt without jeopardizing the idealized woman she retrospectively becomes. That this structural and ideological rewriting of the mother is explicitly represented as the story of David's psychological maturation—his education in how to know his own heart and choose the proper partner—masks the extent to which his identity depends on the contradictions repressed by this symbolic work.

David's first adult attempt to re-create his relationship with his mother comes when he falls in love with Dora Spenlow. Dora is explicitly presented as another version of Clara Copperfield. Just as David's mother was a "wax doll" who was proud of her prettiness (p. 3), so Dora is doll-like, "diminutive" (p. 360), and harmlessly vain. Just as David's mother was a charming but inept housekeeper, so Dora's French education has given her grace but no practical knowledge or skill. The counterpart to these similarities is the likeness between David and his father. Like his father, David initially finds Dora's childlike aversion to life's practicalities attractive, and he imagines, as his father did, that he can teach his wife what she does not know. When David and Dora marry with nothing to support them but David's "earnestness," however, David begins to see what neither he nor, presumably, his father recognized about Clara— that a childish woman imperils the domestic ideal she is supposed to incarnate and superintend. When the younger Copperfields fall prey to their servants' petty larceny and to the casual exploitation of tradesmen, it seems to be simply a manifestation of the emotional ruin David suffers. In such an environment, he must "discipline" his desire so that his unhappiness will not trouble his pretty wife, just as he must squelch complaints about the servants, lest Dora realize how incompetent she is.

David may try to hide the emotional and financial cost of Dora's childishness from her, but he does not hide it from the reader. In fact, the way David masks his misery calls attention to other episodes in the novel that reveal what is really at risk in such domestic misdemeanors. The first two traces of this other story are the phrases that initially expose David's unhappiness. Annie Strong utters these phrases in chapter 45, which immediately follows the first depiction of David's domestic woes. Both phrases—"the final mistaken impulse of an undisciplined heart" and "unsuitability of mind and purpose" (pp. 611, 610)—refer explicitly to Annie's immature infatuation with Jack Maldon, from which she was "saved" by Dr. Strong's proposal of marriage. These phrases are also metonymically linked to earlier references to the Strongs, which, when read in relation to David's history, disclose an uncanny similarity between the Strongs' troubled marriage and the idealized union between David's parents. In the first place, the Strongs' December-May marriage reproduces David's parents' marriage in the sense that the partners are "not equally matched" in terms of class or age. Also, both marriages are motivated by a man's infatuation with a woman who wants out of an unpleasant situation (Annie's "situation" is her emotional entanglement with Maldon; Clara's is her class position, which is reflected in her employment as a nursery maid). In the second place, Dr. Strong, as a "sheep for the shearers" (p. 220) and an unworldly, "unprotected" man, is very like David's father, the man who named a house the "Rookery" simply because, despite all contrary evidence, "he liked to think that there were rooks about it" (p. 5). Dr. Strong is also like David's father in leaving his property to his wife "unconditionally." In the Doctor's case, this trust is eventually corroborated by the fidelity Annie reveals in this scene; the entire issue of fidelity, however, is shadowed by the outcome of that earlier trust: it was because Mr. Copperfield injudiciously trusted his wife to marry wisely if she married again that he placed no restrictions on his bequest to her and therefore made no independent provision for his son.

These explicit connections between the Strongs and David's parents underscore the implicit link between Annie Strong and Clara Copperfield. The significance of this link emerges when David first glimpses what Mr. Wickfield (and the narrator) have repeatedly insinuated—that Annie's affection for Jack Maldon might not be as innocent as it seems. Suddenly recalling the moment when Maldon left for India, David describes his awakening doubts.

> And now, I must confess, the recollection of what I had seen on that night when Mr. Maldon went away, first began to return to me with a meaning it had never had, and to trouble me. . . . I cannot say what an impression this made upon me, or how impossible I found it, when I thought of [Annie] afterwards, to separate her from this look, and remember her face in its innocent loveliness again. It haunted me when I got home. I seemed to have left the Doctor's roof with a dark cloud lowering on it. The reverence that I had for his grey head, was mingled with commiseration for his faith in those who were treacherous to him, and with resentment against those who injured him. The impending shadow of a great affliction, and a disgrace that had no distinct form in it yet, fell like a stain upon the quiet place where I had worked and played as a boy; and did it a cruel wrong. . . . It was as if the tranquil sanctuary of my boyhood had been sacked before my face, and its peace and honour given to the winds. (P. 260)

The real victim of this "stain" is David; the specter of Annie's unworthiness makes it impossible for him to seek imaginative comfort in an unsullied "sanctuary" of the past. But the phrases David uses to describe this past—"the quiet place where I had worked and played as a boy," "the tranquil sanctuary of my boyhood"—are phrases that refer not only to David's school days in Canterbury, but also to his childhood in Blunderstone. This image of a pretty young woman susceptible to the flattery of a dashing man (if not explicitly sexually aggressive) is a displaced version of the mother whose vanity betrayed both David's father's unworldly trust and the boy's unsuspecting love. Knowledge of the possibility that what seems like innocent prettiness and pride might actually signify (or be susceptible to) sexual desire is the "stain" that David refers to here. That this "stain" interrupts the story of David's first marriage suggests that it forms one of the repressed links between Clara and Dora, the two women whose domestic incompetence seems an innocent extension of their vanity and youth. Neither Clara nor Dora, however, is explicitly figured as a sexual woman, nor is their household mismanagement explicitly linked to sexual infidelity. Instead, the link between vanity, domestic misery, and sexual infidelity emerges in relation to another female character—David's childhood sweetheart, Little Emily.

When David (and, following him, almost every reader) refers Annie Strong's comment about "the first mistaken impulse of [an] undisciplined heart" to his love for Dora, he obscures the other, and in some ways more obvious, emotion to which this phrase applies— his love for the fisherman's daughter, Little Emily. Dora may call herself David's "child-wife," but Emily is as literally the "child" of this compound phrase as Dora is the "wife." Of his youthful adoration of Emily, David comments: "Of course I was in love with Little Em'ly. . . . I am sure my fancy raised up something round that blue-eyed mite of a child, which etherealised, and made a very angel of her" (p. 34). It is this "etherealisation" to which Rosa Dartle refers in the episode about Emily that appears in chapter 46. "This devil whom you make an angel of," Rosa sneers, "I mean this low girl whom he [Steerforth] picked out of the tide-mud . . . may be alive,—for I believe some common things are hard to die" (p. 621). Whether men like David simply "rais[e] up" "devils" into "angels" when they fall in love is exactly the point; for the problematic role Emily plays in David's maturation suggests that she—and through her, all the women in the novel—is as threatening as she is affirming to a man's adult identity.

David greets Rosa Dartle's "vaunting cruelty" with a "kind" wish that echoes another, similarly punitive fantasy. "To wish [Emily] dead," he halfmocks Rosa, "may be the kindest wish that one of her own sex could bestow upon her" (p. 616). In the episode to which this sentence alludes, the passage in chapter 3 where Emily is introduced, young David watches helplessly as Emily darts onto a "jagged timber" that overhangs the sea. David's reaction to the girl's rashness explicitly belongs to the older narrator, not to the boy, and his comment develops the idea of the "stain" to which I have already referred.

> The light, bold, fluttering little figure turned and came back safe to me, and I soon laughed at my fears. . . . But there have

been times since, in my manhood, many times there have been, when I have thought, Is it possible, among the possibilities of hidden things, that in the sudden rashness of the child and her wild look so far off, there was any merciful attraction of her into danger, any tempting her towards him permitted on the part of her dead father, that her life might have a chance of ending that day. There has been a time since when I have wondered whether, if the life before her could have been re- vealed to me at a glance, and so revealed as that a child could fully comprehend it, and if her preservation could have de- pended on a motion of my hand, I ought to have held it up to save her. There has been a time since—I do not say it lasted long, but it has been—when I have asked myself the question, would it have been better for little Em'ly to have had the waters close above her head that morning in my sight; and when I have answered Yes, it would have been. (Pp. 33–34)

The judgment implied by the phrase the "merciful attraction of her into danger" is here projected by the adult narrator onto Emily's dead father; it will later be repeated by Ham Peggotty as well (p. 415). What crime does this "blue-eyed mite" commit to merit such pu- nitive "mercy"? Emily's obvious fall, of course, is to Steerforth: in eloping with him she betrays not only her fiancé, Ham, but, perhaps more critically, her surrogate father, Peggotty. But I want to suggest that this transgression is really only the logical extension of other transgressions, crimes of which Emily is guilty even before Steerforth hurries her into his carriage. Only the persistence of these more recondite transgressions can account for the fact that the narrative's treatment of Emily is so much more punitive than is its treatment of the woman who presumably actually becomes a prostitute, Mar- tha. Emily's punishment is multifaceted and extreme: she is almost completely exiled from the novel after her fall (unlike Martha, whose sexual error is the basis for her role in the novel); she is subjected to Rosa Dartle's vicious verbal scarification, of which both David and the reader are horrified observers (while Martha is forgiven and comforted first by Emily herself, then by Mr. Peggotty and David); and she is denied marriage, even in Australia (as Martha is not). Such elaborate punishment suggests not only that her crimes exceed Martha's, but also that after her transgression her mere presence would contaminate the narrative of David's life.[7]

From one perspective, Emily's punishment follows from the position she occupies in David's maturation; from another, it can be seen as an inextricable part of Dickens's representation of sexuality. In David's history, Emily is the first substitute for David's mother, and she seems to offer the boy his best chance to recapture the imaginary plenitude he associates with his mother: "What happiness," David thinks of his childhood courtship, "if we were married, and were going away anywhere to live among the trees and in the fields, never growing older, never growing wiser, children ever" (p. 136). But Emily also stands at the threshold that irrevocably bars access to this innocence, for David's first enchanted visit to Emily makes him feel "ungrateful" in forgetting his mother and his home. He returns to Blunderstone to find that his mother has been as unfaithful to him as he has been to her, that she is married and his no more.

That Emily is intimately connected both to David's fantasies of a childish "marriage" and to his fears about his own and his mother's infidelity points to the way the novel implicates women in its complex and ambiguous representation of sexuality. Because Emily stands for both innocence and sexuality, she precipitates the contradictory effects of both. On the one hand, her initial innocence promises both pleasure and death: David's vision of his Edenic marriage to Emily ends with the two children "laying down our heads on moss at night, in a sweet sleep of purity and peace, and buried by the birds when we were dead" (p. 136). On the other hand, the sexual response she provokes in David on his second visit to Yarmouth excites the boy but leaves him frustrated, confused, and angry as well. The more Emily "captivate[s]" David, the more elusive she seems: "she seemed to have got a great distance away from me," David comments ruefully, "in little more than a year" (p. 133).

The way David's relationship with Emily is narrated—with the fact of sexuality a secret shared by the adult narrator and the reader—effaces any connection between young David and sexual knowledge. Even though David's maturation is implicit in his responses to Emily, the narrative assigns to woman—in this case, Emily—responsibility for the "stain" of sexual provocation, even though the extent to which Emily is conscious of her sexuality is left unclear. In *David Copperfield*, then, woman is the site at which sexuality becomes visible: not only does her provocation make men conscious of their own sexuality, but her vanity and willfulness show that no man can be sure of securing her affections. In *David Copperfield*, as in the medical texts I have already examined, woman is made to bear the burden of sexuality and to be the site of sexual guilt because the problematic aspects of sexuality can be rhetorically (if not actually) mastered when they are externalized and figured in an other. In

Dickens's novel, this mastery entails both the punitive exile whereby Emily's sexuality is "cured" and the symbolic substitutions of less explicitly sexual women for ones who are more closely linked to sexuality.

Even though Emily's sexual transgression can be punished and "cured," however, she also poses another, more indirect threat to the identity of the hero—a threat that will ultimately prove resistant even to such elaborate narrative treatment. Specifically, the possibility that David's childhood infatuation with Emily might mature into love introduces into the rhetoric of affection the specter of class. Class difference exists as a threat in *David Copperfield* because "innocence" in this novel entails not only sexual ignorance, but also the indifference to class distinctions that enables David to befriend and bring together "chuckle-headed" Ham Peggotty and the well-born Steerforth. For reasons I discuss in the third section of this chapter, such indifference to class is as crucial to David's heroism as is his boyish "freshness," and one important sign of this is precisely David's affection for Emily, the fisherman's daughter. One promise of the liberal rhetoric of Victorian individualism was that every individual had the "right" to follow the heart; according to this logic, class difference should not stand between David and Emily. And yet other incidents in the novel suggest that a sexual relationship between the two could only lead to harm: if he seduced but did not marry her, it would ruin David's honor; if he made Emily his wife, it would exclude David from the social position he "deserves." Both of these possibilities are made explicit in the representation of Steerforth, the character who takes over the infatuation from which David professes to have recovered. Steerforth brings dishonor on himself by seducing Emily, but, as his mother suggests, marriage might have been worse: "Such a marriage," Mrs. Steerforth informs Mr. Peggotty, "would irretrievably blight my son's career, and ruin his prospects" (p. 431). Steerforth's presence in the novel enables Dickens to levy this admonitory lesson without contaminating David's "freshness" by an overly self-protective consciousness of class. Through Steerforth, Dickens has it both ways: on the one hand, in carrying out an infatuation initially associated with David, Steerforth acts out the complex of desire and punitive anger of which hostility toward sexuality is the cause and Emily the object; on the other hand, in actually doing what David will not do, Steerforth underscores David's honorable innocence.

As a nursery maid, of course, David's mother posed precisely the same threat to David's father that Emily does to David, just as

David's father's indifference to class marked him as another "fresh" and romantic young man. The "blight" Clara Copperfield confers, however, falls not so much on her husband as on her son; as I have already argued, Clara Copperfield is indirectly to blame for David's being sent to the bottling warehouse, that degradation that momentarily threatens to "blight [his] . . . career, and ruin his prospects." In *David Copperfield,* the "stain" that seems to be a function simply of sexual knowledge is actually this "blight": the possibility not just that innocence might grow into knowledge but that a desire conceptualized as sexual and irrational might be oblivious to class distinctions. In terms of the ideological operations of the novel, this possibility proves to be even more intractable than the "simple" problem of sexuality, for too much attention to class rather than feeling smacks of callous self-interest just as too little threatens dishonor or ruin. To protect his hero from both of these disasterous fates, Dickens simply effaces this unresolvable dilemma: Ham and Steerforth intercede between David and Emily, and the problem of sexuality is transferred from the arena of class relations onto the figure of woman, where it can be symbolically addressed in the substitutions I have been describing. The symbolic "solution" the novel offers to both the explicit problem of sexual knowledge and the implicit problem of the way in which desire can cross class lines is Agnes.

In repeating the "angelic" qualities David associates with Clara Copperfield, Agnes preserves what is best about David's mother, but, because she is not vain, she "cancels" the faults of the mother more completely than Emily, Annie Strong, or Dora can. Because Agnes's love involves self-discipline rather than self-indulgence, she incarnates fidelity and is therefore proof against the kinds of temptation that drew poor Clara into that disasterous second marriage, Annie Strong to Jack Maldon, and Emily to Steerforth. David's turn to Agnes does not "stain" him because he never has to see in her sexuality that exceeds or strays from her relation to him, and his love for her does not "blight" his prospects because she brings to David the dowry of her middle-class virtue and efficient housekeeping skills. Transferring David's affection from his mother to Emily to Dora to Agnes thus works through the constellation of desire, anger, and anxiety structurally associated with but narratively distanced from the mother. By means of these substitutions, Dickens splits off and leaves behind the contradiction written into the mother that threatened to subvert the boy's happiness and to undermine the home. Emily and, to a lesser extent, Annie Strong and Dora

carry the pernicious effects of female vanity with them as they disappear from the novel. In Dickens's final representations of Agnes
she might as well be David's mother, so perfectly does she make
him what he is. "Clasped in my embrace," David exults to the reader,
"I held the source of every worthy aspiration I had ever had; the
centre of myself, the circle of my life, my own, my wife." "What I
am," David cries, "you have made me, Agnes" (p. 802).

Because the process I have been describing is represented as a
series of ever more judicious choices made by a maturing hero, the
imaginative work carried out on the various incarnations of woman
is subsumed by the effect it creates—that of (male) "psychology"
and development. That this effect is literally the work of the (male)
novelist and not a mimetic description of either an emotional development or the power of a woman's influence is underscored by
the fact that David Copperfield has become a professional writer by
the time he chooses Agnes; even at the level of the novel's fictive
world, the extraordinary image that inscribes Agnes as both the
center and circumference of David's identity is itself contained within
the autobiographical narrative that Copperfield has written (which
is, in turn, contained within Dickens's autobiographical novel). This
narrative division of labor, whereby the (male) novelist's responsibility for his own self-creation is transferred to the woman he also
creates but claims to describe, repeats the process by which contaminating sexuality is rhetorically controlled by being projected onto
the woman. I return in a moment to the ramifications of this division.
For now, I look briefly at the representation of writing that permits
this work to remain almost invisible and therefore effective.

In marked contrast to his other representations of work in this
novel, Dickens's references to David's writing are all euphemistic or
nonchalant. Whereas David's work in the bottling warehouse was
concretely detailed and his various jobs in Doctors' Commons, Dr.
Strong's study, and Parliament were metaphorically figured, the work
involved in writing is explicitly effaced. When David becomes a
writer, he advises the reader that he will not discuss his work. Expect
only references to his "earnestness," he tells the reader, not to "the
aspirations, the delights, anxieties, and triumphs of [his] art" (p. 783).
The one time David's aunt asks about the labor involved in writing,
David brushes the question aside: "It's work enough to read sometimes. . . . As to the writing, it has its own charms" (p. 797).

The closest equivalent to this representation of work is Agnes's
description of teaching in her "school": "The labour is so pleasant,"
she explains, "that it is scarcely grateful in me to call it by that name"

(p. 779). Agnes's other work does not receive even this much narrative elaboration; despite numerous references to Agnes as her father's housekeeper, whatever domestic tasks she performs or oversees are signified only by her basket of keys. That these keys stand for actual labor is suggested only indirectly—by Dickens's comic rendition of Dora's domestic blunders. In both his representations of David's writing and Agnes's housekeeping, in other words, Dickens displaces the material details and the emotional strain of labor onto other episodes—thereby conveying the twin impressions that some kinds of work are less "degrading" and less alienating than others and that some laborers are so selfless and skilled that to them work is simultaneously an expression of self and a gift to others.

The narrative transformation of Clara into Agnes functions not only to "solve" the problem of sexuality and to cover over the problem of class, but also, and as an integral part of these effects, to construct the domestic sphere as an arena where work is performed as selflessly and effortlessly as love is given. This construction proceeds alongside of the other kind of labor that is effaced in the novel, the work of writing. The two images—of effortless housekeeping and effortless writing—are interdependent at every level: not only is the Copperfields' domestic security a function of David's material success as a writer, not only does his success as a writer (as he describes it) depend on the selflessness Agnes's example inspires, but the representation of the domestic sphere as immune to the alienation of work is produced by the very writing with which it is compared. To work through the causes and effects of this complex interdependence and to explain the relationship between these representations and David's psychological maturation, I turn for a moment to the mid-nineteenth-century discussion in which this novel participated—the discussion about what role a literary man might play in a society where most work was neither effortless nor hidden and the "hero" was a figure everywhere under seige.

II

During the 1840s and 1850s, as the British book trade first began to expand its market to the mass reading public, the literary profession became the subject of numerous middle-class periodical essays and several popular novels. Part of this public attention was devoted to the "problem" of the literary man's social status; part of it focused on the inadequacy of domestic and international copyright laws; and part of it was concerned with the issue of whether literary men could or should organize themselves into a single professional association. All of these approaches to the problem of literary labor, however, ultimately derived from and eventually addressed the vexed issue of the relationship between this kind of labor and other kinds of professional or waged work. While novels like *David Copperfield* and *Pendennis* tended to formulate their responses to the writer's market situation less directly than did the essays in *Blackwood's* or *North British Review,* all of these discussions of literary men struggled to define the place the writer occupied in Britain's increasingly secular, capitalist society.[8]

Writers' claims to merit more respect than they felt they currently received almost all addressed the issues of work and money directly. Frequently, they conceptualized their work as contributing inestimable benefits to society; part of this representation was the image of the selfless writer, whose altruism generously canceled the "debt" his grateful readers incurred. This, at least, is the image offered by J. W. Kaye, in a long review essay of *Pendennis* and the literary profession. "It is no small thing," Kaye declared,

> to influence public opinion—to guide men to light from darkness, to truth from error—to inform the ignorant, to solace the unhappy, to afford high intellectual enjoyment to the few, or healthy recreation to the many. Of all professions, worthily pursued, it is the least selfish. It brings the worker for his daily bread into constant fellowship and communion with thousands of his fellow-creatures. Thousands are indebted to him for a share of the instruction and amusement of their lives.[9]

Kaye's assessment of the writer's altruism was by no means universal, however. In fact, his representation of writing as less selfish than other professions was partly a corrective to Thackeray's cynical send-up of the literary establishment in *Pendennis.* Partly, moreover, it offset Kaye's own recognition that literary men often did suffer (and even deserve) reputations for money-grubbing, antisocial behavior. The literary man, Kaye admits, "cannot afford to drop his ideas by the way-side: he must keep them to himself, until the printing-press has made them inalienably his own. . . . Even puns are not to be distributed gratis. . . . The smallest jokelet is a marketable commodity."[10]

That the literary man was viewed both (or alternately) as a disinterested sage and a mannerless miser points to the decidedly mixed lineage of the Victorian image of the writer. On the one hand, the Victorian writer could claim as ancestors leisured men of letters, those medieval court scribes and Renaissance intellectuals whose education marked them as privileged men, even if their daily meat came from patrons. On the other hand, the professional writer was descended from the early and mid-eighteenth-century hacks who sold ideas by the word and fought off competitors for every scrap of work. This second image understandably carried over into the Victorian period, for, as the continued extension of literacy accelerated the demand for newspapers and as printing innovations made it possible to meet this demand, more and more men scrapped for positions in what had become an economically viable, if not universally lucrative, profession.[11] It is perhaps more surprising that the first image also survived (indeed, accompanied) the takeoff of the publishing industry, but the late eighteenth-century valorization of "genius" had given it new life by revising the terms of the writer's prestige; according to Romantic poets like Shelley and Wordsworth, the writer's wisdom was an expression of a God-given gift, not social privilege.[12] Dr. Johnson's "general challenger" could only derive his authority from the virtue of hard work, but Thomas Carlyle's "man-of-letters hero" could claim the authority of the prophet. According to Carlyle, the writer deserved a place in a "perpetual Priesthood," for he was "*inspired;* for what we call 'originality,' 'sincerity,' 'genius,' the heroic quality we have no name for, signifies that. The Hero is he who lives in the inward sphere of things, in the True, Divine and Eternal, which exists always, unseen to most, under the Temporary, Trivial: his being is in that; he declares that abroad, by act or speech as it may be, in declaring himself abroad."[13] In keeping with Carlyle's image, the writer was credited with halting the "decline, which the influx of wealth, and the prevalence of commercial ideas, might otherwise have a tendency to produce."[14]

When mid-Victorian writers thought or wrote about their own work, then, they voiced the confusion generated by what must have felt to many like an incomprehensible contradiction. On the one hand, they were called prophets; on the other, they felt they had "no rank or position at all."[15] On the one hand, they were touted as superior to the "commercial ideas" that threatened a cultural "decline"; on the other, they felt themselves hostage to the rise and fall of taste and the good will (or business sense) of publishers, advertisers, and booksellers. Beginning in the 1830s, this contradiction was exacerbated for some writers in particular by the development of a new mode of publication, which jeopardized the writer's ability to claim immunity to the commercial transformation of society. This form of publication, which was the mode in which *David Copperfield* was initially printed and sold, was the part-issue, serial publication. Almost single-handedly, it made the novel into a valuable commodity by expanding the purchasing public beyond collective institutions (like circulating libraries) to a nation of individual buyers.[16]

Monthly part-issue publication, in which a complete novel was published in eighteen one-shilling parts and one double part costing two shillings, first gained popularity when Charles Dickens took over an illustrated serial about a sporting club and reversed the priority between the text and the illustrations. Because it made publishing costs more flexible, increased advertising revenues, and enabled publishers to adjust production runs to sales, Dickens's innovation reduced the previously prohibitive cost of an illustrated triple-decker novel to £1, and it distributed the cost for both publisher and purchaser over an entire year. The success of this publishing innovation was immediately registered in sales: by its fifteenth number, the press run of *Pickwick Papers* had increased from four hundred to forty thousand copies.

Part-issue publication appealed to many writers as well as publishers and readers, for it guaranteed a steady income, lowered the initial risk of piracy, and enabled the author to establish a personal relationship with his audience, what Thackeray (speaking of Dickens) called "a communion between the writer and the public . . . something continual, confidential, something like personal affection."[17] The individualization of the reader and the personalization of the text were, however, the effects of exactly the opposite transformation at the site of the novel's production. Because of the absolute standardization of the form—the fact that each serial part had to contain exactly thirty-two pages, which had to be produced according to an inflexible schedule and internal form—the writer was constructed not as an individual, much less a "genius," but as just one instance of labor, an interchangeable part subject to replacement in case of failure or to repair in case of defect.[18] One sign of this notion was that when a novel was serialized in a magazine, as many mid-Victorian novels were, the editor (or editors) might direct the plot into more marketable channels or even rewrite parts of it, with or without the author's permission.[19]

The conditions by which novels were serialized made absolutely clear the extent to which "literature" was part of the market economy and literary work was alienated labor—both in the author's subjection to another's schedule and the requirements of the form and in the triumph of profit over quality. Although not all kinds of mid-Victorian writing were so obviously bound by these factorylike conditions of production or so visibly tied to consumer demand, the market relations that dominated serial publication implicitly governed all texts written for publication and sale. Even the apparent exceptions to the law of supply and demand—those single-volume works issued in small numbers and sometimes financed by the author—confirmed the rule that the publication of a literary work depended on either its projected ability to make money for a publisher or else its author's capital.[20]

Just as the serial mode of publication highlighted the inscription of writing in the capitalist market economy, the problematic status of the "genius," and the alienated nature of literary labor, so literary work of all kinds rendered some of the other problematic facets of capitalist production more prominent than did most other kinds of waged or professional labor. In the first place, because of the peculiarities of literary composition, this activity exposed the arbitrariness of the definition of labor to which wages were affixed. If, for example, literary labor was defined as the conceptualization of an idea, then was another writer's influence part of the work or not? If literary labor was the physical writing of the manuscript, then were copyists equal partners? If literary work was completed when the manuscript was delivered, then was the work of the editor, printer, and bookseller expendable? In the second place, the problematic nature of literary property revealed how slippery a concept "private property" could be. If literary property resided in the original idea for an article or book, and not in the physical object in which the idea was produced, marketed, and consumed, then how could this property be defined and owned? If the idea was not distinct from the paper on which it was printed, then why did it not belong to the printer? What was the relationship between the "original" manuscript the author produced and all the other copies that were mechanically reproduced? If they were somehow the same, then how could one assess so as to reward the contributions of publishers, printers, and booksellers? If they were somehow different, then how could one determine the author's interest in the thousands of copies actually sold?

Precisely because literary labor exposed the problematic nature of crucial capitalist categories, writing, and specifically the representation of writing, became a contested site during this period, a site at which the instabilities implicit in market relations surfaced, only to be variously worked over and sometimes symbolically resolved. The representation of writing also became the site of this ideological work because of the contradictions inherent in the image of literary labor itself. Because it was conceptualized simultaneously as superior to the capitalist economy and as hopelessly embroiled within it, literary work was the work par excellence that denied *and* exemplified the alienation written into capitalist work. Even though the majority of authors continued to earn marginal money and prestige, then, in writing about writing, literary men played a central role in the consolidation and interrogation of capitalist work relations.

I do not discuss in detail the manner in which all the problems that surfaced at the site of the writer were rhetorically, legally, and practically addressed or resolved. Instead, I focus on one of the kinds of ideological work performed upon and by mid-nineteenth-century representations of the literary man: the construction of the worker-reader-writer as an autonomous individual. Given the anti-individualizing effect of serial publication, the range of jobs involved in producing a physical book, and the various claims that could be made on its ownership, it was by no means inevitable that authorship would be conceptualized as an individualistic activity.[21] But because of a paradox central to the concept of the individual in class society, the individualization of authorship actually "solved" the contradiction between the two images of writer—the "genius" and the cog of the capitalist machine—at the same time that it assured the writer a constructive and relatively lucrative social role.

Most of the rhetorical work of individualizing authorship was performed by literary men themselves, in the kinds of essays I have been discussing and in novels like *David Copperfield*. One of the critical components of this work was the reconceptualization of the meaning and effects of competition. Whereas by midcentury, other occupational groups such as medical men had begun to feel the pernicious effects of unregulated competition and to organize so as to control it, many literary men celebrated competition as the only certain index to literary merit and they resisted professional organization. The individual author, in other words, by these writers' definition, participated in a free trade of ideas that inevitably rewarded the best man. According to J. W. Kaye, for example, a writer's "competitors are, or may be, the world. There is no protection for him to claim; no exclusiveness to defend him from an overwhelming array of rivals." For Kaye, the literary profession's lack of regulation ennobled the victor: "All the more honourable," he claims, "to succeed in it."[22] A writer for *Westminster Review* in 1852 also applauded literature's lack of professional perquisites as supplying an absolute measure of a writer's worth. "In other professions," he writes, there are definite advantages, offices, and gains, which ability, perseverance, and vigilance in the seizure of favourable opportunities, may ultimately hope to achieve. . . . But literature presents none of these temptations in prospect; it has no offices to give away, no sinecures, no penalties, no snug retreats from work and poverty, for the idle, the profligate, and the incapable; interest can do nothing, patronage can do nothing in literature; the appeal lies direct from the author to the public, and distinction must be won and carved out by merit alone.[23]

The laissez-faire image of writing reaches its logical conclusion in Thomas Carlyle's critical assessment of the "democracy" that writing allows. "Printing," Carlyle declared in his lecture "The Man-of-Letters Hero," "which comes necessarily out of Writing . . . is equivalent to Democracy: invent Writing, Democracy is inevitable. . . . Whoever can speak, speaking now to the whole nation, becomes a power, a branch of government, with inalienable weight in law-making, in all acts of authority. It matters not what rank he has, what revenues or garnitures: the requisite thing is, that he have a tongue which others will listen to; this and nothing more is requisite."[24]

If Carlyle's equations had been true, of course, everyone *could* have competed for a literary voice and a slice of the book-trade pie. But in the mid-nineteenth century, Carlyle's complaint was no more accurate than Kaye's claim that writing required "no qualifications," or the *Westminster* reviewer's boast that authorship offered "no sinecures" or "retreats from work." In fact, just as it was a microcosm of some of the most problematic aspects of capitalist work relations, so writing was a showcase for the restrictions unofficially but systematically institutionalized in class society. Even though literacy was increasingly available to members of the lower classes, access to the world of professional letters was still determined in the first instance by one's ability to write in a certain way, with an acceptable breadth of allusion, and according to recognized paradigms, genres, and modes of address. Until education was required and standardized across class lines, these conventions and this idiom were simply unavailable to most members of the working class. Then, as now, what counted as "publishable literature" was at least partly a function of class.[25]

To the extent that such informal checks on publishing were masked by a rhetoric of "free trade," the literary profession simultaneously reinforced and disguised the differences among individuals created by class. Arguments about the salutory effects of competition, in other words, and the accessibility of literature to

the "world" created the illusion of free trade and unlimited opportunities even as they depended on such internal limitations controlling the number of competitors by delimiting the terms of
success. Given this implicit institutionalization of class difference,
it seems paradoxical that the individual writer was represented as
unique and the new incarnation of the self-made, self-sufficient man
(if not always a "prophet" or "genius") by virtue of the fact that
he was *like*—not different from—the other men with whom he was
free to compete. This paradox, whereby (class) difference is represented as (human) likeness, and this likeness becomes the ground
of one's unique identity, is essential to the structure of individualism
in class society. In the mid-nineteenth century, it was mobilized as
the basis for the literary man's social authority and in the defense
of his special role.

This paradox appears, for example, in another of the critical
components of the individualization of authorship, the commercial
marketing of books by linking a writer's name to a unique and
recognizable image—often an "autobiographical" image derived from
the writer's work. On the one hand, by its very nature, the successful
promotion of a marketable "name" depended on distinguishing between this writer and all other competitors. But on the other hand,
arguments advanced to discriminate a writer's personality so as to
enhance the value of his work often referred to his ability to appeal
to or represent the taste of all his readers—to be, in other words,
like everybody else.

As in so many other respects, Dickens was the master of this
dimension of literary production: he expertly used new advertising
techniques to produce an iconography of "Dickens" and a market
for his books.[26] The success with which Dickens created and capitalized on his own public image was highlighted—and reinforced—
by the review of *David Copperfield* that appeared in *Fraser's Magazine*
in 1850. Like many other mid-nineteenth-century "reviews," this piece
functions as an advertisement for the novel, but because it is presented as a critical evaluation, it generates the effect of describing
the value it actually helped create. This review is particularly interesting, however, not only for its participation in the circular economy
of marketing, but also because it sets out the paradox of individualism I have just described. "Probably there is no single individual
who, during the last fourteen years, has occupied so large a space
in the thoughts of English folk as Charles Dickens," the reviewer
declares, thereby distinguishing between Dickens and all his rivals.
But when he comes to "account for this widespread popularity," the

reviewer reveals the likeness upon which this recognition of difference depends. Dickens is popular, he asserts, "because of his kindly, all-pervading charity, which would cover a multitude of failings, because of his genial humour and exquisite comprehension of the national character and manners, because of his tenderness, because of his purity, and, above all, because of his deep reverence for the household sanctities, his enthusiastic worship of the household gods."[27] In this description, Dickens understands and represents ("comprehends") the "national character," and this constitutes the basis for his social authority as well as his popularity. As the reviewer elaborates Dickens's social role, however, the differences beneath the likeness (beneath the difference) reappear. Charles Dickens, the reviewer continues,

> has done more, we verily believe, for the promotion of peace and goodwill between man and man, class and class, nation and nation, than all the congresses under the sun. . . . Boz, and men like Boz, are the true humanizers, and therefore the true pacificators, of the world. They sweep away the prejudices of class and caste, and disclose the common ground of humanity which lies beneath factitious, social, and national systems. They introduce the peasantry to the peerage, the grinder at the mill to the millionaire who owns the grist.[28]

To argue that Dickens—and, by extension, "men like Boz" (i.e., other writers)—can anchor social stability and class harmony better than "congresses" can is explicitly to assume that a "common humanity," which can be defined and mobilized rhetorically better than it can be officially policed, lies beneath economic and national differences. But this reviewer's reference to the "national character and manners" makes it clear that this "humanity" could be mobilized only because (and to the extent that) it was not actually "common" but specifically English: Dickens's popularity within England is represented as a function of his ability to recognize what is characteristically English in his readers. What this description institutes but does not confess is the coercive construction of the likeness it claims to locate beneath superficial differences. That is, the argument that Dickens "comprehends" what makes his readers alike actually creates this likeness—by alluding to, so as to dismiss, the (national and class) differences on which it depends.

Other representations of Dickens and writers in general explicitly acknowledged the role authors played in constructing either the "common ground of humanity" or the English "national character." An article in *Blackwood's* in 1842 defined literature as that which constitutes the bond among men, making them into a single nation with a common share in the national wealth.

> Sentiments such as these immortal [literary] works embody, "thoughts that breathe, and words that burn," are the true national inheritance; they constitute the most powerful elements of national strength, for they form the character, without which all others are unavailing; they belong alike to the rich and the poor, to the prince and to the peasant; they form the unseen bond which links together the high and the low, the rich and the poor; and which, penetrating and pervading every class of society, tends both to perpetuate the virtues which have brought us to our present greatness, and arrest the decline, which the influx of wealth, and the prevalence of commercial ideas, might otherwise have a tendency to produce.[29]

As this quotation makes clear, the image of writers like Dickens comprehending the national character was constructed in a dialectical relationship with that image *of* national character: Dickens is a popular and important writer because he "comprehends" what everyone knows to be the national character; readers know what the national character is because Dickens "comprehends" (represents) it. One function of "literature," then, was to identify (construct) the "national character" by representing (defining) what was common to all Englishmen; by the same token, "literature" included those works that represented these "national" traits. In this circular economy, one Englishman can stand for all others, just as Dickens can stand for all other contributors to the national "literature." In fact, the work of the literary man was to make all Englishmen like each other—or, more precisely, like the literary man. This is one of the contradictions masked by the paradox of individualism: the representative (literary) man was simultaneously considered unique (a "genius") and like every other man (interchangeable) because he made his readers in his own image. This definition of the "national character" implicitly constructed the middle-class male as the norm by obliterating class (and gender) differences, but the hypocrisy inherent in this reproduction of the same—the fact that all individuals did not have the same opportunities or access to the "national inheritance"—was obscured by the appeal to national identity.

This paradox appears again in arguments advanced to promote stricter domestic and international copyright laws. If any issue might have been expected to unite literary men in a common cause or to expose the contradictions and inequities of individualism, it was that of copyright; despite the benefits literary men as a group might have gained from professionalization, however, they could agree on neither whom to unite with or against, nor which actions would enhance their common good. As a consequence, all the alliances they formed were short-lived, and their efforts were effective primarily in establishing a legal basis for the individualized author.[30]

The question of domestic copyright engaged Parliament's attention for five straight sessions between 1837 and 1841. The most important provision of the act that finally became law on 1 July 1842 was the extension of the period writers were protected by copyright beyond the twenty-eight years guaranteed by the act passed under George III.[31] Even though the period initially proposed by this legislation (sixty years) was eventually cut (to forty-two years), the Domestic Copyright Act recognized that, in the first instance, authors and not publishers or booksellers were entitled to the profits from their intellectual property. Writers who supported this bill in print, however, subordinated discussions of what was actually a contest between themselves and publishers to arguments about the advantages *England* would enjoy from stricter copyright laws. It was in the context of debates about this bill that the *Blackwood's* essayist advanced his thesis about writers defining England's national character and defending its "national inheritance"—specifically against foreign competitors. "A nation which aspires to retain its eminence either in arts or in arms," this writer begins, "must keep a-breast of its neighbours; if it does not advance, it will speedily fall behind, be thrown into the shade, and decline. . . . To every empire which has made intellectual triumphs, is prescribed the same law which was felt by Napoleon in Europe and the British in India, that conquest is essential to existence."[32] Such "conquest," the author suggests, will only be possible if writers devote their efforts to serious literature; this will only occur if writing is linked to "the purest and most elevated matters which, in sublunary matters, can influence mankind." These "pure" and "elevated" matters turn out to be the dynastic hopes and expectations associated with the (patriarchal) family. "The hope of transmitting his fortune to his children . . . the desire of founding a family" motivates the writer to produce his best work—*if* this effort is protected by domestic copyright laws that guarantee him and his family proceeds from his labor. This writer declares that such dynastic ambition is "the secret unobserved cause of the greatest individual and national efforts that have ever been achieved among mankind."[33]

The *Blackwood's* writer uses the equation between an individual's and his nation's dynastic ambitions to legitimize—and obscure—the self-interest of his own claim. That is, because what is good for the individual writer is represented as essential to England's well-being, the writer's economic self-interest seems like patriotism and the contest between his interest and that of other Englishmen (publishers and booksellers) simply disappears. Emphasizing likeness here functions to obscure the differences that are actually being defended.

A similar strategy appears in arguments about international copyright laws. Initially at least, this controversy promised to unite everyone involved in the English book trade against foreign publishers, for cheap foreign reprints, often imported back into England for resale, cut into British authors' and publishers' profits and helped keep the price of books within England prohibitively high. Such piracy was a constant source of anger to Dickens, in particular, and during his U.S. tour in 1842 he repeatedly lambasted American audiences for enjoying the fruits of unremunerated English labor.

Partly because publishers had not united against it, Parliament had been able to pass an International Copyright Act in 1838, but the act was completely ineffectual because no other nation could be persuaded to ratify the treaty. In May 1842, encouraged by the passage of the Domestic Copyright Act, a group of writers, publishers, and booksellers met in London to organize support for protective international legislation. Even though the meeting, which was chaired by Dickens, succeeded in founding an association of authors, publishers, printers, and stationers to lobby for improved enforcement, the Association for the Protection of Literature almost immediately splintered into rival factions. The issue that caused Dickens, among others, to withdraw support from the group was an offer by a Leipzig publisher to pay popular British writers a modest fee for reprint rights. When the association denounced the offer, arguing in favor of a more regular and binding agreement for all its members, Dickens, Bulwer, and other successful writers resigned in protest.[34]

Despite the fact that Dickens, in particular, actively promoted his own interest over the combined interests of British literary men, the arguments he advanced for international protection were couched in the same language of *national* interest with which the *Blackwood's* writer defended domestic copyright. Without some international agreement, Dickens proclaimed to a Boston audience in 1842, "you never can have, and keep, a literature of your own."[35] This language was echoed by *Blackwood's* in 1848, this time in an article about U.S.

copyright laws. Even though England had passed the International Copyright Act in 1844, U.S. law continued to protect its own but not foreign writers against piracy. This policy, the *Blackwood's* essayist declared, undermined the United States' ability to establish a national literature. "The selfish and short-sighted policy of our American brethren," he charged, "is found to operate in the most prejudicial manner upon their native literature; as no American publisher is likely to pay its due price for any composition of domestic genius, when he can please his customers and fill his pocket by reprinting, without any remuneration to the author, the most successful productions of the British press."[36] Just as the appeal to family and empire submerged self-interested claims in the arguments about domestic copyright, so the appeal to establishing a national literature obscures the self-interest operative in this position. In his Boston speech, in fact, Dickens specifically disclaimed all selfish motives for his position: "I would rather have the affectionate regard of my fellow men," he modestly declared, "than I would have heaps and mines of gold."[37]

By promoting the ideas of a "national character" and a "national literature," the two British copyright laws reinforced and fed off of the paradoxical image of the writer I have already discussed: in these representations, the writer is simultaneously an individual distinct from all others and a representative (English)man. These arguments also present individual profits as incidental effects of the contributions writers make to a "national inheritance," thereby obscuring the different degrees to which different individuals profited from or had access to this inheritance. Arguments for domestic copyright legislation, in equating the individual man and his family, obliterated the (legal, economic, and social) differences among members of that family; by the same token, arguments for international legislation equated the individual writer with Englishmen (or Americans), thereby repressing the disagreements among writers, or among various branches of the literary establishment. That the obliteration of these differences theoretically undermines the uniqueness of the individual went unremarked because the rhetoric of free trade and competition continued to prevail. These arguments divided these two components of capitalist market relations, however; free trade was represented as flourishing unproblematically within England, and international competition was depicted as a means of national self-definition and defense.

For the purposes of my argument, the important differences that are repressed by this logic are the difference of gender and the difference of class. This repression is a crucial component of the legitimatization of capitalist relations, for the Victorian market economy (like the industry of writing) depended on the illusion (but not the fact) of equal opportunity for everyone. Liberal rhetoric could proclaim that every individual was a subject and every subject had equal opportunities precisely because some individuals were situated and defined as not-subjects and nonequals. For even though gender and class differences were repressed in these arguments, residual assumptions about gender and class continued to operate in the workings of this economy; in fact, these assumptions constituted the basis for the effective ideological work of individualism. As just one example, take the complex roles gender plays in the argument about a national character. The slippage between arguments about the British Empire (in which all Englishmen could be at least imaginatively invested) and individual dynastic rights (in which authors' interests would clearly displace the interests of publishers) was masked by the presence within this equation of dialectically related assumptions about legitimacy and the role of the (legitimate) family in England. "The desire of founding a family," to which the *Blackwood's* writer assigns such power, could anchor an individual's dynastic efforts only if the individual man could be assured that his children were legitimate. This argument therefore depends on institutionalizing women's sexual fidelity (although not necessarily men's), for only the woman's fidelity could guarantee legitimacy and thus the (patriarchal) identity of the family. Assumptions about the chastity of women and the fidelity of wives remained invisible here, but the argument worked precisely *because* fidelity was assumed to be the natural condition of wives and because faithful wives were taken as the sign of England's moral superiority. Faithful wives therefore guaranteed the legitimacy of England's dynastic claims, just as they facilitated the individual man's dynastic ambition.

The representation of woman as a faithful wife played yet another role in the ideological work I am describing. The paradox of individualism defused the potentially pernicious effects of competition, not only by foregrounding its role in establishing a national identity while implicitly limiting those who could compete, but also by rewriting competition as an integral part of the individual—as one of the forces behind personal development. As mother, then, the woman was the origin of the boy's growth, not only for the psychological reasons I have already discussed, but also because she first taught him the habits of industry. But in this system of representation, the woman also served as the stopping point for desire and therefore as another check on competition. Because her domestic authority—indeed, her self-realization—depended on her ability to regulate her own desire, the faithful woman as wife anchored her husband's desire along with her own, giving it an object as she gave him a home. In this model, self-regulation was a particularly valuable and valued form of labor, for it domesticated a man's (sexual) desire in the private sphere without curtailing his ambition in the economy.[38]

The representation of woman as the selfless, self-regulating, faithful wife therefore occupied the same position in relation to arguments about the "national character" as it did to the construction of the legal subject and the man as a developmental individual. In both of these cases, the fidelity of the woman guaranteed legitimacy and neutralized the effects of the internal division essential to this paradigm of identity—whether the identity was of the individual, the family, or the nation. Stabilizing this representation of woman depended on writing out of the image the possibility of promiscuous (or autonomous) sexuality—not only because an unfaithful woman could introduce literal illegitimate offspring, but also because if all women were capable of independent desire, there would be no possibility that any desire could be domesticated or that there would be any natural limit to competition.[39] This is the work performed in *David Copperfield* by the changes rung upon woman in the process I have described. But stabilizing this image of woman *also* depended on normalizing assumptions about class. That is, the legitimacy and domestication that the woman's fidelity reinforced required another kind of support: they required that desire not cross class lines because the integrity of one's class—and, by extension, the difference be-tween this class and others—was as essential to individual (middle-class) identity as the fidelity of one's wife. This is why domestic mismanagement is linked to sexual infidelity in *David Copperfield:* a middle-class woman who did not manage her servants efficiently (as Dora does not) jeopardized the ground of middle-class male identity as surely as did a woman who was sexually unfaithful, because she made it clear that class exploitation was integral to middle-class domesticity. One way to manage her servants without seeming to enforce her will was to inculcate in them middle-class values, but the good example the middle-class housekeeper set had to contain ambition rather than inspire it. Paradoxically, the identity and eco-nomic well-being of the middle-class man depended on reinforcing the very class differences that the middle-class housewife (and the rhetoric of individualism) seemed to overcome. But the moral in-tegrity of the individual middle-class male was not troubled by this paradox as long as he remained unconscious of the contradictions that anchored his identity. To see the troubling ramifications of individualistic rhetoric, which the debates I have been discussing adumbrate but do not so clearly show, I now turn back to *David Copperfield*.

III

Despite both the extensive narrative work performed upon the representation of woman in *David Copperfield* and the less prominent but no less essential rewriting of David's work, Dickens's novel does not completely efface the contradictions these representations repress. For reasons I now explore, the site at which the traces of class issues return is Uriah Heep—or, more specifically, Heep's proximity to the novel's exemplary heroine and hero, Agnes and David Copperfield.

Heep's proximity to Agnes and to David is, in the first instance at least, physical. As her father's articled clerk, Uriah Heep spends most of his time in Agnes's house, and from this association grow both Heep's designs on Agnes and his entanglement in her father's business affairs. David's first introduction to Heep is marked by an even more startling physical image, the handshake that both "attract[s]" David to the red-eyed clerk and leaves him trying to rub Heep from his skin. But despite the fact that Heep's desire to marry Agnes yokes a particularly revolting image to the picture of Heep's clammy hands and writhing body, the physical chill that Heep's bony fingers exude metonymically stands for a much more degrading contamination: the moral corruption Heep's manipulations insinuate—first into Wickfield's financial dealings, then into Mr. Micawber's honesty and self-respect. Through their complicity with Heep, even these good characters lose their moral integrity; once in Heep's power, the good man betrays another's "trust" (as Wickfield does), for he feels (as does Micawber) that he harbors an enemy within. "My heart is no longer in the right place," Micawber mourns as he sinks into complicity with Heep. "The canker is in the flower" (p. 648).

Uriah Heep, again to quote Micawber, is an "interminable cheat, and liar," a "transcendent and immortal hypocrite and perjurer" (p. 658). He is, in short, duplicitous: he shows one false, obsequious smile and hides his sniveling smirk of ambition, hatred, and greed. Not until Micawber explodes Heep's nefarious plot does the reader know what Heep's machinations and motivations have been, even though their effects have reverberated throughout the actions we see. In this, as in almost every other sense, Heep seems to stand as David Copperfield's opposite: whereas Heep's schemes are hidden, David's actions and self-commentary are always present to the reader; whereas Heep is false, David is true both to himself and the reader. The sign of David's truthfulness is the honesty with which he discloses even the embarrassments of his youth—his drunkenness, his boyish love, and the galling memory of his disappointment with Dora.

Yet the contamination of that first touch lingers, and its corrosive effect becomes visible when David strikes Heep to punish him for his pretensions to Agnes. This blow draws David into odious complicity with Heep, both because Heep's revelation makes David the guardian of his trust and because Heep's pretensions are no more audacious than David's own. This blow is the mark of David's likeness to Heep: not only do the two characters share some relatively superficial traits—intense filial attachment, for example, and some experience of being dependent on others' charity—but they also have in common the more sinister tendency to manipulate others for their own self-serving ends. Here, in fact, their relative positions in relation to honesty seem reversed, for whereas Heep's connivances are eventually clearly revealed, David's manipulations remain obscure. Only when the reader reads against the narrator's disarming claims do certain actions appear as what they are: self-aggrandizing attempts to better himself at someone else's expense. When David exposes Mr. Mell's old mother at Mr. Creakle's school, for example, and when he introduces Emily to Steerforth, David is using other people to win respect for himself.

At least once, David acknowledges his "unconscious part" in what comes of Steerforth's acquaintance with Emily (even calling it "the desolation I had caused," p. 418). But for the most part, David's role in such plots is revealed to the reader not by David but by Uriah Heep. It is David's "unconscious part," for example, that Heep fingers when he accuses him of having been "the first to kindle the sparks of ambition in [Heep's] umble breast" by suggesting that Heep might someday be a partner in Mr. Wickfield's business (pp. 348, 216). Heep exposes this "part" again when he tells the Doctor that David harbors suspicions about Annie Strong, thereby shaking the old man's confidence in his wife and his own innocent trust. This, then, constitutes Heep's real threat in the moral scheme of the novel—not that he is fundamentally different from David Copperfield, but that he is, in some important respects, the same. To the extent that he is the same, Heep speaks for Copperfield; Heep is David's "unconscious part." In this sense, the homoeroticism mobilized by the physical contacts between Heep and Copperfield further blurs the boundary between them. Just as Heep's machinations conflate sexual and economic motives in his ambition to cross class boundaries, so the uncertainty of his sexuality exposes in David a responsiveness he cannot control—a responsiveness not only to another man's touch, but also to his ambition and moral ambiguity.

Despite these similarities, however, the crucial—and apparently morally decisive—difference between David's self-serving acts and Heep's manipulations is that the former are unconscious. Whereas Heep sets out to use and hurt others, David's transgressions are, for the most part, unwitting indiscretions. David is immune even to the moral blight that contaminates Wickfield and Micawber because David does not know what he is doing or even what he has done. In emphasizing this distinction between Heep and Copperfield, the novel symbolically reverses the paradox of individualism, whereby likeness covers over difference. In his representation of Heep and Copperfield, Dickens invokes the self-evident fact that people *are* (psychologically) different; some individuals *are* mean and self-serving, while others are generous and good. But in the world of the novel, this difference proves unstable. The sign that there is some difficulty with difference is the contradiction inherent in the narrative device necessary to create its effect—the autobiographical narration.

Given the autobiographical narrative of *David Copperfield,* the effect of a difference between Heep and Copperfield depends on there being a difference between the narrator-David and the character-David. The narrator must know Heep's evil as he retrospectively narrates David's life, even though the young David remains innocent of this knowledge. But while this effect merely capitalizes on the paradigm of development and change, the narration of David's self-serving actions as something other than what they can retrospectively be read to be depends on even the adult narrator not fully knowing what he says or being responsible for what he has done; it depends, in other words, on the narrator and the character being in some fundamental sense the same, even if their obvious difference hides this. Structurally, in fact, the young David Copperfield and the narrator are simultaneously the same and different—just as, in another sense, Copperfield and Heep are both alike and different. And it is the internal complexity in the first pair that transforms the unstable combination Heep-Copperfield into an apparently stable binary opposition.

Yet this complexity seems ominously like duplicity when we come to the matter of David's role in Annie Strong's exposure or Little Emily's fall. The duplicity is masked (and exposed) by the narrator's attempts to distract the reader's attention from young David's actions through misrepresentations so harmless or slight that they almost pass unnoticed. Immediately after David begins to suspect Annie Strong (p. 260), for example, he insists that he feels "dreadfully young" (p. 262), that he is "painfully conscious of [his] youth" (p. 262), that he feels "younger than [he] could have wished" (p. 267; see also pp. 276, 277, 283). The actual occasion of this embarrassment is simply David's first attempt to assert himself as an adult, a difficulty exacerbated by David's reunion with the older and more sophisticated Steerforth. But the fact that these statements occur when they do has the additional effect of distancing from the character the knowledge with which David has just been "stained" and therefore of reinforcing the innocence that contributes to make David's part in Emily's fate "unconscious." In other words, having acknowledged enough imaginative familiarity with illicit sexual desire to feel it as a "stain," the character downplays that familiarity and therefore the responsibility that might be assumed to follow from it.

In a sense, here as elsewhere, David is protecting himself with silence, just as Miss Mowcher protects herself by silently colluding with her customers. But this "self-protection" is possible only because the "hero" of the novel is split into two parts. The narrative persona protects that part of his "self" that is figured as the character by shielding him from both contaminating knowledge and the judgment of irony. The effects of this division are to split agency from knowledge in such a way as to detach responsibility from action, to deny intention, and to defer responsibility so that self-serving means never show themselves as what they are. By the end of the nineteenth century, this division would be reified and the "other" of the self dignified as the unconscious; in Dickens's novel, however, the rudimentary notion of some "unconscious part" cannot account for or accommodate the difference within David. In fact, these differences do not even remain within David but reappear outside him— as if the entire landscape of the novel were a series of mirrors, each of which reflects some "unconscious part" of David Copperfield. Thus Heep is David's selfishness, Steerforth his feckless sexuality, and Micawber his foolishness.

What we have in *David Copperfield*, then, is a novel in which the identity of the "hero" is never completely stabilized or fully individuated because the main character is split and distributed among so many other characters and parts. Given Dickens's presentation of sexuality, and Little Emily in particular, this split may *seem* to be a function of sexual knowledge and of female sexuality in particular. But as I have already argued, this representation of sexuality is itself an *effect,* not a cause, of something else—specifically, it is an effect of the deployment and denial of the structure of the individual in class society. The irrepressible cause of this character's fragmentation, as the issues that Heep brings into the novel reveal, is the difference built into the individual in this society—a difference that readily becomes hypocrisy when it is engaged in the hierarchy of class. This effect of class society is revealed by the duplicitous Uriah Heep, the character who emerges, fittingly, as the novel's conscience, the figure whose effects the narrator cannot contain.

When Micawber and Traddles "explode" Uriah Heep, the sniveling clerk retaliates with a vicious attack on his assailants. David describes this outburst as cowardice, but Heep's words cut uncomfortably close to the collective bone. To David's bland platitude— "there never were greed and cunning in the world yet, that did not do too much, and overreach themselves. It is as certain as death"— Heep responds,

> Or as certain as they used to teach at school (the same school where I picked up so much umbleness), from nine o'clock to eleven, that labour was a curse; and from eleven o'clock to one, that it was a blessing and a cheerfulness, and a dignity, and I don't know what all, eh? . . . You preach, about as consistent as they did. Won't umbleness go down? I shouldn't have got round my gentleman fellow-partner without it, I think. (P. 704)

In this passage, Heep reveals the two lessons the narrative otherwise conceals. The first is that hypocrisy is built into the individualist rhetoric of class society. The second is that David is complicitous with this society in the very morality he espouses and the success he enjoys. The same society that dispenses guilt to contain (working-class) ambition goads all men to work by calling it "a dignity" and "a blessing." But Heep's rhetorical "I don't know what all" points to the carrot that the stick of guilt holds out—the promise, unspoken here but everywhere evident in the novel, that material success will reward labor, that one will receive one's "blessing" on earth. The same society that offers this blessing to everyone, however, sets limits to the achievements of all but a few. The same society that rewards the self-made David Copperfield punishes the self-made Uriah Heep.

The same society that proclaims the likeness of all humans institutes class difference and calls it moral character.

That Heep's hypocrisy simply reproduces the duplicity that is built into class society is driven home to the reader by David's visit to Mr. Creakle's Middlesex prison. In the prison (as was not true in Mr. Creakle's school), everything reveals itself simultaneously as what it is and what it pretends to be. Individualism is perfected in the form of solitary confinement, which is represented as equality and justice. Heep's hypocrisy serves his own interests, even though it is lauded as wisdom. In the prison Heep is the "Model Prisoner"; as such, he can tell the visiting "gentlemen" the truth that David did not want to hear. Heep's words smack of rank hypocrisy, but they simply reproduce the hypocrisy society both produces and rewards. "I should wish," Heep piously declares, in a revealing parody of filial concern, "I should wish mother to be got into my state. I never should have been got into my present state if I hadn't come here. I wish mother had come here. It would be better for everybody, if they got took up, and was brought here" (p. 792).

Even though David Copperfield dismisses Heep's "profession" as a "rotten, hollow, painfully suggestive piece of business," neither he nor the reader can so easily leave behind the system that inculcates and rewards hypocrisy. Or, more precisely, the reader cannot leave this system behind because its duplicity is inscribed in the very narrative device that attempts to deny it—the splitting of the protagonist into an innocent hero, who does not know such deceitfulness because he is too young and good, and a worldly narrator, who knows but will not tell. When *David Copperfield* simply relegates the prison episode to the marginal position of "social commentary," the novel perpetuates the hypocrisy it seems to deny. The operative difference among the characters—the difference of class—is repressed (but not erased) by the vocabulary of emotion and development that subordinates class difference to the individual's upbringing and his personal, moral growth.

The possibility of David's not knowing—even provisionally—the extent to which class difference is institutionalized alongside—and as part of—alienation and psychological complexity as the very conditions of the individual in the society Dickens describes depends on there being some alternative to the deceit, self-interest, and hypocrisy that otherwise seem the very stuff of society itself. The possibility that David's innocence, the difference between Copperfield and Heep, and the happy ending of the novel will be believable, in other words, depends on Dickens constructing as part of his representation of this society his vision of Agnes's home. Only if class difference is first psychologized as an inherent difference in moral character and then projected outward as the difference (of sexuality) among or within women can it be (symbolically) "treated" and "cured" in the process I have described. Only if woman can be so "cured" can a sphere exist that is outside and different from the sphere of market relations. Only then will there be a place in which the (male) individual's desire can be produced as an acquisitive drive and then domesticated as its economic aggression is rewritten as love.

If Agnes and the home implicitly collude in covering over the hypocrisy and alienation that pervade class society, then so does the literary man. In fact, the literary man derives the terms of his ideological work from the idealized vision of domestic labor epitomized in Agnes. Like a good housekeeper, the good writer works invisibly, quietly, without calling attention to his labor; both master dirt and misery by putting things in their proper places; both create a sphere to which one can retreat—a literal or imaginative hearth where anxiety and competition subside, where one's motives do not appear as something other than what they are because self-interest and self-denial really are the same. But even though they seem to provide an alternative to the alienation endemic to class society, the creation and maintenance of the domestic sphere and the work of the literary man actually reproduce the very society from which they seem to offer escape: in creating the illusion of equality on which the false promises of capitalism depend, both contribute to (and depend on) a rhetoric of individualism and likeness that hides the facts of class difference and alienated labor. Indeed, both produce the illusion that class society *could* end and alienation *could* be overcome through their efforts to make others like themselves and work a selfless act. Because of the middle-class woman's influence, the working-class servant could be encouraged to aspire to bourgeois virtues; by the writer's pen, the English "national character" could be presented as what it should be—domestic and middle class; by the exemplary exception of literary labor, all workers could imagine that some kinds of work lay outside the inexorable logic of market relations, even if they were not so lucky in their own work-a-day lives.

That this ideological work was performed at midcentury upon the two sites of the woman and the literary man points to the critical—and highly problematic—position these two figures occupied in Victorian society. On the one hand, representations of the woman and the literary man could disguise the inequities and hypocrisies of class society because these figures carried the symbolic authority of moral superiority in a society everywhere else visibly permeated by self-interest and exploitation. On the other hand, the extent of symbolic work necessary to deploy these figures as markers of morality revealed that they were not really outside of the market economy or class society. The effort necessary to construct and maintain the separate spheres of the home and literary labor reveals itself in its failure: the reappearance elsewhere of what has had to be displaced—the "stain" of sexuality, the "blight" of class, the "degradation" of work.

IV

I conclude this chapter by addressing specifically but briefly two ramifications of the argument I have been presenting. The first concerns the place of "imaginative" texts like *David Copperfield* in the production and reproduction of ideology. For literary critics, this is a particularly vexed and volatile issue, because one source of the "value" of our work has been held to be literature's unique immunity to ideology, politics, and power. Even many critics who have not argued that literature articulates universal values have maintained that literature can expose the operations of power in or even to a society otherwise mystified or blind, that literature tells truths other discourses can or do not. I have two responses to this position. One is to argue that this formulation of the position and effect of literature is itself both historically specific and ideological. To maintain that literature resists ideology is to cover over its participation in and dependence on the kinds of commercial relations I have been discussing here, not to mention its coercive reproduction of likeness (a "national character," "universal" values, shared kinds and degrees of access to print) and its obliteration of (class and gender) differences. "Literature" cannot exist outside a system of social and institutional relations, and in a society characterized by systemic class and gender inequality, literature reproduces the system that makes it what it is. In resurrecting some of the issues raised in the debates about the social role of literary men at midcentury I have tried to remind readers that *David Copperfield* reproduced the rhetoric and representations of class and gender that covered over the writer's problematic place in the market economy and the proprietary form of the subject. By restoring to visibility the material conditions that these debates simultaneously addressed and displaced, I have tried to suggest how these debates were themselves complicitous in the universal instrumentalization that works of "genius" like *David Copperfield* seem to transcend.

My second response, however, to the argument that literature can expose the operations of ideology within class society is to agree. Because imaginative texts do not wield the same kinds of social authority or produce the same kinds of social effects that some other discourses (like law or medicine, for example) do, they occupy a different social position and perform their ideological work in a slightly different way. Because literary texts mobilize fantasies without legislating action, they provide the site at which shared anxieties and tensions can surface as well as be symbolically addressed. In fact, if one of the functions of literary work is, as I have argued, to work through material or ideological contradictions so as to produce such symbolic resolutions, then one component or stage of this working through will necessarily involve exposing to view the very contradictions the text manages or resolves. This is not to say that the literary man is necessarily more free, moral, or wise than his contemporaries or that he can read in his own works what subsequent readers read. But it is to say that the slippage produced by the double narration of *David Copperfield* is a property of all texts and that literary texts in particular often exploit such inconsistencies as part of their double duty of voicing and silencing ideological contradictions.

The second issue this discussion of *David Copperfield* raises is the fallout from the term I have repeatedly used—"literary men." By the middle of the nineteenth century, it was patently not true that all writers *were* "literary men." So numerous were literary *women,* in fact, that one (male) commentator was led to complain in 1866 that "of late . . . the women have been having it all their own way in the realm of fiction."[40] To another (female) writer this fact was cause for celebration, not complaint. "Literature," Jessie Boucherett remarked in the *English Woman's Journal,* "is followed, as a profession, by women, to an extent far greater than our readers are at the moment aware of. Magazines of the day are filled by them; one of the oldest and best of our weekly periodicals owes two-thirds of its content to their pens."[41] Whether either of these assessments was accurate is less important than the fact that such opinions were widely held. Indeed, the perception and the fact were dialectically related, for the perception that literature *was* a profession open to women encouraged women to write and publish in increasingly large numbers.

I have been arguing that to enhance the social status of the literary man, Dickens constructed and appropriated a representation of work that rested on and derived its terms from the ideological separation of spheres and from the representation of women's domestic labor as nonalienated labor. In this sense, Dickens may be said to have participated in what Nancy Armstrong has called "the rise of feminine authority in the novel"—that process by which literary discourse became a "feminized" discourse by the mid-nineteenth century.[42] But even if literary discourse did acquire its moral authority by its (putative) distance from the "masculine" sphere of alienation and market relations, what effect did this "feminization" have on actual women who did or wanted to write? The answer to this question is obviously complex, and it is not my aim to enter now into those discussions feminists have already undertaken in order to address it.[43] I simply want to point out that the same process that helped clear the way for women to write and publish also erected barriers against all but limited access to such "self-expression." If the feminization of authorship derived its authority from an idealized representation of woman and the domestic sphere, then for a woman to depart from that idealization by engaging in the commercial business of writing was to collapse the boundary between the spheres of alienated and nonalienated labor. A woman who wrote for publication threatened to collapse the ideal from which her authority was derived and to which her fidelity was necessary for so many other social institutions to work.

What Sandra Gilbert and Susan Gubar have called women's "anxiety of authorship" seems to me to be the effect of this ideological double bind, the result of the contradiction between the work theoretically—and actually—available to women and a set of values that rendered this work off-limits or necessitated that it be conceptualized as something other than money-getting labor. Rather than address this problem directly, however, I subordinate my treatment of the "feminization" of authorship to a discussion of the more general issue to which the mid-Victorian discussions of women writers belong. The issue that exposes why women writers were potentially so problematic was the issue of women and work. I focus on only two facets of this discussion and two kinds of work, but by addressing the mid-Victorian "problem" of the governess and the emergence of nursing as a profession for women, I suggest how women working imperiled the middle-class male hero that novels like *David Copperfield* so painstakingly constructed.

CHAPTER FIVE

The Anathematized Race:
The Governess and *Jane Eyre*

THE GOVERNESS WAS A FAMILIAR figure to midcentury middle-class Victorians, just as she is now to readers of Victorian novels.[1] Even before Becky Sharp and Jane Eyre gave names to the psychological type of the governess, her "plight" was the subject of numerous 1830s novels; by the 1840s, the governess had become a subject of concern to periodical essayists as well. In part, the attention the governess received in the 1840s was a response to the annual reports of the Governesses' Benevolent Institution, the charity founded in 1841 and reorganized in 1843.[2] But the activities of the GBI were also responses to a widespread perception that governesses were a problem of—and for—all members of the middle class. For many women, the problem was immediate and concrete; after all, as one editor of the *English Woman's Journal* remarked in 1858, every middle-class woman knows at least one governess, either because she has been taught by one or because she has "some relative or cherished friend . . . actually engaged in teaching, or having formerly been so engaged."[3] For most men, the governess represented a more abstract—but no less pressing—problem. As a competitor for work in an unregulated and increasingly overcrowded profession, the governess epitomized the toll capitalist market relations could exact from society's less fortunate members.

Modern historians do not generally dispute that governesses suffered increasing economic and social hardships after the 1830s. The bank failures of that decade combined with the discrepancy between the numbers of marriageable women and men and the late marriage age to drive more middle-class spinsters, widows, and daughters of respectable bankrupts into work outside the home. At the same time that the economic pressure to work increased, the range of activities considered socially acceptable for middle-class women decreased; whereas in the 1790s, middle-class women had worked as jailors, plumbers, butchers, farmers, seedsmen, tailors, and saddlers, by the 1840s and 1850s, dressmaking, millinery, and teaching far outstripped all other occupational activities.[4] Of these occupations, private teaching was widely considered the most genteel, largely because the governess's work was so similar to that of the female norm, the middle-class mother. The overcrowding these conditions produced within the teaching profession drove salaries down and competition for places up; at the same time, employers could and often did demand an increasingly wide range of services from would-be governesses, ranging from childcare for the very youngest children to instruction in French, music, and paper-flower-making for older daughters.

Despite these very real hardships, however, modern historians also point out that, given the relatively small number of women affected by the governess's woes, the attention this figure received in the 1840s and 1850s was disproportionate to the problem.[5] The 1851 Census lists 25,000 governesses, for example, but at the same time there were 750,000 female domestic servants, whose working conditions and wages were often more debilitating but markedly less lamented than the distress of the governess. In this chapter, I address some of the reasons why the governess received so much attention during these decades. I argue that the social stress the governess suffered aroused so much concern when it did at least partly because the economic and political turmoil of the "hungry forties" drove members of the middle class to demand some barrier against the erosion of middle-class assumptions and values; because of the place they occupied in the middle-class ideology, women, and governesses in particular, were invoked as the bulwarks against this erosion.[6] The governess is also significant for my analysis of the ideological work of gender because of the proximity she bears to two of the most important Victorian representations of woman: the figure who epitomized the domestic ideal, and the figure who threatened to destroy it. Because the governess was like the middle-class mother in the work she performed, but like both a working-class woman and man in the wages she received, the very figure who theoretically should have defended the naturalness of separate spheres threatened to collapse the difference between them. Moreover, that discussions of the governesses' plight had dovetailed, by the mid-1850s, with feminist campaigns to improve both employment opportunities for women and women's education reveals the critical role representations of the governess played, not, as conservatives desired, in defending the domestic ideal, but in capitalizing on the contradiction it contained.

I

The periodical essayists of the 1840s justified the attention they devoted to the distressed governess by emphasizing the central role
she played in reproducing the domestic ideal. As a teacher and
example for young children, they argued, the governess was charged
with inculcating domestic virtues and, especially in the case of young
girls, with teaching the "accomplishments" that would attract a good
husband without allowing the sexual component of these accomplishments to get the upper hand. The governess was therefore
expected to preside over the contradiction written into the domestic
ideal—in the sense both that she was meant to police the emergence
of undue assertiveness or sexuality in her maturing charges and that
she was expected not to display willfulness or desires herself.[7] Theoretically, the governess's position neutralized whatever temptation
she, as a young woman herself, might have presented to her male
associates; to gentlemen she was a "tabooed woman," and to male
servants she was as unapproachable as any other middle-class lady.[8]

If the governess was asked to stabilize the contradiction inherent in the middle-class domestic ideal by embodying and superintending morality, then she was also expected to fix another, related
boundary: that between "well-bred, well-educated and perfect
gentlewomen," on the one hand, and, on the other, the "low-born,
ignorant, and vulgar" women of the working class.[9] The assumption
implicit in these conjunctions, as in the middle-class preference for
governesses from their own class, was that only "well-bred" women
were morally reliable. In this reading of contemporary affairs, the
unfortunate circumstances that bankrupted some middle-class fathers were critical to the reproduction of the domestic ideal, for
only such disasters could yield suitable teachers for the next generation of middle-class wives.

One reason the governess was a figure of such concern to her
middle-class contemporaries, then, was simply that she was a middle-
class woman in a period when women were considered so critical
to social stability. Especially in the "hungry forties," women became
both the focus of working-class men's worries about competition
for scarce jobs and the solution advanced by middle-class men for
the social and political discontent hard times fostered. If only women
would remain in the home, men of all classes argued, work would
be available to men who needed it and both the family wage and
morality would be restored. The assumptions implicit in this argument are those I have already discussed: that morality is bred and

nurtured in the home as an effect of maternal instinct, and that if lower-class women were to emulate middle-class wives in their deference, thrift, and discipline, the homes of rich and poor alike would become what they ought to be—havens from the debilitating competition of the market.

A second reason the governess was singled out for special attention was that she did not seem to be fulfilling this critical social task. In fact, contemporaries openly worried that the governess was not the bulwark against immorality and class erosion but the conduit through which working-class habits would infiltrate the middle-class home. One source of this anxiety was the widespread belief that more tradesmen's daughters were entering the ranks of governess, therefore heralding the "degradation of a body so important to the moral interest of the community."[10] Against such "degradation," middle-class commentators proposed a range of defenses, including most of the solutions formulated to end the governesses' plight.[11] Whatever their practical value, all of the suggested remedies functioned to defend the class barrier that was also assumed to mark a moral division; even the Governesses' Benevolent Institution reinforced the distinction between ladies "with character" and other women by providing the former with a separate residence and source of charity.[12]

A second source of the anxiety about governesses surfaces in discussions of the hardships of their situation. As these hardships were most vividly imagined, they were not primarily physical or economic but emotional; the threat they posed was to the governess's self-control and, even more ominously, to her sexual neutrality. This danger surfaces most explicitly in fictional representations of the governess, and I pursue it in a moment in relation to one of the period's most famous governess novels, Charlotte Brontë's *Jane Eyre*.[13] In periodical essays about the governess, allusions to her sexual susceptibility are more indirect, but precisely because of this indirection, they direct our attention to the governess's place in the complex system of associations in which the domestic ideal was also embedded. Two of the figures to which the governess was repeatedly linked begin to suggest why her sexlessness seemed so important—and so unreliable—to her contemporaries. These figures are the lunatic and the fallen woman.

The connection contemporaries made between the governess and the lunatic was, in the first instance, causal. According to both the author of the 1844 "Hints on the Modern Governess System" and Lady Eastlake's 1847 review of the GBI's annual report, gov-

ernesses accounted for the single largest category of women in lunatic asylums.[14] Lady Eastlake attributes this unfortunate fact to the
"wounded vanity" a governess suffers, but the author of "Hints"
connects this "wound" more specifically to sexual repression. Citing
"an ordinary case," this author describes a young girl trained for her
governess position in "one of those schools which are usually mere
gymnasia for accomplishments and elegant manners." There her "animal spirits" are indulged, and her youthful "elasticity" becomes a
"craving for pleasures." Once she leaves the school, however, and
takes up her governessing work, this "craving" is subject to the
frustration and denial her position demands.

> She must live daily amidst the trials of a home without its
> blessings; she must bear about on her heart the sins she wit-
> nesses and the responsibilities that crush her; without any con-
> sent of her will, she is made the *confidante* of many family
> secrets; she must live in a familial circle as if her eyes did not
> perceive the tokens of bitterness; she must appear not to hear
> sharp sayings and *mal-a-propos* speeches; kindly words of cour-
> tesy must be always on her lips; she must be ever on her guard;
> let her relax her self-restraint for one moment, and who shall
> say what mischief and misery might ensue to all from one
> heedless expression of hers?[15]

If the allusion to some mischievous "expression" hints at the governess's latent feelings, this author will not elaborate the nature of
these feelings; instead, the writer turns to the "nervous irritability,
dejection, [and] loss of energy" that result from repressing them
(*FM* 575). The "twisted coil of passion and levity," the author concludes, "may be moved into sobriety by the help of forbearance and
long-suffering," but too often the very girls who have sprung up
"like plants in a hot-house," fade before their "bloom" is gone. "It
is no exaggeration to say that hundreds snap yearly from the stalk,
or prolong a withered, sickly life, till they, too, sink, and are carried
out to die miserably in the by-ways of the world" (*FM* 575, 574).
    The image of the short-lived or barren plant elaborates the
causal connection between the governess and the lunatic by metaphorically tying both to a vitality stunted, silenced, driven mad by
denial and restraint. This vitality may not be explicitly represented
as sexuality here, but its sexual content *is* present in the images to
which this last phrase alludes. The representation of the governess
"carried out to die miserably in the by-ways of the world" meto-

nymically links the governess to the victim of another kind of work that was also represented as "white slavery" at midcentury—the distressed needlewoman "forced to take to the streets."[16] The association between the two figures is further reinforced by the fact that the governess and the needlewoman were two of the three figures that symbolized working women for the early and mid-Victorian public; the third was the factory girl.[17] Significantly, both of the working-class members of this trio were specifically linked by middle-class male commentators to the danger of unregulated female sexuality. Henry Mayhew's determination to expose (and, by extension, control) the "prostitution" he identified among needlewomen in 1849 expresses the same concern to curtail female promiscuity that Lord Ashley voiced in the 1844 parliamentary debate about factory conditions.[18] For both Mayhew and Lord Ashley, the relevant issue was any extramarital sexuality, not just sex for hire; Mayhew's interviews make it clear that for him any woman who lived or had sexual relations with a man outside of marriage was a prostitute.

That representations of the governess in the 1840s brought to her contemporaries' minds not just the middle-class ideal she was meant to reproduce, but the sexualized and often working-class women against whom she was expected to defend, reveals the mid-Victorian fear that the governess could not protect middle-class values because she could not be trusted to regulate her own sexuality. The lunatic's sexuality might have been rhetorically contained by the kind of medical categories I have already discussed, after all, but the prostitute's sexual aggression was undisguised; to introduce either such sexuality or such aggression into the middle-class home would have been tantamount to fomenting revolution, especially in a period in which both were imaginatively linked to the discontent expressed by disgruntled members of the working class and by the "strong-minded women" who were just beginning to demand reform. The conjunction of economic, moral, and political anxieties that could be mobilized by the image of an army of aggressive, impoverished governesses emerges in the warning advanced by the author of "Hints": if someone does not remedy the current injustices, this writer worries, "the miseries of the governess may even swell that sickening clamour about the 'rights of women' which would never have been raised had women been true to themselves" (*FM* 573).

This author's wishful plea that women be "true to themselves" explicitly enjoins middle-class employers and employees to unite in defense of the domestic ideal that the governesses' distress threatens to disturb. Implicitly, however, the plea for women to unite has more subversive implications because it calls attention to the fact that middle-class women have something in common, which is epitomized in the governesses' plight. This more controversial reading of the governesses' situation was made explicit in 1847 by Elizabeth Rigby, later Lady Eastlake, in her review of *Vanity Fair, Jane Eyre,* and the 1847 report of the Governesses' Benevolent Institution. Like many other essayists, Lady Eastlake's express concern was the fate of governesses who could no longer find work, for, as she phrases it, their situation more "painfully expresses the peculiar tyranny of our present state of civilization" than any other social ill.[19] The governess was so affecting to Lady Eastlake, as to many male commentators, because she epitomized the helplessness unfortunate individuals experienced, not just from ordinary poverty but from the volatile fluctuations of the modern, industrializing economy; the toll these fluctuations exacted had become starkly visible in the depression of the 1840s, and contemporaries feared such hardship lay behind working-class discontent. But to Lady Eastlake, the governess was a special kind of victim, for, unlike lower-class men, she was born to neither discomfort nor labor. "The case of the governess," she explains, "is so much the harder than that of any other class of the community, in that they are not only quite as liable to all the vicissitudes of life, but are absolutely supplied by them." What was distressing to Lady Eastlake in this fact was that the governess's plight could be any middle-class woman's fate. Lady Eastlake recognized, however reluctantly, that the governess revealed the price of all middle-class women's dependence on men: "Take a lady, in every meaning of the word, born and bred, and let her father pass through the gazette, and she wants nothing more to suit our highest *beau ideal* of a guide and instructress to our children. We need the imprudencies, extravagancies, mistakes, or crimes of a certain number of fathers, to sow that seed from which we reap the harvest of governesses" (*QR* 176).

Such a recognition could have led Lady Eastlake to identify fully with the "lady" whose imprudent, extravagant, or criminal father has squandered her security; it could have led her, as it did women like Barbara Bodichon, to urge women to unite against the dependence that tied them to their fathers' luck and business sense. Instead, however, Lady Eastlake explicitly rejects such a conclusion; she defends against her identification with the governess by simply asserting the necessity of women's dependence, which she bases on the natural difference between men's work and the "precious" work of women. "Workmen may rebel," Lady Eastlake writes, "and tradesmen may combine, not to let you have their labour or their wares under a certain rate; but the governess has no refuge—no escape; she is a needy *lady*, whose services are of too precious a kind to have any stated market value, and is therefore left to the mercy, or what they call the *means,* of the family that engages her" (*QR* 179).

In the law that places the governess's "precious" work above market value but beneath a fair wage, Lady Eastlake sees that moral superintendence is simultaneously devalued and exploited. Still, she insists that things must be this way: after all, the difference between work whose value can be judged and work that is too "precious" to be subjected to market evaluation is what saves ladies from being like men. But if the difference between working men and leisured ladies is obvious to Lady Eastlake, the definition of ladies becomes problematic when one must establish some difference *among* them. The problem, as she formulates it, is that the difference among ladies is difficult to see because it is not based on some natural distinction. The difference among ladies, she complains,

> is not one which will take care of itself, as in the case of a servant. If she [the governess] sits at table she does not shock you—if she opens her mouth she does not distress you—her appearance and manners are likely to be as good as your own— her education rather better; there is nothing upon the face of the thing to stamp her as having been called to a different state of life from that in which it has pleased God to place you; and therefore the distinction has to be kept up by a fictitious barrier which presses with cruel weight upon the mental strength or constitutional vanity of a woman. (*QR* 177)

Because neither sex nor class "stamp[s]" the governess as different from the lady who employs her, Lady Eastlake is once more drawn toward identifying with her. Yet even though she realizes the barrier between them is "fictitious" and "cruel," Lady Eastlake will not lower it for a moment. Instead, she turns away again, this time decisively, by appealing to another kind of nature—"the inherent constitution of English habits, feelings, and prejudices": "We shall ever prefer to place those immediately about our children who have been born and bred with somewhat of the same refinement as ourselves. We must ever keep them in a sort of isolation, for it is the only means for maintaining that distance which the reserve of English manners and the decorum of English families exact" (*QR* 178).

Lady Eastlake's appeal to "the inherent constitution" of the English is meant to resolve the paradox whereby two persons who

are by class and sex the same must be treated differently. Her in-
vocation of national character therefore extends the work we have
already seen this concept perform. Like the discussions of Dickens
I have already examined, Lady Eastlake's appeal to the unassailable
authority of national character generalizes middle-class "reserve" and
"decorum" to all "English families." Beyond this, however, it also
rationalizes a difference among members of the middle class that is
otherwise unaccountable: the difference of circumstances or luck.

Lady Eastlake's discussion of governesses follows her reviews
of two recently published governess novels, *Vanity Fair* and *Jane
Eyre*.[20] The substance of these reviews highlights both the conservatism and the potential subversiveness of Eastlake's position. In
general, Lady Eastlake approves of Thackeray's novel, despite the
immorality of Becky Sharp, but she declares the heroine of *Jane Eyre*
to be "vulgar-minded," a woman "whom we should not care for as
an acquaintance, whom we should not seek as a friend, whom we
should not desire for a relation, and whom we should scrupulously
avoid for a governess" (*QR* 176, 174). Eastlake formulates her objections in religious language, but she focuses specifically on the
threat this heroine poses to the barrier she will soon admit is "fictitious"—the barrier between one wellborn (if penniless) lady and
another. "It is true Jane does right," Lady Eastlake begrudgingly
admits, in discussing Jane's decision to leave Rochester,

> and [she] exerts great moral strength, but it is the strength of
> a mere heathen mind which is a law unto itself. . . . Jane Eyre
> is proud, and therefore she is ungrateful too. It pleased God
> to make her an orphan, friendless, and penniless—yet she thanks
> nobody, and least of all Him, for the food and raiment, the
> friends, companions, and instructors of her helpless youth. . . .
> The doctrine of humility is not more foreign to her mind than
> it is repudiated by her heart. It is by her own talents, virtues,
> and courage that she is made to attain the summit of human
> happiness, and, as far as Jane Eyre's own statement is concerned,
> no one would think that she owed anything either to God above
> or to man below. (*QR* 173)

As Lady Eastlake continues, her religious argument explicitly becomes a warning against the political upheavals threatened by
working-class discontent. What has happened here is that the difference of circumstance that Lady Eastlake acknowledges to be a
matter of chance has become a matter of class, which is a difference

she assumes to be authoritative because it is appointed by God. "Altogether the auto-biography of Jane Eyre is pre-eminently an anti-Christian composition," she asserts.

> There is throughout it a murmuring against the comforts of the rich and against the privations of the poor, which, as far as each individual is concerned, is a murmuring against God's appointment. . . . There is a proud and perpetual assertion of the rights of man . . . a pervading tone of ungodly discontent which is at once the most prominent and the most subtle evil which the law and the pulpit, which all civilized society in fact has at the present day to contend with. We do not hesitate to say that the tone of mind and thought which has overthrown authority and violated every code human and divine abroad, and fostered Chartism and rebellion at home, is the same which has also written Jane Eyre. (*QR* 173–74)

If this objection targets the class issues contemporaries asso-ciated with the governess, then Lady Eastlake's other complaint about *Jane Eyre* centers on the second anxiety this figure aroused. The protagonist's "language and manners . . . offend you in every particular," she asserts, especially when Rochester "pours into [Jane's] ears disgraceful tales of his past life, connected with the birth of little Adele," and the governess "listens as if it were nothing new, and certainly nothing distasteful" (*QR* 167, 164). What offends Lady Eastlake here is the "perpetual disparity between the account [Jane Eyre] herself gives of the effect she produces, and the means shown us by which she brings that about"—the gap between Jane's pro-fessed innocence and the sexual knowledge the author insinuates in the language and action of the novel. What this implies is that the author of the novel knows more about sexual matters than the character admits and that the novel is "vulgar" because it makes the hypocrisy of women's professed innocence legible.

Despite Lady Eastlake's strenuous complaint about *Jane Eyre*'s "gross vulgarity"—or, rather, precisely because of this complaint—she draws out the similarities rather than the differences between herself and the author of the novel. If Lady Eastlake sees sexuality in Jane's "restlessness," after all, there is little to distinguish her from the writer who created this sexuality in the first place. Just as Lady Eastlake inadvertently exposes her likeness to the governess, then, so she betrays her resemblance to the author she disdains. If we turn for a moment to Brontë's novel, we can begin to identify some of the implications of this similarity and some of the reasons discussions of the governesses' plight sparked other controversies that eventually challenged the domestic ideal.

Jane Eyre may be neither a lunatic nor a fallen woman, but when she refuses Rochester's proposal in chapter 27 that she become his mistress, her language specifically calls to mind the figures to whom the governess was so frequently linked by her contemporaries. Despite her passion, Jane says, she is not "mad," like a lunatic; her principles are "worth" more than the pleasure that becoming Rochester's mistress would yield.[21] The two women metaphorically invoked here are also dramatized literally in the two characters that precede Jane Eyre as Rochester's lovers—the lunatic Bertha and the mistress Céline Varens. But if the juxtaposition of these characters calls attention to the problematic sexuality that connects them, the way Brontë works through Jane's position as governess seems to sever the links among them. Read one way, Brontë's novel repeats such conservative resolutions of the governesses' plight as Lady Eastlake's, for Jane's departure from Rochester's house dismisses the sexual and class instabilities the governess introduces, in a way that makes Jane the guardian of sexual and class order rather than its weakest point. When considered in terms of the entire novel, however, Brontë's treatment of the governess problem does not seem so conservative. In introducing the possibility that women may be fundamentally alike, Brontë raises in a more systematically critical way the subversive suggestions adumbrated by Lady Eastlake.

The issues of sexual susceptibility and social incongruity that contemporaries associated with the governess are inextricably bound up with each other in Jane's situation at Thornfield Hall: Jane is vulnerable to Rochester's advances because, as his employee, she lacks both social peers and the means to defend herself against her attractive, aggressive employer. But Brontë symbolically neutralizes both of these problems by revising the origin, the terms, and the conditions of Jane's employment. While Jane seeks employment because she has no one to support her, Brontë makes it clear that, in this case, the social incongruity that others might attribute to her position as governess precedes Jane's taking up this work. It is, in part, a family matter; Jane is "less than a servant," as her cousin John Reed sneers, because she is an orphan and a dependent ward (p. 44). In part, Jane's "heterogeneity" comes from her personality; she is called "a discord" and "a noxious thing," and she thinks that her temperament makes her deserve these names (p. 47).

The effect of making Jane's dependence a function of family and personality is to individualize her problems so as to detach them from her position as governess. Brontë further downplays the importance of Jane's position by idealizing her work. Not only is there no mother to satisfy at Thornfield and initially no company from which Jane is excluded, but Adele is a tractable, if untaught, child, and Jane's actual duties are barely characterized at all. Beside the physical and psychological deprivations so extensively detailed in the Lowood section of the novel, in fact, what Jane terms her "new servitude" seems luxurious; the only hardship she suffers as a governess is an unsatisfied craving for something she cannot name— something that is represented as romantic love.

When Rochester finally appears at Thornfield, Brontë completes what seems to be a dismissal of Jane's employment by subsuming the economic necessity that drove Jane to work into the narrative of an elaborate courtship. Rochester's temperamental "peculiarities," for which Mrs. Fairfax has prepared us, lead him to forget Jane's salary at one point, to double, then halve it, at another. By the time Blanche Ingram and her companions ridicule the "anathematized race" of governesses in front of Jane, Brontë has already elevated her heroine above this "race" by subordinating her poverty to her personality and to the place it has earned her in Rochester's affections. "Your station," Rochester exclaims, "is in my heart." The individualistic and psychological vocabulary Rochester uses here pervades Brontë's characterization of their relationship: "You are my sympathy," Rochester cries to Jane at one point (p. 342); "I have something in my brain and heart," Jane tells the reader, "that assimilates me mentally to him" (p. 204).

When Rochester proposes marriage to Jane, the problems of sexual susceptibility and class incongruity that intersect in the governess's role ought theoretically to be solved. In this context, Mrs. Fairfax's warning that "gentlemen in [Rochester's] station are not accustomed to marry their governesses" (p. 287), Blanche Ingram's admonitory example of the governess dismissed for falling in love (pp. 206–7), and Jane's insistence that she still be treated as a "plain, Quakerish governess" (p. 287) all underscore the alternative logic behind Jane's situation—a logic that eroticizes economics so that class and financial difficulties are overcome by the irresistible (and inexplicable) "sympathy" of romantic love. But if so translating the class and economic issues raised by the governess resembles the psychologizing gesture I have just examined in *David Copperfield*,

Brontë's novel here takes a different turn. For the very issues that foregrounding personality and love should lay to rest come back to haunt the novel in the most fully psychologized episodes of *Jane Eyre*: Jane's dreams of children.[22]

According to Jane's exposition in chapter 21, emotional affinity, or "sympathy," is a sign of a mysterious but undeniable kinship: "the unity of the source to which each traces his origin" (p. 249). But Jane's discussion of sympathy here focuses not on the bond of kinship, which she claims to be explaining, but on some *disturbance* within a family relationship. Specifically, Jane is recalling her old nursemaid Bessie telling her that "to dream of children was a sure sign of trouble, either to oneself or to one's kin" (p. 249). Jane then reveals that Bessie's superstition has come back to her because every night for a week she has dreamed of an infant, "which I sometimes hushed in my arms, sometimes dandled on my knee, sometimes watched playing with daisies on a lawn. . . . It was a wailing child this night, and a laughing one the next: now it nestled close to me, and now it ran from me" (p. 249). This revelation is immediately followed by Jane's discovering that the obvious "trouble" presaged by her dream is at her childhood home, Gateshead: John has gambled the Reed family into debt and is now dead, probably by his own hand, and Mrs. Reed, broken in spirit and health, lies near death asking for Jane.

The implications of this "trouble" surface when this reference is read against the other episodes adjacent to the dream. Jane's journey to Gateshead follows two scenes in which Rochester wantonly taunts Jane with his power: in chapter 20 he teases her that he will marry Blanche Ingram, and in chapter 21 he refuses to pay her her wages, thereby underscoring her emotional and financial dependence. Once at Gateshead, Jane discovers that Mrs. Reed has also been dreaming of a child—of Jane Eyre, in fact, that "mad," "fiend"-like child who was so much "trouble" that Mrs. Reed has withheld for three years the knowledge that Jane has other kin and that her uncle, John Eyre, wants to support her (pp. 260, 266–67). Mrs. Reed's malice has thereby prolonged Jane's economic dependence while depriving her of the kinship for which she has yearned. Jane explicitly denies feeling any "vengeance . . . rage . . . [or] aversion" toward Mrs. Reed, but her very denial calls attention to the rage she expressed when she was similarly helpless at Lowood. Foregrounding the structural similarities among the scenes conveys the impression that John Reed's suicide and the stroke that soon kills Mrs. Reed are displaced expressions of Jane's anger at them for the

dependence and humiliation they have inflicted on her. These symbolic murders, which the character denies, can also be seen as dis-
placements of the rage at the other figure who now stands in the
same relation of superiority to Jane as the Reeds once did: Rochester.
That both the character and the plot of the novel deny this anger,
however, leads us to the other "trouble" adjacent to this dream of
a child: Bertha's attack on her brother, Richard Mason.

As soon as Mason enters the narrative, he is rhetorically linked
to Rochester: he appears when and where Rochester was expected
to appear, and in her description of him Jane compares him explicitly
to Rochester (pp. 218, 219). Like the sequence I have just examined,
Mason's arrival punctuates a series of painful reminders of Jane's
dependence and marginality; he interrupts the engagement party
(when Jane, obsessed with watching Rochester and Blanche, specifically denies that she is jealous, p. 215), and his arrival is immediately followed by the gypsy scene, in which Rochester so completely
invades Jane's thoughts that she wonders "what unseen spirit" has
taken up residence in her heart (p. 228). When the gypsy reveals that
s/he is Rochester, Jane voices more rage toward her "master" than
at any other time: "It is scarcely fair, sir," Jane says; "it was not
right" (p. 231). Jane's hurt is soon repaid, however, even if what
happens is not acknowledged as revenge. Jane suddenly, and with
a marked carelessness, remembers Mason's presence. The effect on
Rochester is dramatic. Leaning on Jane as he once did before (and
will do again), Rochester "staggers" and exclaims, "Jane, I've got a
blow—I've got a blow, Jane!" (p. 232). The "blow" Jane's an-
nouncement delivers is then graphically acted out when Bertha, who
is Jane's surrogate by virtue of her relation to Rochester, attacks
Mason, whose textual connection to Rochester has already been
established. As before, anger and violence are transferred from one
set of characters to another, revenge is displaced from Jane's character, and agency is dispersed into the text.

The text—not as agent but as effect—turns out to be precisely
what is at stake in these series, for in each of them Rochester's most
serious transgression has been to usurp Jane's control over what is,
after all, primarily her story. In the gypsy scene he has told her what
she feels, in words as "familiar . . . as the speech of my own tongue"
(p. 231), and in the scene immediately following Bertha's assault on
Mason, he has usurped her authority even more, first commanding
her not to speak (p. 239), then asking her to imagine herself "no
longer a girl . . . but a wild boy"—to imagine she is Rochester, in
other words, while he tells *his* story to her as if she were telling her

own story to herself (pp. 246–47). The precarious independence Jane earned by leaving Gateshead has been figured in the ability to tell (if not direct) her own story; thus, the measure of autonomy gained by translating Jane's economic dependence into a story of love is undercut by Rochester's imperious demand that she listen to him tell his story and hers, that she be dependent—seen and not heard, as women (particularly governesses) should be.

Jane's second reference to dreaming of children extends and elaborates this pattern of enforced dependence and indirect revenge. Once more, Jane's narration of the dream is temporally displaced from the moment of her dreaming. When she does disclose to Rochester and the reader what frightened her, Jane also reveals that when Bertha awakened her, Jane had twice been dreaming of a child. In the first dream, "some barrier" divided her and Rochester. "I was following the windings of an unknown road," Jane explains; "total obscurity environed me; rain pelted me; I was burdened with the charge of a little child. . . . My movements were fettered, and my voice still died away inarticulate; while you, I felt, withdrew farther and farther every moment" (p. 309). In the next dream, of Thornfield Hall in ruins, the child still encumbers Jane. "Wrapped up in a shawl," she says,

> I still carried the unknown little child: I might not lay it down anywhere, however tired were my arms—however much its weight impeded my progress, I must retain it. I heard the gallop of a horse. . . . I was sure it was you; and you were departing for many years, and for a distant country. I climbed the thin wall with frantic, perilous haste. . . . The stones rolled from under my feet, the ivy branches I grasped gave way, the child clung round my neck in terror, and almost strangled me. . . . I saw you like a speck on a white track, lessening every moment. . . . The wall crumbled; I was shaken; the child rolled from my knee, I lost my balance, fell, and woke. (P. 310)

To this "preface" Jane then appends the story of the "trouble" that followed: Bertha's rending Jane's wedding veil. This is immediately followed by the much more devastating "trouble" of Mason's denunciation in the church, Rochester's revelation that he is already married, and the obliteration of Jane's hopes to formalize her "kinship" with Rochester.

Alone in her bedroom, Jane surveys her ruined love—which she likens to "a suffering child in a cold cradle"; once more she denies that she is angry at Rochester ("I would not ascribe vice to him; I would not say he had betrayed me," p. 324), but even more explicitly than before, the plot suggests that the person who has hurt Jane is now indirectly suffering the effects of the rage that follows from such hurt: Jane's letter to John Eyre, after all, led her uncle to expose to Mason her planned marriage, and Jane's desire for some independence from Rochester led her to write her uncle in the first place. In this instance, of course, Jane initially suffers as much as—if not more than—Rochester does: not only is she subjected to the humiliating offer of his adulterous love, but she also forces herself to leave Thornfield and she almost dies as a consequence. Jane's suffering, however, turns out to be only the first stage in her gradual recovery of kinship, independence, money, and enough mastery to write both her story and Rochester's. By contrast, Rochester is further reduced by the novel's subsequent action; when he is blinded and maimed in the fire Bertha sets, the pattern of displaced anger is complete again.[23]

Why does dreaming of children signify "trouble" in these sequences, and why does the trouble take this form? When Jane dreams of children, some disaster follows that is a displaced expression of the anger against kin that the character denies. In the sense that narrative effect is split off from psychological cause, *Jane Eyre* becomes at these moments what we might call a hysterical text, in which the body of the text symptomatically acts out what cannot make its way into the psychologically realistic narrative. Because there was no permissible plot in the nineteenth century for a woman's anger, whenever Brontë explores this form of self-assertion the text splinters hysterically, provoked by and provoking images of dependence and frustration.

Dreaming of children, then, is metonymically linked to a rage that remains implicit at the level of character but materializes at the level of plot. And *this* signifies "trouble" both because the children that appear in these dreams metaphorically represent the dependence that defined women's place in bourgeois ideology (and that was epitomized in the governess) *and* because the disjunction that characterizes these narrative episodes shows that hysteria is produced as the condition in which a lady's impermissible emotions are expressed. What Jane's dreams of children reveal, then, in their content, their placement, and their form, is that the helplessness enforced by the governess's dependent position—along with the frustration, self-denial, and maddened, thwarted rage that accompanies it—marks every middle-class woman's life because she is not allowed to express (or possess) the emotions that her dependence provokes. The structural paradigm underlying the governess's sexual vulnerability and her social incongruity—her lunacy and her class ambiguity—is dependence, and this is the position all middle-class women share.

From one perspective, Brontë neutralizes the effects of this revelation and downplays its subversive implications. By making Jane leave Thornfield, Brontë seems to reformulate her dilemma, making it once more an individual, moral, emotional problem and not a function of social position or occupation. As soon as Jane stops being a governess, she is "free" to earn her happiness according to the paradoxical terms of the domestic ideal: even the skeptical Lady Eastlake conceded that the self-denial Jane expresses in renouncing Rochester's love and nearly starving on the heath gives her a right to earthly happiness. When Jane discovers she has both money and kin, then, the dependence epitomized by the governess's position seems no longer to be an issue—a point made clear by the end to which Jane puts her newfound wealth: she liberates Diana and Mary from having to be governesses and so frees them to a woman's "natural" fate—marriage.

From another perspective, however, Brontë's "resolution" of the governess's dilemma can be seen to underscore—not dismiss— the problem of women's dependence. That only the coincidence of a rich uncle's death can confer on a single woman autonomy and power, after all, suggests just how intractable her dependence really was in the 1840s. Brontë also calls attention to the pervasiveness of this dependence in the very episode in which Jane ceases to be a governess, the episode at Whitcross. As soon as Jane is not a governess, her irreducable likeness to other women returns with stark clarity—and in the very form that relieving Jane of her economic dependence should theoretically have displaced: the sexual vulnerability and class uncertainty epitomized in the lunatic and the fallen woman. "Absolutely destitute," "objectless and lost," Jane is mistaken for an "eccentric sort of lady," a thief, and a figure too "sinister" to be named: "you are not what you ought to be," sneers the Riverses' wary servant (pp. 349, 355, 361).

The return of these other women at the very moment at which Jane is least of all a governess functions to reinscribe the similarity between the governess and these sexualized women. At the same time, it lets us glimpse both why it was so important for contemporaries like Lady Eastlake to insist that the governess was different from other women and why it was so difficult to defend this assertion. For the fact that the associations return even though Jane is *not* a governess suggests the instability of the boundary that all the nonfiction accounts of the governess simultaneously took for granted and fiercely upheld: the boundary between such aberrant women as lunatic, prostitute, and governess and the "normal" woman—the woman who is a wife and mother.

That the governess was somehow a threat to the "natural" order superintended by the middle-class wife is clear from essayists' insistence that the governess's availability kept mothers from performing their God-given tasks. This interruption of nature, in turn, was held responsible for the "restless rage to push on" that was feeding class discontent (*FM* 572). If "ladies of the middle rank resume[d] the instruction of their own children, as God ordained they should," the author of "Hints" asserted, "if mothers would obey their highest calling, many who now fill their places would be safer and happier in their lower vocation" (*FM* 581). At stake, according to this writer, is not only the happiness of those "daughters of poor men" who are now "crammed by a hierling" instead of being taught domestic skills, but also the "depth and breadth of character" all women should display. "Surely it must be acknowledged," the author continues, "that women whose lesson of life has been learned at mothers' knees, over infant's cradles, will be more earnest and genuine than those taught by a stranger, however well qualified" (*FM* 581).

This intricate weave of assumptions about class relations and female nature reproduces the ideological equation I have already examined: that morality and class stability will follow the expression of maternal instinct—a force grounded in God's order and the (middle-class) female body. In this representation, maternal instinct is paradoxically both what distinguishes the mother from the governess and what naturally qualifies the former to perform the services the latter must be trained to provide.

> New difficulties and responsibilities meet [the governess] every day; she is hourly tried by all those childish follies and perversities which need a mother's instinctive love to make them tolerable; yet a forbearance and spring of spirits is claimed from the stranger, in spite of the frets she endures, which He who made the heart knew that maternal affection only could supply, under the perpetual contradictions of wilful childhood. This strength of instinct has been given to every mother. It enables her to walk lightly under a load which, without it, she could not sustain. (*FM* 574)

Positioning the governess against a normative definition of woman as wife and mother reinforced the complex ideological system I have set out in this book. This juxtaposition shored up the distinction between (abnormal) women who performed domestic (in this case maternal) labor for wages and those who did the same work for free, as an expression of a love that was generous, noncompetitive, and guaranteed by the natural force of maternal "instinct." The image of an arena of "freedom" for women was, in turn, central to the representation of domesticity as desirable, and this representation, along with the disincentive to work outside the home that it enforced, was instrumental to the image of women as moral and not economic agents, antidotes to the evils of competition, not competitors themselves. Finally, the picture of a sphere of relative freedom was crucial to establishing some boundary to the market economy; the wife, protected and fulfilled by maternal instinct, was living proof that the commodification of labor, the alienation of human relations, the frustrations and disappointments inflicted by economic vicissitudes stopped at the door of the home. From this complex ideological role, we can see that laments about the governess's plight in the 1840s belonged primarily to a discourse about domestic relations—which was necessarily a discourse about gender, class, and the nature of labor as well.

The problem was that governesses—especially in such numbers and in such visibly desperate straits—gave the lie to the complex of economic and domestic representations that underwrote this ideology. Not only did the governess's "plight" bring the economic vicissitudes of the market economy into the middle-class home, thereby collapsing the separation of spheres, but the very existence of so many governesses was proof that, whatever middle-class women might want, not all of them could be (legitimate) mothers because they could not all be wives. As the 1851 Census made absolutely clear, there simply were not enough men to go around. Moreover, there was something dangerously unstable even about the putatively reliable force of maternal love. Moralists admitted that "love" was a notoriously difficult emotion to define and that the distinction between one kind of love and another required constant defense. What, they worried, could prevent "the key-stone of the stupendous arch which unites heaven to earth, and man to heaven" from becoming *"morbid sentimentality—an ungovernable, tumultuous passion"*—especially if the person who should incarnate the former was distinguished from the victim of the latter only by maternal instinct, which even the most optimistic moralists admitted was unstable.[24] According to the logic of these fears, the governess not only revealed what the mother might otherwise have been; she also actively freed mothers to display other desires that were distinctly *not* maternal. This set up the unsettling possibility that a mother's "jealousy" and her energies might find an object other than the one "nature" had decreed. "If more governesses find a penurious maintenance by these means," Lady Eastlake warned, "more mothers are encouraged to neglect those duties, which, one would have thought, they would have been as jealous of as of that first duty of all that infancy requires of them" (*QR* 180).

These warnings suggest that, even though the unemployed mother functions as the norm in the essays I have been examining and in the symbolic economy of which they are a part, motherhood had to be rhetorically constructed *as* the norm in defiance of real economic conditions and as a denial of whatever additional desires a woman (even a mother) might have. In my reading of *David Copperfield*, I have suggested that securing the middle-class mother as norm necessitated elaborate symbolic reworking, one version of which involved differentiating between the idealized mother and other, sexualized, and often lower-class women. My reading of *Jane Eyre* suggests that articulating the "problem" of female sexuality upon class difference was not always sufficient to repress the contradiction written into the domestic ideal. Brontë's novel reveals that the figure from whom the mother had to be distinguished was not just the lower-class prostitute but the middle-class governess as well, for the governess was both what a woman who should be a mother might actually become and the woman who had to be paid for doing what the mother should want to do for free. If the fallen woman was the middle-class mother's opposite, the middle-class governess was her next-of-kin, the figure who ought to ensure that a boundary existed between classes of women but who could not, precisely because her sexuality made her like the women from whom she ought to differ.[25]

This is the ideological economy whose instabilities Brontë exposes when she "resolves" the problem of the governess by having Jane marry Rochester. Jane's marriage imperils this symbolic economy in two ways. In the first place, despite her explicit disavowal of kinship, Jane has effectively been inscribed in a series that includes not just a lunatic and a mistress, but also a veritable united nations of women. In telling Jane about these other lovers, Rochester's design is to insist on difference, to draw an absolute distinction between some kinds of women, who cannot be legitimate wives, and Jane, who can. This distinction is reinforced by both racism and nationalist prejudice: that Bertha is West Indian "explains" her madness, just as Céline's French birth "accounts for" her moral laxity. But Jane immediately sees that if she assents to Rochester's proposal, she will become simply "the successor of these poor girls" (p. 339). She sees, in other words, the likeness that Rochester denies: *any* woman who is not a wife is automatically like a governess in being dependent, like a fallen woman in being "kept."

Emphasizing the likeness among women is subversive not merely because doing so highlights all women's dependence—although this is, of course, part of the point. Beyond this, the fact that the likeness Brontë stresses is not women's selflessness or self-control but some internal difference suggests that the contradiction repressed by the domestic ideal is precisely what makes a woman womanly. This internal difference is figured variously as madness and as sexuality. Jane's own descriptions of herself show her growing from the "insanity" of childhood rebellion to the "restlessness" of unspecified desire: "I desired more," she says, ". . . than I possessed" (p. 141). In the passage in chapter 12 in which Jane describes this "restlessness," she compares it specifically to the "ferment" that feeds "political rebellions" and she opposes it explicitly to the self-denial that caring for children requires. This passage returns us once more to Jane's dreams of children, for the manifest content of the majority of those dreams reveals how carrying a child burdens the dreamer, impeding her efforts to reach her lover or voice her frustrated love. "Anybody may blame me who likes," Jane says of the "cool language" with which she describes her feelings for Adele, but caring for the child is not enough; "I believed in the existence of other and more vivid kinds of goodness, and what I believed in I wished to behold" (pp. 140, 141). Even when Jane has her own child at the end of the novel, her only reference to him subordinates maternal love to the sexual passion that Rochester's eyes have consistently represented.[26]

Positioning Jane within a series of women and characterizing her as "restless" and passionate transform the difference among women that Dickens invoked, to "cure" the problematic sexuality written into the domestic ideal, into a difference within all women—the "difference" of sexual desire. This similarity thus subverts the putative difference between the governess and the lunatic or mistress, just as it obliterates the difference between the governess and the wife. Having Jane marry Rochester—transforming the governess into a wife—extends the series of aberrant women to include the figure who ought to be exempt from this series, who ought to be the norm. The point is that, as the boundary between these two groups of women, the governess belongs to both sides of the opposition: in her, the very possibility of an opposition collapses.

The second sense in which Jane's marriage is subversive follows directly from this relocation of difference. If all women are alike in being "restless," then they are also like—not different from—men. Charlotte Brontë makes this point explicitly in chapter 12, in the passage I have been quoting. "Women are supposed to be very calm generally," Jane notes, "but women feel just as men feel; they need exercise for their faculties, and a field for their efforts as much as their brothers do; they suffer from too rigid a restraint, too absolute a stagnation, precisely as men would suffer; and it is . . . thoughtless to condemn them, or laugh at them, if they seek to do more or learn more than custom has pronounced necessary for their sex" (p. 141). The implications of this statement may not be drawn out consistently in this novel, but merely to assert that the most salient difference was located within every individual and not between men and women was to raise the possibilities that women's dependence was customary, not natural, that their sphere was kept separate only by artificial means, and that women, like men, could grow through work outside the home. Even though Jane marries Rochester, then, she does so as an expression of her desire, not as the self-sacrifice St. John advocates; the image with which she represents her marriage fuses man and woman instead of respecting their separate bodies, much less their separate spheres. "Ever more absolutely bone of his bone and flesh of his flesh," Jane represents herself as taking the law of coverture to its logical extreme.

What Lady Eastlake objected to in *Jane Eyre* is exactly this subversive tendency. But despite her objection, Eastlake's intermittent—and irrepressible—recognition that the governess's plight is, theoretically at least, that of every middle-class woman repeats Brontë's subversive move. Moreover, Eastlake's charge that the "crimes of fathers" sow the crop of governesses fingers men as the villains behind women's dependence even more specifically than Brontë was willing to do.[27] This charge—that men are responsible for the fetters women wear—also appears in the bitter myth recounted in "Hints on the Modern Governess System." " 'Twas a stroke of policy in those ranty-pole barons of old," the author writes, "to make their lady-loves idols, and curb their wives with silken idleness. Woman was raised on a pinnacle to keep her in safety. Our chivalrous northern knights had a religious horror of the Paynim harems. They never heard of Chinese shoes in those days, so they devised a new chain for the weaker sex. They made feminine labour disgraceful" (*FM* 576). The implicit accusation here is that women had to be idolized and immobilized for some men to think them safe from other men's rapacious sexual desire and from their own susceptibility. Just as some medical men attempted to regulate medical practice so as to control fears about sexuality, so our "chivalrous northern knights" curtail women's honorable labor to protect men from the appetite they represent as uncontrollable and destructive.

Neither Lady Eastlake nor the author of "Hints on the Modern Governess System" developed this indictment of men into an extended argument; instead, they continued to see the problem in terms of a natural difference between the sexes and the inevitability of women's dependence. So fixed did these writers imagine women's dependence to be, in fact, that the only solution they could devise was to defer their criticism of men, to make women responsible for remedying the trouble they identified: Lady Eastlake yokes her plea that upper-class employers pay their governesses higher wages to an argument that middle-class women—not to mention those in lesser ranks—resume their maternal duties; the author of "Hints" explicitly states that "the modern governess system is a case between woman and woman. Before one sex demands its due from the other, let it be just to itself" (*FM* 573).

II

Lady Eastlake's formulation of the governess's plight is as explicit as anything written in the 1840s about the class and moral concerns that dovetail in the governess—and, more specifically, about the fact that her situation epitomizes that of the middle-class mother whom she ought to reproduce but not displace. As I have suggested, in exposing the contradictions it sets out to defend, this text is itself contradictory; it illuminates, even as it ostentaciously denies, the tensions inherent in a domestic ideal that simultaneously invoked and denied female sexuality as *the* basis for social differences. Other texts from the 1840s draw out even more explicitly the contradiction inherent in this ideal as they elaborated the normative definition of woman. Already in the 1840s, the issue was whether it was "natural" for women to be dependent. In "Hints," for example, the author not only indicts male sexual anxiety for enforcing women's dependence; he—or (surely) she—also momentarily envisions a future in which marriage and motherhood will not be a woman's only fate: "A few generations hence, . . . when female energy has scope, . . .

an 'old maid' will be a useful, honoured personage. . . . When a woman, who is neither wife nor mother, may use the faculties God has given her, as her necessities require, she may sing a paean which has not been heard since the golden age, when Ceres gave bread to man" (*FM* 576).

In characterizing the governess's work as a "profession" rather than a duty or a necessity, Sarah Lewis—herself once a governess—also boldly claimed respect for women's independence and work. In an 1848 essay entitled "On the Social Position of Governesses," Lewis argues that salary should be fixed to training and skill, not hardship or rank, and recommends that governesses form "a professional combination" to eliminate the unqualified and to dispense annuities in lieu of charity.[28] In one sense, Lewis was only responding logically to one of the complaints made against governesses; if governesses were underpaid because they were unqualified, then internal organization might enhance their market value by limiting competition and imposing uniform qualifications on successful applicants. But in another sense, Lewis's suggestion completely violated the way the governess problem was typically conceptualized. By substituting for the moral categories in which it was usually formulated a set of terms that recast the governess as a worker rather than a mother manqué, Lewis rewrote the governess's plight as a problem of work rather than domestic relations. Lewis's reconceptualization of the governess makes explicit what the arguments I have been discussing suggest but do not pursue: that *work* was the site upon which "nature" was being constructed—and not vice versa. As the discussion about governesses was subsumed into the more wide-ranging debate that Lewis adumbrates, two of the commonplaces of the ideology I have discussed came under more direct scrutiny and attack. The first was the issue I have just discussed—the representation of female desire as exclusively maternal; the second was the notion that some kinds of work were not characterized by alienation and, as a consequence, that a sphere separate from the alienated sphere of work existed in the home. The emergence of these issues in the 1850s was signaled and greeted by a proliferation of discussions about work and nature, on the one hand—some of which openly challenged the normative definition of female nature on which the middle-class ideology was based—and, on the other hand, by an increasingly vehement defense of the "naturalness" of the very idealized domesticity currently under material and rhetorical siege.

In the 1850s, the first organized attempt to expand employment opportunities for women was launched by the so-called ladies of

Langham Place, led by Bessie Rayner Parkes and Barbara Leigh Smith Bodichon.[29] This collaboration originated partly in the growing recognition among middle-class reformers that the plight of governesses would never be solved unless other jobs were opened to middle-class women; partly, it was a response to Parliament's rejection of the Married Women's Property Bill in favor of the Matrimonial Causes Bill in the autumn of 1856 and the winter of 1857. As a result, the campaign was simultaneously a pragmatic response to an immediate social problem and the first expression of an organized, political feminist movement. Barbara Bodichon's pamphlet entitled *Women and Work* was critical in linking the issue of legal reform to the problem of work. Published in April 1857, this pamphlet made explicit what Brontë's novel only implied: in so far as they were legally and economically positioned as dependents, all women were governesses to their children, prostitutes to their husbands, and the victims of their father's crimes. "Fathers have no right to cast the burden of the support of their daughters on other men," Bodichon charges. "It lowers the dignity of women, and tends to prostitution, whether legal or in the streets. As long as fathers regard the sex of a child as a reason why it should not be taught to gain its own bread, so long must women be degraded. Adult women must not be supported by men, if they are to stand as dignified, rational, beings before God."[30]

Bodichon, Parkes, and the other women who had formed the Married Women's Property Committee in 1855 established a journal in March 1858 with the express goal of advocating employment for women and lobbying for legal reforms. The *English Woman's Journal* not only became the vehicle for linking the ladies of Langham Place to sympathizers throughout the country; it also began to draw women who wanted work—especially unemployed governesses—to its offices in Cavendish Square. Partly in response to these women, and with the support of the influential National Association for the Promotion of the Social Sciences, Bodichon and Parkes founded a Society for the Promotion of the Employment of Women in July 1859. This society, the first pragmatic feminist effort to train lower-middle-class women for work, drew Jessie Boucherett to London, and in 1860 she opened a business school for girls, under the auspices of the society.[31] The work of the Women's Employment Society continued after the *English Woman's Journal* ceased publication in 1864.

In their arguments in favor of expanding women's employment, the ladies of Langham Place were essentially capitalizing on one component of the argument by which moralists and medical men attempted to defend the mother as the female norm. That is, the argument that some women were (unfortunately) forced by financial necessity to be independent could easily be given another emphasis: if some women were *able* to be independent, feminists argued, then women were not necessarily by *nature* dependent. Two effects followed from this position: the first, to which I return in a moment, is that as the argument that more women could work was borne out in practice, the notion that "maternal nature" was the norm seemed increasingly suspect and in need of defense; the second is that arguments began to be formulated about the kind of education women might want or need—arguments that paradoxically both undermined and reinforced the idea that the unwaged mother was the female norm.

Viewed from the perspective of feminists, some reconceptualization of women's education was necessary to break into what otherwise threatened to remain a vicious circle. As long as education was conceptualized as training and training was primarily directed toward obtaining better jobs, women would not need education unless jobs were available to them; yet until women were better trained, even the most outspoken feminists admitted that they would not be qualified for skilled work. One approach to this problem, which was adumbrated as early as 1844 in the *Athenaeum*, was simply to formalize improved training for women. This position was elaborated in Bessie Parkes's *Remarks on the Education of Girls,* published in 1854 (with a revised edition issued in 1856), and it received concrete form in four training schools established for women: Queen's College (established 1848), Bedford College (1848), the North London Collegiate School for Women (1850), and the Ladies' College at Cheltenham (1850).

The second attempt to break into this vicious circle involved the effort to detach training from a more broadly conceived notion of "education." One of the first women to elaborate this approach was Emily Shirreff, who was to become mistress of Girton College in the 1860s. Initially, Shirreff directed her attention to the kind of education most obviously aligned with the domestic norm—what she and her contemporaries called "self-culture," the self-improvement any girl with sufficient leisure could undertake at home.[32] By 1858, however, Shirreff had undertaken a more ambitious consideration of the nature and purposes of education. Her primary goal in *Intellectual Education and Its Influence on the Character and Happiness of Women* (1858) was to prove that education was intrinsically valu-

able in "disciplining the mind" and was therefore desirable for everyone, not just leisured ladies or male wage earners. "Now, the
fundamental truth to start from appears to me to be this," she wrote,
"—that education, apart from all secondary objects (that is, all objects which have reference to peculiar circumstances or positions),
has one and the same purpose for every human being; and this
purpose is systematic and harmonious development of his whole
moral and intellectual nature."[33] One effect of Shirreff's position was
to expand middle-class women's education beyond "self-culture." "If
we argue upon grounds of mere worldly utility," Shirreff pointed
out,

> we can never get rid of petty squabbles as to the amount of
> arithmetic, grammar, or history which may or may not turn
> out to be profitable to them [working-class men]; and it must
> ever remain an open question whether industrial schools are
> not better than those of a more intellectual character. But if we
> take our stand upon the ground that the human being remains
> a mutilated creature if the capacities of his mind are left dor-
> mant, or if, when awakened by circumstances, he has no com-
> mand over them, then it becomes at once apparent that every
> study which tends to exercise those powers is useful in the
> highest sense of the word, and that the only limitations to this
> mental discipline and to the knowledge which it is good for all
> human beings to acquire are those imposed by time and means.[34]

Even if Shirreff argued for expanding girls' education, however,
she did not intend this education to prepare girls for paid work or
the public sphere. Instead, she aligned knowledge with domestic
duties and moral influence. "It is not indeed difficult to show how
many of woman's home duties, both as wife and mother, would be
far better discharged by more cultivated minds," she wrote, "and
how far her sphere of enjoyment and influence is increased by extending to man's intellectual life the power of sympathy she exercises
so strongly within the range of feelings and affections."[35]

Sherriff's argument that "society will suffer in proportion as
women . . . join the noisy throng in the busy markets of the world"[36]
separated her from Parkes and Boucherett, who considered economic or social independence the proper goals of education.[37] Paradoxically, moreover, it aligned her with one of the most consistently
outspoken opponents of expanding women's sphere, the *Saturday
Review*. From its founding in 1856, the *Review* professed sympathy
for "women's rights" and women's welfare, but its writers so dra-

matically redefined "women's rights" that this term completely lost its feminist edge. "We are, we believe, the truest advocates of women's rights," one author proclaimed in 1857, "when we say that, as a rule, it is [any woman's] misfortune that she is ever compelled to earn money." That this writer was actually protecting not women's rights but men's jobs becomes clear as soon as his solicitude turns to threat. "Woman, to the end, must remain the weaker vessel," he declares; if women seek independence, "the coarser muscles and tougher mental fibres of the dominant sex" will simply drive them out of work. "Hitherto her true strength has been in her dependence, but it may come to pass that, if she calls attention to the fact, her natural weakness will invite oppression."[38]

The implicit connection this writer makes between the increasing numbers of women entering the labor force and the threat they potentially posed to male employment was most often submerged in arguments about social stability, a natural division of labor, and the welfare of marriage as an institution. Articles in the *Review*, many specifically ridiculing the work of Bodichon, Parkes, and proponents of women's education, alternated between denying that any middle-class women had to work, asserting that they should not work under any conditions, and complaining that, if they did work, they would undermine the state, morality, and nature. In the rhetoric of these writers, women working signaled social degeneration. "The interest of a State is to get as many of its citizens married as possible," one reviewer responded to Bessie Parkes in 1859. "And we add that man, in European communities, has deliberately adopted the view that, as much as possible, women should be relieved from the necessity of self-support. The measure of civilization is the maximum at which this end is attained in any given community or nation. Women labourers are a proof of a barbarous and imperfect civilization." For this author, the reason for this maxim is clear: "wherever women are self-supporters, marriage is, *ipso facto*, discouraged. . . . And where there are fewer marriages, there is more vice."[39]

In this comment we see the same projection of anxieties about the promiscuity and/or susceptibility of sexuality that we saw in the statements of medical men, but here the anxieties are conceptualized in relation to women's work rather than their bodies. The assumption here is that economic independence will automatically lead to sexual independence; if women are "self-supporters," they will not marry; if they do not marry, sexuality will no longer be controlled. What is not clear in this statement is what this writer assumes would cause the "vice." Would it follow from *women's* increased independence? Or would it follow from women's "natural" vulnerability and men's retaliatory anger? The reviewer's assertion that for a woman not to marry is to fail in her "profession" assigns responsibility for this state of things to the woman, but his subsequent threat makes it sound like men would punish women for their failure by withdrawing the option of marriage. In expressing his uncertainty about whose sexuality threatens to escape control, this writer alludes to the sexuality implicit in the domestic ideal and to its resemblance to the sexual aggression he acknowledges in men.

> Married life is women's profession; and to this life her training—that of dependence—is modelled. Of course by not getting a husband, or losing him, she may find that she is without resources. All that can be said of her is, she has failed in business; and no social reform can prevent such failures. The mischance of the distressed governess and the unprovided widow, is that of every insolvent tradesman. . . .
>
> Men do not like, and would not seek, to mate with an independent factor, who at any time could quit—or who at all times would be tempted to neglect—the tedious duties of training and bringing up children, and keeping the tradesmen's bills, and mending the linen, for the more lucrative returns of the desk or counter.

This author goes on to link explicitly his disapproval of women's work to a fear about the dissolution of sexual difference, which only keeping women dependent can protect. "We do not want our women to be androgynous," he asserts. "We had rather do what we can for the Governesses' Institution, and, if need be, subscribe to a dozen more such institutions, than realize Miss Parkes' Utopia of every middle-class girl taught some useful art."[40] As long as women remained objects of charity, in other words, and middle-class women's work remained the exception and not the rule, the "natural" difference between the sexes would not be imperiled. What the *Saturday Review* rejected was any form of organized response that might replace the image of women's dependence, which deserved protection, with a model of sexual equality, in which women, like men, would become self-reliant individuals with responsibilities and rights. The importance of seeing economically distressed women as isolated cases rather than challenges to the sexual division of labor and rights was stated clearly in the *Review's* 1857 response to Brougham's proposed Married Women's Property Bill: "Let the occasional and accidental defects of law be treated with occasional and accidental

remedies—let individual and exceptional cases be dealt with indi-
vidually and exceptionally . . . but let there be no interference with
the law of God and nature."[41]

If treating distressed working women as "individual and exceptional cases" constituted one way of containing the challenge
they posed to the "law of God and nature," then keeping all women
ignorant of anything beyond the home was another, more extreme
remedy. In 1859 the *Review* was willing to grant women the right to
education as long as their knowledge was ultimately devoted to their
domestic duties. "So long as the solidity of education is limited by
the consideration that the girls, when they have become women,
must exercise their special gifts, there can be no objection to it," one
writer generously conceded in a survey of "The Intellect of Women."[42]
By 1865, however, the *Review* drew the curtains much more closely
around the home. The sexual double standard, this writer insists,
must not only protect women from the world of work, it must even
keep them ignorant of the dangers they avoid.

> No woman can or ought to know very much of the mass of
> meanness and wickedness and misery that is loose in the wide
> world. She could not learn about it without losing the bloom
> and freshness which it is her mission in life to preserve. Her
> position is somewhat peculiar, and to her unsophisticated eyes
> may seem partly unintelligible. In order to protect itself, society
> is compelled to punish a woman's faults and transgressions
> more severely than it punishes the failings of the stronger sex;
> and yet it is necessary that the very sex which is to be so
> disproportionately punished should be left in ignorance of the
> dangers and characteristic features of transgression. . . . The
> code [the double standard] has a relative apart from its positive
> value, and . . . it exists, not for the sake of itself, but as a warning
> against other evils that are designedly kept veiled from the
> common gaze.[43]

The increasingly vehement tone of the *Saturday Review* reveals
that by the mid-1860s the threat posed to the equation of female
nature and domesticity or maternity was perceived to be increasingly
serious (a perception no doubt strengthened by the election of John
Stuart Mill to Parliament that year). If even middle-class women
could and did work outside the home, then women might not be
naturally dependent or destined (or content) to be mothers; if they
did not always marry, then marriage might not be the only unit of
social organization. And given the position female dependence, ma-

ternity, and marriage occupied in assumptions about morality and class stability, to question this definition of female nature was to shake the foundations on which middle-class ideology was based. That unmarried women were figured not just as "unnatural" but also as business failures suggests the extent to which "God's laws" had already begun to be rewritten in economic language by the 1850s, but while the laws of the capitalist economy might increasingly be conceded as governing men's lives, conservative essayists still struggled to keep women's "nature" affixed to the supposedly more stable, more moral laws of God. Paradoxically, however, as the last passage I quoted reveals, the effect of this defensive effort was to construct woman's "nature" as increasingly fragile at the same time that it was assigned an increasingly serious "mission": the greater the "meanness . . . and misery" woman defies, in other words, the more protection she requires to remain the hothouse flower whose fragility (theoretically) keeps the misery out.

This author's allusion to "other evils" that must be kept veiled points to a second effect of such efforts to contain the threat posed by working women. If characterizing the public sphere as containing a "mass of meanness and wickedness and misery" was intended to discourage women from wanting to work in or even know about this world, it also articulated a pervasive ambivalence on the part of even the most rabid antifeminists toward the labor they so jealously protected. In disparaging the public sphere so as to enhance the desirability of the home, writers such as this essayist voiced the same ambivalence toward work that surfaces in depictions of literary labor and the literary man. On the one hand, professional work—and even, at least in the case of literary labor, competition—was celebrated as the means by which an individual (man) achieved self-fulfillment and social status and the avenue by which society recognized and rewarded merit. But on the other hand, in novels like *David Copperfield* and essays like those in the *Saturday Review,* we see the implication, at least, that work could be degrading instead of ennobling, an imposition on rather than an expression of one's "self." Discussions of work that denigrated all paid labor for the purpose of discouraging women constituted one site at which the alienation I described in chapter 3 emerged into visibility. And it was this depiction of work that mandated the production of its alternative—the image of some kinds of work that were exempt from alienation because they seemed completely outside the system of wages and surplus value. Only the existence of such "creative" work—even as an exception—made the rule of waged slavery tolerable.

As I have already suggested, literary and domestic labor were examples par excellence of such "creative" work. But just as the symbolic work necessary to cover over the place literary labor occupied in the capitalist economy betrayed its affinity to other kinds of alienated labor, so the arguments advanced to construct the domestic sphere as an arena of nonalienated labor occasionally reveal the extent to which even the writers who extolled it as such recognized the fiction they created. The *Saturday Review*'s reference to the "tedious details of training and bringing up children" constitutes one conservative's recognition that work in the domestic sphere might be as trying, in its own way, as work for money. On the other side of the political divide, John Stuart Mill articulated the same perception in 1861. "The superintendence of a household," he wrote, "even when not in other respects laborious, is extremely onerous to the thoughts; it requires incessant vigilance, an eye which no detail escapes, and presents questions for consideration and solution, foreseen and unforeseen, at every hour of the day, from which the person responsible for them can hardly ever shake herself free."[44]

The contradictions inherent in arguments against expanding women's sphere emerge in almost all of the *Saturday Review*'s essays. On the one hand, the more woman's moral mission was emphasized, the clearer it became that the "nature" essential to this mission had to be protected against or even constructed in defiance of the sexual assertiveness also feared to be innate in women. On the other hand, the more insistently "nature" was articulated upon the sexed division of labor, the more obvious it became that work and the public sphere were simultaneously glorified (for young men) and denigrated (for women) as part of what seemed like an increasingly desperate campaign to keep women in the home. By the 1860s, the artificiality of both of these truisms could at least occasionally be recognized. "Why," Mary Taylor asked rhetorically in an article published in the feminist *Victoria Magazine*,

> is [woman] not to seek, and to be helped and taught to find some lucrative employment? Because her life is not to be made too easy, lest she should be less willing for the matrimony which is already what she likes best. It is surprising how often in men's schemes for ameliorating feminine evils one meets with this contradiction. Never a philanthropist takes the subject in hand

but he begins by vigorously asserting that [women's] first wish
is for marriage, and that their main happiness in life must come
from their husbands and children, as if the point were doubtful.
Seldom, however, does he write long without betraying the
belief that they adopt their career because all others are artifi-
cially closed to them, and that if a single life is made too pleasant
they will not adopt it at all.[45]

An author for the less irreverent *Fraser's Magazine* noted the problem
as early as 1860. "It is not in the nature of things," this author remarks,
"that we should teach young women to look upon non-domestic
employments as a privilege, and then expect that they will value
home leisure; that we should kindle ambition, and expect them to
cherish obscurity, and to give themselves cheerfully to petty household details, and the patient, laborious training of children."[46]

If the contradictions in definitions of female "nature" and attitudes toward work riddled conservative arguments, they also helped
delimit the kinds of solutions that women's supporters could devise
for women's plight. Because of the assumptions I have been discussing about female nature and the public and private spheres,
feminists in the 1850s confronted two images that dissuaded most
women from questioning their social role. One was the image epitomized in the prostitute but also raised by Caroline Norton in the
specter of Hannah Brown, the image of a sexualized, and therefore
vulnerable, woman who could not find protection in marriage or
the law; the other was the picture of women "failing" at the moral
mission that supposedly proved their superiority to sexuality simply
because they sought economic independence. These two images set
the limits to the kinds of remedies midcentury feminists were generally able to propose, not merely because they discouraged women
from rejecting domesticity, but also because the solutions they encouraged undermined the possibility that women would recognize
what was common about their plight by reinforcing the difference
that so obviously divided them—the difference of class.

Almost every advocate of expanding women's employment
shared two crucial assumptions with her (or his) opponents: that
women would work only out of necessity and that every occupation
was appropriate to a specific class. Even if Barbara Bodichon or
Jessie Boucherett was willing to suggest that a woman might *choose*
not to marry, both these women and almost every other feminist
cast her (or his) argument about women's work as a solution to a
problem: because there were not enough husbands or solvent fathers,

women had to work; therefore there should be more jobs.[47] The conceptualization of paid work as a problem women faced perpetuated the belief voiced by conservatives that women's *proper* work was moral superintendence and (unpaid) domestic labor. This position retained the power it did partly because it could so easily be articulated upon two commonplaces about class.

The first of these truisms was that leisure represented social status. As capitalism pervaded all sectors of society, much of the burden of representing privilege was transferred from men's possessions or attributes (a landed estate, a title) to women's activities and appearance. The paradoxical place leisured women occupied in the economy, which was based on their economic redundancy and their conspicuous consumption, made them uniquely appropriate for this role, for their consumption simultaneously fueled the home market and enabled them visibly to incarnate the leisure most men could not afford to enjoy. As a consequence, it was in his ability to support the leisured woman that the middle-class man could most clearly identify his success. The second commonplace was that some kinds of work were more "genteel" than others. In spite of feminists' explicit attempts to debunk the social opprobrium placed on women earning money, they almost all retained the notion that nonmanual and noncommercial work was more suited to women of the middle class. This class bias runs throughout arguments that the governesses' plight will be alleviated by opening other jobs to women; like oil and water, feminists argued, women would then seek and find their "natural" places. As Jessie Boucherett asserts, the governesses' problems would disappear once that "army" was purged of its socially inferior members.

> If women of the trading classes were thus enabled to become clerks and accountants, and to take part in commercial business, the number of candidates for places as governesses would be much diminished, and would consist principally of ladies who had known better days, and of daughters of the clergy and professional men left without fortunes; and as the competition would diminish with the numbers seeking engagements, these could ask sufficiently high salaries to enable them to live in tolerable comfort during their old age, without being beholden to charity; and being principally gentlewomen by birth and manners, the unfavorable impressions now existing against governesses would gradually fade away. The profession would rise in public estimation, and those following it would receive the respect and consideration due to them.[48]

These two assumptions—that work was gendered and classed—reinforced the connection between work and moral contamination. In so far as they were constructed *in relation to women,* in other words, the images of lower class and work bore a reciprocal relation to each other, just as did the representations of middle-class domesticity and morality: each was simultaneously cause and effect of the other. Moreover, assumptions about class "solved" the problem of women's work for middle-class women by discriminating among kinds of work, and assumptions about gender "solved" the problem of work for men by making some kinds of work simultaneously morally superior and economically inferior to others. As long as feminists retained these assumptions, then, they remained blind to the fact that privileging women's moral role kept women as a "class" in an economically disadvantaged place, the position of dependence that unequal property laws and the sexual double standard also defined as theirs.

Articulating assumptions about work and morality onto assumptions about gender was therefore one aspect of the paradox of individualism I have already discussed. These assumptions produced as part of the representation of woman the illusion of one kind of likeness (moral nature, which followed from maternal instinct), while both reinforcing class difference *and* obscuring the positional likeness (legal and economic dependence) all women actually shared. This rhetorical construction was the basis for the equally paradoxical definition of man: if the moral nature of woman *did* follow from nature and if it *could* stabilize the aggressive, naturally sexualized nature of man, then the class and economic inequalities among men that fueled competition would be less important than the domestic character women enabled men to share. The problem was, of course, that as more working-class women entered paid labor, the possibility that domesticity could ever be their "natural" state seemed increasingly remote. This is why by the 1850s, the argument about women's domestic nature, in so far as it was successful at all, worked only for the middle class; it also explains why the increase in numbers of middle-class women working outside the home provoked increasingly elaborate defenses of women's "nature."

Given the assaults on female nature, the domestic sphere, and the domestic national character inflicted by women working, it is not surprising that the difficulties inherent in these assumptions became visible in the discussion about what kind of education working-class girls should receive. Middle-class women might still be celebrated as innately moral because the middle-class woman who had to work was still the exception; but if woman's *nature* were to be considered moral, then something had to be done about working-class women, among whom paid work was *not* exceptional. To ensure that domesticity could be represented as the norm, the state—in the form of the educational system—intervened. The goal of this project, not surprisingly, was the reproduction of England's (domestic) national character. This is a member of the Committee of the Council of Education, speaking in the mid-1850s.

> But there are other evil results arising from the neglect of girls' education, far more serious that the want of good servants;— as the girl is, so will the woman be; and as the woman is, so will the home be; and as the home is, such, for good or for evil, will be the character of our population. . . . No amount of mere knowledge, religious or secular, given to boys, will secure them from drunkenness or crime in after life. It may be true that knowledge is power, but knowledge is not virtue. . . . If we wish to arrest the growth of national vice, we must go to its real seminary, *the home*. Instead of that thriftless untidy woman who presides over it, driving her husband to the gin palace by the discomfort of his own house, and marring for life the temper and health of her own child by her own want of sense, we must train up one who will be a cleanly careful housewife, and a patient skillful mother. Until one or two generations have been improved, we must trust mainly to our schools to effect this change in the daughters of the working classes. We must multiply over the face of the country girls' schools of a sensible and practical sort.[49]

If Dickens and other literary men were able to "comprehend" that the national character was a domestic character, it was only because women made it so by making the home moral, tidy, and more attractive than the public sphere or the public house. But just as *David Copperfield* makes clear that Dickens's image of domesticity required the displacement of both domestic labor and the capitalist work relations in which the writer and the woman were implicitly involved, so this quotation reveals that the image of the woman reproducing domesticity entailed symbolically generalizing the values of middle-class "nature" and institutionally implanting this nature in women who were not middle class. Despite all the rhetoric to the contrary, then, the nature of the national character was not necessarily domestic, and the sign of this was that working-class women did not automatically reproduce middle-class virtues—or, read another way, that more women of all classes increasingly worked outside the home.

The argument that institutionalized education for working-class girls would inculcate morality eventually helped achieve higher levels of more standardized education for both sexes and all classes. But in the short run at least, the assumptions operative here also worked against reconceptualizing woman's social role, the nature of education, and—as part of these—the governess's duties and her relevant qualifications. As long as a (girl's) teacher's primary responsibility was conceptualized as the superintendence of morality, then class position would remain more important than academic knowledge or educational training; as long as *teacher* was considered "synonymous with *mother*," the governess's sex would be more important than her training, and whatever education girls received was likely to be conducted for—if not in—the home.⁵⁰

The interdependent representations of middle-class women as the natural guardians of the national character and the domestic sphere, and the public sphere as an arena of "misery . . . and meanness," worked against professionalizing any middle-class women's work. For to professionalize women's work would be to erode the distinctions between separate spheres, between classes, and—as a consequence—between moral and immoral arenas of life. Therefore, maintaining—even in the face of changing material conditions—that marriage was a middle-class woman's only "natural" "business" had the double and paradoxical effects of reinforcing the devaluation of work and the public sphere from which men sought to exclude women and ensuring that the guardians of the private sphere had no alternative but to superintend morality or else consider themselves failures in the very terms by which men measured their success.

By the end of the 1850s, the governess no longer marked the border between one class and another or between immorality and morality because she no longer symbolized working middle-class women in the same way that she had in the 1840s. That is, the problem of women's work had been reconceptualized as involving more than one *kind* of women's work. By the late 1850s, what had begun as concern for individual cases of economic suffering had yielded the recognition that the governesses' "plight" articulated the contradiction between the moral role women had been assigned in capitalist society and the economic position into which they were being driven in increasing numbers. The extent to which the governesses' plight had been recast as part of a larger issue can be seen from Harriet Martineau's 1859 essay entitled "Female Industry." Here Martineau reviews the report of the Governesses' Benevolent Institution not with novels, as Lady Eastlake had done a decade earlier, but with nine other nonfiction treatments of contemporary social problems; the texts include the 1851 Census, four texts on work, and two texts on education. Of the forty-three pages in the essay, the governess receives only two paragraphs, whose point, according to Martineau, is self-evident. "We need not go on," Martineau concludes. "The evil is plain enough. The remedies seem to be equally clear;—to sustain and improve the modern tests of the quality of educators; and to open broad and new ways for the industrial exertions of women; or at least to take care that such as open naturally are not arbitrarily closed."[51]

Despite the fact that by the end of the 1850s the governess had become just another instance of the working woman, her "plight" had thrust into prominence the instability of those middle-class assumptions about female nature and the separation of spheres on which the identity of the bourgeois subject was rhetorically and legally based. Because discussions of the governess implicitly or explicitly equated the sexuality written into the domestic ideal with economic independence, they adumbrated another reading that could be given to this contradictory image. The other side of women's dependence—the capacity that celebrants of domesticity conceptualized as moral energy—*could* be represented as sexual aggression—especially by those who feared the consequences of female promiscuity. But it could also be represented as women's "capability," their capacity to accomplish tasks and acquire independence that ultimately undermined the hegemony of the domestic ideal and questioned this particular definition of the meaning of sexual difference. The way this reading of the contradictory domestic ideal allowed for an expansion of women's sphere was set out dramatically at midcentury by Florence Nightingale.

CHAPTER SIX

A Housewifely Woman: The Social Construction of Florence Nightingale

In the Summer of 1856, when all of England feared that Florence Nightingale was dying from a fever contracted in the Crimea, Harriet Martineau composed her obituary. This obituary makes it clear that, in the twenty months since she had first captured public attention by her nursing expedition to the East, Florence Nightingale had come to embody her contemporaries' complex ideas about what a woman should—and could—be.[1] "Florence Nightingale," Martineau writes,

> had perhaps the highest lot ever fulfilled by woman, except by women sovereigns who have not merely reigned but ruled. . . . It is no small distinction to our time that it produced a woman who effected two great things;—a mighty reform in the care of the sick, & an opening for her sex into the region of serious business, in proportion to their ability to maintain a place in it.
>
> This is all true; & it is very important truth: but it is not what can satisfy us at such a moment as this. We shall grieve too bitterly at such a loss to care for any estimate of the position held by her whom the nation mourns. We think of her today as the nurse, & the dispenser of comfort and relief; & we care little for her greatness, while conscious that her gentle voice will never more rouse the sufferer to courage, nor her skilled hand administer ease. We think of her dressing wounds, bringing wine & food, carrying the lamp through miles of sick soldiers in the middle of the night, noting every face, & answering the appeal of every eye as she passed. We think of her spending precious hours in selecting books to please the men's individual wish or want; & stocking her coffee-house with luxuries and innocent pleasures, to draw the soldiers away from poisonous drinks and mischief. We think now of the poor fellow who said that he looked for her coming in hospital, for he c^d at least kiss her shadow on his pillow as she passed. We think today of the

little Russian prisoner, the poor boy who c^d not speak or be spoken to till she had taken him in, & had taught him & made useful; & how he answered when at length he c^d understand a question. When asked if he knew where he w^d go when he was dead, he confidently said "I shall go to Miss Nightingale." . . .

Many of the wisest of men & women said that talk about the powers & position of women is nearly useless, because all human beings take rank, in the long run, according to their capability. But it is true & will remain true, that what women are able to do they will do, with or without leave obtained from men. Florence Nightingale encountered opposition,—from her own set as much as the other; & she achieved, as the most natural thing in the world, & without the smallest sacrifice of her womanly quality, what w^d beforehand have been declared a deed for a future age. She was no declaimer but a housewifely woman;—she talked little, & did great things. When other women see that there are things for them to do, & train themselves to the work, they will get it done easily enough. There can never be a more unthought-of & marvellous career before any working woman than Florence Nightingale has achieved; & her success had opened a way to all others easier than any one had prepared for her.[2]

Florence Nightingale did not, of course, die in 1856. In fact, despite numerous undiagnosable illnesses and an almost constant personal conviction that she was dying, Nightingale lived until 1910; she spent most of the fifty-four years after her return from the East lying on a couch in London, seeing almost no one, and issuing reams of directives and reports about sanitary conditions in India, the reform of the War Office, and the organization of military and civilian hospitals and nursing. The hagiographical construction of Florence Nightingale, of which Martineau's obituary is a piece, therefore misrepresents Nightingale—not only in being prematurely laudatory, as Martineau's eulogy most obviously is, but also in understating the range of projects Nightingale actually undertook, while crediting her with things she did not do. Despite the impression her contemporaries give us, for example, Nightingale was not the first nurse, nor did she single-handedly found modern nursing; her accomplishments in the Crimea and in nursing were not her only or even her primary interests, and her success in the hospital at Scutari was neither complete nor strictly a function of either her exemplary feminine virtues or her iron will and indominable spirit.[3] In this chapter I look at some of the reasons why Nightingale was so misrepresented, why she emerges from mid-nineteenth-century accounts as the figure almost solely responsible for creating modern nursing and almost solely as a nurse. I argue that Nightingale's own writings authorized this misrepresentation and that these writings, along with the misrepresentation they underwrote, capitalized on the contradiction inherent in the domestic ideal in order to make even more radical claims for women than contemporary feminists did. At the same time that Florence Nightingale was able to exploit contradictory assumptions about gender, however, she also contributed to the construction of an image of the English national character, which deployed the domestic ideal to support both Britain's imperial designs in India and the expansion of state administrative control over the poor at home.

In focusing primarily on the place an individual occupies in ideological and material changes, this discussion of Florence Nightingale continues the inquiry I set out in chapter 3, but it also picks up on my discussions of the chloroform debate, on the one hand, and governesses and middle-class women's employment, on the other. In the first place, nursing—especially given the female autonomy Nightingale institutionalized in its every facet—came closer than any other branch of the medical profession to providing some resistance to the male domination I examined in chapter 2.[4] Even though women were almost completely excluded from scientific research and medical discourse during this period, Nightingale's conceptualization of nursing ultimately challenged the basis of medical men's power—the right to define who was a patient in need of health care.[5] But in the second place, unlike many of the occupations the feminists I discussed in chapter 5 wanted to open to women, nursing was from its earliest modern organization a profession that proudly claimed a supportive, subordinate relationship to its male counterpart. Part of my argument here is that this self-proclaimed subordination helped enhance the reputation of an activity overwhelmingly dominated by women, because it helped neutralize the specter of female sexuality contemporaries associated with independent women. But I also argue that, in so doing, this representation of nursing helped preserve the domestic ideal it seemed to undermine.

I

The idealized and idealizing narrative we see invoked in the obituary by Martineau first obtained a heroine and an opening episode in late October 1854, just after Nightingale and her thirty-eight nurses set sail for the Crimea. Nightingale herself was responding to rather than creating this idealized image, for her decision to go to the Crimea followed a series of newspaper accounts that outlined the kind of hero the war required. On 9 October, the *London Times* began publishing W. H. Russell's detailed reports of the gratuitous suffering bureaucratic mismanagement was causing at the Baltic front. The public response to these revelations was immediate and intense: something must be done, declared letters and outraged editorials, if not to reform the army, then at least to help the wounded, who lay neglected and diseased in hopelessly inadequate facilities. On 14 October, a "Sufferer by the Present War" complained bitterly in a letter to the *Times* that the suffering soldier had become not only a symbol of national disgrace but also a source of domestic misery. "We sit at home," this writer lamented, "trying to picture the last moments of those dear to us, and our agony is increased by the fear that all was not done that might have been done to relieve their sufferings. . . . The strongest man becomes helpless and dependent like a child in his hour of need, and we all know how, in such a case, a humble nurse, with no other recommendations than a kind heart and skilful hands, appears to the sufferer as a saving angel."[6]

The figure of the "humble nurse" as "saving angel" was already present at the front, in fact; she just was not with the English troups. Indeed, the haunting refrain of the English correspondent—"Why have we no Sisters of Charity?"—simply brought before English readers the French Sisters of Charity, which the English hospitals so signally lacked. Florence Nightingale's response to this well-publicized English deficiency was in many ways merely a more energetic and politically astute version of her contemporaries' letter writing. Despite having no systematic training in nursing, the thirty-year-old eldest daughter of a wealthy liberal family wrote the wife of her old friend Sidney Herbert, then secretary at war, offering to organize and lead nurses to the East.[7] Sidney Herbert's letter inviting Nightingale to do just that crossed hers in the mail, thereby providing her contemporaries with the first public episode in a history that could easily be read as proclaiming Nightingale's mystical election to this mission.[8] Nightingale herself embraced the idea of a divine calling, which helped parry her family's objections and lent legitimacy to her ambition. She answered the call without delay, recruiting her nurses wherever she could find them; they set sail on 27 October, only eighteen days after Russell's first reports appeared in the *Times* and eight days after she had received her official instructions from the War Office On 28 October the *Examiner* published an article entitled "Who Is Mrs. Nightingale?" which was reprinted in the *Times* two days later. Before Nightingale even reached the hospital at Scutari, then, the myth was being constructed in the image of national fantasies and fears.

As it is set out in Martineau's obituary, the mythic figure of Florence Nightingale had two faces. One was obviously allied with the normative definition of the middle-class woman that I have been discussing; it was the image of the English Sister of Charity, the self-denying caretaker—a mother, a saint, or even a female Christ.[9] Martineau's depiction of Nightingale nursing, tutoring, and converting the little Russian prisoner epitomizes this version of Nightingale. The prisoner is rhetorically rendered a child by the adjective "little," and, as Nightingale gives him speech (the English language), "useful" work (caring for English casualties), and religion (albeit a version of Christianity mediated through her), she conquers the enemy as a mother schools her son. This is the Nightingale of "gentle voice" and the lamp, the Nightingale who draws brute soldiers away from drink, the Nightingale whose passing shadow is medicine enough.

The second face of Florence Nightingale bore a greater likeness to a politician or a soldier than a gentle mother; it was the image of the tough-minded administrator who "encountered opposition" but persevered. This Nightingale was popularized largely by the lectures and reports circulated by C. Holte Bracebridge, Nightingale's chaperone to Scutari. In a speech printed in the *Times* on 16 October 1855, for example, Bracebridge told of his own attempts to remedy the scarcities he witnessed. After going to the purveyor ("the answer he got was, 'It is not my business; it is very hard on my department to have to find such things [as knives and forks]' ") and the commandant of the hospital (who "would have nothing to do with it, who said that soldiers had always knives and forks as well as spoons in their knapsacks"), Bracebridge almost despaired. "It was in vain that he informed the gentlemen that the soldiers had been ordered to throw away their knapsacks by the direction of Lord Raglan—that some of the poor men had not a clean shirt for six weeks, and that many of them were even without a shirt. . . . Miss Nightingale, however, took a different view of the subject, and managed to supply between November and February 10,537 shirts and 6,823 flannel shirts; and from February to Midsummer 2,549 more."[10] In this sentimentalized representation, the numerical specificity of Nightingale's contribution is set in stark contrast to the official indifference and red tape. The two images are constructed dialectically, of course: without the purveyor and the hospital commandant, Nightingale's shirts would have been mere charity; and without Florence Nightingale the officials would have remained—as they had in other wars—largely invisible to the public and the soldiers as well.

These two versions of Florence Nightingale most obviously consolidated two narratives about patriotic service that were culturally available at midcentury—a domestic narrative of maternal nurturing and self-sacrifice and a military narrative of individual assertion and will.[11] The heroine of the first narrative was typically self-effacing, gentle, and kind; her contribution was to fit others to serve; her territory was the home. The hero of the military narrative, by contrast, was characteristically resolute, fearless, and strong willed; his service often entailed excursions into alien territory, the endurance of great physical hardships, and the accomplishment of hitherto unimagined deeds.[12] On the surface at least, these two narratives seemed so pervasive and powerful at midcentury because they were versions of the fundamental Victorian narratives of gender; they constituted the basic stories of how the girl grew up to be a woman and the boy a man. But even though the opposition between the sexes apparently underwrote and was bolstered by the difference between these stories, that they converged in Florence Nightingale suggests that the military narrative was always at least compatible with—if not implicit in—the domestic narrative.

The domestic and military narratives *could* converge in a single individual for three reasons. In the first place, Florence Nightingale's own exploits neatly reproduced the most important features of both stories. On the one hand, as a woman who vociforously shunned publicity, she was self-effacing; as a nurse, she was gentle, kind, and capable of making any place she visited seem a home.[13] On the other hand, as steward of the *Times's* relief fund and an administrator who got things done, she was resolute and efficient; as England's envoy to the land of the Turkish infidel, she was a courageous Christian soldier; and as a survivor of the squalid Scutari hospital, she undoubtedly possessed remarkable strength and determination.

The second condition that supported the convergence of these narratives was the crisis of faith generated by the unprecedented publicity that accompanied the Crimean War. This collapse of Britain's self-confidence was partly a function of the high expectations with which the English public initially greeted the fighting—expectations that gained their momentum from the grandiose parallels made between this and the Napoleonic Wars, their moral force from

England's claim to be defending Christian liberty, and their political and nationalistic overtones from the contrasts contemporaries repeatedly made between England's parliamentary government and the autocracy of the Russian foe.[14] Partly, it was a function of the discrepancy between the technological expertise that proclaimed one kind of English superiority and the administrative incompetence that announced another, more debilitating weakness. As the first war in English history to be covered by the modern technologies of telegraphy and photography, the Crimean War became a symbol of the democratizing effects of British scientific expertise; thanks to this technology, ordinary men could debate military strategy with almost as much knowledge as statesmen in Parliament.[15] What this technology revealed to the common man, however, was a devastating and pervasive lack of English leadership, which daily jeopardized the sons of the very men who rejoiced in being able to know what was happening at the front. Not only was Lord Raglan, commander in the East, a sixty-six-year-old bureaucrat who had not seen active duty for forty years, but every English institution seemed marred by a similar "fatal mediocrity" among its leaders. As Sir George Sinclair remarked, there was "in the Cabinet, no Chatham; in the Navy, no Nelson; in the Army, no Wellington; in the Church, no Luther."[16] For both of these reasons, the Crimean War opened a vertiginous ideological rift—in which the very conditions that generated pride also provoked despair, and the imaginative engagement that the media mobilized found no hero on whom to fix the anxious public gaze.

The third—and, from the perspective of my argument, the most important—reason the domestic and military narratives could converge is that the domestic ideal always contained an aggressive component. I have already pointed to female sexuality as the form in which this aggression was castigated and to women's capability as the version that midcentury feminists invoked to expand the discussion of women's work. In representations of Florence Nightingale, we see the aggressiveness implicit in the allusions to female sexuality placed in the service of work that was simultaneously conceptualized as a service and rewarded with pay. The militant component of this aggression was explicit in some representations of women's work, as, for example, in Isabella Beeton's *Book of Household Management*. "As with the Commander of an Army," Beeton writes in her introduction, "or the leader of any enterprise, so it is with the mistress of a house."[17] Because this militancy carried overtones of masculinity, however, it was most frequently neutralized by some form of rhetorical or symbolic revision. In this 1856 celebration of Florence Nightingale, for example, John Davies transports the mother onto the battlefield in the guise of a goddess healing her favored son, thereby simultaneously acknowledging her power and effectively placing it beyond the scope of mortal women. Behind this representation of the mother on the battlefield is Athena magically healing Achilles.

> Yet grateful monuments now walk the earth,
> Who love thee as if thou didst give them birth;
> They sing thy virtues, and of thy bright deeds,
> At which Imagination starts—recedes.
> There! is the form once doubled in the fight,
> And left for dead, made by thy skill upright;
> Thy plastic hand has healed the shattered arm—
> Thy magic touch did each dead muscle charm![18]

Depicting Nightingale as a goddess addressed the anxieties that were raised by a woman's assuming even temporary superiority over an infantalized male patient, for in construing her power as magic or even divine, it removed this woman not only from her mortality, but also from competition with medical men. Representing Nightingale as a queen also addressed fears about female power, for Queen Victoria herself was compared less frequently to a patriarchal commander than to a loving mother. Comparisons to the housewifely monarch served another function as well: as Nightingale's likeness to the queen was played out, royalty became the site at which problems of class difference could be introduced so as to be dismissed. The *Examiner* biography, for example, opens with this description: "Young (about the age of our Queen), graceful, feminine, rich, and popular, [Nightingale] holds a singularly gentle and persuasive influence over all with whom she comes in contact. Her friends and acquaintances are of all classes and persuasions, but her happiest place is at home, in the empire of a very large band of accomplished relatives, and in the simplest obedience to her admiring parents."[19] In this popular ballad, Nightingale's royalty is once more linked to both her benign power and her indifference—or superiority—to class.

> Her heart it means good, for no bounty she'll take,
> She'd lay down her life for the poor soldier's sake;
> She prays for the dying, she gives peace to the brave,
> She feels that a soldier has a soul to be saved.

The wounded they love her as it has been seen,
She's the soldiers' preserver, they call her their Queen.[20]

By birth and wealth, of course, Florence Nightingale was affiliated not with the common soldiers whose interests she was seen
to represent, but with the generals and cabinet ministers to whom
she was commonly contrasted. Indeed, this class position and the
privileges it entailed were crucial factors in the considerable power
Nightingale wielded within the barrack hospital and the War Office;
had Sidney Herbert not already been a family friend, for example,
her willingness to serve in the Crimea would doubtless have gone
unheard, and had her family and the Bracebridges not exerted such
a relentless barrage of public and private pressure on officials in high
places, Nightingale's demands for hospital reforms would certainly
have had less effect. In representations of Nightingale, however, her
wealth appears not as the ground of privilege, but as an index of
what she has given up for a life of service: all the advantages that
accrue to wealth were thereby rewritten as sacrifices, which, when
laid at the bedside of the suffering soldier, became a measure of his
worth and her heroism. As the "Iphegenia of the day," the wellborn
Nightingale paradoxically ennobled the common man.[21] And finally,
the class basis of Nightingale's power was further effaced by the
myth of her irresistable personality—at the same time that those
personality traits considered "masculine" or abrasive simply disappeared from popular representations.[22]

The representation of Florence Nightingale therefore worked
like a Freudian compromise formation, joining what could be seen
either as two apparently antithetical narratives or as the manifest
and latent contents of the same narrative by reworking or repressing
their discordant features. The momentum behind this compromise
came from a number of sources at midcentury. In addition to providing a particularly compelling "solution" to the public debacle in
the Crimea, Nightingale and the image of nursing she came to
represent also "fit"—and partially took their definition from—other
ideological "spaces" opened by mid-nineteenth-century controversies. Like Bracebridge's construction of Nightingale and the hospital
officials, this process of definition was dialectical; just as the popularized image of Nightingale the nurse was constructed in opposition to controversial figures she did *not* represent, so those figures
acquired their definition partly through the contrast her image
stabilized.

The first relevant controversy is the one I have already examined from another perspective—the intraprofessional dispute within the medical community. In medicine, as I have already argued, the 1850s was a decade of professional consolidation, marked by the struggle of members of the lower ranks to disassociate themselves from trade by claiming a place within a recognized, organized profession. In one sense, women who contemplated health care at midcentury faced another version of the problem relatively successfully surmounted by general practitioners, for they too had to dislodge a culturally devalued stereotype to win social and medical recognition. Just as general practitioners had to sever their historical associations with tradesmen and female midwives, so the nurse's historical link with domestic servants had to be effaced before respectable women could contemplate this work. But the symbolic reworking of the nurse was, in one sense at least, more complex than that of the general practitioner or even the apothecary. The image of the nurse had to be freed not only from the taint of its lower-class origins, but also from the contemporary specter of those "strong-minded women" who aspired to be doctors. The two disreputable figures who flank the Nightingale nurse—the old monthly nurse and the lady doctor— were therefore inextricably bound up with—and, in part at least, constructed alongside of—the image of the nurse that the public embraced.

It is difficult to tell whether Dickens's *Martin Chuzzlewit* created or capitalized on a cultural stereotype, but it is certain that Sairey Gamp galvanized the prejudices and anxieties of a large sector of the English public. "Mrs. Gamp may be a caricature," notes one writer for *Fraser's Magazine*, "but the likeness is very tracable. . . . There are some [nurses] whose honesty and temperance may be trusted, but they make up for the restraint in one direction by a greater license in another. They are the scolds and termagants of a hospital. Others are easy and good-tempered, but the assistant in attendance must go his round at night to see that the wine or beer ordered for the patients is not abstracted by the nurses. These two classes comprise, perhaps, the great mass of the whole body."[23] Bad temper and drunkenness—sometimes these qualities alternate, sometimes they coincide; despite occasional acknowledgments that good nurses did exist before Florence Nightingale, however, most commentators revile nurses for these and their companion faults. "A paid nurse of the old school!" snorts a writer for the *Medical Times and Gazette*. "We in the Profession well know what that means,—a hard-minded, ignorant, lazy, drunken woman, who upsets the whole establishment with her whims; sleeps when she should be awake; is cross when she should be patient; and is constant only in a persevering attempt to make the job as lucrative as possible."[24] The medical establishment was not the only group liable to represent the traditional nurse as an irresponsible, money-grubbing fool. Reformers who wanted to redefine modern nursing also lumped all old nurses together into a homogeneous mass, distinguished only by its variety of failings. Nurses, according to Nightingale, were women "who were too old, too weak, too drunken, too dirty, too stolid, or too bad to do anything else."[25]

Whatever individual nurses were really like at midcentury, as a group they undeniably lacked training; the reason was not simply that English training facilities were few in number and religious in nature, but also that, until cleanliness and good bedside care came to seem important to the public and, more specifically, to medical practitioners, there was no consensus about what nursing training should entail. The overcrowded and unsavory urban conditions made visible by the cholera epidemic of the 1840s was instrumental in drawing the attention of a worried middle class to the role of sanitation in the health and morality of the poor; this, along with an increased emphasis within the medical establishment on the importance of monitoring the patient's vital signs, mandated an attendant who was moral, observant, obedient, and capable of superintending sanitation. The modern nurse that Nightingale came to symbolize was, then, one effect of a reorientation within both public opinion and medical practice—a reorientation that displaced anxieties about the inexplicability of death and the limitations of medicine onto class and gender prejudices by foregrounding a complex set of assumptions about the salutary effects of middle-class morality and science.[26]

By the 1840s, spokesmen for the medical profession had begun to sketch out the kind of medical attendant doctors felt they needed, but it was still not necessarily the case that women would be considered appropriate to these tasks.[27] Working against women becoming medical attendants was not only the traditional prejudice against nurses that medical reformers mobilized and that discouraged educated women from considering this work, but also class-specific prejudices about women's paid labor, which I have already discussed and to which I return in a moment. Working in favor of feminizing nursing, however, was an even more compelling set of factors: the increasing economic and social pressure on unmarried women of all but the highest classes to work, the reluctance of the medical profession to countenance an organization of male medical attendants that might eventually infiltrate the medical hierarchy, and the availability—at least in Nightingale's writings on the subject—of a representation of nursing as subordinate to, but also wholly different from, medical practice. This image of the obedient nurse, who could never challenge medical authority on the basis of expertise or threaten the medical establishment with competition, was therefore constructed on top of assumptions about the social relations between men and women and alongside class-laden assumptions about the unreliability of the women who had previously done this work. It also gained support—especially from the medical establishment—by its distance from the other form in which women actively sought to enter the medical profession—the lady doctors.

Among the feminists who campaigned in the 1850s for increasing employment opportunities for middle-class women, some, like Emily Davies, scorned nursing; only the practice of medicine, she argued, was sufficiently respectable and lucrative to be a profession for well-educated women.[28] Davies's vision of successful women doctors was given concrete form by the one woman who had trained as a medical doctor, Elizabeth Blackwell. While Blackwell, an American, had trained at Geneva College in New York, she was allowed to register in England because she had practiced medicine before the qualifying date of 1 October 1858.[29] But the medical establishment left no doubt that this case was going to remain the exception to the rule that women could not be doctors. Indeed, the institutional response had already begun in 1851, when Emily Blackwell, attempting to repeat her sister's course of medical training, was told that Geneva College was not willing to consider her sister's admission a precedent for admitting women students.[30] In 1856, Jessie Meriton White was denied access to the examinations for both the Colleges of Physicians and Surgeons, and, while Elizabeth Garrett was able to obtain a license from the Apothecaries' Society in 1865 because the 1815 act used the word "persons," this provision was soon changed. The lengths to which the medical profession was willing to go to exclude women are clear in its response to the 1875 attempt by Sophia Jex-Blake and two other women to earn the midwifery diploma. Because this diploma was not explicitly limited to practicing members of the Royal College of Surgeons, the women were theoretically eligible to sit the examination; if they had passed, they would have been qualified to register under the 1858 act. When the Royal College was advised that it had no legal grounds for refusing the women registration if they qualified, it acted decisively to block this and all such applications: all the midwifery examiners resigned and were not replaced, and the examination was not administered again until 1881.[31]

Partly because admitting women into the wards as nurses could be used—rhetorically at least—to head off this threat by would-be women doctors, and partly because the increasingly specialized practice of medicine demanded some body of trained, obedient attendants, the medical establishment as a whole generally supported the establishment of female nursing. Spokesmen for the profession were quick to admit their interest in this project. "No class," asserted a writer for the *Medical Times and Gazette* in 1852, "is more directly concerned in promoting any scheme for the supply of good nurses than the Medical Profession."[32] Still, a difficulty remained in even supportive contemporaries' minds, for the work of nursing was sadly at odds with the conventional image of the middle-class domestic ideal, and lower-class women who consented to nurse were suspect by definition. What, skeptics worried, could possibly motivate a moral, responsible, conscientious woman—much less an educated "lady"—to undertake this exacting, tedious, and often distasteful work? The following slip of the pen in the *Medical Times and Gazette* reveals the two equally problematic answers available to midcentury reformers. "Increased funds are now only wanting," this writer optimistically claims, "for the completion of these most necessary as well as charitable works; for creating a calling—we had almost said a profession—by which an intelligent and worthy female may, at an early age, gain an honourable independence; by which a most useful and important class will be formed for services of great trust among the wealthy; by which messengers of charity and of hope will be sent among the poor."[33] A calling or a profession? This was the pertinent question for those who advocated that women nurse. Those feminists who supported opening nursing to women of all classes argued that nursing should be a profession, with some form of regular training, adequate wages, and sufficient provisions for retirement. Other commentators, however, advocated conceptualizing nursing as a vocation. Only some form of religious vows, they argued, would bind nurses to those tasks that are "repugnant to the senses." As one writer argued in 1848, nurses "must be awakened to a sense of the dignity of their calling, and taught what it requires; and all this must be done under the guidance of the religion which is to supply the motive. They must be taught to feel that they, as well as the chaplains of hospitals, have a religious work to do." This author explicitly sets his argument against the case for professionalization. Nurses "must be an order, working for the love of God and man," he asserts, "not a class, working for their livelihood."[34]

Paying nurses was controversial simply because the idea of middle-class women working for wages was controversial, as I discussed more fully in relation to governesses.[35] But the issue of whether nurses should be paid at all remained alive in a way it did not for governesses, where the debate was always about the rate of wages, not whether the work should be undertaken for free. One source of this controversy was the common conceptualization of nursing as a sacrifice, which linked it with philanthropic and even religious service rather than money. This association persisted partly because there were historical precedents for philanthropic and religious nursing; partly, it reflects the cultural assumption that attending to the intimate bodily functions of another person is degrading (a prejudice that did not carry over to a mother's performing these same tasks for her children); and partly, it suggests that nursing required the renunciation of some component of those social relations that might be assumed to obtain when contact is both intimate and physical—that nursing, in other words, both intimated and specifically sacrificed sexuality.

The proximity of sexuality to nursing appears not just in contemporaries' assumptions about sacrifice, but also in popular fictions that variously described a woman's turn to nursing as a compensation for thwarted love or depicted the nurse marrying the soldier whom she has lovingly restored to health.[36] Given the anxieties about female sexuality I have already discussed and the concomitant prejudices against allowing either sexual interest or the desire for economic independence to attract women to nursing, it would not have been surprising if the image of nursing as a religious vocation had triumphed; conceptualizing nursing as a religious calling, after all, would have simultaneously provided a familiar antidote to the sexuality inherent in the domestic ideal and supported the image of women's dependence—this time to a divine master. But even though the idea of vocation became an important component of mid-nineteenth-century conceptualizations of nursing, as Katherine Williams has argued, it was potentially as controversial an image to promote as advocating that women nurse for pay.[37] The word *vocation*, especially when voiced within the comparison between the French Sisters of Charity and an English nursing corps, all too readily conjured up the image of Catholic sisterhoods. This association was especially damaging in the early 1850s because of the controversy aroused by Edward Pusey's Tractarianism, which brought the specter of Catholicism home to the Anglican church. Pusey and his supporters argued that the Church of England was a divine institution and its clergymen direct descendants of the apostles; in so doing, they reinstated the High Church ideals of the seventeenth century, which, to the more worldly Anglicans, seemed to pose a moral as well as a spiritual threat. This threat was partly a function of the Tractarians' endorsement of women working outside the home, which Anglicans interpreted as a challenge to the nuclear family. Despite their essential conservatism, Tractarians supported expanding employment opportunities for women for very practical reasons: when High Church clergymen were banished for their unpopular stance to poorer parishes, they often found women more willing than men to assist with parish visiting, running orphanages, and organizing ragged schools. Tractarians therefore encouraged the foundation of Anglican sisterhoods, whose members accomplished social and religious reforms that the Low Church middle-class clergy could not, at the same time that they found opportunities for teaching, welfare work, or nursing that individual women were often denied.[38]

Florence Nightingale's early efforts to formulate an acceptable image of nursing were haunted by the specter of this religious controversy. Nightingale herself inadvertently contributed to the religious furor aroused by nursing when she was forced by the scarcity of volunteers to recruit nurses for her Crimean venture from both Anglican sisterhoods and Catholic orders; her original party included fourteen secular nurses, six Puseyites (from St. John's), eight Anglican Sisters of Mercy, and ten Catholic nuns.[39] At Scutari, the storm continued; during her twenty-odd months in the barrack hospital, Nightingale weathered a succession of complaints about proselytizing and religiously motivated feuds, and even the attempt by one Catholic matron, the Rev. Mother Frances Brickman, to oust Nightingale from power.

Despite the circumstantial and ideological controversy generated by nursing's religious affiliation, Nightingale insisted throughout her life that nursing was a "calling"—a secular vocation, to be sure, but a calling none the less.[40] In this sense, as in the others I have been outlining, Nightingale's conceptualization of nursing constituted a compromise, which mobilized and repressed various parts of the domestic ideal and its militancy so as to negotiate the treacherous waters of popular prejudice. Neither the newly professionalized doctor's competitor nor simply the untrained monthly nurse, neither a fully professional woman nor just a religious sister, the Nightingale nurse combined womanly self-sacrifice with a more aggressive image of work that deserved fair pay. If we turn for a moment to Nightingale's own writings, we see how the way in which she capitalized on the contradictions inherent in the domestic ideal helped tailor the Nightingale nurse to contemporaries' assumptions about women and domesticity. In the evolution of Nightingale's ideas we see not only which elements of this image she reworked, but also why this symbolic compromise could both authorize Nightingale's own dynastic ambitions and be enlisted for a national campaign that had nothing to do with nursing.

II

Florence Nightingale's publications on nursing are extremely heterogeneous. They range from her most popular work—*Notes on Nursing* (1859), which was written for a general audience and sold fifteen thousand copies in just one month—to a series of reports written for Royal Commissions, which were only publicly available in the extremely limited numbers Nightingale had privately printed. That Nightingale's observations on nursing are so various and unsystematic partially reflects the lack of public or official interest in this subject at midcentury: even within the medical community, there was no consensus about what good nursing entailed, and no educated woman who was not called to a religious vocation was likely to take an interest in the subject. Through her writings, Nightingale therefore had to create an interested and sympathetic audience for nursing (including a body of potential recruits) as well as to answer to the bureaucratic specifications and political crosscurrents of the official groups she often addressed.

The material conditions in which Nightingale organized her first nursing corps also indelibly marked her conceptualization of nursing. By definition, shepherding thirty-eight variously trained women into a military hospital in a war zone for the first time in English history constituted a unique opportunity, but it also meant that Nightingale had to accommodate her ideas to the organizations that preceded her. The administrative inefficiency she encountered at Scutari impressed on Nightingale the necessity for a clearly specified, rigidly enforced chain of command in her nursing corps, just as the rigor and lapses of army discipline turned her attention to strict regimentation, discipline, and unflagging surveillance. Given her experience with the army medical corps, it is not surprising that the militaristic strain she emphasized focused not on the career of heroism so much as on the administrative prowess the good housekeeper could perfect. The organizing concepts of Nightingale's vision are discipline, subordination, surveillance, punishment, training, and regimentation; her favorite story chronicled the transformation of the raw recruit into an efficient nursing machine.

These things—and not medical training—preoccupied Nightingale in her first treatment of nursing. In an essay entitled "Subsidiary Notes as to the Introduction of Female Nursing into Military Hospitals," appended to her long report for the 1857 Royal Commission on the Sanitary Conditions of the Army, Nightingale set out the qualifications any hospital nurse must learn to value; notably, her list entails a set of deferential attitudes rather than medical skills: "obedience, discipline, self-control, work understood as work, hospital service as implying masters, civil and medical, and a mistress, what service means, and abnegation of self.[41] To inculcate these attitudes, Nightingale argued that a two-part approach was necessary: the respectable character of working-class women must be ensured by "leavening" the mass of nurses with "ladies," and the entire operation must be well governed and closely watched.[42] "Rule, system, and superintendence"—these principles and not religious vows bind the Nightingale nurse. If these principles are strictly observed, she suggests, her nursing corps could effectively combat not only disease but also what emerges as an equally dangerous enemy—the moral infection that breeds where people "congregate" promiscuously.

In so far as disease is the enemy that must be treated in a hospital, Nightingale's solution was to allow the patients plenty of space and clean air.[43] Her insistence on the importance of adequate ventilation reflects her belief in Dr. William Farr's theory of "zymotic" disease: the theory, roughly speaking, that disease breeds as yeast ferments and that it is spread through the patient's inhalation of the "noxious matter" his own or another nearby body has excreted.[44] "As it is a law," she states, "that all excretions are injurious to health if reintroduced into the system it is easy to understand how the . . . reintroduction of excrementitious matter into the blood through the functions of respiration will tend to produce disease. This will be still more the case in sick wards overcrowded with sick, the exhalations from whom are always highly morbid and dangerous, as they are nature's method of eliminating noxious matter from the body, in order that it may recover health" (SN 65). The zymotic disease theory was antithetical to the germ theory, which Nightingale resisted throughout her life, despite increasing medical acceptance. Instead of seeing diseases as discrete entities (as proponents of the germ theory did), she conceptualized the human body as an organism so attuned to and dependent on its environment that a disorder in the latter produced a disease in the former as surely as heat made mercury rise. The nurse's job was therefore simply to monitor the patient and his environment to ensure, as far as possible, that "morbid matter" was rapidly carried away.

A large squad of disciplined nurses, presumably, emptying bedpans and changing sheets, could effectively combat zymotic disease in a large, airy ward. But the problem Nightingale saw with military hospitals was not just that they lacked such wards, but also that if these wards were built, they would require more nurses and more superintendence. After considering various architectural schemes, Nightingale advocated the "Vincennes modification of the Pavilion plan" because of "the greater facility of supervision it affords." Her description of this system suggests that her supervisors were involved in an elaborate counterespionage scheme rather than the work of healing. In this design, she writes approvingly,

> the Military Superior, the Surgeon, the Matron, can at any instant pop in upon any ward of a Hospital. . . . Each pavilion may, unless the matter be specially considered with a view to providing this effectual supervision, perceive the approach of the inspector. The system of secrets, watch, alarm, is well understood in many hundred wards, whose patients would be puzzled to give the things names. Remember that Ward-Masters, Orderlies, and Nurses require inspection as well as patients. (SN 75)

Nightingale's concern here is with misconduct in the wards—most explicitly, with drinking: "remember," she writes, "there is such a thing as quiet drinking, as well as noisy drinking" (SN 106). But here, as in many nineteenth-century texts, alcohol consumption is metonymically connected to an unnameable (sexual) indulgence, which Nightingale suspects in every unlit hospital corner and from every inmate of the ward. "The orderly must never enter the Nurse's room," she insists twice in one paragraph. "Guard against too many closets, sinks, &c., &c., &c.," she writes; "endeavour to prevent the system of holes and corners. It is best that the Nurse's door should command the view of those who come in or out of the lavatory, and in and out of the water-closet. This whole section," Nightingale grimly concludes, "is both ugly and important" (SN 47, 92, 94).

These passages suggest that the unnameable activities include masturbation and homosexuality as well as heterosexual liaisons. To

Nightingale, all such permutations of immorality are conceivable because the patients—as soldiers—are not moral beings. Despite the popular image of Nightingale championing the common man, her own writings reveal a distrust of soldiers bordering on scorn. "In contemplating a Military Hospital," she comments, "we contemplate a place through which, one year with another, all characters, including a few of the vilest, pass" (SN 92). As a consequence,

> a Military Hospital must, and should ever remain, essentially different from a Civil Hospital; both different in discipline and detail, and altogether a rougher and ruder place. It should never for a moment be forgotten that the soldier is a very peculiar individual, old and stern as is his trade. A regiment, if one thinks *into* it, is a curious thing. . . . The moral standard of the patients of the Military Hospital, their readiness to obey, their good feeling to each other, are strikingly higher than in the Civil Hospital; but the soldier is what, amidst all his faults, he has been made by the habit and spirit of discipline, which has become an instinct and a second nature, and which ennobles his own. Relax discipline, and in proportion as you do so, there remains of the soldier a being with as much or more of the brute than the man. (SN 37)

In many ways, Nightingale aspired to make her little squadron of nurses into a regiment—obedient and loyal, with discipline an "instinct and a second nature." But, as this quotation suggests, discipline was always in danger of breaking down; given the sexuality implicit in the domestic ideal, the "brute" was nearly as likely to materialize in a woman as a man. Nightingale, in her distrust of every unsupervised encounter, betrays her sensitivity to the sexuality contemporaries feared in women. Do not let nurses "congregate" with the orderlies *or* each other, she writes: "associating the nurses in large dormitories tends to corrupt the good, and make the bad worse." "Give the Nurse plenty to do" so that mischief will not tempt her. Keep the number of nurses as low as possible; "the fewer women are about an Army Hospital the better," Nightingale curtly remarks (SN 11, 81, 73). Above all, never let vigilance cease. Nightingale stopped just short of advocating spying, but this was with palpable regret. "Nurses trusted to do their duty in wards," she begrudgingly admits, "must be trusted to walk out alone if they choose, and I would not attempt to restrict it, though the Superintendent must see to this, so far as she can without doing or encouraging spy-work, a thing which has many advantages, and is

often done in various, very various ways, but which in the long run
brings no blessing, and *pro tanto,* degrades all who are concerned
with it" (SN 115–16).

Nightingale's caution is understandable from many points of
view. Given the contemporary ambivalence toward female nature
and the prejudice against introducing women into military hospitals
in particular, it was imperative for her to protect her charges from
suspicions about their characters. Moreover, given the administrative
inefficiency at Scutari, the competing and complex chains of command, and the practice of employing convalescent soldiers as orderlies, Nightingale had to overcome hospital laxity as well as to
accustom her own nurses to difficult and tiring labor. Then, too,
those soldiers recovering from wounds were often hospitalized for
several months, some weeks of which they were sufficiently ambu-
latory (and bored) to test hospital rules. But above and beyond these
practical considerations, Nightingale's conceptualization of the
problem also reflects the contradictions inherent in her own middle-
class assumptions, as well as the difficulties these assumptions posed
for the nursing squad she wanted to organize.

The problem that conceptualizing sexuality as both pernicious
and pervasive constituted for nursing was that it not only implied
but institutionalized a constantly circulating, ungovernable mistrust:
in such a system there could be no effective government because no
individual could be free of the system that reproduced what it was
designed to police. Thus, as Nightingale explores the solutions, the
problems simply proliferate: if the superior spies on her nurses, then
everyone is degraded; if she does not, "congregation" or worse goes
unchecked; if one increases the size of wards, ventilation is improved
but supervision becomes more difficult; if one reduces the number
of nurses, women's morality is protected, but the patients go un-
watched; if one locks the nurses in a common room at night, orderlies can be kept out, but all the dangers of female congregation
creep in again. Ultimately, the solution Nightingale institutionalized
for these problems was a training program in which discipline could
be ceaselessly monitored and indiscretions effectively punished; this
was the system instituted in the Nightingale Training School at St.
Thomas's Hospital (established 1860), where nurses were evaluated
weekly in twenty-one subjects (from enema giving to sobriety and
punctuality).[45] In 1858, however, and in a military hospital in Turkey,
no such systematic discipline was possible. In its absence, Nightingale simply relinquished the entire dilemma to a higher authority—
even though this admitted religious sisterhoods, which she wanted

to exclude, back into the wards. "Let the female service obtain, please God," she writes, and then she opens this long, torturously qualified parenthesis:

> (I do not write these words *pro forma,*—if possible, I feel every day more intensely how solely it is to Him we must trust in this difficult work,—the more so that, if possible, I feel every day more intensely the importance of, if He grants it success, improving secular Hospital nursing, leaving the English Sisterhoods, which will always have great advantages, and, I believe, great disadvantages, with reference to Hospital nursing, to take their share of this great field, which has plenty of room for both), let, I say, the female service obtain a firm footing in the Army Hospitals, and with it, by cautious degrees, sundry ameliorations will creep in insensibly as to decorum among other things. (SN 118)

What Nightingale's early conceptualization lacks, quite obviously, is any morally reliable figure to superintend the other inmates. The source of this problem is that, in foregrounding only one side of the domestic ideal, she has collapsed the difference between men and women and therefore the possibility that sexual appetite will submit to control. Nightingale's halting reference to the "sundry ameliorations" that will "creep in" with women suggests how she will soon solve this problem: by emphasizing the other side of the domestic ideal, she will capitalize on the assumption that, no matter how debauched some nurses may currently be, all women are more capable of moral improvement than any man. To stabilize this representation, Nightingale subordinates her preoccupation with class to a more resolute focus on gender and on women's maternal nature in particular. This reorientation accompanies Nightingale's turn from wartime nursing to private nursing in the home.

Taking up the subject of nursing in the home enabled Nightingale to solve the problems endemic to the military hospital because it let her displace what she assumed to be the locus of those problems: the lower-class status of the patients and nurses she supervised at Scutari. The basis of this rhetorical displacement is at least partly material: because private nursing was typical of *middle-class* care, setting her discussion in the home implies that the patient and nurse are governed by middle-class standards of morality. The patient in *Notes on Nursing* is no "brute," but a tractable, silent man too preoccupied with the enemy of ill health to cause trouble himself.[46] "Remember," Nightingale remarks of this patient, "he is face to face with his enemy all the time, internally wrestling with him, having long, imaginary conversations with him" (*N* 38). The relationship between such a patient and his caretaker is also transformed by the domestic setting. What had been a volatile, ungovernable relation between two sexual (and always potentially immoral) beings now becomes a familial relationship, in which the difference between the sexes holds sway because the nurse can be represented as a literal or a metaphorical (middle-class) mother. Once more, this revision alludes to the stereotypical image of domesticity, which Nightingale reinforces in the opening to her slender volume: "Every woman," Nightingale proclaims, "or at least almost every woman, in England has, at one time or another of her life, charge of the personal health of somebody, whether child or invalid—in other words, every woman is a nurse" (*N* 3).

While the dismissal of class that I am describing had a material basis in the actual differences between private nursing and nursing in a military hospital, it derived its cultural appeal from the assumptions about female morality that the domestic narrative mobilized. These assumptions were so powerful partly because they cloaked a controversial set of assumptions about class beneath the less controversial set of assumptions about gender: the feminine path to glory epitomized in Agnes Wickfield's self-fulfilling self-denial and inscribed in the domestic narrative *assumed* a middle-class family and middle-class values while concentrating on the difference between the sexes. When the apparent classlessness of this narrative was further enhanced by the classlessness conferred on Nightingale by images of divinity and royalty, the domestic narrative seemed to underwrite a tension-free society, imperceptibly governed by moral influence, where everyone was happy in his or her allotted place. So effective did this narrative and the national image it supported prove as a symbolic solution to the problems of creating a nursing corps that Nightingale retained it, and the revision it implied, in all her subsequent nursing schemes—even though the literal setting of these schemes was never again a middle-class home.

If invoking the asexual, apparently classless image of woman by which her own exploits were publicly represented enabled Nightingale to solve rhetorically most of the problems introduced by her original conceptualization of nursing, it added one new difficulty. If "every woman is a nurse," then why should nurses earn money for what ought to be a labor of love? Because of its implicit middle-class bias and its position within the symbolic economy of separate spheres, the domestic ideal and the narrative that accompanied it were positioned outside of the system of waged labor, professional commitment, and the "public"; yet to accede to that exclusion would have been ruinous to any attempts to make nursing training systematic. Nightingale acknowledged this dilemma when she adamantly rejected attempts by popular novelists to blur the boundary between middle-class domestic life and nursing work. "It seems a commonly received idea among men and even among women themselves," she complains,

> that it requires nothing but a disappointment in love, the want of an object, a general disgust, or incapacity for other things, to turn a woman into a good nurse. Popular novelists of recent days have invented ladies disappointed in love or fresh out of the drawing-room turning into the war-hospitals to find their wounded lovers, and when found, forthwith abandoning their sick-ward for their lover, as might be expected. Yet in the estimation of the authors, these ladies were none the worse for that, but on the contrary were heroines of nursing. (*N* 134)

Nightingale's scorn for the lovelorn girl, whose susceptibility made visible the sexuality implicit in the domestic ideal, was equaled by her insistence that the nurse not err in the opposite direction—that she not be too manly, as strong-minded women were. So intent was Nightingale on reinforcing the difference between the sexes that she ends *Notes on Nursing* with a long note commanding the nurse to resist that "jargon . . . about the 'rights' of women, which urges women to do all that men do, including the medical and other professions, merely because men do it, and without regard to whether this *is* the best that women can do" (*N* 135n). Her solution to avoiding both of these extremes was to reproduce the ideological separation of spheres that supposedly characterized society as a whole within medicine and to insist on the autonomy of each sphere. Within the separate sphere of their expertise, women would address problems of sanitation and hygiene (and midwifery), not medicine or surgery; establishing this separate sphere would therefore eliminate the risk of competition with medical men.[47] As Nightingale developed this idea, it becomes clear that, despite her mollifying rhetoric, she had launched a territorial campaign—one that would eventually eliminate altogether the need for medical men and expand nursing's domain outside the middle-class home. Nightingale justified the ambitiousness of this campaign by invoking the militaristic component of the domestic ideal, for the assertiveness sanctioned in the middle-class housewife not only accorded with the disciplined training Nightingale required for her nursing corps, but also rhetorically sanctioned her territorial design.

Nightingale elaborated the domestic and militaristic sides of the domestic ideal by aligning her nurse with a representation of the middle-class wife as commander in chief of a servant army. In the home, surveillance could be conceptualized as educative observation; discipline could be linked to cleanliness and hence to cure; and the military system of subordination and command could be represented as what Nightingale calls "petty management"—the art of household administration. "All the results of good nursing, as detailed in these notes," she cautions, "may be spoiled or utterly negatived by one defect, viz.: in petty management, or in other words, by not knowing how to manage that what you do when you are there, shall be done when you are not there" (N 35).

Nightingale's emphasis on domestic management makes clear that the militant strain implicit in the domestic ideology derived its authority from the morality that maternal instinct was assumed to bestow on all women: because it represented all women as middle class and invested them with commensurate moral power, the domestic ideology elevated every woman over every man. In Notes on Nursing, the patient is the first man to be dwarfed by this power. Representing the patient as a silent, immobile man obviously appealed to Nightingale's female readers, who bought the book in large numbers. One reviewer found the weakness Nightingale wrote into the patient so flattering that she further embroidered his emaciation and wistfulness, as if to enhance her own health, her prestige, and her rightful power. "Always before you," she remarks, describing the source of her fascination with the book, "there is the hero of the tale, an emaciated being, with sad wistful eyes, who depends upon good nursing as his best, perhaps his only chance of life."[48]

Medical men are also dwarfed in this representation of domestic authority. In one sense, they are simply redundant: "Did Nature intend mothers to be always accompanied by doctors?" Nightingale rhetorically asks (N 11). In another sense, as mere visitors to the domestic sphere, doctors are ineffective. "Now the medical man who sees the patient only once a day or even only once or twice a week, cannot possibly tell [how the patient is] without the assistance of the patient himself, or of those who are in constant observation on the patient. The utmost the medical man can tell is whether the patient is weaker or stronger at this visit than he was at the last visit" (N 75). Given Nightingale's definition of disease as a "reparative process," medical expertise is less relevant to cure than good housekeeping: it is the nurse cum commander who transports noxious exhalations away from the patient, the nurse who protects an environment conducive to repair. Nightingale is outspoken on this point:

> It is often thought that medicine is the curative process. It is no such thing; medicine is the surgery of functions, as surgery proper is that of limbs and organs. Neither can do anything but remove obstructions; neither can cure; nature alone cures. Surgery removes the bullet out of the limb, which is an obstruction to cure, but nature heals the wound. So it is with medicine; the function of an organ becomes obstructed; medicine, so far as we know, assists nature to remove the obstruction, but does nothing more. And what nursing has to do in either case, is to put the patient in the best condition for nature to act upon him. . . . You think fresh air, and quiet and cleanliness extravagant, perhaps dangerous, luxuries, which should be given to the patient only when quite convenient, and medicine the *sine qua non,* the panacea. If I have succeeded in any measure in dispelling this illusion, and in showing what true nursing is, and what it is not, my object will have been answered. (*N* 133)

If Nightingale's exploitation of the militancy inherent in the domestic ideal helped authorize the supremacy of nursing, it also aligned her vision of the nurse with another enterprise gaining momentum at midcentury. To appreciate the connection between these two campaigns, it is helpful to cast Nightingale's project in terms only slightly more militaristic than the ones she provided. If we view her campaign for nursing as an imperialistic program, we can see that it had two related fronts. The first was the "domestic" front within medicine; in this battle, Nightingale's opponents were medical men; her object was to carve out an autonomous—and ultimately superior—realm for female nursing. The second front was the "foreign" front of class; in this skirmish, her enemies were the "dirt, drink, diet, damp, draughts, drains" that made lower-class homes unsanitary; her object here was to bring the poor and their environment under the salutary sway of their middle-class betters.[49] Nightingale's strategy was to foreground the second campaign, which was a project shared by middle-class men, to mask the subversive character of the first, domestic campaign, which decidedly was not. But the rhetoric in which this strategy was accomplished made Nightingale's vision of nursing particularly amenable to appropriation by English politicians and imperialists, who had their own foreign front to conquer. The texts that chronicle this development go beyond the specific years of my study, for they were all written after the founding of the Nightingale Training School in 1860. Enlarging the scope of my subject is important at this point, however, because it enables me to suggest the almost limitless potential the domestic ideology contained to authorize aggressive projects that far exceeded the boundaries of the home and even of England itself. The texts I draw on include Nightingale's report to the 1859 Royal Commission appointed to inquire into the sanitary state of the army in India (*Suggestions on a System of Nursing for Hospitals in India*, 1865); another paper prepared for a government committee, her 1867 *Suggestions on the Subject of Providing, Training, and Organizing Nurses for the Sick Poor in Workhouse Infirmaries;* the pamphlet entitled "On Trained Nursing for the Sick Poor" (1876), which was originally published as a letter to the *Times;* two entries to Sir Robert Quain's *A Dictionary of Medicine,* published in 1882 ("Nurses, Training of" and "Nursing the Sick"); and the paper Nightingale prepared for the 1893 Chicago Exhibition, later published in *Woman's Mission,* entitled "Sick-Nursing and Health-Nursing."

In her works written after 1860, Nightingale continued to emphasize discipline, but because the problematic aspects of class had disappeared from her representation of nursing, the object—and nature—of this discipline has changed. Discipline is no longer necessary to control the crafty, lascivious "brute"; as an aspect of moral training, discipline now more closely resembles female self-regulation, or even Christian resignation, than punitive or cautionary regimentation. Here, for example, is Nightingale's 1882 description of discipline. *"Discipline,"* Nightingale writes, "is the essence of training."

> People connect discipline with the idea of drill, standing at attention—some with flagellating themselves, some with flagellating boys. A lady who has, perhaps, more experience in training than anyone else, says: "It is education, instruction, training—all that in fact goes to the full development of our faculties, moral, physical, and spiritual, not only for this life, but looking on this life as the training-ground for the future and higher life. Then discipline embraces order, method, and, as we gain some knowledge of the laws of nature ('God's laws'), we not only see order, method, a place for everything, each its own work, but we find no waste of material or force or space; we find, too, no hurry; and we learn to have patience with our circumstances and ourselves; and so, as we go on learning, we

become more disciplined, more content to work where we are placed, more anxious to fill our appointed work than to see the result thereof; and so God, no doubt, gives us the required patience and steadfastness to continue on our 'blessed drudgery,' which is the discipline He sees best for most of us."[50]

Nightingale's earlier nightmare of a hospital filled with immoral inmates lingers in the first sentence of this passage. But under the influence of her nameless "lady" authority, this nightmare gives way to a vision of a world where efficient government perfectly reconciles the needs of the governed with the plan of a benevolent, watchful God. The implicit model for this world is the orderly, happy, middle-class home. This model becomes explicit when Nightingale institutionalizes discipline in a training home for nurses.

Nightingale first elaborates her scheme for nursing homes in 1876, in her letter to the *Times*. Initially, she has in mind literal dwelling places—homes to which district (or "visiting") nurses can return after their day's work. These homes obviously carry the metaphorical valence of the domestic ideology, but they also retain militant connotations. As Nightingale elaborates her scheme, the home becomes the command post for a holy war against the "dirt and fever nests" that she now defines as the enemies. "The beginning has been made," she proclaims triumphantly,

> the first crusade has been fought and won, to bring a truly "national" undertaking—real nursing, trained nursing—to the bedsides of cases wanting real nursing among the London sick poor; and this is by providing a real home, within reach of their work, for the nurses to live in—a home which gives what real family homes are supposed to give—materially, a bedroom for each, dining and sitting-rooms in common, all meals prepared and eaten in the home; morally, direction, support, sympathy in a common work; further training and instruction in it; proper rest and recreation; and a head of the home, who is also and pre-eminently trained and skilled head of the nursing; in short, a home where any good mother, of whatever class, would be willing to let her daughter, however attractive or highly educated, live.[51]

The head of this domesticated command post is the matron-mother, who combines training with love so as to nurture her daughter-nurses into medical expertise. The matron, Nightingale writes, must exercise "a constant, motherly, intangible supervision" in the home. "She must know how to make it a real 'home,' with constant supply of all wants and constant *sympathy,* which must be taught by example and precept." "The probationers must really be the matron's children," Nightingale continues. "A training school without a mother is worse than children without parents" (NT 329, 330). This home does have a nominal father—the medical instructor from the hospital staff—but his presence is intermittent and his influence indirect (NT 332). In fact, despite Nightingale's nod to this figure, the home she envisions is really run by and for women. Like a religious sisterhood, it avoids male interference, domination, and competition. But because its metaphorical basis is familial, it is politically and religiously neutral—a bulwark of secular society instead of a potential threat to national unity, as all religious orders were thought to be.

The crusade that Nightingale originated in this autonomous, middle-class, female home was explicitly colonial: its aim was to "reform and re-create . . . the homes of the sick poor" in its own image. With the complacency of an imperialist, Nightingale assumed that bourgeois domesticity and cleanliness were universally desired. As a consequence, victory was assumed to be easy, and the "glory" of good nursing was promised to every young recruit. "Every home she has thus cleaned has always been kept so. This is her glory. She found it a pig-sty; she left it a tidy, airy room" (SP 312). In this image we see the stages of what, by the late 1870s, Nightingale explicitly represented as nursing's territorial expansion. From the patient's body, the nurse turns her attention to the room in which he lies: the nurse, Nightingale proclaims, must "nurse the room as well as the patient." The next step for the nurse is to monitor the alleyways of crowded slums, the narrow streets where sewage runs, entire neighborhoods and urban districts so that she can bring "such sanitary defects as produce sickness and death . . . to the notice of the public officer whom it concerns" (SP 314).

As monitor of the poor family's home environment, the nurse therefore becomes a public agent of moral reform. Just as Martineau represented Nightingale coaxing soldiers from "poisonous drinks and mischief," so Nightingale represents her nurses luring wayward men away from gin shops and public houses, back to the home where morality begins, back into the sphere of women's influence. "What efforts such a man will make *not* to drink, when his wife is sick, if you help him to help himself and her; to maintain his independence—and if you make his home by cleanliness and care less intolerable" (SP 315). As caretaker, sanitary warden, and moral reformer, the nurse deploys the cultural authority granted to (middle-class) women in the service of the reform middle-class men also wanted to effect. But Nightingale did not stop here. Because hers was also a domestic war against medical men, she yoked the conquest of the poor to the nurse's gradual usurpation of the doctor's authority. In her representation, the nurse becomes a complete medical staff—apparently from necessity: "she has not the doctor always at hand. . . . She is his staff of clinical clerks, dressers, and nurses" (SP 316). But necessity generates opportunity; from her position as helpmaid, the nurse can launch a social and medical revolution: after this revolution, all homes will be like the orderly, middle-class home she describes in *Notes on Nursing;* hospitals will completely disappear (except as training schools for nurses); and nurses will become the agents of health and morality in all classes, in all parts of the civilized world. "Hospitals are but an intermediate stage of civilization," she writes. "The ultimate object is to nurse all sick at home" (SP 317).

Nightingale's vision of a classless, hospital-less society is actually a vision of society as a network of middle-class families dominated if not run by women, penetrated and linked by nurses who emanate from the central hospital-homes where they are disciplined and trained. This panoptical plan, which is the Nightingale Nursing School writ large, reaches its logical conclusion in Nightingale's scheme of "health missioners," which she set out in 1893. The work of these health missioners undermines the doctor's hegemony within medicine precisely by doing what women do best—tidying up the homes and superintending the morals of the poor. In focusing on society's health, not individuals' diseases, the health missioner dispenses with the diagnosis as a means for determining who needs medical care, and she eliminates the present system that brings only some people under the doctor's supervision. In Nightingale's scheme, everyone comes under the health missioners' jurisdiction: "the art of health," she writes, "is an art which concerns every family in the world" (SH 355). Within this family, not surprisingly, the mother rules: "upon womankind," Nightingale declares, "the national health, as far as the household goes, depends" (SH 356). At least as an idea, Nightingale's health missioners therefore complete the "peaceful revolution" she inaugurated in the Crimea.[52] In their work, women's domestic labors of love are translated into nationwide housekeeping: in this vision, class tension and immorality can both be conquered through woman's aggressive domestic work, not just by the example she passively sets.

Paradoxically, given her emphasis on women's work, Nightingale vehemently opposed the campaign to professionalize nursing that was launched in the 1880s and 1890s. Nightingale rejected state nursing registration on the grounds that nursing was a calling that registration would debase.[53] Nightingale's increasingly insistent deployment of familial metaphors and the vocabulary of altruism that went with them was partly aimed at bolstering her arguments against professionalization: in a family, after all, responsibilities and rewards follow from love, not contracts or certificates. This is the positive sense in which the domestic sphere lies outside the marketplace; according to Nightingale, the true nurse nurses not for money but for some higher, abstract ideal—"to satisfy the high idea of what is the *right*, the *best*" (SH 363). For this, no certification will serve: "You might as well register mothers as nurses," she proclaims (SH 367). Above all, Nightingale wanted nursing to remain aloof from that motor of free enterprise—competition.

> Competition, or each man for himself, and the devil against us all, may be necessary, we are told, but it is the enemy of health. Combination is the antidote—combined interests, recreation, combination to secure the best air, the best food, and all that makes life useful, healthy, and happy. There is no such thing as independence. As far as we are successful, our success lies in combination. (SH 367)

Nightingale's deployment of familial metaphors and her fierce antipathy to both nursing registration and competition were part of her effort to displace the domestic struggle in which her nurses were actually engaged by foregrounding what I have called the "foreign" conflict—the moralization of the poor, here idealized as the working class's "combination" with their middle-class advisers. That is, Nightingale disavowed competition between nurses and medical men for the same reason that she resisted nursing registration: she wanted to preserve an autonomous sphere for nursing, a sphere whose superiority was proved by women's greater efficacy with the poor. Furthermore, the domestic metaphors that underwrote both her domestic and foreign campaigns disguised the implications of Nightingale's own insistence that nurses be paid a fair market wage for their labor. If she were not rhetorically disentangled from the specter of the professional woman, the paid nurse could have jeopardized the existence of a separate sphere of (womanly) altruism, the idea of which was critical to Nightingale's elevation of female nurses over medical men.

III

From Nightingale's denunciation of competition I turn to what will seem in every sense a completely different scene—India. It will become clear why this geographical and cultural leap is worth making, but first I need to outline England's relationship to India in the nineteenth century. For the first half of the century, until 1858, India was a British colony governed by the East India Company. Long a captive source of some of England's most important raw materials, India was both a supplier of cotton and a market for textiles and, increasingly, a prime field for capital investment; India was, therefore, critical to the early nineteenth-century expansion of the British economy that both produced and was supported by the ideology of separate spheres. The commercial relationship between the two countries, like the relationship between the domestic public and private spheres, was couched in a discourse of moral and economic necessity, which, in this case, assumed the superiority of Christianity, the English language, and the white race. In 1857–58, just after the end of the Crimean War, this discourse of Western supremacy was intensified by the outbreak of a mutiny in the Indian army. This uprising, which was marked by extreme violence and racial hatred, culminated in the transfer of power over India from the private East India Company to the British Crown.

This transfer of power was accompanied by the revision of the prevalent language of "trusteeship" into a discourse about familial relations and altruism, which disguised the English commercial interests that were still very much alive under Crown rule.[54] This revised discourse emphasized the Crown's benevolent, efficient administration and its contributions to India's sanitation and morality by rhetorically constructing the new government in opposition to both the East India Company, which was represented as corrupt, greedy, and inefficient, and the native population, which was represented as childlike, dirty, immoral, and sick. In other words, the India Company was rhetorically rewritten as an inefficient, profiteering administration (which Victoria's government was supposedly not) and India was rhetorically transformed into a tractable patient, a sickly child (which the English prided themselves on no longer being).

From these formulations, we see that the two fronts on which Florence Nightingale waged her war for nursing supremacy had their counterparts in the two fronts on which England's middle-class men waged their war for cultural and economic supremacy.

The relationship between the two, however, was not one of homology but of mutual rhetorical construction. In other words, just as Nightingale's campaign for nursing's power was authorized by a language borrowed from the imperial campaigns England waged throughout the second half of the century, so those nationalistic campaigns appropriated the terms of the domestic ideology that underwrote the separation of spheres, male identity, and female nature, and by which Nightingale masked her own territorial ambitions.

The first link between the Nightingale nursing project and the expansion of England's middle-class hegemony is explicit: in 1859, just after the Indian mutiny, Nightingale wrote a long report for the Royal Commission appointed to investigate sanitary conditions in the Indian army. In this report she explicitly advocated importing English head nurses to Indian hospitals to ensure discipline and morality in the colony. Her contention here is that one cannot remedy the unsanitary conditions in the hospital unless one addresses the moral environment of the entire country. In the metaphor with which she explains this, India becomes a diseased body that only a continuous transfusion of healthy English blood can preserve. "No one," she writes, "who is acquainted with European life in India will doubt that such a continuous stream of fresh blood and advanced knowledge will be necessary to prevent progressive deterioration."[55] In this document, Nightingale consistently presented India as if it were the brute soldier of her "Subsidiary Notes"—India, in other words, was the lower-class enemy as much as a suffering, helpless patient.

The second link between Nightingale's nursing campaign and England's nationalistic enterprise is more tenuous and will take us back to England by way of one more critical nineteenth-century development—the general reform and gradual centralization of the British state. By the 1830s, the process that transformed the traditional decentralized society of English localities into the modern state was already well underway. Although it was uneven and multifaceted, this process gradually transformed a relatively stratified society in which power was held by right of birth into a somewhat less stratified society where power could be earned by achievement or merit. This transformation also entailed the gradual separation of the political from the administrative faculties of government, the rationalization of tasks within such agencies as the Mental Health Board or the War Office, and both the establishment of a rudimentary educational system and the creation of a system of paid inspectors to oversee and report back on operations in local districts.[56] In a process too complex to detail here, the formation of this state was simultaneously a cause and an effect of its imperial expansion: centralization at home was a necessary condition of efficient administration and effective surveillance in the colonial field, just as the campaign to provide a trained corps of civil servants for India helped rationalize civil service training at home. Nightingale's concern with defining and deploying effective administration in hospitals and poor districts was part and parcel of this process; her army of health missioners—like the numerous questionnaires by which she surveyed and tabulated conditions in English and Indian hospitals—was just one of the many mid-nineteenth-century attempts to map, and colonize, the hitherto uncharted territories of the private and the lower class. As with the state government, centralization and effectiveness within her nursing organization facilitated—and depended on—extending nursing's influence beyond its domestic environment into the "foreign" territory of the poor.

The two fronts of Florence Nightingale's nursing reforms were inextricably implicated, then, in the two fronts on which England waged its war for international domination. What I have described as Nightingale's foreign front, of course—the English poor—was England's domestic front; England's foreign front consisted of her colonies, most notably India. The important point here is that Nightingale's rhetoric of a healthy nation (the necessity of which was "proved" by the Crimean War) could be appropriated and deployed in the service of a healthy empire, so as to mask England's economic design, just as parliamentary discussions of a "crusade" could be adopted by Nightingale to mask her war against medical men. The two discourses actually employed exactly the same terms in different social registers: the patient (read: India, the poor) is really a brute (a native, a working-class man) who must be cured (colonized, civilized) by an efficient head nurse cum bourgeois mother (England, middle-class women). The ultimate goal in both projects is a tidy society where there is "no waste of material or force or space," where "we learn to have patience with our circumstances and ourselves," where "we become more disciplined, more content to work where we are placed." In both cases, surveillance, discipline, and good administration are the keys to this transformation; in each case, a housewifely, regal, classless woman presides.

Nightingale's discourse could be so appropriated by apologists for the empire because of the way the twin compromises she represented and forged mobilized and deployed gender. In mobilizing

the Victorian domestic narrative to reform the poor, Florence Nightingale activated the altruistic language that women's maternal nature
underwrote, so as to free paid nursing from the contamination of
greed and competition by transforming it into a "sacrifice" or a
quasi-religious calling; when this language was linked to England's
colonization of India, it masked the economic motivation behind
territorial expansion. When she displaced class so as to transform
the brute soldier into a tractable, infantalized patient, she provided
a strategy that could also displace race by transforming the Indian
from a dirty foreigner into a sickly child. In Nightingale's sanitized
vision, discipline could be rewritten as womanly self-regulation; in
England's imperial dream, conquest and colonial rule could also be
written as the government of love, which was superintended by a
motherly monarch. In the image of Florence Nightingale, as in the
image of the queen, the contradiction between an aggressive, economically interested war and the mother's curative tutelage of the
child was symbolically resolved and the tensions it provoked could
magically disappear.

In one sense—in her *own* terms—Florence Nightingale failed
at nearly every nursing scheme she devised. Nightingale's plan for
nursing homes, for example, came to naught; her health missioners
were never recruited and organized on the scale she envisioned; and
her effort to reform workhouse nursing yielded only a cruel parody
of her original grandiose scheme.[57] But these failures did not preclude
Nightingale and her representation of nursing from being enlisted
in the nationalistic project I have been describing. In fact, in *these*
terms, Nightingale triumphed: her signal "success" was in creating
the conditions for the deployment of an image—an image that was
produced and reproduced as England's empire grew, because it legitimized middle-class England's domestic and colonial imperialism
while disguising the profoundly and violently racist and classist bases
of these campaigns. The misrepresentation of Florence Nightingale
can best be understood as one crucial facet of the building and
defense of the empire at home, as part of England's construction of
its own national character and value in the eyes of its people and
the peoples of the world.

In May 1855, while Nightingale was still at Scutari, reports reached
England that she was dying of the fever she had gone out to the
Crimea to cure. These reports sparked a sentimental and commercial
explosion of Nightingale's already considerable popularity: writing
paper watermarked with her portrait, waxwork dolls, penny ballads,

and Staffordshire figurines vied to capture the public's desire for some commemorative item to immortalize Florence Nightingale. Because no official portraits were available, however, the images these figures presented were all different. Florence Nightingale had become—quite literally—a public figure; like the female body silenced by the medical profession, she had become the vehicle for the aspirations and fantasies of the national character she helped construct.

The fate of Florence Nightingale in this anecdote is exemplary. The different Florence Nightingales that were produced, marketed, and consumed in the summer of 1855 bore the same relation to the real woman as did the reputation that grew throughout the century to her immobilized, increasingly corpulent body: by the end of the century, her image had so dwarfed the bedridden woman that most people in England were shocked to learn that Nightingale was still alive. In a very real sense, it had ceased to matter that she was: her image had become far more powerful than anything she could say or write, and it had long escaped her control. Because of the ideological "fit" I have discussed—the intersection in Nightingale of the two Victorian narratives and the way that her own vision of nursing underwrote, elaborated, and neutralized the militancy inherent in the domestic ideology—her image and her writings could be part of both a public discourse about political solutions and a private discourse that provided moral solutions to these same problems. But while Nightingale could thereby demonstrate the power of the domestic ideology to conquer worlds beyond the home, she could not put her own plans into action or control how her image was used; like Caroline Norton, Nightingale could not single-handedly determine the ends that her efforts and her image would serve.

Yet precisely *because* she was displaced by her own image, Florence Nightingale could also be appropriated by feminists who sought proof of women's capabilities. For Harriet Martineau and others, Florence Nightingale planted a flag upon a new territory, a "woman's battle-field" that others could now defend.[58] As these women read her, Florence Nightingale gave the lie to arguments about women's natural limitations; she proved beyond a doubt that women could work in the public sphere. Because her image displaced her own antifeminist sentiments, the name of Florence Nightingale could be enlisted in the feminist cause the woman herself refused to support.

Conclusion

Examining the ideological work performed by representations of woman across a variety of social institutions and during a relatively short period of time has led me to formulate several general conclusions and to feel acutely the need for specific kinds of future research. In the first place, I have come to see more clearly than before that the location and organization of difference are crucial to a culture's self-representation and its distribution of power. Recognizing that middle-class Victorians at midcentury organized difference in a binary opposition and that they mapped this opposition onto the "natural" difference between men and women has helped me understand their moralization of women, the idealization of the home, and the resistance—even by some very assertive women—to such causes as Josephine Butler's campaign against the Contagious Diseases acts or Barbara Bodichon's effort to change property laws for married women. So much depended on maintaining the oppositional, gendered organization of social relations at midcentury that challenges to it seemed to threaten the most fundamental principles of the social and natural orders. Thus it is no surprise that the changes whose beginnings I have just traced here—women's organized resistance to a sexual division of waged labor, for example—initially at least took their terms from the ideological system they were eventually to subvert.

A second conclusion prompted by this investigation involves the instability of ideological formulations—even one as apparently secure as the binary formulation of difference. The mid-Victorian tendency to foreground a binary representation of sex as the fundamental definition of difference was unstable partly because it depended on other conceptualizations of difference whose importance it seemed to supplant. Only because the differences of class, race, and national identity produced real, if occluded, effects, in other words, could sexual difference seem decisive and the anchor of all social relations. In the preceding chapters I have illuminated some of the intracacies of this structural interdependence, but I have not been able to trace all of its ramifications. My brief, concluding discussion of India, for example, can only allude to the place the dark-skinned Indians occupied in self-representations of middle-class Englishmen; to sketch this more fully would entail returning to some of the other texts I have already examined, so as to analyze how Jack Maldon's exile to India or St. John Rivers's martyrdom there helped underwrite the sexual and moral relations in which these two figures are more obviously involved.

The interrelation of such determinants as gender, class, race, and national identity is clearly one area that calls for more attention from feminists. If we could chart the changing relation of symbolic and institutional representations of class, race, and gender, for example, or the changing prominence of symbolic and institutional representations of gender in relation to other determinants, we could produce a history of ideological formulations that might help us understand the impetus behind and resistances to change in ways our old histories have failed to do. This would necessarily entail not only identifying the way that various formulations of difference were played off against or used to construct each other, but also analyzing the competitions among various institutions for the right to articulate and legislate difference. As my discussion of the chloroform debate suggests, the uneven operation of representations is sometimes an effect of this competition. Even if medical men and clergymen agreed that women were naturally dependent on men, for example, the fact that doctors saw themselves as competing with clergymen for the authority to explain this dependence led doctors to conflate moralistic and scientific arguments in their discussions of female bodies. Further analysis could highlight the way such competition helped direct arguments about and articulations of difference; it could also map the reliance of one kind of institutional authority on another—as, for example, when M.P.s debating the rights and wrongs of divorce invoked Dickens's *Hard Times* as an authoritative treatment of marital stress.

Some feminists will argue that the danger of such an inquiry is that it risks losing sight of the history of real women. Because my project examines the social organization of difference rather than taking that difference for granted, I might be seen as abandoning the task in which many twentieth-century feminists have been engaged and from which many of us have gained self-consciousness and collective identification—the task of excavating and reevaluating the lives of forgotten women. To reveal the artificiality of the Victorian definition of difference, after all, as I have done in this book, is implicitly to challenge the importance of the category "woman"; to give this category a history is implicitly, at least, to call its future into question.

I do mean to call into question the future of this conceptualization of difference because in the long run it reproduces the problem it claims to subvert. In the short run, however, it seems to me important for feminists to work on two fronts: to recognize, on the one hand, that articulating difference onto sex *has* dominated the culture we have inherited and does set the terms in which we can work; to investigate, on the other hand, the effects those terms have produced, the artificiality and *politics* of difference, and the possibilities for change contained within the kinds of unevenness I have examined here. To write the history of difference is not necessarily to govern its future, of course, but it is to identify the ideological work such representations have performed and to glimpse the possibilities they have excluded.

Notes

Chapter 1. The Ideological Work of Gender

1. W. R. Greg, "Why Are Women Redundant?" *National Review* 14 (1862): 436.

2. Ibid., pp. 438, 440.

3. Contemporary feminists often distinguish between biological sex and gender, the social organization of sex. In this book, I use this distinction. The most influential discussion of this concept is Gayle Rubin, "The Traffic in Women," in Rayna R. Reiter, ed., *Toward an Anthropology of Women* (New York: Monthly Review Press, 1975).

4. Louis Althusser, "Ideology and Ideological State Apparatuses (Notes towards an Investigation)," in Louis Althusser, *Lenin and Philosophy and Other Essays*, trans. Ben Brewster (New York: Monthly Review Press, 1971), p. 162. See also Raymond Williams, *Marxism and Literature* (Oxford: Oxford University Press, 1977), p. 175.

5. Roger Smith quotes C. Taylor on this subject: "It is not just that people in our society all or mostly have a given set of ideas in their heads and subscribe to a given set of goals. The meanings and norms implicit in the practices are not just in the minds of the actors but are out there in the practices themselves, practices which cannot be conceived as a set of individual actions, but as essentially modes of social relation, of mutual action." From C. Taylor, "Interpretation and the Sciences of Man," *Review of Metaphysics* 25 (1971); quoted in Roger Smith, *Trial by Medicine: Insanity and Responsibility in Victorian Trials* (Edinburgh: Edinburgh University Press, 1981), p. 8. See also Althusser, "Ideology," p. 182.

6. For a discussion of the 1851 Census, see Constance Rover, *Women's Suffrage and Party Politics in Britain, 1866–1914* (London: Routledge and Kegan Paul, 1967), p. 14.

7. See Barbara Leigh Smith Bodichon, *Women and Work* (London: Bosworth and Harrison, 1857); and [Harriet Martineau], "Female Industry," *Edinburgh Review* 109 (April 1859): 293–336.

8. Greg, "Why Are Women Redundant?" pp. 454–55.

9. Ibid., p. 460. Greg's "Prostitution" was published in the *Westminster Review* 53 (July 1850): 238–68.

10. Greg, "Prostitution," p. 242.

11. Ibid., p. 267.

12. Notable exceptions to this generalization include William Thompson and Anna Wheeler, George Drysdale, Orson S. Fowler, and Elizabeth Cady Stanton. For a discussion of this topic, see Elizabeth K. Helsinger, Robin Lauterbach Sheets, and William Veeder, eds., *The Woman Question: Social Issues, 1837–1883*, vol. 3 of *The Woman Question: Society and Literature in Britain and America, 1837–1883* (New York: Garland Publishing, 1983), pp. 58–75.

13. The analysis of the Victorian symbolic economy that bears closest affinity to my analysis is Leonore Davidoff's "Class and Gender in Victorian England: The Diaries of Arthur J. Munby and Hannah Cullwick," *Feminist Studies 5* (Spring 1979): 86–141. I use the phrase *symbolic economy* to refer to the characteristic organizational principle in an ideological formulation.

14. For a discussion of clergymen's formulation of this dichotomy, see Leonore Davidoff and Catherine Hall, *Family Fortunes: Men and Women of the English Middle Class, 1780–1850* (Chicago: University of Chicago Press, 1987), pp. 104–48.

15. See Thomas Laqueur, "Orgasm, Generation, and the Politics of Reproductive Biology," *Representations* 14 (Spring 1986): 1–41.

16. Ibid., pp. 1–2. Laqueur points out that medical men since the end of the Enlightenment had discounted the traditional assumption that female orgasm was essential to conception.

17. *Lancet* 1 (1856): 4.

18. Peter Gaskell, *The Manufacturing Population of England, Its Moral, Social, and Physical Conditions, and the Changes Which Have Arisen from the Use of Steam Machinery; with an Examination of Infant Labour* (1833; reprint, New York: Arno Press, 1972), pp. 144–45.

19. Ibid., p. 165.

20. From "The Comparison," Canto V of *The Angel in the House*, in *The Poems of Coventry Patmore*, ed. Frederick Page (London: Oxford University Press, 1949). Quoted in Carol Christ, "Victorian Masculinity and the Angel in the House," in Martha Vicinus, ed., *A Widening Sphere: Changing Roles of Victorian Women* (Bloomington: Indiana University Press, 1977), p. 148. Christ's essay is extremely interesting in relation to this point, as is Stephen Heath's *The Sexual Fix* (New York: Schocken Books, 1984), esp. p. 47.

21. See Ellen Pollak, *The Poetics of Sexual Myth: Gender and Ideology in the Verse of Swift and Pope* (Chicago: University of Chicago Press, 1985; Felicity A. Nussbaum, *The Brink of All We Hate: English Satires on Women, 1660–1750* (Lexington: University of Kentucky Press, 1984); and Mary Poovey, *The Proper Lady and the Woman Writer: Ideology as Style in the Works of Mary Wollstonecraft, Mary Shelley, and Jane Austen* (Chicago: University of Chicago Press, 1984), chap. 1.

22. For relevant discussions of the evolution of the domestic ideal, see Catherine Gallagher, *The Industrial Reformation of English Fiction: Social*

Discourse and Narrative Form, 1832–1867 (Chicago: University of Chicago Press, 1985), pt. 2; and Nancy Armstrong, *Desire and Domestic Fiction: A Political History of the Novel* (New York: Oxford University Press, 1987), chap. 2.

23. See Davidoff and Hall, *Family Fortunes,* chap. 6.

24. See Nina Auerbach, *Woman and the Demon: The Life of a Victorian Myth* (Cambridge: Harvard University Press, 1982), esp. chap. 3; and Eric Trudgill, *Madonnas and Magdalenes: The Origins and Development of Victorian Sexual Attitudes* (New York: Holmes and Meier, 1976).

25. See Jacques Derrida, "Structure, Sign, and Play in the Discourse of the Human Sciences," in *Writing and Difference,* trans. Alan Bass (Chicago: University of Chicago Press, 1978), pp. 284, 285.

26. In the introduction to the 1851 Census, the registrar general declared: "The possession of an entire house is strongly desired by every Englishman, for it throws a sharp well-defined circle round his family and hearth—the shrine of his sorrows, joys and meditations." Quoted in Leonore Davidoff, "The Separation of Home and Work? Landladies and Lodgers in Nineteenth- and Twentieth-Century England," in Sandra Burman, ed., *Fit Work for Women* (New York: St. Martin's Press, 1979), p. 69.

27. See Rover, *Women's Suffrage,* p. 14.

28. See Henry Mayhew, *London Labour and the London Poor* (New York: Dover, 1968), 4: 35–272. For a brief but provocative discussion of Mayhew's position, see Armstrong, *Desire and Domestic Fiction,* p. 182.

29. More canonical structuralists refer to these basic units as nodes or matrices. See Tzvetan Todorov, "How to Read?" in *The Poetics of Prose,* trans. Richard Howard (Ithaca: Cornell University Press, 1977), pp. 234–46; and Michael Riffaterre, "Interpretation and Descriptive Poetry: A Reading of Wordsworth's 'Yew-Trees,' " in Robert Young, ed., *Untying the Text: A Post-Structuralist Reader* (Boston: Routledge and Kegan Paul, 1981), pp. 103–32. For related post-structuralist readings of novels, see Peter Brooks, *Reading for the Plot: Design and Intention in Narrative* (New York: Alfred A. Knopf, 1984).

30. The best discussion of these features and ideological operations is Roland Barthes, *S/Z: An Essay,* trans. Richard Miller (New York: Hill and Wang, 1974).

31. See especially Michel Foucault, *Language, Counter-Memory, Practice: Selected Essays and Interviews,* ed. Donald F. Bouchard, trans. Donald F. Bouchard and Sherry Simon (Ithaca: Cornell University Press, 1977); Etienne Balibar and Pierre Macherey, "On Literature as an Ideological Form," in Young, *Untying the Text,* pp. 79–99; and Fredric Jameson, *The Political Unconscious: Narrative as a Socially Symbolic Act* (Ithaca: Cornell University Press, 1981).

32. Gerald L. Bruns, "Law as Hermeneutics: A Response to Ronald Dworkin," in W. J. T. Mitchell, ed., *The Politics of Interpretation* (Chicago: University of Chicago Press, 1983), pp. 319–20.

33. Jameson, *Political Unconscious,* p. 81.

34. Caroline Norton, *Caroline Norton's Defense: English Laws for Women in the Nineteenth Century* (Chicago: Academy Press, 1982), p. 165.

35. Another example of unforeseen consequences is provided by the workings of the divorce court. Whatever conservative intentions legislators might have had in passing this legislation, by 1859 its well-publicized operations were making public (or rather, official) the numbers of women whose earnings were supporting their families and the extent of domestic cruelty women suffered. For two different responses to this state of affairs, see Martineau, "Female Industry," p. 335; and "The Divorce Court at Work," *Saturday Review*, 31 December 1859, p. 809.

36. This is a complex debate among contemporary feminist historians, and my schematization admittedly does not do either side full justice. In one sense, the distinction I want to make is between feminists committed to an idea of women's culture and those who are wary of such idealization; in another, the relevant distinction is between those who have argued that women's emancipation has begun in women's manipulation of their ideology's dominant terms and those who have maintained that women's use of these terms has always remained within the dominant ideology. One reason it is difficult to make this distinction stick is that most feminists recognize that the relationship between the "public" and "private" spheres has historically been extremely complex, and many critics have been justifiably wary of retaining the terms that are part of the historical problem in the first place. Nevertheless, some general groupings may be useful. Among the feminist historians who have emphasized women's ability to construct communities within the terms of the dominant ideology are Carroll Smith-Rosenberg and Mary Ryan; those who have emphasized the limitations imposed by this ideology include Alice Kessler Harris and Sally Alexander.

Chapter 2. The Medical Treatment of Victorian Women

1. James Miller, *The Principles of Surgery* (1858). Quoted in A. J. Youngson, *The Scientific Revolution in Victorian Medicine* (New York: Holmes and Meier, 1979), p. 69.

2. Barbara M. Duncum, *The Development of Inhalation Anaesthesia, with Special Reference to the Years 1846–1900* (London: Oxford University Press, 1947), p. 253.

3. See Thomas Laqueur, "Orgasm, Generation, and the Politics of Reproductive Biology," *Representations* 14 (Spring 1986): 1–41.

4. See the discussion by Leonore Davidoff and Catherine Hall of the role clergymen continued to play in the early nineteenth century in defining the roles of men and women, in *Family Fortunes: Men and Women of the English Middle Class, 1780–1850* (Chicago: University of Chicago Press, 1987), pt. 1.

5. "The word *anaesthesia*, implying loss of sensation as a result of disease or injury, but not loss of consciousness, was quite frequently used

during the eighteenth and early nineteenth centuries." Duncum, *Inhalation Anaesthesia*, p. 562. For an account of the discovery of the anesthetic properties of ether and the establishment of chloroform, see Duncum, pp. 9–26 and *passim*.

6. *Lancet* 2 (1847): 549–50.

7. See Duncum, *Inhalation Anaesthesia*, pp. 9–10. She quotes John Snow as stating: "Besides the great benefit conferred by chloroform in the prevention of pain, it probably confers still greater advantages by the extension which it gives to the practice of surgery" (p. 10).

8. The *O.E.D.* cites instances of the adjective *obstetric* (or *obstetrical*) from the seventeenth and early eighteenth centuries. Interestingly, these early uses are almost all metaphorical and refer to a man aiding in the "delivery" of an idea, text, or event. Examples include: "there all the Learn'd shall at the labour stand, And Douglas lend his soft, obstetric hand" (1742; Pope, *Dunciad* 4: 394); "this you protect their pregnant hour; . . . Exerting your obstetric pow'r" (c. 1750; Shenstone, *To the Virtuosi*, vii). One non-metaphorical use depicts a male frog, the "obstetrical toad" (Alytes obste-tricians), who aids the female in birth: "They spawn like frogs; but what is singular, the male affords the female obstetrical aid" (1776; Pennant, *Zoology* 3: 17). By the end of the eighteenth century, the word was generally used in its medical sense: "The obstetric art . . . began to emerge from its barbarity during the sixteenth century" (1799; *Medical Journal* 2: 453). Instances of figurative usages continue to appear, however, as when Byron wrote to Scott in 1822 that "Mr. Murray has several things of mine in his obstetrical hands." The word *obstetrician* first appears in 1828, when Dr. Michael Ryan calls attention to its novelty: "It may be necessary to say a few words apologetic, for my adoption of the word obstetrician" (1828; *Man Midwifery*, p. v). In 1819, the word *obstetrics* already referred to a medical practice more extensive than the simple delivery in which even untrained women could assist: "*Obstetrics*, the doctrines or practice of midwifery. . . . Employed in a larger signification than mid-wifery in its usual sense" (1819; *Pantalogia*). The *O.E.D.* cites the first appearance of *accoucheur* as Laurence Sterne's *Tristram Shandy* (1759–67): "Nothing will serve you but to carry off the man-midwife," says Tristram's father. "*Accoucheur*,—if you please," responds Dr. Slop (2: xii).

W. Tyler Smith was intent on eliminating the very word *midwife* from medical language and in sharply distinguishing between scientific, male-administered obstetrics and unscientific, female-dominated "midwifery": "We may confidently hope," he states in his first obstetric lecture, "that hereafter the sign of the escape of midwifery from the midwife will be . . . obscure and insignificant, and that the very term *midwifery* will be rejected on account of its derivation." *Lancet* 2: 371. See also "Obstetrics a Science, Midwifery an Art," *British and Foreign Medico-Chirurgical Review* 4 (1849): 501–10.

9. See Margarete Sandelowski, *Pain, Pleasure, and American Childbirth: From the Twilight Sleep to the Reed Method, 1914–1960* (Westport, Conn.:

Greenwood Press, 1984), pp. 29–30. Simpson also acknowledged this when he stated that "the application of anaesthesia to midwifery involves many more difficult and delicate problems that its mere application to surgery" (quoted in Sandelowski, p. 28).

10. See Ann Oakley, *Women Confined: Towards a Sociology of Childbirth* (New York: Schocken Books, 1980), pp. 8–9.

11. As one clergyman phrased it, chloroform was "a decoy of Satan, apparently offering itself to bless women; but in the end . . . it will harden society, and rob God of the deep earnest cries which arise in time of trouble for help." Quoted by James Young Simpson, "Same Subject Continued, in a Letter to Dr. Protheroe Smith, of London," in *Anaesthesia: Or the Employment of Chloroform and Ether in Surgery, Midwifery, etc.* (Philadelphia: Lindsay and Blakiston, 1849), p. 123. One glimpse into the spiritual significance childbirth might have had in this period is provided by this extract from W. E. Gladstone's diary, written after watching the birth of his first child in 1840. "This is to me a new scene & lesson in human life. I have seen her endure today—less than the average for first children, says Dr L, yet six times as much bodily pain as I have undergone in my whole life. . . . How many thoughts does this agony excite: the comparison of the termination with the commencement: the undergoings of another for our sakes: the humbling & sobering view of human relations here presented: the mixed & intricate considerations of religion which may be brought to bear upon the question of the continuation of our wayward race. Certainly the woman has this blessing that she may as a member of Christ behold in these pains certain especially appointed means of her purification with a willing mind, & so the more cheerfully hallow them by willing endurance into a thank offering." Quoted in F. B. Smith, *The People's Health, 1830–1910* (New York: Holmes and Meier, 1979), p. 59, n. 20.

12. *Lancet* 1 (1848): 614. Simpson made the presumption of such "medical" arguments explicit when he called these speakers "London medical divines" ("Same Subject Continued," p. 125).

13. Ibid. Meigs states earlier, "I have been accustomed to look upon the sensations of pain in labour as a physiological relative of the power or force; and notwithstanding I have seen so many women in the throes of labour, I have always regarded a labour-pain as a most desirable, salutary, and conservative manifestation of life-force" (p. 613). Stanley Joel Reiser discusses the transformation of "theory-bound, patient-dependent scholastics" into "touch-oriented, observation-bound" practitioners who no longer depended on the patient's observations and accounts. See Reiser, *Medicine and the Reign of Technology* (Cambridge: Cambridge University Press, 1978), pp. 4–29. See also M. Jeanne Peterson, *The Medical Profession in Mid-Victorian London* (Berkeley: University of California Press, 1978), p. 14.

14. James Young Simpson, "Answer to the Religious Objections Advanced against the Employment of Anaesthetic Agents in Midwifery and Surgery," in Simpson, *Anaesthesia*, pp. 120, 122. This essay also cites many of Simpson's opponents.

15. James Young Simpson, "Results of the Practice of Anaesthesia in Medicine," in Simpson, *Anaesthesia*, pp. 140—41.

16. Simpson, "Answer," p. 117.

17. Here is Simpson on the double nature of pain: "Each so-called labour pain consists, as you well know, of two distinct and separate elements; viz. *first*, of contraction of the uterus and other assistant muscles; and, *secondly*, of sensations of pain, more or less agonizing, accompanying these contractions, and directly resulting from them. Now, I have been often struck, as you must have been, in chloroform labours, with the fact that, in the anaesthetic state, not only does the uterus contract powerfully, but that the abdominal muscles do so also, and even the face of the patient will sometimes betoken strong expulsive actions, while all accompanying suffering is quite annulled. We abrogate the second element of the so-called labour pain, without destroying the first. We leave intact the expulsive muscular efforts, but remove the sense and feeling of pain accompanying these efforts. It is only of late that these two elements or constituents of labour pains have been recognised and studied by the Profession as *two* separate objects. But it is surely, as I have above stated, worthy of remark and wonder, that the language of the Bible is, on this as on other points, strictly and scientifically correct, and long ago made, with perfect precision, the very distinction which we are now-a-days only recognising. For the Hebrew noun, *etzebh,* distinctly signifies the muscular contraction or effort, and the nouns, *hhil* and *hhebhel,* as distinctly signify the sensations of pain accompanying these efforts." It is all right, of course, for the doctor to alleviate the latter, for "sorrow" is derived from the former, Simpson argues. See "Answer," pp. 124—25.

18. Simpson, "Results," p. 144. Simpson also states that the "manageableness" of an anesthetized patient can be "as perfect as if she had been a wax doll or a lay figure." *Lancet* 2 (1847): 550.

19. For an account of Simpson's revulsion from the pain he had to inflict, see *Lancet* 2 (1847): 625. Here he describes "that great principle of emotion which both impels us to feel sympathy at the sight of suffering in any fellow-creature, and at the same time imparts to us delight and gratification in the exercise of any power by which we can mitigate and alleviate suffering." Accounts of appreciative patients appear throughout "Report of the Results," in Simpson, *Anaesthesia*, pp. 151—79.

20. Simpson, "Report of the Results," p. 157.

21. Ibid., pp. 159, 164, 156.

22. This experiment was conducted in 1847 and reported in *Lancet* 1 (1848): 19—25. The many variables in these experiments include different animals (ranging from horses to hedgehogs to pigeons), different amounts of chloroform or ether, different conditions of administration, and different periods of inhalation. Wakley concludes that chloroform is more dangerous than ether, but he offers no physiological explanation. Another unscientific set of experiments is reported in *Lancet* 1 (1851): 505—6.

23. Snow stated: "I use chloroform for the same reason that you use

phosphorus matches instead of the tinder box. An occasional risk never stands in the way of ready applicability." Quoted in Duncum, *Inhalation Anaesthesia*, p. 180. Duncum states that Snow "brushed aside evidence which ran counter to his theory (proved to his own satisfaction by experiments on animals in the laboratory), that if the vapour were sufficiently diluted with air then it could not cause death without warning" (p. 203). In 1911, A. Goodman proved conclusively that Snow was mistaken. Light chloroform *could* kill without warning from ventricular fibrillations of the heart (p. 203).

24. See Dr. S. Gower's judgment against chloroform in *London Lancet* 2 (1848): 124. Gower admits that his preference for ether is primarily based on its odor. "Ether as inhaled as from a sponge not only acts on the patient, but diffuses a grateful fragrance around, which makes both Dr. and nurse—what doctors and nurses ought to be—cheerful." Gower's more "scientific" conclusions about ether and chloroform are, incidentally, wrong. Simpson's response to the argument that chloroform was unsafe was not to refer even to pseudoscientific experiments, but to attack the putative fallacy of the logic. "If there were any soundness in the reasoning," he declaimed, "a thousand things beside would require to be abandoned. Railways, steamboats, stage-coaches, &c., when used as substitutes for the natural and physiological function of human progression, are ever and anon attended with accidents to limb and life. But surely no one would, from this, maintain that these means of conveyance should in consequence be abandoned. Many persons are annually drowned in bathing.—Should bathing, therefore, be prohibited and this powerful means of maintaining and restoring health be entirely forsaken?" "Objections to Anaesthesia in Midwifery," in Simpson, *Anaesthesia*, p. 187.

25. James Young Simpson, "Discussion on the Employment of Chloroform in Midwifery and Surgery before the Medico-Chirurgical Society of Edinburgh," in Simpson *Anaesthesia*, p. 189.

26. See *Lancet* 1 (1848): 26; *Lancet* 2 (1847): 389. Havelock Ellis, writing more than fifty years later, continued to assert that women were more likely to experience sexual excitation under anesthesia. He cites a series of experiments in which Dr. J. F. W. Silk administered anesthesia to 5,119 patients, 3,400 of whom were women. "Erotic phenomena occurred 18 times, but only once in a man; to preserve the male ratio they should only have occurred twice among the women." Ellis, *Man and Woman: A Study of Human Secondary Sexual Characters* (London: Walter Scott, 1904; New York: Arno Press, 1974), p. 273.

Here is Dr. W. Martin Coates's description of his patient's and his own response to chloroform: "I own that I never witnessed the sudden suffused countenance, the foaming mouth, the injected conjunctivae, the dilated pupil, the convulsive movements of the extremities, the stertorous breathing, and, at a subsequent stage, the pallid face, the slow, laboured respiration, and the very feeble pulse of the patient under the ordinary dose inhaled, without a dread of a suddenly fatal result, and a conviction that chloroform, to be safely administered, must be inhaled in much smaller doses." *Lancet* 1 (1851): 505.

27. *London Lancet* 1 (1847): 377. Smith allows a disturbing ambiguity to insinuate itself into this account when he fails to report that Dubois specified that the attendant the woman kissed was female. Dubois's account also emphasizes the woman's modesty. " 'What did you dream of?' was my question; but the patient turned her face aside with a smile, the peculiarity of which having drawn my particular attention, I renewed my question; but on her having again refused to let me know the nature of her dream, I had recourse, in order to ascertain it, to the intermediary communication of a respectable person of her own sex, and who was present at the operation of inhaling ether. To the same question being renewed, she answered, she had dreamt she was beside her husband, and that he and herself had been simultaneously engaged, going through those preliminaries which had led her to the state in which we now beheld her." *London Lancet* 1 (1847): 411, 412.

W. Tyler Smith, who had arrived in London in 1840 after a scanty education in Bristol, had no influence or connections, yet he rose to such prominence that in 1859 he became one of the founders of the Obstetrical Society. His degree was an M.B.; he was not a member of any of the Royal Colleges. See Youngson, *Scientific Revolution in Victorian Medicine,* pp. 77–78; and W. Tyler Smith, "On the Founding of the Obstetrical Society of London (1859)," *Transactions of the Obstetrical Society of London* (1859): 5–14.

28. *London Lancet* 2 (1848): 207.

29. *London Lancet* 1 (1847): 377.

30. For discussions of the domestication of this image, see Nancy Armstrong, *Desire and Domestic Fiction: A Political History of the Novel* (New York: Oxford University Press, 1987), esp. chap. 2; Susan Staves, *Players' Scepters: Fictions of Authority in the Restoration* (Lincoln: University of Nebraska Press, 1979), chap. 3; and Mary Poovey, *The Proper Lady and the Woman Writer: Ideology as Style in the Works of Mary Wollstonecraft, Mary Shelley, and Jane Austen* (Chicago: University of Chicago Press, 1984), chap. 1.

31. *Lancet* 1 (1849): 212. In 1853, Dr. Robert Lee and Dr. Gream were still making this point. See *Lancet* 1 (1853): 611.

32. *Lancet* 1 (1849): 212.

33. Ibid., p. 395. Dr. Syme added that "he had never witnessed any sexual excitement produced by the exhibition of chloroform, but that he and others had frequently heard patients in the operating theatre swearing, when excited by chloroform, and that, sometimes, in patients whose friends had seldom or ever heard using such language. Possibly these improper expressions were only a true exhibition of the state of the patients' mind, and it was always stopped by throwing him deeply asleep" (p. 395).

34. *Lancet* 1 (1855): 499. One way of construing the quarrel about how to administer chloroform is to see it as part of the ongoing debate about whether Edinburgh-trained medical men were superior or inferior to London-trained men. The "Edinburgh method" of chloroform appli-

cation was considered by many English doctors as irresponsible and unsafe; in England, lighter doses were applied, and often doctors used an inhaler—not a rag or handkerchief—to administer the anodyne. In Edinburgh, all medical men were trained in surgery and pharmacy and were therefore what would be called general practitioners in England. When they began coming to England in larger numbers in the second half of the eighteenth century, they helped swell the ranks of general practitioners, many of whom wanted—but were denied—representation in the Royal Colleges. Scottish physicians were not formally recognized in England, but the Royal Colleges had no mechanism for effectively limiting their practice. See Noel Parry and José Parry, *The Rise of the Medical Profession: A Study of Collective Social Mobility* (London: Croom Helm, 1976), pp. 105–7.

35. This phrase appears in *Lancet* 1 (1856): 424.

36. See Youngson, *Scientific Revolution in Victorian Medicine*, p. 78. In England, a medical student training for general practice was generally required to attend lectures on midwifery for three months (which would have included only a part of Smith's course) and to be present for at least six deliveries in a lying-in hospital. The latter part of this regulation was almost always curtailed because there were never enough women confined in the hospitals to enable each student to witness six births. See F. B. Smith, *People's Health*, p. 24. By 1827, some training in midwifery was required by the Society of Apothecaries; by 1855, this was also true of the College of Surgeons; by 1884, midwifery and women's diseases were also part of the required curriculum of the Royal College of Surgeons. See Peterson, *Medical Profession*, pp. 62–63; and Ivan Waddington, "General Practitioners and Consultants in Early Nineteenth-Century England: The Sociology of an Intra-Professional Conflict," in John Woodward and David Richards, eds., *Health Care and Popular Medicine in Nineteenth Century England* (New York: Holmes and Meier, 1977), p. 180.

As late as the 1850s, licenses from all three colleges could be obtained from extremely varied systems of training, including that provided by universities, hospitals, dispensaries, provincial schools, private schools, special institutions, and independent courses of lectures. See Ian Inkster, "Marginal Men: Aspects of the Social Role of the Medical Community in Sheffield, 1790–1850," in Woodward and Richards, *Health Care and Popular Medicine*, pp. 132–35. Inkster also discusses the institution of private lecturing. See pp. 133–34.

37. *Lancet* 2 (1847): 544.

38. Ibid., p. 595.

39. Ibid.

40. Dr. M. L. Holbrook, *Parturition without Pain: A Code of Directions for Escaping from the Primal Curse* (1882). Quoted in Carroll Smith-Rosenberg and Charles E. Rosenberg, "The Female Animal: Medical and Biological Views of Woman and Her Role in Nineteenth-Century America," in Judith Walzer Leavitt, ed., *Women and Health in America: Historical Readings* (Madison: University of Wisconsin Press, 1984), p. 13.

41. *Lancet* 2 (1847): 371.

42. Thomas Laycock, *An Essay on Hysteria: Being an Analysis of Its Irregular and Aggravated Forms; Including Hysterical Hemorrhage, and Hysterical Ischuria* (Philadelphia: Haswell, Barrington, and Haswell, 1840), p. 63. Laycock differed from many other mid-nineteenth-century medical men in maintaining that "the uterus is an appendage to the ovaries" (p. 64), but he agreed that the female reproductive system was central to the organism.

43. From Dr. Charles Taylor in 1882. Quoted in Carl N. Degler, "What Ought to Be and What Was: Women's Sexuality in the Nineteenth Century," in Leavitt, *Women and Health in America*, p. 41.

44. See G. J. Barker-Benfield, "The Spermatic Economy: A Nineteenth-Century View of Sexuality," *Feminist Studies* 1 (1972): 45–74; Smith-Rosenberg and Rosenberg, "Female Animal," pp. 13–14; and Barbara Ehrenreich and Deidre English, *For Her Own Good: 150 Years of the Experts' Advice to Women* (Garden City, N.Y.: Anchor Press/Doubleday, 1979), p. 27. Here is Dr. Beard on reflex action: "When any part or point of the body, external or internal, on the periphery, or at the center, is irritated, some other part is liable to be in some way changed for the better or worse; but there are *par excellence* three great centers of reflex action—the *brain,* the *stomach* and *digestive apparatus,* and the *genital* or *reproductive* system. When any one of these three reflex centers is irritated by over-use or direct abuse, the injury is likely to radiate or reverberate in any or in all directions; we can not tell just where, any more than we can tell where lightning will strike. . . . This accounts, in part, for the immense number and variety of symptoms and abnormal sensations from which the nervously exhausted suffer. . . .

"Disorders of the genital apparatus in either sex are continually exciting disease in remote organs; and it is observed that as in women mild irritation—slight and limited disturbance—produces severer reflex trouble than coarse and grave lesions. In females, superficial disorder of the cervix, for example, often induces more annoying pains and distresses in the head than incurable cancers." "The Nature and Diagnosis of Neurasthenia (Nervous Exhaustion)," *New York Medical Journal: A Monthly Record of Medicine and the Collateral Sciences* 29 (March 1979): 233–35. One of the most extensive treatments of reflex insanity in women is Horatio Storer, *The Causation, Course, and Treatment of Reflex Insanity in Women* (1871: reprint, New York: Arno Press, 1972). Storer was a student of Simpson's and was surgeon to St. Elizabeth's and St. Francis's hospitals for women (in Boston) when he delivered this treatise to the AMA in 1865.

45. See W. Tyler Smith, *London Lancet* 2 (1848): 326.

46. Thomas Laycock, *A Treatise on the Nervous Diseases of Women: Comprising an Inquiry into the Nature, Causes, and Treatment of Spinal and Hysterical Disorders* (London: Longman, Orme, Brown, Green, and Longmans, 1840), p. 150.

47. In 1860, Dr. Stephen Tracy remarked of women: "The nerves themselves are smaller, and of a more delicate structure. They are endowed with greater sensibility, and, of course, are liable to more frequent and

stronger impressions from external agents or mental influences." Tracy, *The Mother and Her Offspring,* quoted in Smith-Rosenberg and Rosenberg, "Female Animal," p. 13.

48. See Laycock, *Treatise,* pp. 76, 126.

49. See *London Lancet* 2 (1848): 208. Here is Dr. Robert Brudenell Carter, writing in 1853 on female emotionalism: "If the relative power of emotion against the sexes be compared in the present day, even without including the erotic passion, it is seen to be considerably greater in the woman than in the man, partly from that natural conformation which causes the former to feel, under circumstances where the latter thinks; and partly because the woman is more often under the necessity of endeavouring to conceal her feelings. But when sexual desire is taken into account, it will add immensely to the forces bearing upon the female, who is often much under its dominion; and who, if unmarried and chaste, is compelled to restrain every manifestation of its sway." Quoted in Ilza Veith, *Hysteria: The History of a Disease* (Chicago: University of Chicago Press, 1965), pp. 201–2. Here is Thomas Laycock on female cunning: "One of the most remarkable of the faculties developed during the gererative nisus, and peculiar to the females of the higher classes of animals, is their artfulness; and this seems to be given them in place of those weapons of offence and defence with which the males are so generally provided. Indeed the less muscular power, want of defensive weapons, and exalted perceptive faculties of females, would naturally excite into action timidity and cunning. This is strikingly obvious in the human female in general." (*Treatise,* p. 72).

50. *London Lancet* 2 (1848): 208.

51. Horatio Storer remarks: "The wise old physician was not far wrong in his judgment: 'What is woman? Disease, says Hippocrates' " (*Reflex,* p. 152).

52. *London Lancet* 2 (1848): 330.

53. From "Insanity Produced by Seduction" (1866), quoted G. J. Barker-Benfield, *The Horrors of the Half-Known Life: Male Attitudes towards Women and Sexuality in Nineteenth-Century America* (New York: Harper and Row, 1976), p. 83. Storer refers to John Charles Bucknill as saying: "Every medical man has observed the extraordinary amount of obscenity in thought and language which breaks forth from the most modest and well-nurtured woman under the influence of puerperal mania; and although it may be courteous and politic to join in the wonder of those around, that such impurities could ever enter such a mind, and while he repudiates Pope's slander, that 'every woman is at heart a rake,' he will nevertheless acknowledge that religious and moral principles alone give strength to the female mind; and that, when these are weakened or removed by disease, the subterranean fires become active, and the crater gives forth smoke and flame" (*Reflex,* p. 109). For a view of twentieth-century ideas about hysteria, see Pierre Janet, *The Major Symptoms of Hysteria: Fifteen Lectures Given in the Medical School of Harvard University,* 2d ed. (1920; reprint, New York: Hafner Publishing, 1965); Thomas S. Szasz, *The Myth*

of Mental Illness: Foundations of a Theory of Personal Conduct (New York: Harper and Row, 1961), pp. 21–163; and Alec Roy, ed., *Hysteria* (Chichester, England: John Wiley and Sons, 1982).

54. *London Lancet* 1 (1848): 376.

55. *Lancet* 2 (1854): 495.

56. Samuel Gregory, *Man-Midwifery Exposed* (1848), in *The Male-Midwife and the Female Doctor: The Gynecology Controversy in Nineteenth-Century America* (reprint, New York: Arno Press, 1974), Preface, Frontispiece, p. 46. Here is George Gregory, writing in 1852: "The distinction of sex is laid in human nature, fixed by the creating hand, and on it are founded many of the most interesting relations and duties of life; it must, therefore, be preserved inviolate, or the social fabric will be overthrown. God has decreed that every man shall have his own wife free from mercenary or other pollution, and no tampering of the medical faculty can for a moment be permitted without destruction to the marriage compact." George Gregory, *Medical Morals, Illustrated with Plates and Extracts from Medical Works; Designed to Show the Pernicious Social and Moral Influence of the Present System of Medical Practice, and the Importance of Establishing Female Medical Colleges, and Educating and Employing Female Physicians for Their Own Sex,* in Samuel Gregory, *The Male-Midwife and the Female Doctor,* p. 47. See also Samuel Dickson, *The Destructive Art of Healing, or, Facts for Families,* 3d ed. (London, 1853), esp. pp. 39–45; and John Stevens, *Man-Midwifery Exposed; or, the Danger and Immorality of Employing Men in Midwifery Proved; and the Remedy for the Evil Found* (London, 1865).

57. *Lancet* 2 (1847): 371.

58. Ibid. James Hobson Aveling cites an 1869 report of the Council of the Obstetrical Society of London as finding that among the agricultural poor, "a large proportion, varying from thirty to ninety percent, is attended by midwives." In small, nonmanufacturing towns, the percentage was lower; in large provincial and especially in manufacturing towns, the rate was again 30 percent to 90 percent. In London, in the east 30 percent to 50 percent of the poor were attended by midwives; in west London only 2 percent or fewer women were attended by midwives. See Aveling, *English Midwives: Their History and Prospects* (1872; reprint, London: Hugh K. Elliott, 1967), p. 164. For discussions of midwives, see also Jean Donnison, *Midwives and Medical Men: A History of Inter-Professional Rivalries and Women's Rights* (New York: Schocken, 1977); and Jane B. Donegan, *Women and Men Midwives: Medicine, Morality, and Misogyny in Early America* (Westport, Conn.: Greenwood Press, 1978).

59. *Lancet* 2 (1847): 371. Margaret Versluysen argues that an important part of this transformation in obstetrics involved the doctor's access to lower-class patients in lying-in hospitals. These patients could not afford to exercise modesty to the same extent as women paying for the doctor's attendance, so medical men could develop techniques of "touching" and physical examinations in these hospitals that they then took to middle-class patients. See Versluysen, "Midwives, Medical Men and 'Poor Women La-

bouring of Child': Lying-in Hospitals in Eighteenth-Century London," in Helen Roberts, ed., *Women, Health and Reproduction* (London: Routledge and Kegan Paul, 1981), pp. 18–49. The first lying-in hospitals in London were the British Lying-in Hospital (1749), the City of London Lying-in Hospital (1750), Queen Charlotte's (1752), the Royal Maternity Hospital (1759), and the General Lying-in Hospital (1765). For a discussion of admission procedures to these charity hospitals, see F. B. Smith, *People's Health,* pp. 34–40.

60. William Harvey, Peter Chamberlen, and William Hunter are the "fathers" of obstetrics, according to Smith. *Lancet* 2 (1847): 458–60.

61. For a typical antimidwife account, see *Lancet* 1 (1848): 122–23. Here the midwife, acting "in a supercilious, half-drunken ignorant manner," is unable to deliver the child because of its presentation. Dr. Moore is called in by worried neighbors, and, once he surveys the situation, he tries to leave to get his equipment. But "there was no egress for me, the door being locked, as they feared I should perhaps leave them in the lurch." Dr. Moore administers chloroform and delivers the child alive. He concludes his account by stating that "there can, I think, be scarcely a doubt that the midwife's conduct deserves the severest reprehension."

W. Tyler Smith advocates "principles" in his first obstetric lecture. *Lancet* 2 (1847): 373.

62. One correspondent to the *Lancet* remarked in 1842 that "the information of the medical profession, generally, on matters of natural science, is very little greater than that of the people at large. This is an extremely humiliating fact." Quoted in Youngson, *Scientific Revolution in Victorian Medicine,* p. 16. On the limitations of the authority accorded to medical men, see Peterson, *Medical Profession,* 34–39; and Youngson, *Scientific Revolution in Victorian Medicine,* pp. 9–41.

63. See Peterson, *Medical Profession,* pp. 5–29. For a discussion of the limits of the power of various colleges and licensing bodies, see *Lancet* 2 (1847): 480–81, 483, 507.

64. See Peterson, *Medical Profession,* pp. 30–39. When the Medical Act was finally passed in 1858, it was not the reform generally hoped for by general practitioners. The act created a General Council of Medical Education and Registration, which for the first time united representatives of all three medical corporations and gave a single governing body responsibility for supervising medical education throughout Great Britain. But the act also left intact the hierarchical organization of the profession and the powers of the corporations because it left the power to grant licenses in the hands of the corporations. The General Medical Council's role was largely supervisory and advisory. See also *Lancet* 2 (1858): 124–29, for an article on the Medical Registration Act.

65. See Peterson, *Medical Profession,* pp. 5–39; and Waddington, "General Practitioners," pp. 165–68.

66. Waddington, "General Practitioners," pp. 170–72; and S. W. F.

Holloway, "Medical Education in England, 1830–1858: A Sociological Analysis," *History* 49 (1964): 299–324.

67. Remarking on the importance of women to the general practitioner, J. H. Aveling noted that "women, as you know, enjoy, and always find time for, gossip with one another. . . . Woe to the unhappy practitioner who has failed in his treatment of their troubles; his condemnation will be widely heard. On the other hand he who has been successful will have the trumpet of fame sounded with extravagant force." Quoted in Peterson, *Medical Profession,* p. 129.

68. Quoted in Donnison, *Midwives and Medical Men,* p. 47. Here is Sir Henry Halford, president of the Royal College of Physicians, in 1834: "I think it [midwifery] is considered rather as a manual operation and that we should be very sorry to throw anything like a discredit upon the men who have been educated at the Universities, who have taken time to acquire their improvement of their minds in literary and scientific acquirements, by mixing it up with this manual labour. I think it would rather disparage the highest grade of the profession, to let them engage in that particular branch, which is a manual operation very much." Quoted in Waddington, "General Practitioners," p. 177. Aveling gives a sense of the longevity of this male aversion to female bodies when he cites the translator's introduction to Roesslin's *The Birth of Mankynde,* the first midwifery book to be translated from Latin to English (1540). "Many think that it is not meete ne fitting such matters to be intreated of so plainly in our mother and vulgar language, to the dishonour (as they say) of womanhood and the derision of their own secrets, by the detection and discovering whereof, men it reading or hearing, shall be moved thereby, the more to abhorte and loathe the company of women, every boy and knave reading them as openly as the tales of 'Robin Hood' " (*Midwives,* pp. 10–11).

69. *Lancet* 2 (1847): 451–54. See also pp. 479–83, 533–36, and 559–63.

70. Ibid., p. 371.

71. The only quotation I have found from a woman that approaches a description of how labor or chloroform felt appears in 1848. "I give the patient's description of her feelings in her own words," John Beaumont writes. " 'Up to the time of inhaling, the pains were most severe, and were becoming insupportable; but they appeared to do no good. I felt as if there were an insuperable bar across, which effectually resisted the force of the pains, and I felt in despair; but from the moment that I became under its [chloroform's] influence, that resistance appeared to give way, and every effort seemed successful' " *London Lancet* 2 (1848): 398. Despite this quotation, this letter to the *Lancet* is typical in Beaumont's assertion that it is the "province of the physician" to decide whether to administer chloroform *and* in his implicit anxiety that such control will not remain with the doctor if patients have their way. Note his final reference to "a lady of high moral and religious feeling" who "did not scruple to make [the administration of chloroform] almost the condition of [his] attending her." Luckily, Beau-

mont's compliance still left him authority, for it made the woman "thankful" rather than assertive.

The argument against asking women to report on their own sensations under chloroform was not, incidentally, based on a person's inability to narrate unconsciousness. Many patients were not anesthetized into complete unconsciousness, for insensibility to pain could be induced before the disruption of consciousness by administering a light dose. Moreover, some doctors do report on the sensations chloroform caused when they administered it to themselves, and these descriptions are certainly not distinguished by language more technical or detailed than an intelligent layperson might have been able to provide. See *London Lancet* 2 (1848): 122.

72. See Simpson, "Report on the Results," p. 164; *Lancet* 2 (1847): 122; *Lancet* 1 (1853): 609. Here is W. Tyler Smith on the link between the female reproductive system and maternal instinct: "In the higher mammalia, a true vascular connexion is formed between the ovum and the mother by means of . . . the mucous membrane of the uterus; and the embryo, after a prolonged term of inter-uterine development, is expelled to pass through another protracted phase of maternal nutrition from the mammae. . . . The generative organs reach their greatest state of development in the human species, and consist of parts adapted to coitus, ovulation, menstruation, impregnation, utero-gestation, parturition, and lactation—functions which are placed in relation to the highest affection and parental love." *Lancet* 1 (1856): 4. Thomas Laycock links reproductive physiology and maternal instinct with this statement: "The desire for sexual congress, the secretion of milk, and the love of offspring, are equally the results of the same reproductive effort" (*Essay on Hysteria,* p. 64).

73. Here is Dr. John Conolly, whom Storer cites with approval, on the extension of a physician's domain: "The physician's office is assuming in these times a higher character in proportion as he ceases to be a mere prescriber of medicines, and acts as the guardian or conservator of public and of private health; studious of all agencies that influence the body and the mind, and which, affecting individual comfort and longevity, act widely on societies of human beings." Quoted in Storer, *Reflex,* p. 174. This extension of a physician's territory is also intimately connected to the definition of various nervous or mental afflictions as diseases. Thomas Laycock, for example, wants to treat a woman's bad temper as a medical disorder: "Irritability of temper in the nervous and delicate should always be treated *as a disease;* that is, by medicine, regimen, air and exercise, soothing kindness, and gentle authority. . . . Irritability of temper is as much a disease as insanity" (*Treatise,* p. 352). See also Vieda Skultans, *Madness and Morals: Ideas on Insanity in the Nineteenth Century* (London: Routledge and Kegan Paul, 1975), pp. 9–23.

74. *Lancet* 2 (1847): 481. Burrows estimated that there were four hundred to five hundred unlicensed physicians practicing in London and the provinces (p. 561).

75. The threat perceived by the medical men who attended nervous or hysterical women is discussed in Carroll Smith-Rosenberg, "The Hysterical Women: Sex Roles and Role Conflict in Nineteenth-Century America," *Social Research* 39 (1972): 663 and 674, esp.

76. *Lancet* 1 (1855): 205, 206. Skey recommends examining a patient's spine for pain as a means of detecting true (organic) disorder.

77. Jules Falret, *Etudes cliniques sur les maladies mentales et nerveuses,* 1890. Quoted in Veith, *Hysteria,* p. 211.

78. Quoted in S. Weir Mitchell, *Fat and Blood: An Essay on the Treatment of Certain Forms of Neurasthenia and Hysteria,* 1st ed., 1877; 4th ed. (Philadelphia: J. B. Lippincott, 1885), p. 49.

79. *Lancet* 2 (1847): 574.

80. Simpson, "Report of the Results," p. 165. See also pp. 160−63, 166, 169, and 170.

81. *Lancet* 1 (1848): 163.

82. *Lancet* 2 (1847): 677.

83. Ibid., p. 626. Protheroe Smith seconds this warning when he says: "Accoucheurs will, ere long, have to submit to the demand of their patients to be relieved from the agony of childbirth . . . the question will no longer be whether anaesthetic agents shall be employed, but which of them shall be preferred" (p. 574).

84. *Lancet* 1 (1853): 609.

85. Veith, *Hysteria,* p. 204.

86. George Gregory, *Medical Morals,* p. 47.

87. The debate about *whether* women experience sexual feelings, and orgasm in particular, emerges in this period partly because of the ambiguity inherent in conceptualizing female sexuality according to a model of male sexuality. Strictly speaking, if female sexuality is analogous anatomically, then women should have erections and ejaculate; many medical men, in fact, asserted that this was the case. But if women do not have these physical signs, as other medical men asserted, then they must not experience sexuality at all. This is the position held by Dr. William Acton. See *The Functions and Disorders of the Reproductive Organs in Youth, in Adult Age, and in Advanced Life: Considered in Their Physiological, Social, and Moral Relations* (London:John Churchill, 1857). See also Degler, "What Ought to Be," pp. 40−53; Nancy F. Cott, "Passionlessness: An Interpretation of Victorian Sexual Ideology," *Signs* 4 (1978): 219−36; Peter T. Cominus, "Innocent Femina Sensualis in Unconscious Conflict," in Martha Vicinus, ed., *Suffer and Be Still* (Bloomington: University of Indiana Press, 1972), pp. 155−72; and Jean L'Esperance, "Doctors and Women in Nineteenth-Century Society: Sexuality and Role," in Woodward and Richards, *Health Care and Popular Medicine,* pp. 112−16.

Chapter 3. Caroline Norton and the 1857 Matrimonial Causes Act

1. Leonore Davidoff and Catherine Hall, *Family Fortunes: Men and Women of the English Middle Class, 1780–1850* (Chicago: University of Chicago Press, 1987), p. 275. See also chap. 4 and 6.

2. See Paul Q. Hirst, "Introduction," in Bernard Edelman, *Ownership of the Image: Elements for a Marxist Theory of Law,* trans. Elizabeth Kingdom (London: Routledge and Kegan Paul, 1979), p. 1. For an introduction to some of the complexities of the British legal system, see William Geldart, *Introduction to English Law,* 9th ed., ed. D. C. M. Yardley (Oxford: Oxford University Press, 1984).

3. See Susan S. M. Edwards, *Female Sexuality and the Law: A Study of Constructs of Female Sexuality as They Inform Statute and Legal Procedure* (Oxford: Martin Robertson, 1981), p. 49.

4. The three best recent studies of the history of divorce and the 1857 Matrimonial Causes Act are Dorothy M. Stetson, *A Woman's Issue: The Politics of Family Law Reform in England* (Westport, Conn.: Greenwood Press, 1982), chap. 1; Lee Holcombe, *Wives and Property: Reform of the Married Women's Property Law in Nineteenth-Century England* (Toronto: University of Toronto Press, 1983), chap. 5; and Mary Shanley, " 'One Must Ride Behind': Married Women's Rights and the Divorce Act of 1857," *Victorian Studies* 25 (Spring 1982): 355–76.

5. The ecclesiastical courts could also grant divorce *a vinculo matrimonii* (from the bonds of matrimony) when either the husband or the wife petitioned that the marriage was null and void because of some defect existing from its beginning. Relevant defects included kinship within the prohibited degrees, physical incompetence, and insanity. Such divorces allowed both parties to remarry and declared their children illegitimate. See Holcombe, *Wives and Property,* p. 94.

6. Parliamentary divorce was created in part because of the difficulty propertied men experienced in obtaining a divorce, when children and property were concerned, in a period in which property and legitimate, patrilinear inheritance were critical to the economic consolidation of families. What is generally held to be the first petition to Parliament for divorce *a vinculo* was not actually a bill for divorce, but a bill to allow Lord Roos (John Manners) to set aside the bond required by the ecclesiastical court when it granted him divorce *a mensa* so that he could remarry. Entitled "An Act for Lord Roos to Marry Again," the bill was passed in 1669.

The first genuine divorce bill was passed in 1697 to enable Lord Macclesfield to divorce the countess of Macclesfield, Richard Savage's mother. The first divorce bill granted after an ecclesiastical judgment granting divorce *a mensa* was for Mr. Box in 1701. According to a mid-nineteenth-century commentator, this precedent-setting case "gave rise to an opinion that nothing short of an Act of Parliament could dissolve an English marriage—an opinion which, though owing its birth to an accident, is now as firmly settled as if it had been determined upon solemn deliberation by the highest court of justice in the realm." *Law Review, and Quarterly Journal of British and Foreign Jurisprudence* 1 (1844–45): 365; see also pp. 362–66. On the general history of divorce, see William Latey, *The Tide of Divorce* (London: Longman, 1970); O. R. McGregor, *Divorce in England: A Centenary Study* (London: Heinemann, 1957); and Gellert Spencer Alleman, *Matrimonial Laws and the Materials of Restoration Comedy* (Wallingford, Pa.: privately published, 1942), esp. pp. 113–14.

7. Sybil Wolfram disputes this figure. Her painstaking research suggests, in fact, that divorce was not nearly as costly as almost all official commentators claimed and that it was sought and obtained by members of the middle and working classes. The fact remains, however, that the misperception about the expense of divorce was repeated by legislators, lawyers, and judges; whether the mistake was intentional or not is unclear. See Wolfram, "Divorce in England, 1700–1857," *Oxford Journal of Legal Studies* 5 (1985): 155–86.

8. Quoted in Stetson, *A Woman's Issue*, p. 27. Holcombe states that "only one or two divorces were granted by parliament each year—134 in the eighteenth century, and 90 in the nineteenth century (before the reform of 1857)" (*Wives and Property*, p. 96). Wolfram disputes this. See "Divorce in England."

9. *Hansard's Parliamentary Debates*, 3d series, vol. 84; 5/20/56, 414. All future references to the *Parliamentary Debates* are cited in the text by date and column number.

10. See *Hansard* 8/13/57, 1552.

11. This argument is forcefully made by Rachel Harrison and Frank Mort in "Patriarchal Aspects of Nineteenth-Century State Formation: Property Relations, Marriage and Divorce, and Sexuality," in Philip Corrigan, ed., *Capitalism, State Formation and Marxist Theory: Historical Investigations* (London: Quartet Books, 1980), pp. 79–109. One of the primary nineteenth-century arguments about the divorce procedures was that the established Church should not have jurisdiction over divorce when fewer than one-third of the population belonged to the Anglican church and when the state recognized both civil marriage and marriages solemnized by Nonconformist ministers.

12. *Hansard* 5/19/57, 501–2. Lyndhurst also argues that, even though women *can* introduce "spurious offspring," they should not be denied the right to petition for divorce on that basis alone. Because of this legal restriction, wives might have no recourse whatsoever against their husbands' cruelty, flagrant adultery, or desertion.

13. J. W. Kaye, "The 'Non-Existence' of Women," *North British Review* 18 (August 1855): 292.

14. Lyndhurst quoted Caroline Norton in the Lords but referred to her only as "an eloquent writer." See *Hansard* 5/20/56, 415; for other allusions to Norton, see 5/25/57, 780–85 and 6/9/57, 1411. Stetson discusses Norton's influence in *A Woman's Issue*, pp. 31–36, 41, and 47–50.

15. For biographical discussions of Caroline Norton, see Alice Acland, *Caroline Norton* (London: Constable, 1948); and Jane Gray Perkins, *The Life of the Honourable Mrs. Norton* (New York: Henry Holt, 1909).

16. Caroline Norton, *A Letter to the Queen on Lord Chancellor Cranworth's Marriage and Divorce Bill* (London: Longman, Brown, Green and Longmans, 1855), pp. 4, 13; reprinted in *Selected Writings of Caroline Norton: Facsimile Reproductions with an Introduction and Notes by James O. Hoge and Jane Marcus* (Delmar, N.Y.: Scholar's Facsimiles and Reprints, 1978).

17. *Caroline Norton's Defense: English Laws for Women in the Nineteenth Century* (1854; reprint, Chicago: Academy Press, 1982), p. 3. All future references cited in the text by page number.

18. For a pertinent discussion of nineteenth-century melodrama, see Peter Brooks, *The Melodramatic Imagination: Balzac, Henry James, Melodrama, and the Mode of Excess* (New Haven: Yale University Press, 1976), chaps. 1 and 2. Brooks argues that melodrama "tends to become the dramaturgy of virtue misprized and eventually recognized" (p. 27). "In a striking number of cases," he continues, "this recognition requires a full-fledged trial, the public hearing and judgment of right against wrong, where virtue's advocates deploy all arms to win the victory of truth over appearance and to explain the deep meaning of enigmatic and misleading signs" (p. 31). Brooks's comment about the villain of melodrama could be a description of the threat George Norton poses: "the force of evil in melodrama derives from its personalized menace, its swift execution of its declaration of intent, its reduction of innocence to powerlessness" (p. 34); his discussion of the source of melodrama's hyperbole sheds an interesting light on the psychological underpinnings of Caroline Norton's self-presentation in the Westminster courtroom: "Evil's moment of spectacular power—when it imposes its rule and drives out innocence—provides a simulacrum of the 'primal scene.' It is a moment of intense, originary trauma that leaves virtue stunned and humiliated. . . . The familial structure that melodrama (like Greek tragedy) so often exploits contributes to the experience of excruciation: the most basic loyalties and relationships become a source of torture" (pp. 34–35). On the subject of melodrama in the nineteenth century, see also Judith Walkowitz, *Jack the Ripper's London* (Chicago: University of Chicago Press; copublished with Virago Press, forthcoming). Davidoff and Hall point out that the Queen Caroline adultery scandal was represented by the press as a melodrama. See *Family Fortunes,* pp. 150–55.

19. I am indebted for this point to a paper by Teri Silvio, "The Male Representing the Female Representing Herself: Wilkie Collins and Caroline Norton," Bryn Mawr College, 1985, pp. 6–7.

20. In 1856, Barbara Bodichon's Married Women's Property Committee secured thirty thousand signatures on a similar petition, and in 1857 she presented twenty-four thousand more. For a reprint of the 14 March 1856 petition, see Holcombe, *Wives and Property,* appendix 1, pp. 237–38.

21. Quoted in Holcombe, *Wives and Property,* p. 88.

22. Holcombe, *Wives and Property,* contains the best recent discussion of the various married women's property bills and the debates surrounding their passage; see especially pp. 88–165. Other twentieth-century discussions of this issue include Albert Venn Dicey, *Lectures on the Relation between Law and Public Opinion in England during the Nineteenth Century* (London: Macmillan, 1905), pp. 369–93; and Stetson, *A Woman's Issue,* pp. 54–96. Mid-nineteenth-century articles of special interest include "Property of Married Women," *English Woman's Journal* 1 (1858): 58–59; and "The Property of Married Women," *Westminster Review* 66 (October 1856): 181–97.

23. Quoted in Dicey, *Lectures,* p. 373.

24. Davidoff and Hall, *Family Fortunes,* pp. 209–11.

25. Ibid., chap. 6.

26. Ibid., p. 511, n. 13.

27. See Stetson, *A Woman's Issue,* pp. 61–62; Holcombe, *Wives and Property,* p. 91.

28. While the explicit legal opposition is between men and *married* women, the implicit opposition is between men and women—not only because an unmarried woman was legally her father's ward, but also because marriage was generally held to be the natural destiny of all women, that legal state in which a woman became what she was biologically destined to be. The normative status of married women helps account for the distress provoked by the 1851 Census, which revealed a "surplus" of women—hence that every woman could not possibly become a "normal" woman.

A related discussion of the position women occupied in the Victorian symbolic economy can be found in Nancy Cott, *The Bonds of Womanhood: "Woman's Sphere" in New England, 1780–1835* (New Haven: Yale University Press, 1977) chap. 2.

29. Here is Sir Henry Sumner Maine in 1861: "The child before years of discretion, the orphan under guardianship, the adjudged lunatic, have all their capacities and incapacities regulated by the Law of Persons. But why? The reason is differently expressed in the conventional language of different systems, but in substance it is stated to the same effect by all. The great majority of Jurists are constant to the principle that the classes of persons just mentioned are subject to extrinsic control on the single ground that they do not possess the faculty of forming a judgment on their own interests; in other words, they are wanting in the first essential of an engagement by Contract." Maine, *Ancient Law,* quoted in Tony Tanner, *Adultery in the Novel: Contract and Transgression* (Baltimore: Johns Hopkins University Press, 1979), pp. 4–5. The justification typically offered for including women in this category is that their interests are identical to those of their father or husband. That Maine's argument about the inability to recognize or act on their own interests *actually* underwrites including women in this group is argued forcefully by William Thompson. See *Appeal of One-Half the Human Race, Women, against the Pretensions of the Other Half, Men, to Retain Them in Political, and Thence in Civil and Domestic, Slavery* (London: Virago Press, 1983), pp. 25–113.

30. Before abolition, slaves were commodities too, and the analogy between slaves and women was a staple of arguments for extending women's rights. Caroline Norton makes this analogy in the beginning of *English Laws;* see pp. 15–17. For a discussion of nineteenth-century arguments about slavery and workers, on the one hand, and slavery and women, on the other, see Catherine Gallagher, *The Industrial Reformation of English Fiction: Social Discourse and Narrative Form, 1832–1867* (Chicago: University of Chicago Press, 1985).

31. Davidoff and Hall, *Family Fortunes,* pp. 211–13.

32. "Protective legislation" is a phrase that was used at midcentury to refer both to labor legislation like the 1840s mining and Short Hours legislation and to laws that recognized "a parent's interest in respect to his daughter's chastity." This phrase is from a review, published in the *Law Review* in 1854, of a book entitled *Prize Essay on the Laws for the Protection of Women* by James Edward Davies, barrister. The book treats the subjects of seduction, rape, and prostitution in terms of the father's rights to his daughter's services or the equivalent monetary compensation. "If the father loses the benefit or profit of his daughter's services through the act of her seducer, his right to damages accrues, and a jury is directed to award him compensation for the consequential injury he has sustained." "The Laws Relating to Women," in *Law Review* 20 (1854): 10, 11. For recent discussions of such protective legislation, see Susan Staves, "British Seduced Maidens," *Eighteenth-Century Studies* 14 (Winter 1980–81): 109–34; idem, "Money for Honor: Damages for Criminal Conversation," in Harry C. Payne, ed., *Studies in Eighteenth-Century Culture* (Madison: University of Wisconsin Press, 1982) 11: 179–97.

33. John Locke, *The Second Treatise of Government: An Essay concerning the True, Original, Extent, and End of Civil Government,* ed. Thomas P. Peardon (Indianapolis: Bobbs-Merrill, 1952), p. 17.

34. See Wai-che Dimock, *Empire of Liberty* (Princeton: Princeton University Press, forthcoming).

35. Peter Gaskell, *The Manufacturing Population of England, Its Moral, Social, and Physical Conditions, and the Changes Which Have Arisen from the Use of Steam Machinery; with an Examination of Infant Labour* (1833; reprint, New York: Arno Press, 1972), p. 270.

36. Here is W. R. Greg on the differences between male and female sexual desire. "Women's *desires* scarcely ever lead to their fall; for (save in a class of whom we shall speak presently) the desire scarcely exists in a definite and conscious form, till they *have* fallen. In this point there is a radical and essential difference between the sexes: the arrangements of nature and the customs of society would be even more unequal than they are, were it not so. In men, in general, the sexual desire is inherent and spontaneous, and belongs to the condition of puberty. In the other sex, the desire is dormant, if not non-existent, till excited; almost always till excited by actual intercourse. . . . Women whose position and education have protected them from exciting causes, constantly pass through life

without ever been [*sic*] cognizant of the promptings of the senses. Happy for them it is so! . . . Were it not for this kind decision of nature, which, in England, has been assisted by that correctness of feeling which pervades our education, the consequences would, we believe, be frightful. If the passions of women were ready, strong, and spontaneous, in a degree even remotely approaching the form they assume in the coarser sex, there can be little doubt that sexual irregularities would reach a height, of which, at present, we have happily no conception." When women do fall into pros-titution, Greg continues, it is because "they yield to desires in which they do not share, from a weak generosity which cannot refuse anything to the passionate entreaties of the man they love. There is in the warm fond heart of woman a strange and sublime unselfishness, which men too commonly discover only to profit by,—a positive love of self-sacrifice,—an active, so to speak, an *aggressive* desire to show their affection, by giving up to those who have won it something they hold very dear." *Westminster Review* 53 (July 1850): 241–43, 244. In the parliamentary debates about divorce, the bishop of Oxford gives another version of this commonplace about female desire when he says that women desire "only the desire of the man." "In the man," he con-tinues, "the great temptation [is] the gratification of appetite; but it [*is*] not so in the woman. . . . The woman is led astray, not by the direct temptation of sensual appetite, but by the proffer of affection" (6/9/57, 1417). Gladstone re-peats much the same formula in the Commons on 8 July 1857.

37. Lord St. Leonards, ex-chancellor, insisted on including in the Divorce Act a provision protecting deserted wives from their husbands' taking their property, because, he said, this would prevent "a greater evil"—passage of the Married Women's Property Bill. Quoted in Holcombe, *Wives and Property,* p. 102.

38. Kaye, " 'Non-Existence' of Women," p. 295.

39. For a discussion of the relationship between gender and genre during this period, see Nancy Armstrong, "The Rise of Feminine Authority in the Novel," *Novel* 15 (Winter 1982): 127–45.

40. The review of Caroline Norton's *Letter to the Queen* in *Law Review* points to the potentially subversive nature of her emotional lan-guage. "Such are the charms of her style that, we may have cause to dread, lest, where we agree with the writer, we may be led away by our feelings, and not influenced by our judgment. . . . We must take some time, as it were to cool, before we find out what we think on the subject, as distin-guished from what we feel: we have to separate the logician from the poetess, the law-reformer from the woman, before we can even re-arrange our own theories." "Woman's Law.—Mrs. Norton's *Letter to the Queen,*" *Law Review* 23 (1855): 334.

41. Susan Staves, *Players' Scepters: Fictions of Authority in the Resto-ration* (Lincoln: University of Nebraska Press, 1979), p. 151.

42. Ibid., p. 155.

43. In "The 'Non-Existence' of Women," J. W. Kaye makes this ab-solutely clear when he argues that no "evil" can come of granting what

Norton wants because the laws will still be administered by men. "As sentence of divorce can only be pronounced by a competent tribunal, and that tribunal, whatever the law may be, will consist of men, we do not see what evil, which cannot practically be held in check, can result from the equalization for which Mrs. Norton contends" (p. 293).

44. Here is Caroline Norton on the sexual double standard: "Now it is consistent with all the discretion of justice, that far greater leniency should be *practically* extended, to a sex whose passions, habits of life, and greater laxity of opinions, make their temptations greater and their resistance less, than is the case among women; and a proportionate severity may well be shewn to that other sex, whose purity is of infinitely greater importance" (*English Laws,* pp. 152–53).

45. For the interesting parliamentary debate about this point, see *Hansard* 8/7/57, 1262–63, 1265–66.

46. Interesting debates about this issue are in *Hansard* 5/25/57, 796–97; 8/7/57, 1230–35; 8/13/57, 1587–90.

47. See "Property of Married Women," *English Woman's Journal* 1 (1858): 58; and "The New Law of Divorce," *English Woman's Journal* 1 (1858): 186.

48. When the first Married Women's Property Act was passed in 1870, it did not really disturb this alignment, for in maintaining the provision of coverture and the category of separate property, it continued to equate married women and the property they owned. By the 1880s, economic, social, and ideological factors had finally combined to pose a substantial challenge to the sexual double standard so crucial to these oppositions. The midcentury religious revival that focused the middle classes' attention on prostitution initiated this challenge, and, by the 1860s, the campaign for repeal of the Contagious Diseases Acts had sharpened this challenge into a specific, well-publicized campaign. Couching its arguments in medical and moral language, the Ladies National Association capitalized on widespread anxieties about the relationship between male and female promiscuity, social problems like disease and urban overcrowding, and unstable class relations. The public campaign against the acts, which continued into the 1880s, demonstrated the extent to which the conceptualization of sexuality could be effectively challenged by a determined, organized special interest group. See Judith R. Walkowitz, *Prostitution and Victorian Society: Women, Class, and the State* (Cambridge: Cambridge University Press, 1980), esp. pp. 42–45, 70–100. The language of sexual relations continued to function as a discourse for discussing other kinds of social and power relations, but by the 1880s the terms of the discourse no longer derived unproblematically from what seemed to be a fixed binary opposition of male and female. This was made clear by the emergence of sexology as a medical speciality in the 1880s and by the proliferation of sexual discussions that tried to reestablish the nature of sexual desire according not just to male and female oppositional norms, but also to a range of "perversions," "inversions," and "neurosis." See Jeffrey Weeks, *Sexuality and Its Discontents:*

Meanings, Myths and Modern Sexualities (London: Routledge and Kegan Paul, 1985), esp. pp. 61—95. The passage of the 1882 Married Women's Property Act was just one sign of the extent to which the realignment of social, legal, economic, and sexual oppositions opened a space for consideration of women's legal and economic autonomy that was unthinkable two decades previously.

49. Jane Perkins says that Caroline Norton wrote letters to her husband signed "Hannah Moore"—in other words, that she participated in the joke. But Caroline never refers to these letters, and, since Perkins has the victim's last name wrong, I don't know whether this is true or not. In any case, Norton presents the joke as George's; this is clearly part of her vision of him as villain. See Perkins, *Life of the Hon. Mrs. Norton*, pp. 102.

50. This brief excerpt from one of George's Greenacre letters gives a sense of why Caroline was so outraged by his joke: "You had better make haste to seize the 500£. I offered, as I assure you it is in dangerous hands,—those of a man trying to furnish two houses at once, and of one very tired of his own lame legs, and arguing thus:—I Iave I not a stable with two delicious loose boxes? and have I not daily run from this place of Wilton to the Omnibus of Charing Cross? Am I not weary of my legs? and is there any more pleasure in my life? No, there is not; and I'll spend the money in horse flesh and curtains, if you don't look sharp. Pray *Mrs Brown*, how many chairs have you got—also tables? Have you e're a dining one? 'Pray come on Friday night; bring all you have got, and we'll be married on Christmas Day.' Your affectionate intended, 'GREENACRE.' " The Greenacre letters are reprinted in the section entitled "Letters, etc. Dated from June, 1836, to July, 1841. (Privately Printed)" in [Caroline Norton], *The Separation of Mother and Child by the Law of "Custody of Infants," Considered* (London: Roake and Varty, 1838).

51. [Caroline Norton], *Taxation, by an Irresponsible Taxpayer*, n.p., n.d., p. 30. I assume this pamphlet is privately printed; a note in Caroline Norton's hand in the copy in Yale University's Beinecke Library is dated 3 July 1874 and refers to the fact that the pamphlet is "only for parliamentary circulation."

52. The freedom of expression Norton enjoyed can be judged by contrasting her uninhibited self-justification to the censorship imposed on M.P.s by the rules of parliamentary discourse. These rules include both *Roberts' Rules of Order* and more specific injunctions—such as the rules against speaking Greek and against statements of too personal a kind. When, for example, the marquess of Westmeath began to rail in the Lords against his estranged wife, who had published a libelous attack on him, Lord Redesdale called him to order, reminding him that "it was hardly allowable to permit the noble Marquess to introduce matters in which he was personally concerned" (*Hansard* 5/25/57, 810—11).

The manner of reporting speeches made in Parliament constitutes another form of censorship—this time not on what M.P.s could say but on the form in which the speeches were available to the public (and posterity). The relative uniformity of tone and absence of idiosyncratic speech patterns or metaphorical language in *Hansard's Parliamentary Debates* is a function of the rules governing parliamentary reporting. Here is a description of these rules; note the kinds of revision that are considered "necessary": "Revision is limited to the correction of grammar, spelling, and punctuation, ensuring that the correct parliamentary forms are observed, striking out superfluous repetition, and making any amendments necessary in the interests of clarity, common sense, and good English. No material alterations may be made, nor any amendments which would in any way tend to change the sense of what has been spoken. The transcript must remain an accurate, and as far as possible an exact, report of what has been said. A certain amount of revision is bound to be necessary, however. For instance, the tangled sentence and confusion of ideas which are such common features of extempore speaking, particularly when subject to interruption, must be sorted out if they are to make sense when committed to paper; the split infinitive and other solecisms which frequently occur in speech must be corrected; the mixed metaphor and other varieties of *lapsus linguae,* those dreadful pitfalls in public speaking, must not be perpetrated in print; and the Member who refers to 'the Honourable and gallant Member' must have his error corrected in the transcript. The speeches of the poor speaker must be made to read as intelligibly as those of the master orator." N. Wilding and P. Laundry, "Hansard," in *An Encyclopaedia of Parliament* (London, 1958), p. 255. Such corrections, of course, confound the reader who is looking for slips of decorum, solecisms, and other "dreadful pitfalls" of unintended self-expression; this accounts, in large part, for the relative scarcity of textual analysis in my discussion of the parliamentary debates. For a history of the reporting of these debates, see H. Donaldson Jordan, "The Reports of Parliamentary Debates, 1803–1908," *Economica* 11 (1931): 437–49.

53. I am indebted for this observation to Anna Clark and Judith Walkowitz.

54. See Davidoff and Hall, *Family Fortunes,* pp. 272–315, for a discussion of the very real material and ideological restrictions on women's economic activities.

Chapter 4. *David Copperfield* and the Professional Writer

1. Raymond Williams discusses the history of "literature" in *Keywords: A Vocabulary of Culture and Society* (New York: Oxford University Press, 1976), pp. 15–54. See also Patrick Parrinder, *Authors and Authority: A Study of English Literary Criticism and Its Relation to Culture, 1750–1900* (London: Routledge and Kegan Paul, 1977), esp. pp. 20–21, 104; and Nancy Armstrong, *Desire and Domestic Fiction: A Political History of the Novel* (New York: Oxford University Press, 1987), chap. 3.

2. On the importance of the public press, see David Musselwhite,

"The Trial of Warren Hastings," in Francis Barker, Peter Hulme, Margaret Iversen, and Diana Loxley, eds., *Literature, Politics, and Theory: Papers from the Essex Conference, 1976–84* (London: Methuen, 1986), p. 92. See also Etienne Balibar and Pierre Macherey, "On Literature as an Ideological Form," in Robert Young, ed., *Untying the Text: A Post-Structuralist Reader* (Boston: Routledge and Kegan Paul, 1981), pp. 79–99.

3. Critics who have begun to investigate the historicity of subjectivity include Armstrong, *Desire and Domestic Fiction;* Clifford H. Siskin, *The Historicity of Romantic Discourse* (New York: Oxford University Press, 1988); Walter Benn Michaels, *The Gold Standard and the Logic of Naturalism* (Berkeley: University of California Press, 1987); and Catherine Belsey, "The Romantic Construction of the Unconscious," in Barker et al., *Literature, Politics and Theory,* pp. 57–76.

4. For a relevant discussion of this paradigm, see Armstrong, *Desire and Domestic Fiction,* Introduction and chap. 1.

5. Charles Dickens, *David Copperfield* (New York: Bantam Books, 1981), pp. 12, 14 15. All subsequent references to this edition will be cited by page number in the text. For a critical essay that complements my discussion of *David Copperfield,* see John O. Jordan, "The Social Sub-Text of *David Copperfield,*" *Dickens Studies Annual: Essays on Victorian Fiction* 14 (1985): 61–92.

6. I quote Wordsworth because this is the paradigm of individual growth that the English Romantic poets celebrated. See Siskin, *Historicity,* chap. 4. This paradigm becomes the basis for the Freudian model of subjectivity, which was articulated in the late nineteenth century.

7. Mr. Peggotty explicitly and repeatedly forgives Emily, but even his love becomes part of her punishment because it exacerbates her guilt.

8. At the end of this chapter and again in the next I return briefly to the concept of "literary men" to show how the efforts of women to become professional writers were limited and facilitated by this representation. For my more extended treatment of this subject, see *The Proper Lady and the Woman Writer: Ideology as Style in the Works of Mary Wollstonecraft, Mary Shelley, and Jane Austen* (Chicago: University of Chicago Press, 1984).

9. [J. W. Kaye], "*Pendennis:* The Literary Profession," *North British Review* 13 (August 1850): 371.

10. Ibid., p. 343.

11. See Parrinder, *Authors and Authority,* chap. 1. For a brief discussion of the technological developments in printing and papermaking, see Richard D. Altick, *The English Common Reader: A Social History of the Mass Reading Public, 1800–1900* (Chicago: University of Chicago Press, 1957), pp. 277–78.

12. See Parrinder, *Authors and Authority,* chap. 2.

13. Thomas Carlyle, "The Hero as Man of Letters: Johnson, Rousseau, Burns," in Archibald MacMechan, ed., *On Heroes, Hero-Worship, and the Heroic in History* (Boston: Ginn, 1901), p. 179. Carlyle earned two hundred guineas for the six lectures in this series.

14. "The Copyright Question," *Blackwood's Magazine* 51 (January 1842): 109.

15. "Public Patronage of Men of Letters," *Fraser's Magazine* 33 (January 1846): 58.

16. See Kathleen Tillotson, *The Novels of the Eighteen-Forties* (Oxford: Clarendon Press, 1954), p. 28; and Altick, *English Common Reader,* pp. 279–80. One of the most interesting discussions to date of the way in which Dickens's innovation transformed the book into a commodity is by N. N. Feltes in *Modes of Production of Victorian Novels* (Chicago: University of Chicago Press, 1986), chap. 1.

17. Quoted in Tillotson, *Novels,* p. 33.

18. See John A. Sutherland, *Victorian Novelists and Publishers* (Chicago: University of Chicago Press, 1976), chaps. 2 and 3.

19. As one sign of the extent to which novelists became interchangeable, note Dickens's comment that, if necessary, he could supply the next number of the Wilkie Collins novel being published in *All the Year Round.* "If [Collins] should break down," Dickens bragged, "I would go on with his story so that nobody should be any the wiser." Quoted in Sutherland, *Victorian Novelists,* p. 170. For a discussion of Dickens as a publisher, see Sutherland, chap. 8.

20. Ibid., chap. 1; and Altick, *English Common Reader,* chaps. 12 and 13.

21. To show just how possible—even logical—it would have been for the concept of intellectual property *not* to have been conceptualized so individualistically, Martha Woodmansee cites a 1753 definition of "book": "*Book,* either numerous sheets of white paper that have been stitched together in such a way that they can be filled with writing; or, a highly useful and convenient instrument constructed of printed sheets variously bound in cardboard, paper, vellum, leather, etc. for promoting the truth to another in such a way that it can be conveniently read and recognized. Many people work on this ware before it is complete and becomes an actual book in this sense. The scholar and the writer, the papermaker, the type founder, the typesetter and the printer, the proofreader, the publisher, the book binder, sometimes even the guilder and the brass-worker, etc. Thus many mouths are fed by this branch of manufacture." From *Allgemeines Oeconomisches Lexicon* by Georg Zinck; quoted in Woodmansee, "The Genius and the Copyright: Economic and Legal Conditions of the Emergence of the 'Author,'" *Eighteenth-Century Studies* 17 (1983–84): 425. See also pp. 445–47.

22. Kaye, *"Pendennis,"* p. 370.

23. "The Profession of Literature," *Westminster Review,* o.s., 58 (October 1852): 525.

24. Carlyle, "Man-of-Letters Hero," pp. 188–89.

25. For a discussion of the limited access members of the working class had to books, see Altick, *English Common Reader,* chap. 11.

26. See Jennifer Wicke, *Advertising Fictions* (New York: Columbia University Press, forthcoming), chap. 2.

27. "Charles Dickens and *David Copperfield*," *Fraser's Magazine* 42 (December 1850): 698.

28. "Charles Dickens," p. 700.

29. "Copyright Question," pp. 108–9.

30. Eight writers' organizations were founded between 1736 and 1843. For a list of these organizations, see Victor Bonham-Carter, *Authors by Profession* (Los Altos, Calif.: William Kaufmann, 1978), 1: 226–27, n. 35. See also 1: 80–86.

31. Robert L. Patten, *Charles Dickens and His Publishers* (Oxford: Oxford University Press, 1978), p. 19.

32. "Copyright Question," p. 108.

33. Ibid., p. 118.

34. See James J. Barnes, *Authors, Publishers and Politicians: The Quest for an Anglo-American Copyright Agreement, 1815–54* (London: Routledge and Kegan Paul, 1974), pp. 131–35.

35. Quoted in Bonham-Carter, *Authors*, 1: 78.

36. [Charles Neaves], "*Blackwood's* and Copyright in America," *Blackwood's Magazine* 63 (January 1848): 127.

37. Quoted in Bonham-Carter, *Authors*, 1: 78.

38. See Armstrong, *Desire and Domestic Fiction*, p. 81.

39. This helps explain both why male desire became the paradigm for Freud's model of "universal" psychological development and why female desire, that "dark continent," was assumed to follow a trajectory different than male desire.

40. E. S. Dallas, *The Gay Science* (London: Chapman and Hall, 1866), 2: 295.

41. "The Profession of the Teacher," *English Woman's Journal* 1 (March 1858): 8. In "What Should We Do with Our Old Maids?" Frances Power Cobbe summarized the situation as follows: "whether doctoresses are to be permitted or not, may be a question; but authoresses are already a guild, which, instead of opposition, has met the kindliest welcome. It is now a real profession to women as to men, to be writers." *Fraser's Magazine* 66 (November 1862): 609. I suggest in the next chapter that this is a simplification of women's place in the literary profession.

42. Armstrong, *Desire and Domestic Fiction* chap. 1 and *passim*.

43. See Elaine Showalter, *A Literature of Their Own: British Women Novelists from Brontë to Lessing* (Princeton: Princeton University Press, 1977); Sandra M. Gilbert and Susan Gubar, *The Madwoman in the Attic: The Woman Writer and the Nineteenth-Century Literary Imagination* (New Haven: Yale University Press, 1979); and Margaret Homans, *Bearing the Word: Language and Female Experience in Nineteenth-Century Women's Writing* (Chicago: University of Chicago Press, 1986).

Chapter 5. The Governess and *Jane Eyre*

1. For discussions of nineteenth-century governess novels, see Wanda F. Neff, *Victorian Working Women: An Historical and Literary Study of Women in British Industries and Professions, 1832–1850* (1929; reprint, New York: Humanities Press, 1966), pp. 153–74; Jerome Beaty, "*Jane Eyre* and Genre," *Genre* 10 (Winter 1977): 619–54; and Robert A. Colby, *Fiction with a Purpose: Major and Minor Nineteenth-Century Novels* (Bloomington: Indiana University Press, 1967); pp. 178–212. More theoretical discussions of the governess include: Shoshana Felman, "Turning the Screw of Interpretation," *Yale French Studies* 55/56 (1977): 94–207; and Jane Gallop, *The Daughter's Seduction: Feminism and Psychoanalysis* (Ithaca: Cornell University Press, 1982), pp. 141–48.

2. For the history of the Governesses' Benevolent Institution, see *The Story of the Governesses' Benevolent Institution* (Southwick, Sussex, England: Grange Press, 1962). The GBI (which was still in existence in 1962) was the second institution to address the governesses' plight. The first, the Governesses' Mutual Assurance Society, founded in 1829 to help governesses save for sickness, unemployment, and old age, did not fare well and dissolved in 1838. The GBI also got off to an uncertain start, and, largely because it had managed to save only about £100 in its first two years, was substantially reorganized in 1843 under the Rev. David Laing, chaplain of Middlesex Hospital and pastor of the Holy Trinity Church of Saint Pancras. The stated goals of the GBI were "to raise the character of governesses as a class, and thus improve the tone of Female Education; to assist Governesses in making provision for their old age; and to assist in distress and age those Governesses whose exertions for their parents, or families have prevented such a provision" (*Story of the GBI*, p. 14). What is interesting about these goals is the way they combine provisions that encourage professional identification and co-operation with more explicitly moral (and implicitly class-specific) aims ("raise the character"). The GBI gave its first annuity in May 1844, and by 1860, ninety-nine governesses were receiving annuities from the GBI, although the annual reports made it clear how dramatically the need exceeded the monies the GBI had at its disposal. See [Jessie Boucherette], "The Profession of the Teacher: The Annual Reports of the Governesses' Benevolent Institution, from 1843 to 1856," *English Woman's Journal* 1 (March 1858): 1–13. Other activities of the GBI included the opening in 1845 of a home in Harley Street to provide cheap, respectable lodgings for governesses who were temporarily unemployed; the establishment at about the same time of a free employment register; and, in 1849, the establishment of a permanent home for aged governesses in the Prince of Wales Road.

3. Boucherette, "Profession of the Teacher," p. 1.

4. Leonore Davidoff and Catherine Hall, *Family Fortunes: Men and Women of the English Middle Class, 1780–1850* (Chicago: University of Chicago Press, 1987), pp. 312–13.

5. See M. Jeanne Peterson, "The Victorian Governess: Status Incongruence in Family and Society," in Martha Vicinus, ed., *Suffer and Be Still: Women in the Victorian Age* (Bloomington: Indiana University Press, 1972), p. 4; and Martha Vicinus, *Independent Women: Work and Community for Single Women, 1850–1920* (Chicago: University of Chicago Press, 1985), pp. 23, 26.

6. Peterson, "Victorian Governess," pp. 3–19.

7. For a discussion of the increasingly problematized conceptualization of Victorian children, see Mark Spilka, "On the Enrichment of Poor Monkeys by Myth and Dream; or, How Dickens Rousseauisticized and Pre-Freudianized Victorian Views of Childhood," in Don Richard Cox, ed., *Sexuality and Victorian Literature* (Knoxville: University of Tennessee Press, 1984), pp. 161–79.

8. The phrase "tabooed woman" comes from Lady Eastlake (Elizabeth Rigby), "*Vanity Fair*—and *Jane Eyre*," *Quarterly Review* 84 (1848): 177, hereafter cited as *QR*. See ibid.; and "Hints on the Modern Governess System," *Fraser's Magazine* 30 (November 1844): 573, hereafter cited as *FM*.

9. *The Governess: Or, Politics in Private Life* (London: Smith, Elder, 1836), p. 310. One of the few departures from the conceptualization of the governess as "genteel" appears in an article entitled "The Governess Question," *English Woman's Journal* 4 (1860). In this essay, the author argues that the governess's position is not considered genteel and is never likely to be elevated in status. "Whatever *gentility* may once have attached to the profession of the governess has long since vanished, and it is impossible to name any occupation, not positively disreputable, which confers so little respectability,—respectability in the worldly sense. . . . The governess, however well-conducted, remains a governess; may starve *genteely*, and sink into her grave friendless and alone" (pp. 163, 170). This is explicitly a polemical article, however, "addressed to parents, who, not having the means of giving their daughters any fortune, seem seized with an epidemic madness to make them governesses" (p. 163). It is, in other words, designed to discourage lower-middle-class women from entering the governesses' ranks by disparaging the social status of this work.

10. The phrase about "degradation" appears in [Sarah Lewis], "On the Social Position of Governesses," *Fraser's Magazine* 34 (April 1848): 414. See also *FM* 581.

11. See *QR* 180; *FM* 173, 580; "Social Position," pp. 413–14.

12. Peterson also makes this point. See "Victorian Governess," p. 17.

13. For an autobiographical report of a governess's sexual vulnerability, see Ellen Weeton, *Miss Weeton's Journal of a Governess*, ed. J. J. Bagley (New York: Augustus M. Kelley, 1969), 1: 209–327.

The sexual exploitation to which the governess was potentially exposed surfaces obliquely at the end of an 1858 essay in the *English Woman's Journal*. "Depths of horror," the author (Jessie Boucherette) warns, "into which men cannot fall" await the unemployed governess ("Profession of the Teacher" p. 13).

14. See *QR* 177; and *FM* 573.

15. *FM* 574.

16. The phrase "white slavery" is the title of a letter about governesses published in the *London Times* and cited by Barbara Leigh Smith Bodichon, *Women and Work* (London: Bosworth and Harrison, 1857), p. 17. The phrase "needlewomen forced to take to the streets" was used by Henry Mayhew in his 1849–50 *Morning Chronicle* series on London, "Labour and the Poor." See *The Unknown Mayhew: Selections from the "Morning Chronicle," 1849–50,* ed. E. P. Thompson and Eileen Yeo (Harmondsworth, England: Penguin Books, 1973), p. 200.

17. See Elizabeth K. Helsinger, Robin Lauterbach Sheets, and William Veeder, eds., *The Woman Question: Social Issues, 1837–1883,* vol. 2 of *The Woman Question: Society and Literature in Britain and America, 1837–1883* (New York: Garland Publishing, 1983), p. 115.

18. Henry Mayhew, "Second Test—Meeting of Needlewomen Forced to Take to the Streets," in *Unknown Mayhew,* pp. 200–16; and Anthony Ashley Cooper (Lord Ashley, later the seventh Earl of Shaftesbury), in *Hansard's Parliamentary Debates,* 3d series, March 15, 1844, cc. 1088–89, 1091–96, 1099–1100.

19. *QR* 181.

20. Other early reviews of *Jane Eyre* include: George Henry Lewes's review in *Fraser's Magazine,* December 1847, pp. 690–93; John Eagles' essay in *Blackwood's Magazine,* October 1848, pp. 473–74; [H. R. Bagshawe], *"Jane Eyre, Shirley," Dublin Review* 28 (March 1850): 209–33; [G. H. Lewes], "The Lady Novelists," *Fraser's Magazine,* o.s., 58 (July 1852): 129–41; and [E. S. Dallas], "Currer Bell," *Blackwood's Magazine* 82 (July 1857): 77–94.

21. Charlotte Brontë, *Jane Eyre,* ed. Q. D. Leavis (Harmondsworth, England: Penguin Books, 1966), p. 344. All future references will be cited in the text by page numbers. *Jane Eyre* was initially published by the firm of Smith, Elder.

22. Other essays on these dreams include Margaret Homans, "Dreaming of Children: Literalization in *Jane Eyre* and *Wuthering Heights,*" in Juliann E. Fleenor, ed., *The Female Gothic* (Montreal: Eden Press, 1983), pp. 257–79; and Maurianne Adams, "Family Disintegration and Creative Reintegration: The Case of Charlotte Brontë and *Jane Eyre,*" in Anthony S. Wohl, ed., *The Victorian Family: Structure and Stresses* (London: Croom Helm, 1978), pp. 148–79.

23. See Sandra M. Gilbert and Susan Gubar, *The Madwoman in the Attic: The Woman Writer and the Nineteenth-Century Literary Imagination* (New Haven: Yale University Press, 1979), pp. 336–71.

24. "Love," *The Governess: A Repertory of Female Education* 2 (1855): 94. This periodical was founded in 1854 and continued publication at least until 1856. In addition to essays on educational theory, it included both practical help for governesses (directions and patterns for "fancy needle work," sample lesson plans, and quizzes for periods of English history) and a correspondence section that elicited extremely pragmatic complaints and

suggestions from governesses (as to the poisonous properties of the coloring agent in modeling wax, for example). In 1855 the editors of the periodical described it as Christian but nonsectarian and as "the *first*—and for twelve months . . . the *only* periodical on the subject of Female Education" (*The Governess: A Repertory of Female Education*, p. iii).

25. Nancy Armstrong, in *Desire and Domestic Fiction: A Political History of the Novel* (New York: Oxford University Press, 1987), p. 79, discusses the problematic position the governess occupied. The unstable boundary between the governess and the mother was explicitly explored by Mrs. Henry Wood in *East Lynne*, when the (disfigured) mother returns home as the governess for her own children.

26. The only reference to Jane's child is this sentence: "When his first-born was put into his arms, he could see that the boy had inherited his own eyes, as they once were—large, brilliant, and black" (*Jane Eyre*, p. 476).

27. Jane's father is only obliquely held responsible for her situation—but her maternal grandfather is more directly to blame. Jane's father, a poor clergyman, wooed her mother into marriage against her father's wishes, and it was the old man's inexorable anger that caused him to leave all his money to Jane's uncle, thus leaving her penniless and dependent when her parents died.

28. Lewis, "On the Social Position," pp. 411, 412, 413.

29. Important histories of the nineteenth-century British feminist movement include Ray Strachey, *The Cause: A Short History of the Women's Movement in Great Britain* (1928; reprint, London: Virago Press, 1978); Josephine Kamm, *Rapiers and Battleaxes: The Women's Movement and Its Aftermath* (London: George Allen and Unwin, 1966); and Sheila R. Herstein, *A Mid-Victorian Feminist: Barbara Leigh Smith Bodichon* (New Haven: Yale University Press, 1985).

30. Bodichon, *Women and Work*, pp. 11–12. *Women and Work* was originally published in an obscure Scottish periodical, the *Waverly Journal*, in the February issue. For a discussion of Bodichon's efforts on behalf of women's employment, see Herstein, *Mid-Victorian Feminist*, chap. 5.

31. For Boucherette's ideas about women's work, see "On the Obstacles to the Employment of Women," *English Woman's Journal* 4 (February 1860): 361–75.

32. In 1851, Emily Shirreff and her sister, Maria G. Grey, published *Thoughts on Self-Culture Addressed to Women* (London: Edward Moxon, 1850).

33. Emily Shirreff, *Intellectual Education and Its Influence on the Character and Happiness of Women* (London: John W. Parker and Son, 1858), pp. 7–8.

34. Ibid., p. 8.

35. Ibid., p. 29.

36. Ibid., p. 418. Here is Shirreff on the subject of middle-class women's paid employment: "for women who are above this necessity [to work] to find any career of activity analogous to men's professions, seems to me

utterly chimerical, and of very questionable advantage could it be found. What society wants from women is not labour, but refinement, elevation of mind, knowledge, making its power felt through moral influence and sound opinions. It wants civilizers of men, and educators of the young" (p. 417).

37. Bessie Parkes, for example, insisted that middle-class girls should receive "the Education of Life—the Education of Responsibility," which, for her, meant learning to use money wisely. Parkes, *Remarks on the Education of Girls, with Reference to the Social, Legal, and Industrial Position of Women in the Present Day,* 3d ed. (London: John Chapman, 1856), pp. 17. Jessie Boucherette advocated this education for middle-class girls: "teach them above all, that it is more honorable to depend on their own exertions than to marry for the sake of a maintenance" ("On the Obstacles," p. 366). And Barbara Bodichon flatly asserted that "women should not make *love their profession,*" and that "every human being should work; no one should owe bread to any but his or her parents" (*Women and Work,* pp. 9, 11).

38. "Queen Bees or Working Bees," *Saturday Review,* 21 February 1857, p. 173. Expressions of aversion to women working were not, of course, confined to the pages of the *Saturday Review.* In 1862, W. R. Greg also lamented this modern trend in "Why Are Women Redundant?" published in the *National Review* 14 (April 1862). "To endeavour to make women independent of men; to multiply and facilitate this employment; to enable them to earn a separate and ample subsistence . . . to induct them generally into avocations, not only as interesting and beneficient, and therefore *appropriate,* but specially and definitely as *lucrative;* to surround single life for them with so smooth an entrance . . . that marriage shall almost come to be regarded, not as their most honourable function and especial calling, but merely as one of many ways open to them . . . would appear to be the aim and theory of many female reformers. . . . Few more radical or more fatal errors, we are satisfied, philanthropy ever made" (pp. 42–43).

39. "Queen Bees or Working Bees?" *Saturday Review,* 12 November 1859, p. 576.

40. Ibid.

41. "Queen Bees or Working Bees," p. 173.

42. "The Intellect of Women," *Saturday Review,* 8 October 1859, p. 417.

43. "Conventionalities," *Saturday Review,* 9 December 1865, p. 723.

44. John Stuart Mill, *The Subjection of Women* (1869; reprint, Arlington Heights, Ill.: A. H. M. Publishing, 1980), pp. 73–74. *The Subjection of Women* was written in 1861.

45. From *The First Duty of Women* (1870), reprinted from *Victoria Magazine* and quoted in J. A. Banks and Olive Banks, *Feminism and Family Planning in Victorian England* (New York: Schocken Books, 1964), p. 44. Another writer pointed to another version of this contradiction in 1868. "The possibility that women, if adequately educated, may develop powers adapted to employments monopolized by men, has led to a jealousy for female delicacy and elevation above work which is a little suspicious: men

NOTES TO PAGES 158–65

have never made an outcry against women's entering upon any occupation

have never made an outcry against women's entering upon any occupation however hard or 'degrading,' unless that occupation were one in which they would compete with men!" "The Suppressed Sex," *Westminster Review,* October 1868, quoted in Lee Holcombe, *Victorian Ladies at Work: Middle-Class Working Women in England and Wales, 1850–1914* (Hamden, Conn.: Shoe String Press, 1973), pp. 9–10.

46. "Female Labour," *Fraser's Magazine* 61 (March 1860): 367.

47. See, for example, Boucherette, "Profession of the Teacher," p. 8. Even though Barbara Bodichon argued that "it is much more important to the welfare of a girl's soul that she be trained to work than that she marry," she also believed that women had "moral natures" that would be attracted to "nobler works" instead of such careers as "being in the army, mixing in political life, going to sea, or being barristers" (*Women and Work,* pp. 18, 51).

48. Boucherette, "On the Obstacles," pp. 362, 367. This argument also appears in idem, "Profession of the Teacher," pp. 7–8, 10.

49. Quoted in [Harriet Martineau], "Female Industry," *Edinburgh Review* 109 (April 1859): p. 336.

50. Shirreff, *Intellectual Education,* p. 84.

51. Martineau, "Female Industry," p. 336.

Chapter 6. The Social Construction of Florence Nightingale

1. The date of this document is not clear. Reports of Nightingale's illness in the Crimea reached England in May 1855, but since the title of this obituary indicates that it was written after the war, it probably dates from 1856. Nightingale returned from the Crimea, in great secrecy, in July 1856.

2. Harriet Martineau, "Obituary of Florence Nightingale, written when she was thought to be dying after the Crimean War, and published in part in the 'Daily News' when she actually died in 1910," handwritten manuscript in the Fawcett Library, London, pp. 1–2, 8–9.

3. Among the nursing schools that preceded the Nightingale Training School at St. Thomas's Hospital were the Kaiserwerth Institution in Germany and St. John's House in London (founded 1848); from 1856, pupil nurses were also admitted to King's College Hospital in London. Nightingale's writings also include works on religion, sanitation, and architecture, to name just a few of the subjects she undertook. A comprehensive bibliography of Nightingale's writings can be found in W. J. Bishop and Sue Goldie, *A Bio-Bibliography of Florence Nightingale* (London: Dawsons, 1962). For discussions of the discrepancies between the legend and the facts, see F. B. Smith, *Florence Nightingale: Reputation and Power* (London: Croom Helm, 1982); Elvi Whittaker and Virginia Olesen, "The Faces of Florence Nightingale: Functions of the Heroine Legend in an Occupational Sub-

Culture," in Robert Dingwall and Jean McIntosh, eds., *Readings in the Sociology of Nursing* (Edinburgh and London: Churchill Livingston, 1978), pp. 19–35; Katherine Williams, "Ideologies of Nursing: Their Meanings and Implications," in Dingwall and McIntosh, *Readings,* pp. 36–44; Margaret Goldsmith, *Florence Nightingale: The Woman and the Legend* (London: Hodder and Stoughton, 1937); and Sandra Holton, "Feminine Authority and Social Order: Florence Nightingale's Conception of Nursing and Health Care," *Social Analysis* 15 (August 1984): 59–72.

4. There may be autobiographical reports of childbirth, but after extensive research and numerous inquiries, I have not found them. The most candid and explicit firsthand account of pregnancy I have been able to locate from this period is Eliza B. Duffey, *What Women Should Know: A Woman's Book about Women* (Philadelphia: J. M. Stoddart, 1873; New York: Arno Press, 1974); see especially pp. 151, 159–60. There were pamphlets by midwives, and these can be seen as part of an oppositional voice within medicine. However, since midwives were not part of the official medical establishment, I have chosen not to deal extensively with them. After women began to enter the medical profession as doctors, of course, an oppositional voice within medicine materialized. In 1874, for example, Elizabeth Garrett Anderson adamantly rejected medical men's assertion that menstruation made women permanent invalids. See Anderson, "Sex in Mind and in Education: A Reply," *Fortnightly Review* 15 (1874): 582–94.

5. Eva Gamarnikow makes the point that diagnosis was a critical component of medical men's hegemony within medicine. See Gamarnikow, "Sexual Division of Labour: The Case of Nursing," in Annette Kuhn and AnnMarie Wolpe, eds., *Feminism and Materialism: Women and Modes of Production* (London: Routledge and Kegan Paul, 1978), pp. 97, 107. While I agree with many of her observations, I find her central thesis too simplistic.

6. "Hospital Assistants in the East," *London Times,* 14 October 1857, p. 7.

7. Nightingale had spent several months at Kaiserwerth in 1851, but she received no regular nursing training there. She was later to remark of Kaiserwerth that there "the nursing was nil and the hygiene horrible." Quoted in Monica E. Baly, *Nursing and Social Change,* 2d ed. (London: Heinemann, 1980), p. 117. At the time she volunteered to go to the East, Nightingale was the (voluntary) resident lady superintendent of the Invalid Gentlewoman's Institution in London, but her duties there did not include nursing.

8. F. B. Smith, predictably, gives this the darkest reading, arguing not only that Nightingale pushed herself forward (in the process ousting Lady Maria Forester and the Reverend Mr. Hume, who also offered their services), but also that she "coached" Mrs. Herbert, who "coached" Sidney Herbert, to offer Nightingale what she wanted. See Smith, *Reputation and Power,* pp. 26–27. Harriet Martineau, also predictably, provides a more generous reading in her obituary, when she says that Herbert's letter "was treacherously stolen, + made public by an officious person who subjected

the friends to ungenerous criticism, + to implications of vanity + self-seeking, purely absurd to all who had any knowledge whatever of Florence and her friends" ("Obituary," p. 6). Biographies of Nightingale, which all provide readings of this episode, include: Sir Edward Cook, *The Life of Florence Nightingale* (London: Macmillan, 1913); Cecil Woodham-Smith, *Florence Nightingale, 1820–1910* (London: Constable, 1950); and Goldsmith, *The Woman and the Legend.*

9. Nightingale compares herself to Christ in her fragmentary "Cassandra." See Ray Strachey, *The Cause: A Short History of the Woman's Movement in Great Britain* (1928; reprint, London: Virago, 1978), pp. 416–17. Nightingale is compared to a saint in an anonymous poem (by "A Lady") entitled *Florence Nightingale and the Russian War: A Poem* (London: T. Hatchard, 1856). Here are the relevant lines:

> 'Mid this dire scene of mortal woe,
> The saddest human heart can
>   know,—
> 'Mid mangled limbs and broken
>   bones,
> And heavy sighs and dying groans,
> And the loud shout, the strife, the jar,
> Which follow that sad Demon—War,
> Methinks, I see before my eyes
> A form half bending from the skies;
> I hear a voice divinely sweet
> These words of winning love repeat:
> 'Friend of the brave! on land and sea,
> 'Friend of the brave! I come to thee."
>
> (Pp. 17–18)

John Davies, seeking Nightingale's motivation for volunteering, finds it in an explicit analogy to Christ. Why did she offer herself? he asks; then he triumphantly answers:

> It was to imitate Jehovah's Son!
> Divine Compassion touched thy heart with fire,
> *Then* thou didst unto Calvary aspire!
> Earth-born thou wast, but in High Heaven
>   conceived;
> Thou hast the noblest work of time achieved.

In *Florence Nightingale, or the Heroine of the East, etc., etc., etc. A Poem* (London: Arthur Hall, Virtue, 1856), p. 8.

The title of a penny pamphlet also conveys the analogy between Nightingale and Christ through its allusions: "They were without clothing and she procured it; they were wounded and she nursed them; they were dying and she consoled them, making them happy even in their desolate condition, thus has she not only had and deserved the blessings of the Poor, but Royalty." *The Only and Unabridged Edition of the Life of Miss Nightingale (The Heroine of European Philanthropy)* (London: Coulson, n. d.).

10. "Mr. Bracebridge on the Crimean Hospitals," *London Times,* 16 October 1855, p. 5. This is a report of a lecture Bracebridge delivered on 10 October at St. Mary's Hall in Coventry. In a report that appeared in the *Cambridge Chronicle* in April 1856, Bracebridge narrated this anecdote, which constructs a picture of the poor soldier wronged in the very areas that announce his moral "improvement"—his literacy and his religious faith. "There was a poor fellow who had both his legs taken off: he had a Bible and three books, which by some foolish general order were taken away from him. This struck him as a cruel thing; but of course nobody was to blame for it. Having been done by order, he did not like to undo it. The books were on the table; Miss Nightingale came in, took up the Bible, and gave it to the man again. Nothing could be more simple, but it was an illustration of all that she did—never to make a fuss, but to act, to take away the evil and produce a good effect." "Miss Florence Nightingale at Scutari: A Speech of Mr. Bracebridge, at Cambridge," *Cambridge Chronicle,* 28 April 1856, p. 7.

11. Martha Vicinus does not formulate her argument this way, but she also identifies metaphors of domesticity and militarism in statements about nursing made by Nightingale and others. There are two fundamental differences between Vicinus's account of nursing and mine. The first is that Vicinus argues that the military metaphor is replaced by a domestic metaphor, while I suggest that, while their relative prominence may shift, both metaphors were always present. The second difference is that I emphasize that these metaphors belong to narratives that already existed in Victorian culture and that carried with them meanings and effects. See Martha Vicinus, *Independent Women: Work and Community for Single Women, 1850–1920* (Chicago: University of Chicago Press, 1985), chap. 3. Sandra Holton also discusses the two faces of this image in "Feminine Authority," p. 59.

12. For a discussion of this narrative in boys' fiction, see J. S. Bratton, "Of England, Home, and Duty: The Image of England in Victorian and Edwardian Juvenile Fiction," in John M. MacKenzie, ed., *Imperialism and Popular Culture* (Manchester, England: Manchester University Press, 1986), pp. 73–93.

13. An example of Nightingale creating the stereotype of home is provided by [Frederick Edge], *A Woman's Example and a Nation's Work: A Tribute to Florence Nightingale* (London: William Ridgway, 1864). " 'Soldier,' said a man, 'you cannot have the comforts and the care of "Home" on the grim fields of war': 'Man,' said this brave true woman, 'where I am is "Home"; I bring with me its comforts and its care to the battle-field and camp, and all a mother's love shall tend your aching brow and staunch the oozing blood.' " This passage immediately invokes the divinity Victorians

associated with this image; the next sentence reads: "Thus an angel came and ministered to him" (p. 6).

14. See Olive Anderson, *A Liberal State at War: English Politics and Economics during the Crimean War* (New York: St. Martin's Press, 1967), pp. 1–28. Anderson divides the public response to the war into four phases: the six-month-long, anticlimactic preliminary period (March 1854–September 1854); the period of patriotic excitement and confidence (from the landing in the Crimea in September through the Battle of Balaklava and the charge of the Light Brigade in late October); the period of "hysterical accusations and recriminations" that followed news of the defeat at Inkermann (5 November) and lasted through the winter of 1855; and the period of more sober confidence that began in June 1855, when the successful expedition to Kerch cut off Russia's main supply route (pp. 26–27).

Two of the most popular nonfiction works in the years immediately preceding the war were Sir William Napier's *History of the War in the Peninsula* and Wellington's *Dispatches* (Anderson, p. 2). In light of this, it is interesting to see the narrative implicitly inscribed in twentieth century Bank of England notes: the figure on the £5 note is Wellington; Nightingale is on the £10 note; and Shakespeare is represented on the £20 note.

15. For one discussion of this technology, see Karen W. Smith, *Constantin Guys: Crimean War Drawings, 1854–1856* (Cleveland: Cleveland Museum of Art, 1978), p. 11. Here is a contemporary account of the way in which the publicity about the war generated public pressure: "Public attention was now riveted closely on the war, to the absolute exclusion of all other topics. . . . Private correspondence from the seat of war was eagerly sought and extensively published, and columns set apart for 'Letters from the Camp'; the special correspondence of the daily press was copied into other journals; leading articles in periodicals daily, weekly, and monthly, were founded on the information thus received, and the exaggerated statements were sometimes coloured still more highly; and popular opinion, thus originated and formed, began to exercise [a] powerful . . . pressure on the Parliament and the Government." [E. B. Hamley], "Lessons from the War," *Blackwood's Magazine* 79 (February 1856): 233.

16. *The Croker Papers,* ed. L. Jennings (1855), 4: 354 (20 November 1855). Quoted in Anderson, *Liberal State at War,* p. 37.

17. *Mrs. Beeton's Book of Household Management,* facsimile ed. (1861; reprint, London: Chancellor Press, 1982), p. 1.

18. Davies, *Florence Nightingale,* p. 9.

19. "Who Is Mrs. Nightingale?" *London Times,* 30 October 1854, p. 7. The analogies made between Nightingale and Queen Victoria fed off the actual links between the two women: Victoria not only sent encouragement to the troups via letters to Nightingale, but she also awarded Nightingale a medal (designed by Prince Albert) for her services in the Crimea. See Goldsmith, *The Woman and the Legend,* pp. 181, 189; and Nina Auerbach, *Woman and the Demon: The Life of a Victorian Myth* (Cambridge: Harvard University Press, 1982), p. 120.

20. "Ballad to Florence Nightingale" (ca. 1856), cited in Janet H. Murray, *Strong Minded Women, and Other Lost Voices from Nineteenth-Century England* (New York: Pantheon Books, 1982), p. 301.

21. This is Bracebridge's formulation; he continues: "government had sacrificed a woman to the cause of the army, who had been carried to the same place as her prototype, and had there changed a temple of human sacrifice into a Christian temple of mercy" ("Miss Nightingale at Scutari," p. 8).

22. Nightingale often conceptualized herself in masculine terms, at least partly because there were no other terms available to legitimize her ambition. This is an imaginary speech to her mother recorded in Florence's diary before she won permission to leave home for good. Notice how the narratives of male and female self-realization pull in opposite directions. "Florence to her mother: Well, my dear, you don't suppose that with my 'talents' and my 'European reputation' and my 'beautiful letters,' and all that, I'm going to stay dangling about my mother's drawing-room all my life. I shall go out and look for work, to be sure. You must look upon me as your son. I should have cost you a great deal more if I had married or been a son. You must now consider me married or a son. You were willing to part with me to be married." Goldsmith, *The Woman and the Legend,* pp. 99–100.

23. "Hospital Nurses as They Are and as They Ought to Be," *Fraser's Magazine* 37 (May 1848): 540.

24. "Training Institutions for Nurses," *Medical Times and Gazette: A Journal of Medical Science, Literature, Criticism, and News,* 10 January 1852, p. 40.

25. "Suggestions on the Subject of Providing, Training, and Organizing Nurses for the Sick Poor in Workhouse Infirmaries," quoted in Brian Able-Smith, *A History of the Nursing Profession* (London: Heinemann, 1960), p. 5.

26. Williams, "Ideologies of Nursing," pp. 36–37.

27. In the headnote to Williams's "Ideologies of Nursing," the editors state that Williams acknowledges in a private correspondence that "all the essential features of the post-Nightingale nurses' role are defined in the columns of medical journals of the 1840s" (p. 37).

28. See Emily Davies, "Female Physicians," and "Medicine as a Profession for Women," in *Thoughts on Some Questions Relating to Women, 1860–1908* (Cambridge: Bowes and Bowes, 1910), pp. 19–27 and 34–40; and Elizabeth Blackwell and Emily Blackwell, "Medicine as a Profession," *English Woman's Journal* 5 (May 1860): 145–60. Interestingly enough in light of its staunch antifeminism, the *Saturday Review* supported the position that medicine was a profession suitable to women. It is difficult to tell, however, how much of this support was a function of the unlikelihood that this profession *would* be opened to women. See "Industrial Occupations of Women," *Saturday Review,* 18 July 1857, p. 64.

29. For discussions of women's entry into the medical profession, see E. H. C. Moberly Bell, *Storming the Citadel: The Rise of the Woman Doctor* (London: Constable, 1953); Edythe Lutzker, *Women Gain a Place in Medicine* (New York: McGraw-Hill, 1969); and Noel Parry and José Parry, *The Rise of the Medical Profession: A Study of Collective Mobility* (London: Croom Helm, 1976), pp. 173–76.

30. See "Elizabeth Blackwell," *English Woman's Journal* 1 (1858): 97.

31. Parry and Parry, *Rise of the Medical Profession*, pp. 173–76.

32. "Training Institutions for Nurses," p. 40. There was some opposition to Nightingale and female nursing, of course. At Scutari, the opposition was spearheaded by Dr. John Hall, chief of medical staff of the British Expeditionary Army; at St. Thomas's, Mr. J. F. South was Nightingale's most outspoken adversary. See Zachary Cope, *Florence Nightingale and the Doctors* (London: Museum Press, 1958), esp. p. 109.

33. "Training Institutions for Nurses," p. 41.

34. "Hospital Nurses as They Are," p. 540.

35. In nursing, the debate about class and wages got off to a roaring start in the Crimea, where, despite the attempts of Mary Stanley and others to institute an "equality system," "ladies" objected to being treated like and made to wear the same uniforms as working-class "nurses." For a firsthand account of the failures of the equality system, see [Frances Taylor], *Eastern Hospitals and English Nurses; The Narrative of Twelve Months' Experience in the Hospitals of Koulali and Scutari, by a Lady Volunteer* (London: Hurst and Blackett, 1856), 1: 37, 117–18; 2: 13, 14, 15, 267–73. For another contemporary discussion of this issue, see "Something of What Florence Nightingale Has Done and Is Doing," *St. James's Magazine* 1 (1861): 39. Two modern analyses of the class issue are provided by Anne Summers, "Pride and Prejudice: Ladies and Nurses in the Crimean War," *History Workshop Journal* 16 (1982): 32–56; and Abel-Smith, *History of Nursing Profession*, pp. 21–31.

36. One such "true" story is "The Hospital Nurse: An Episode of the War, Founded on Fact," *Fraser's Magazine* 51 (January 1855): 96–105.

37. Williams, "Ideologies of Nursing," pp. 37–40.

38. For a biography of one such Anglican sister, a contemporary of Florence Nightingale, see Jo Manton, *Sister Dora: The Life of Dorothy Pattison* (New York: Quartet Books, 1977). Vicinus discusses the Puseyite controversy in *Independent Women*, chap. 2.

39. F. B. Smith discusses the recruitment of nurses in *Reputation and Power*, pp. 27–34.

40. "*They* call it a profession," Nightingale smartly remarked, "but I say that it is a calling." Quoted in Williams, "Ideologies of Nursing," p. 39.

41. "Subsidiary Notes as to the Introduction of Female Nursing into Military Hospitals," reprinted in *Selected Writings of Florence Nightingale*, ed. Lucy Ridgely Seymer (New York: Macmillan, 1954), p. 8. Hereafter cited as SN.

42. Ibid., esp. pp. 5–6, 23, 33.

43. Most of the men who were treated (and died) at Scutari were suffering from cholera, not wounds.

44. The best discussion of Florence Nightingale's theory of disease is Charles E. Rosenberg, "Florence Nightingale on Contagion: The Hospital as Moral Universe," in Charles E. Rosenberg, ed., *Healing and History* (New York: Dawson, 1979), pp. 116–36. Sandra Holton also discusses this in "Feminine Authority," pp. 60–61.

45. Nightingale explains the procedures and government of the Nightingale Training School in her report to the Royal Commission appointed to investigate the sanitary conditions of the army in India. See "Suggestions on a System of Nursing for Hospitals in India," in *Selected Writings,* pp. 237–43. The training school at St. Thomas's was financed by the Nightingale Fund, a scheme to honor Nightingale inaugurated by the duke of Cambridge on 29 November 1855. A good measure of the universality of Nightingale's popularity is the fact that Englishmen from all classes contributed to this fund, in sums ranging from six pence to several hundred pounds. The fund eventually raised over £44,000. See Lucy Seymer, *Florence Nightingale's Nurses: The Nightingale Training School, 1860–1960* (London: Pitman Medical Publishing, 1960), chap. 1.

46. Florence Nightingale, *Notes on Nursing: What It Is and What It Is Not* (New York: Dover, 1969), p. 38. Hereafter cited as N. Occasionally in this text, Nightingale does refer to the patient as a female, but these references are all to her own experiences as a patient.

47. In her 1871 text on midwifery, *Introductory Notes on Lying-in Institutions,* Nightingale makes it clear that her argument for excluding women from some medical practices is one facet of her attempt to sidestep competition with medical men. "Why," she asks here, "(in the great movement there is now to make women into medical men) should not this branch, midwifery, which they will find no one to contest against them—not at least in the estimation of the patients—be the first ambition of cultivated women? . . . There is a better thing than making women into medical men, and that is making them into medical *women.*" Nightingale, *Introductory Notes on Lying-in Institutions* (London: Longmans, Green, 1871), p. 106.

48. "A Reverie after Reading Miss Nightingale's *Notes on Nursing,*" *Fraser's Magazine* 61 (June 1860): p. 753. Other early reviews include [Harriet Martineau], "Miss Nightingale's *Notes on Nursing,*" *Quarterly Review* 107 (April 1860): pp. 392–422; and "Something of What Florence Nightingale Has Done."

49. This phrase comes from Nightingale's "Sick-Nursing and Health-Nursing," in *Selected Writings,* p. 362. Hereafter cited as SH.

50. "Nurses, Training of," in *Selected Writings,* p. 334. Hereafter cited as NT. This definition also appears in SH, where Nightingale inserts the word "moral": "What is discipline?" she asks. "Discipline is the essence of moral training" (SH 358).

51. "Suggestions on the Subject of Providing, Training, and Organizing Nurses for the Sick Poor in Workhouse Infirmaries," in *Selected Writings*, p. 311. Hereafter cited as SP.

52. The phrase comes from "Something of What Florence Nightingale Has Done," p. 229.

53. The campaign for state registration was led by Ethel Bedford Fenwick. Nightingale spelled out the basis of her resistance to registration in a letter to Dr. Henry Acland in 1869: "nursing and medicine must never be mixed up. It spoils both. If the enemy wished to ruin our nurses in training at St. Thomas's it would be by persuading me to accept your noble offer of a female special certificate (or any degree) for them. (and I can say quite unaffectedly that it is a noble and generous offer). If I were not afraid of being misunderstood I would almost say—the less knowledge of medicine a hospital matron has the better (1) because it does not improve her sanitary practice, (2) because it would make her miserable or intolerable to the doctors." A few years later Nightingale continued her argument: "Nursing does not come within the category of those arts (or sciences) which may be usefully 'examined' or 'certified' by the agency proposed. . . . Nursing is not only an art but a character, and how can that be arrived at by examination?" Quoted in Cope, *Florence Nightingale and the Doctors*, pp. 121, 122.

54. Edmund Burke introduced the metaphor of trusteeship in his famous 1783 parliamentary speech on India. See John Cell, "The Imperial Conscience," in Peter Marsh, ed., *The Conscience of the Victorian State* (Syracuse, N.Y.: Syracuse University Press, 1979), pp. 186–87.

55. Nightingale, "Suggestions on a System of Nursing for Hospitals in India," p. 230. Martha Vicinus, who is editing Florence Nightingale's letters, notes that Nightingale had "so very little power" in the administration of India. "Even though she was repeatedly consulted, it seems to me to have been more pro forma than with any intention of carrying out her sanitation plans. Most of the British in India seem so aware of the difficulties of enforcing any legal changes that involved a change in religious practice, that they simply preferred a policy of hands-off, no matter how high the death rates were. . . . The interesting thing about FN and India for me is how it represents an example of how limited her power could be in the face of male dominance, no matter how much her ideas might have chimed in with those of the dominant liberal ideology" (private correspondence). I agree with Vicinus and would only add that Nightingale's images and ideas could still be deployed in ways she did not intend or foresee.

56. See Henry Parris, *Constitutional Bureaucracy: The Development of British Central Administration since the Eighteenth Century* (New York: Augustus M. Kelley, 1969), chaps. 2, 3, and 6. The reform of the War Office following the Crimean War entailed dividing the responsibilities of the

secretary of state for colonies and war, so that war and imperialism were at least officially separated.

57. Smith, *Reputation and Power*, pp. 169–78.

58. The phrase is Harriet Martineau's. See "Woman's Battle-field," *Once a Week*, 3 December 1854, pp. 474–79.

Bibliography

Primary Sources

"Act to Amend the Divorce and Matrimonial Causes Act of Last Session." *English Woman's Journal* 2 (1859): 119–22.

Acton, William. *The Functions and Disorders of the Reproductive Organs in Youth, in Adult Age, and in Advanced Life: Considered in Their Physiological, Social, and Moral Relations.* London: John Churchill, 1857.

Adye, Lt. Col. John. *A Review of the Crimean War, to the Winter of 1854–55.* 1860. Reprint. East Ardsley, Yorkshire, England: E. P. Publishing, 1973.

Anderson, Elizabeth Garrett. "Sex in Mind and in Education: A Reply." *Fortnightly Review* 15 (1874): 582–94.

"Association for Promoting the Employment of Women." *English Woman's Journal* 4 (September 1859).

Aveling, James Hobson. *The Chamberlens and the Midwifery Forceps: Memorials of the Family and an Essay on the Invention of the Instrument.* London: J. and A. Churchill, 1882. Reprint. New York: AMS Press, 1977.

———. *English Midwives: Their History and Prospects.* 1872. Reprint. London: Hugh K. Elliot, 1967.

[Bagshawe, H. R.] *"Jane Eyre, Shirley." Dublin Review* 28 (March 1850): 209–33.

"Ballad to Florence Nightingale." In Janet H. Murray, *Strong Minded Women, and Other Lost Voices from Nineteenth-Century England*, pp. 300–301. New York: Pantheon Books, 1982.

Barwell, Mrs. *Advice to Mothers on the Treatment of Infants: With Directions for Self-Management before, during, and after Pregnancy. Addressed to Mothers and Nurses. Revised, Enlarged, and Adapted to Habits and Climate in the United States, by a Physician of New York, under the Approval and Recommendation of Valentine Mott, M.D.* Philadelphia: Leary and Getz, 1853.

Beard, George M. "The Nature and Diagnosis of Neurasthenia (Nervous Exhaustion)." *New York Medical Journal: A Monthly Record of Medicine and the Collateral Sciences* 29 (March 1879): 225–51.

Becklard, Eugene. *Know Thyself: The Physiologist; or Sexual Physiology Revealed.* Trans. M. Sherman Wharton. Boston: Bela Marsh, 1859. Reprinted in *Sex for the Common Man.* New York: Arno Press, 1974.

Beeton, Isabella. *Mrs. Beeton's Book of Household Management.* London, 1861. Reprint. London: Chancellor Press, 1982.

Blackwell, Elizabeth, and Emily Blackwell. "Medicine as a Profession." *English Woman's Journal* 5 (May 1860): 145–60.

Bodichon, Barbara Leigh Smith. *Women and Work.* London: Bosworth and Harrison, 1857.

Boucherette, Jessie. "How to Provide for Superfluous Women." In Josephine Butler, ed., *Woman's Work and Woman's Culture,* pp. 27–48. London: Macmillan, 1869.

———. "On the Obstacles to the Employment of Women." *English Woman's Journal* 4 (February 1860): 361–75.

———. "The Profession of the Teacher: The Annual Reports of the Governesses' Benevolent Institution, from 1843 to 1856." *English Woman's Journal* 1 (March 1858): 1–13.

Bracebridge, C. Holte. "Miss Florence Nightingale at Scutari: A Speech of Mr. Bracebridge, at Cambridge." *Cambridge Chronicle,* 28 April 1856. Reprint.

British and Foreign Medico-Chirurgical Review. 1849.

Brontë, Charlotte. *Jane Eyre.* Ed. Q. D. Leavis. Harmondsworth, England: Penguin Books, 1966.

Bucknill, John Charles. *Unsoundness of Mind in Relation to Criminal Acts: An Essay, to Which the First Sugden Prize Was This Year Awarded, by the King and Queen's College of Physicians in Ireland.* Philadelphia: T. and Q. W. Johnson, 1856. Reprinted in Robert W. Rieber, ed., *Insanity and the Law: Two Nineteenth-Century Classics.* New York: Da Capo Press, 1981.

Carlyle, Thomas. "The Hero as Man of Letters: Johnson, Rousseau, Burns." In Archibald MacMechan, ed., *On Heroes, Hero-Worship, and the Heroic in History.* Boston: Ginn, 1901.

Carter, Robert Brudenell. *On the Pathology and Treatment of Hysteria.* London: John Churchill, 1853.

Cobbe, Frances Power. "What Shall We Do with Our Old Maids?" *Fraser's Magazine* 66 (November 1862): 594–610.

"Conventionalities." *Saturday Review,* 9 December 1865, pp. 722–23.

Coolidge, Bertha. *Some Unrecorded Letters of Caroline Norton in the Altschul Collection of the Yale University Library.* Boston: Marymount Press, 1934.

"The Copyright Question." *Blackwood's Magazine* 51 (January 1842): 107–21.

The Creevey Papers: A Selection from the Correspondence and Diaries of the Late Thomas Creevey, M. P. Born 1768—Died 1838. Ed. the Right Honorable Sir Herbert Maxwell, Bart., Ll.D., F.R.S. London: John Murray, 1912.

[Dallas, E. S.] "Currer Bell." *Blackwood's Magazine* 82 (July 1857): 77–94.
———. *The Gay Science*. 2 vols. London: Chapman and Hall, 1866. Reprint. New York: Johnson Reprint Corp., 1969.
Davies, Emily. *Thoughts on Some Questions Relating to Women, 1860–1908*. Cambridge: Bowes and Bowes, 1910.
Davies, John. *Florence Nightingale, or the Heroine of the East, etc., etc., etc. A Poem*. London: Arthur Hall, Virtue, 1856.
Dickens, Charles. *David Copperfield*. New York: Bantam Books, 1981.
Dickson, Samuel. *The Destructive Art of Healing, or, Facts for Families*. 3d ed. London, 1853.
"The Divorce Court at Work." *Saturday Review*, 31 December 1859, pp. 809–10.
Duffey, Eliza B. *What Women Should Know: A Woman's Book about Women*. Philadelphia: J. M. Stoddart, 1873. Reprint. New York: Arno Press, 1974.
Eastlake, Elizabeth, Lady. *"Vanity Fair—and Jane Eyre." Quarterly Review* 84 (1848): 153–85.
[Edge, Frederick.] *A Woman's Example and a Nation's Work: A Tribute to Florence Nightingale*. London: William Ridgway, 1864.
"Elizabeth Blackwell." *English Woman's Journal* 1 (1858): 80–100.
Ellis, Havelock. *Man and Woman: A Study of Human Secondary Sexual Characters*. London: Walter Scott, 1904. Reprint. New York: Arno Press, 1974.
Esquirol, E. *Mental Maladies: A Treatise on Insanity*. Trans. E. K. Hunt. Philadelphia: Lea and Blanchard, 1845.
Everon, Ernest. "Some Thoughts about Dickens and Novel Writing." *Ladies' Companion and Monthly Magazine* 7 (May 1855): 257–61.
"Female Labour." *Fraser's Magazine* 61 (March 1869): 359–71.
Florence Nightingale and the Russian War—A Poem (by a Lady). London: T. Hatchard, 1856.
Gaskell, Elizabeth. *Mary Barton*. 1848. Reprint. New York: W. W. Norton, 1958.
Gaskell, Peter. *The Manufacturing Population of England, Its Moral, Social, and Physical Conditions, and the Changes Which Have Arisen from the Use of Steam Machinery; with an Examination of Infant Labour*. 1833. Reprint. New York: Arno Press, 1972.
"Going a Governessing." *English Woman's Journal* 1 (August 1858): 396–404.
The Governess: A Repertory of Female Education. London: Darton, 1855.
"The Governess Grinders." *Punch*, 27 October 1855, p. 169.
The Governess: Or, Politics in Private Life. London: Smith, Elder, 1836.
"The Governess Question." *English Woman's Journal* 4 (1860): 163–70.
[Gowing, Timothy.] *Voice from the Ranks: A Personal Narrative of the Crimean Campaign by a Sergeant of the Royal Fusiliers*. Ed. Kenneth Fenwick. London: Folio Society, 1954.
Greg, W. R. "Prostitution." *Westminster Review* 53 (July 1850): 238–68.

————. "Why Are Women Redundant?" *National Review* 14 (April 1862): 434–60.

Gregory, Samuel. *The Male Midwife and the Female Doctor: The Gynecology Controversy in Nineteenth-Century America.* New York: Arno Press, 1974.

Hamilton, Alexander. *A Treatise on the Management of Female Complaints and of Children in Early Infancy.* London: T. Cadell and W. Davies, 1804.

[Hamley, E. B.] "Lessons from the War." *Blackwood's Magazine* 79 (February 1856): 232–42.

Hansard's Parliamentary Debates. 3d series. 1844, 1854–58.

"Hints on the Modern Governess System." *Fraser's Magazine* 30 (November 1844): 571–83.

Hollick, Frederick. *The Marriage Guide; or, Natural History of Generation.* New York: T. W. Strong, 1850. Reprint. New York: Arno Press, 1974.

"Hospital Assistants in the East." *London Times,* 14 October 1857, p. 7.

"The Hospital Nurse: An Episode of the War, Founded on Fact." *Fraser's Magazine* 51 (January 1855): 96–105.

"Industrial Occupations of Women." *Saturday Review,* 18 July 1857, pp. 63–64.

"The Intellect of Women." *Saturday Review,* 8 October 1859, pp. 417–18.

Johnston, William. *England as It Is, Political, Social, and Industrial, in the Middle of the Nineteenth Century.* 2 vols. London: John Murray, Publishers, 1851.

Kaye, J. W. "The 'Non-Existence' of Women." *North British Review* 23 (August 1855): 288–302.

————. "*Pendennis:* The Literary Profession." *North British Review* 13 (August 1850): 335–72.

King, F. A. "A New Basis for Uterine Pathology." *American Journal of Obstetrical Diseases of the Woman and Child* 8 (1875): 237–56.

Lancet. 1847–63.

Law Review 23 (1855).

Law Review and Quarterly Journal of British and Foreign Jurisprudence 1 (1844–45); 20 (1854).

"The Laws Relating to Women." *Law Review* 20 (May 1854): 1–34.

Laycock, Thomas. *An Essay on Hysteria: Being an Analysis of Its Irregular and Aggravated Forms; Including Hysterical Hemorrhage, and Hysterical Ischuria.* Philadelphia: Haswell, Barrington, and Haswell, 1840.

————. *A Treatise on the Nervous Diseases of Women: Comprising an Inquiry into the Nature, Causes, and Treatment of Spinal and Hysterical Disorders.* London: Longman, Orme, Brown, Green, and Longmans, 1840.

[Lewes, G. H.] "The Condition of Authors in England, Germany, and France." *Fraser's Magazine* 35 (March 1847): 285–95.

[————] "The Lady Novelists." *Westminster Review,* o.s., 58 (July 1852): 129–41.

[Lewis, Sarah.] "On the Social Position of Governesses." *Fraser's Magazine* 34 (April 1848): 411–14.

"Literature and Society." *Saturday Review,* 2 May 1857, pp. 400–401.

Locke, John. *The Second Treatise of Government: An Essay concerning the True, Original, Extent, and End of Civil Government.* Ed. Thomas P. Peardon. Indianapolis: Bobbs-Merrill, 1952.

Macnaghten, Angus I. "Some Letters of Caroline Norton." In *Family Roundabout,* pp. 27–65. Edinburgh and London: Oliver and Bond, 1955.

"Marriage Law Reform." *Saturday Review,* 14 February 1857, 147–48.

[Martineau, Harriet.] "Female Industry." *Edinburgh Review* 109 (April 1859): 293–336.

———. "Obituary of Florence Nightingale, written when she was thought to be dying after the Crimean War, and published in part in the 'Daily News' when she actually died in 1910." Manuscript. Fawcett Library, London.

———. "Woman's Battle-field." *Once a Week,* 3 December 1854, pp. 474–79.

"Matrimonial Divorce Act." *English Woman's Journal* 2 (1859): 56–62.

Mauriceau, A. M. *The Married Woman's Private Medical Companion.* New York, 1847. Reprint. New York, Arno Press, 1974.

May, Sir Thomas Erskine. *A Treatise on the Law, Privileges, Proceedings and Usage of Parliament.* 10th ed. 1844. London: William Clowes and Sons, 1893.

Mayhew, Henry. *London Labour and the London Poor.* 4 vols. New York: Dover, 1968.

———. *The Unknown Mayhew: Selections from the "Morning Chronicle," 1849–50.* Ed. E. P. Thompson and Eileen Yeo. Harmondsworth, England: Penguin Books, 1973.

Mill, James. *Essay on Government.* Ed. Currin V. Shields. Indianapolis: Bobbs-Merrill, 1955.

Mill, John Stuart. *The Subjection of Women.* 1869. Reprint. Arlington Heights, Ill.: A. H. M. Publishing, 1980.

[Milne, John.] *Industrial and Social Position of Women, in the Middle and Lower Ranks.* London: Chapman and Hall, 1857.

Mitchell, S. Weir. *Fat and Blood: An Essay on the Treatment of Certain Forms of Neurasthenia and Hysteria.* 4th ed. Philadelphia: J. B. Lippincott, 1885.

[Neaves, Charles.] "*Blackwood's* and Copyright in America." *Blackwood's Magazine* 63 (January 1848): 127–28.

"The New Law of Divorce." *English Woman's Journal* 1 (1858): 186–88.

Nightingale, Florence. "Introduction." In *Memorials of Agnes Elizabeth Jones,* by her sister. London: Strahan, 1871.

———. *Introductory Notes on Lying-in Institutions.* London: Longmans, Green, 1871.

———. *Notes on Nursing for the Labouring Classes.* New ed. London: Harrison, 1868.

————. *Notes on Nursing: What It Is and What It Is Not.* New York: Dover, 1969.

————. *Selected Writings of Florence Nightingale.* Ed. Lucy Ridgely Seymer. New York: Macmillan, 1954.

"The Nightingale of the East." London: Ryle, n.d.

Norton, Caroline. *Caroline Norton's Defense: English Laws for Women in the Nineteenth Century.* 1854. Reprint. Chicago: Academy Press, 1982.

————. *Letter to the Queen on Lord Cranworth's Marriage and Divorce Bill.* 4th ed. London: privately published, 1854.

[————.] *Letters, & c. Dated from June, 1836, to July, 1841.* Privately printed.

————. *The Letters of Caroline Norton to Lord Melbourne.* Ed. James O. Hoge and Clarke Olney. Athens: Ohio State University Press, 1974.

[————.] *Letters to the Mob, by Libertas.* London: Thomas Bosworth, 1848.

————. *Lost and Saved.* London: Hurst and Blackett, 1864.

————. *Observations on the Natural Claim of the Mother to the Custody of Her Infant Children, as Affected by the Common Law Right of the Father.* London: J. Ridgway, 1837.

————. *Old Sir Douglas.* Philadelphia: J. B. Lippincott; London: Macmillan, 1867.

[————.] *A Plain Letter.* Privately published, 1839.

————. *Selected Writings of Caroline Norton: Facsimile Reproductions with an Introduction and Notes by James O. Hoge and Jane Marcus.* Delmar, N.Y.: Scholar's Facsimiles and Reprints, 1978.

[————.] *The Separation of Mother and Child by the Law of "Custody of Infants," Considered.* London: Roake and Varty, 1838.

————. *Stuart of Dunleath: A Story of the Present Time.* 2 vols. Leipzig: Bernhard Tauchnitz, 1851.

[————.] *Taxation, by an Irresponsible Taxpayer.* Privately printed, n.d.

[————.] *The Wife and Woman's Reward.* 3 vols. London: Saunders and Otley, 1835.

"The Nurse in Leading Strings." *Household Words* 17 (June 1858): 602–6.

"Nurses Wanted." *Cornhill Magazine* 11 (April 1865): 409–25.

[Oliphant, Margaret.] "Sensation Novels." *Blackwood's Edinburgh Magazine* 91 (May 1862): 564–84.

"On the Adoption of Professional Life by Women." *English Woman's Journal* 2 (September 1859): 1–10.

The Only and Unabridged Edition of the Life of Miss Nightingale (The Heroine of European Philanthropy). London: Coulson, n.d.

Parkes, Bessie Rayner. *Essays on Woman's Work.* London: A. Strahan, 1866.

————. *Remarks on the Education of Girls, with Reference to the Social, Legal, and Industrial Position of Women in the Present Day.* 3d ed. London: John Chapman, 1856.

"The Profession of Literature." *Fraser's Magazine,* o.s., 58 (October 1852): 507–31.

"Property of Married Women." *English Woman's Journal* 1 (1858): 58–59.

"The Property of Married Women." *Westminster Review* 66 (October 1856): 181–97.

"Public Patronage of Men of Letters." *Fraser's Magazine* 33 (January 1846): 58–71.

"Queen Bees or Working Bees." *Saturday Review,* 21 February 1857, pp. 172–73.

"Queen Bees or Working Bees?" *Saturday Review,* 12 November 1859, pp. 575–76.

Reid, Douglas A. *Soldier-Surgeon: The Crimean War Letters of Dr. Douglas A. Reid, 1855–1856.* Ed. Joseph O. Baylen and Alan Conway. Knoxville: University of Tennessee Press, 1968.

Russell, William Howard. *Russell's Despatches from the Crimea, 1854–1856.* Ed. Nicholas Bentley. London: André Deutsch, 1966.

Ryan, Michael. *The Philosophy of Marriage in Its Social, Moral, and Physical Relations.* 3d ed. London: H. Bailliere, 1839. Reprint. New York: Arno Press, 1974.

"The 'Saturday Review' and the 'English Woman's Journal.' " *English Woman's Journal* 1 (May 1858): 201–4.

Shirreff, Emily. *Intellectual Education and Its Influence on the Character and Happiness of Women.* London: John W. Parker and Son, 1858.

Shirreff, Emily, and Maria G. Grey. *Thoughts on Self-Culture, Addressed to Women.* 2 vols. London: Edward Moxon, 1850.

Simpson, James Young. *Anaesthesia: Or the Employment of Chloroform and Ether in Surgery, Midwifery, etc.* Philadelphia: Lindsay and Blakiston, 1849.

————. *Simpson on Chloroform: An Account of a New Anaesthetic Agent as a Substitute for Sulphuric Ether in Surgery and Midwifery.* 3d ed. New York: Rushton, Clark, 1848.

Skey, F. C. *Hysteria.* London, Longmans, Green, Reader, and Dyer, 1867.

Smiles, Samuel. *Self-Help; with Illustrations of Character, Conduct, and Perseverance.* 1859. Reprint. New York: Harper and Brothers, 1899.

Smith, W. Tyler. "On the Founding of the Obstetrical Society of London (1859)." *Transactions of the Obstetrical Society of London* (1859): 5–14.

"Society for Promoting the Employment of Women, in Conjunction with the National Association for the Promotion of Social Science." *English Woman's Journal* 5 (August 1860): 388–96.

"Something of What Florence Nightingale Has Done and Is Doing." *St. James's Magazine* 1 (1861): 29–40.

Speeches of Lord Campbell, at the Bar, and in the House of Commons; with an Address to the Irish Bar as Lord Chancellor of Ireland. Edinburgh: Adam and Charles Black, and London: Longman, Brown, Green, and Longmans, 1842.

Stevens, John. *Man-Midwifery Exposed; or, the Danger and Immorality of Employing Men in Midwifery Proved; and the Remedy for the Evil Found.* London: J. Caudwell, 1865.

Storer, Horatio. *The Causation, Course, and Treatment of Reflex Insanity in Women.* 1871. Reprint. New York: Arno Press, 1972.

Studley, W. H. "Is Menstruation a Disease." *American Journal of Obstetrics and Diseases of the Woman and Child* 8 (1875): 487–512.

The Talisman, or English Keepsake: A Bouquet of Literature and the Fine Arts. London, n.d.

[Taylor, Frances.] *Eastern Hospitals and English Nurses; The Narrative of Twelve Months' Experience in the Hospitals of Koulali and Scutari, by a Lady Volunteer.* 2 vols. London: Hurst and Blackett, 1856.

Thompson, William. *Appeal of One-Half the Human Race, Women, against the Pretensions of the Other Half, Men, to Retain Them in Political, and Thence in Civil and Domestic, Slavery.* London: Virago Press, 1983.

"Training Institutions for Nurses." *Medical Times and Gazette: A Journal of Medical Science, Literature, Criticism, and News,* 10 January 1852, pp. 40–41.

" 'Wanted, a Governess.' " *Saturday Review,* 3 September 1859, pp. 279–80.

Weeton, Ellen. *Miss Weeton's Journal of a Governess.* 2 vols. Ed. J. J. Bagley. New York: Augustus M. Kelley, 1969.

"Who Is Mrs. Nightingale?" *London Times,* 30 October 1854, p. 7.

"The Working of the New Divorce Act." *English Woman's Journal* 2 (1859): 415–17.

"The Working of the New Divorce Bill." *English Woman's Journal* 1 (1858): 339–41.

Secondary Sources

Abbott, Grace. *The Child and the State.* 2 vols. 1938. New York: Greenwood Press, 1968.

Abbott, Maude Elizabeth Seymour. *Florence Nightingale: As Seen in Her Portraits.* Boston, 1916.

Abel-Smith, Brian. *A History of the Nursing Profession.* London: Heinemann, 1960.

Abraham, Kenneth S. "Statutory Interpretation and Literary Theory: Some Common Concerns of an Unlikely Pair." *Rutgers Law Review* 32 (1979): 676–94.

Abraham, L. A., and S. C. Hawtrey. *A Parliamentary Dictionary.* London: Butterworth, 1956.

Acland, Alice [Anne Marreco (Acland-Troyte)]. *Caroline Norton.* London: Constable, 1948.

Adams, Maurianne. "Family Disintegration and Creative Reintegration: The Case of Charlotte Brontë and *Jane Eyre*." In Anthony S. Wohl, ed., *The Victorian Family: Structure and Stresses.* London: Croom Helm, 1978.

Alexander, Sally. "Women, Class and Sexual Difference in the 1830s and 1840s: Some Reflections on the Writing of a Feminist History." *History Workshop Journal* 17 (1984): 125–49.

———. *Women's Work in Nineteenth-Century London: A Study of the Years 1820–50*. London: Journeyman Press, 1983.

Alleman, Gellert Spencer. *Matrimonial Laws and the Materials of Restoration Comedy*. Wallingford, Pa: privately printed, 1942.

Althusser, Louis. "Ideology and Ideological State Apparatuses (Notes towards an Investigation)." In *Lenin and Philosophy and Other Essays*. Trans. Ben Brewster. New York: Monthly Review Press, 1971.

Altick, Richard D. *The English Common Reader: A Social History of the Mass Reading Public, 1800–1900*. Chicago: University of Chicago Press, 1957.

Anderson, Olive. "The Janus Face of Mid-Nineteenth-Century English Radicalism: The Administrative Reform Association of 1855." *Victorian Studies* 8 (1965): 231–42.

———. *A Liberal State at War: English Politics and Economics during the Crimean War*. New York: St. Martin's Press, 1967.

Armstrong, Nancy. *Desire and Domestic Fiction: A Political History of the Novel*. New York: Oxford University Press, 1987.

———. "The Rise of Feminine Authority in the Novel." *Novel* 15 (Winter 1982): 127–45.

Arney, William Ray. *Power and the Profession of Obstetrics*. Chicago: University of Chicago Press, 1982.

Auerbach, Nina. *Woman and the Demon: The Life of a Victorian Myth*. Cambridge: Harvard University Press, 1982.

Baird, John D. "Divorce and Matrimonial Causes: An Aspect of *Hard Times*." *Victorian Studies* 20 (1977): 400–12.

Balibar, Etienne, and Peter Macherey. "On Literature as an Ideological Form." In Robert Young, ed., *Untying the Text: A Post-Structuralist Reader*, pp. 79–99. Boston: Routledge and Kegan Paul, 1981.

Baly, Monica E. *Nursing and Social Change*. 2d ed. London: Heinemann, 1980.

Banks, J. A. *Prosperity and Parenthood: A Study of Family Planning among the Victorian Middle Classes*. London: Routledge and Kegan Paul, 1954.

Banks, J. A., and Olive Banks. *Feminism and Family Planning in Victorian England*. New York: Schocken, 1964.

Barker-Benfield, G. J. *The Horrors of the Half-Known Life: Male Attitudes towards Women and Sexuality in Nineteenth-Century America*. New York: Harper and Row, 1976.

———. "The Spermatic Economy: A Nineteenth-Century View of Sexuality." *Feminist Studies* 1 (1972): 45–74.

Barnes, James J. *Authors, Publishers and Politicians: The Quest for an Anglo-American Copyright Agreement, 1815–54*. London: Routledge and Kegan Paul, 1974.

———. *Free Trade in Books: A Study of the London Book Trade since 1800*. London: Clarendon Press, 1964.

Barthes, Roland. *S/Z: An Essay*. Trans. Richard Miller. New York: Hill and Wang, 1974.

Basch, Françoise. *Relative Creatures: Victorian Women in Society and the Novel.* New York: Schocken Books, 1974.

Beard, Mary R. *Woman as a Force in History: A Study in Traditions and Realities.* New York: Macmillan, 1946.

Beaty, Jerome. "*Jane Eyre* and Genre." *Genre* 10 (Winter 1977): 619–54.

Bell, E. H. C. Moberley. *Storming the Citadel: The Rise of the Woman Doctor.* London: Constable, 1953.

Belsey, Catherine. "The Romantic Construction of the Unconscious." In Frances Barker, Peter Hulme, Margaret Iversen, and Diana Loxley, eds., *Literature, Politics and Theory: Papers from the Essex Conference, 1976–84,* pp. 57–76. London: Methuen, 1986.

———. *The Subject of Tragedy: Identity and Difference in Renaissance Drama.* London: Methuen, 1985.

Bendix, Reinhard. *Work and Authority in Industry: Ideologies of Management in the Course of Industrialization.* New York: Harper and Row, 1963.

Bennett, Scott. "Revolutions in Thought: Serial Publication and the Mass Market for Reading." In Joanne Shattock and Michael Wolff, eds., *The Victorian Periodical Press,* pp. 225–60. Leicester and Toronto: Leicester University Press and University of Toronto Press, 1982.

Berlant, Jeffrey Lionel. *Profession and Monopoly: A Study of Medicine in the United States and Great Britain.* Berkeley: University of California Press, 1975.

Bishop, W. J., and Sue Goldie. *A Bio-Bibliography of Florence Nightingale.* London: Dawsons, 1962.

Bonham-Carter, Victor. *Authors by Profession.* Vol 1. Los Altos, Calif.: William Kaufmann, 1978.

———, ed. *Surgeon in the Crimea: The Experiences of George Lawson Recorded in Letters to His Family, 1854–1855.* London: Constable, 1968.

Boyle, Thomas F. " 'Morbid Depression Alternating with Excitement': Sex in Victorian Newspapers." In Don Richard Cox, ed., *Sexuality and Victorian Literature,* pp. 212–33. Tennessee Studies in Literature, vol. 27. Knoxville: University of Tennessee Press, 1984.

Bratton, J. S. "Of England, Home, and Duty: The Image of England in Victorian and Edwardian Juvenile Fiction." In John M. MacKenzie, ed., *Imperialism and Popular Culture,* pp. 73–93. Manchester, England: Manchester University Press, 1986.

Briggs, Asa. *Iron Bridge to Crystal Palace: Impact and Images of the Industrial Revolution.* London: Thames and Hudson, 1979.

———. "Middle-Class Consciousness in English Politics, 1780–1846." *Past and Present,* no. 9 (April 1956): 65–74.

Bristow, Edward J. *Vice and Vigilance: Purity Movements in Britain since 1700.* Dublin: Gill and Macmillan, 1977.

Brooks, Peter. *The Melodramatic Imagination: Balzac, Henry James, Melodrama, and the Mode of Excess.* New Haven: Yale University Press, 1976.

————. *Reading for the Plot: Design and Intention in Narrative.* New York: Alfred A. Knopf, 1984.

Brown, Carol. "Mothers, Fathers, and Children: From Private to Public Patriarchy." In Lydia Sargent, ed., *Women and Revolution: A Discussion of the Unhappy Marriage of Marxism and Feminism,* pp. 239–68. Boston: South End Press, 1981.

Bruns, Gerald L. "Law as Hermeneutics: A Response to Ronald Dworkin." In W. J. T. Mitchell, ed., *The Politics of Interpretation,* pp. 315–20. Chicago: University of Chicago Press, 1983.

Bullough, Vern, and Martha Voght. "Women, Menstruation, and Nineteenth-Century Medicine." In Judith Walzer Leavitt, ed., *Women and Health in America: Historical Readings,* pp. 28–37. Madison: University of Wisconsin Press, 1984.

Burman, Sandra, ed. *Fit Work for Women.* New York: St. Martin's Press, 1979.

Burstyn, Joan N. *Victorian Education and the Ideal of Womanhood.* Totowa, N.J.: Barnes and Noble, 1980.

Carr-Saunders, A. M., and P. A. Wilson. *The Professions.* Oxford: Oxford University Press, 1933. Reprint. London: Frank Cass, 1964.

Catalogue of British Parliamentary Papers. Irish University Press 1000-Volume Series; Area Studies Series 1801–1900. Dublin: Irish Academic Press, 1977.

Cecil, David. *Lord M., or the Later Life of Lord Melbourne.* London: Constable, 1954.

Cell, John. "The Imperial Conscience." In Peter Marsh, ed., *The Conscience of the Victorian State,* pp. 173–213. Syracuse, N.Y.: Syracuse University Press, 1979.

Chauncey, George, Jr. "From Sexual Inversion to Homosexuality: Medicine and the Changing Conceptualization of Female Deviance." *Salamagundi* 58–59 (1982): 114–46.

Christ, Carol. "Victorian Masculinity and the Angel in the House." In Martha Vicinus, ed., *A Widening Sphere: Changing Roles of Victorian Women,* pp. 146–62. Bloomington: Indiana University Press, 1977.

Clark, Anna K. "Rape or Seduction? A Controversy over Sexual Violence in the Nineteenth Century." In *The Sexual Dynamics of History: Men's Power, Women's Resistance,* pp. 13–27. London: Pluto Press, 1983.

Colby, Robert A. *Fiction with a Purpose: Major and Minor Nineteenth-Century Novels.* Bloomington: Indiana University Press, 1967.

Cole, Frank. *Milestones in Anaesthesia: Readings in the Development of Surgical Anaesthesia, 1665–1940.* Lincoln: University of Nebraska Press, 1965.

Cominus, Peter T. "Innocent Femina Sensualis in Unconscious Conflict." In Martha Vicinus, ed., *Suffer and Be Still: Women in the Victorian Age,* pp. 155–72. Bloomington: University of Indiana Press, 1972.

Conacher, J. B. *The Aberdeen Coalition, 1852–55.* Cambridge: Cambridge University Press, 1968.

Cook, Sir Edward. *The Life of Florence Nightingale.* 2 vols. London: Macmillan, 1913.

Cope, Zachary. *Florence Nightingale and the Doctors.* London: Museum Press, 1958.

Corrigan, Philip, ed., *Capitalism, State Formation and Marxist Theory: Historical Investigations.* London: Quartet Books, 1980.

Cott, Nancy. *The Bonds of Womanhood: "Woman's Sphere" in New England, 1780–1835.* New Haven: Yale University Press, 1977.

———. "Passionlessness: An Interpretation of Victorian Sexual Ideology." *Signs* 4 (1978): 219–36.

Coveney, Peter. *The Image of Childhood: The Individual and Society: A Study of the Theme in English Literature.* Rev. ed. Harmondsworth, England: Penguin Books, 1967.

Cowan, J. L. *Pleasure and Pain: A Study in Philosophical Psychology.* New York: St. Martin's Press, 1968.

Coward, Rosalind. "Sexual Politics and Psychoanalysis: Some Notes on Their Relation." In Rosalind Brunt and Caroline Rowan, eds., *Feminism, Culture, and Politics,* pp. 171–87. London: Lawrence and Wishart, 1982.

Craft, Christopher. " 'Kiss Me with Those Red Lips': Gender and Inversion in Bram Stoker's *Dracula.*" *Representations* 8 (1984): 107–34.

Crowther, M. A. *Church Embattled: Religious Controversy in Mid-Victorian England.* Newton Abbot, Devon, England: David and Chaves, 1970.

Dabney, Ross. *Love and Property in the Novels of Dickens.* Berkeley: University of California Press, 1967.

Dally, Ann. *Inventing Motherhood: The Consequences of an Ideal.* New York: Schocken Books, 1983.

Davidoff, Leonore. "Class and Gender in Victorian England: The Diaries of Arthur J. Munby and Hannah Cullwick." *Feminist Studies* 5 (Spring 1979): 86–141.

———. "Mastered for Life: Servant and Wife in Victorian and Edwardian England." *Journal of Social History* 7 (1974): 406–28.

———. "The Separation of Home and Work? Landladies and Lodgers in Nineteenth- and Twentieth-Century England." In Sandra Burman, ed., *Fit Work for Women.* New York: St. Martin's Press, 1979.

Davidoff, Leonore, and Catherine Hall. *Family Fortunes: Men and Women of the English Middle Class, 1780–1850.* Chicago: University of Chicago Press, 1987.

Davidoff, Leonore, Jean L'Esperance, and Howard Newby. "Landscape with Figures: Home and Community in English Society." In Juliet Mitchell and Ann Oakley, eds., *The Rights and Wrongs of Women,* pp. 139–75. Harmondsworth, England: Penguin Books, 1976.

Davidson, M. H. Armstrong. *The Evolution of Anaesthesia.* Baltimore: Williams and Wilkins, 1965.

Davies, Celia, ed. *Rewriting Nursing History.* London: Croom Helm, 1980.

Degler, Carl N. "What Ought to Be and What Was: Women's Sexuality in the Nineteenth Century." In Judith Walzer Leavitt, ed., *Women and Health in America: Historical Readings,* pp. 40–56. Madison: University of Wisconsin Press, 1984.

Dentith, Simon. "Political Economy, Fiction and the Language of Practical Ideology in Nineteenth-Century England." *Social History* 8 (1983): 183–99.

Derrida, Jacques. "Structure, Sign, and Play in the Discourse of the Human Sciences." In *Writing and Difference.* Trans. Alan Bass. Chicago: University of Chicago Press, 1978.

Dicey, Albert Venn. *Lectures on the Relation between Law and Public Opinion in England during the Nineteenth Century.* London: Macmillan Publishers, 1905.

Dimock, Wai-che. *Empire of Liberty.* Princeton: Princeton University Press, forthcoming.

Donegan, Jane B. *Women and Men Midwives: Medicine, Morality, and Misogyny in Early America.* Westport, Conn.: Greenwood Press, 1978.

Donnison, Jean. *Midwives and Medical Men: A History of Inter-Professional Rivalries and Women's Rights.* New York: Schocken, 1977.

Duffin, Lorna. "The Conspicuous Consumptive: Woman as an Invalid." In Sara Delamont and Lorna Duffin, eds., *The Nineteenth-Century Woman: Her Cultural and Physical World,* pp. 26–56. London: Croom Helm, 1978.

Dunbar, Janet. *The Early Victorian Woman: Some Aspects of Her Life (1837–57).* London: Harrap, 1953. Reprint. Westport, Conn.: Hyperion Press, 1979.

Duncum, Barbara M. *The Development of Inhalation Anaesthesia, with Special Reference to the Years 1846–1900.* London: Oxford University Press, 1947.

Dworkin, Ronald. "Law as Interpretation." In W. J. T. Mitchell, ed., *The Politics of Interpretation,* pp. 249–70. Chicago: University of Chicago Press, 1983.

Edelman, Bernard. *Ownership of the Image: Elements for a Marxist Theory of Law.* Trans. Elizabeth Kingdom. London: Routledge and Kegan Paul, 1979.

Edwards, Susan. *Female Sexuality and the Law: A Study of Constructs of Female Sexuality as They Inform Statute and Legal Procedure.* Oxford: Martin Robertson, 1981.

———. "Introduction." In Susan Edwards, ed., *Gender, Sex and the Law.* London: Croom Helm, 1985.

Ehrenreich, Barbara, and Deidre English. *Complaints and Disorders: The Sexual Politics of Sickness.* Grass Mountain Pamphlet, no. 2. Old Westbury, N.Y.: Feminist Press, 1973.

———. *For Her Own Good: 150 Years of the Experts' Advice to Women.* Garden City, N.Y.: Anchor Press/Doubleday, 1979.

Ellis, Havelock. *Man and Woman: A Study of Human Secondary Sexual Characteristics.* London: Walter Scott, 1904. Reprint. New York: Arno Press, 1974.

Enloe, Cynthia H. "On Common Ground." *Women's Review of Books* 1 (September 1984): 3–5.

Fee, Elizabeth. "Psychology, Sexuality, and Social Control in Victorian England." *Social Science Quarterly* 58 (1978): 632–46.

Felman, Shoshana. "Turning the Screw of Interpretation." *Yale French Studies* 55/56 (1977): 94–207.

Feltes, N. N. *Modes of Production of Victorian Novels.* Chicago: University of Chicago Press, 1986.

Fish, Stanley. "Working on the Chain Gang: Interpretation in the Law and in Literary Criticism." In W. J. T. Mitchell, ed., *The Politics of Interpretation.* Chicago: University of Chicago Press, 1983.

Foreman, Ann. *Femininity as Alienation: Women and the Family in Marxism and Psychoanalysis.* London: Pluto Press, 1977.

Forster, John. *The Life of Charles Dickens.* 2 vols. London: Chapman and Hall, 1899.

Foucault, Michel. "History of Systems of Thought." In *Language, Counter-Memory, Practice: Selected Essays and Interviews,* pp. 199–204. Ed. Donald F. Bouchard; trans. Donald F. Bouchard and Sherry Simon. Ithaca: Cornell University Press, 1977.

———. "Intellectuals and Power: A Conversation between Michel Foucault and Gilles Deleuze." In *Language, Counter-Memory, Practice: Selected Essays and Interviews,* pp. 205–17. Ed. Donald F. Bouchard, trans. Donald F. Bouchard and Sherry Simon. Ithaca: Cornell University Press, 1977.

———. *Language, Counter-Memory, Practice: Selected Essays and Interviews.* Ed. Donald F. Bouchard; trans. Donald F. Bouchard and Sherry Simon. Ithaca: Cornell University Press, 1977.

———. "Nietzsche, Genealogy, History." In *Language, Counter-Memory, Practice: Selected Essays and Interviews,* pp. 139–84. Ed. Donald F. Bouchard; translated Donald F. Bouchard and Sherry Simon. Ithaca: Cornell University Press, 1977.

———. "A Preface to Transgression." In *Language, Counter-Memory, Practice: Selected Essays and Interviews,* pp. 29–52. Ed. Donald F. Bouchard; trans. Donald F. Bouchard and Sherry Simon. Ithaca: Cornell University Press, 1977.

———. "What Is an Author?" In *Language, Counter-Memory, Practice: Selected Essays and Interviews,* pp. 113–38. Ed. Donald F. Bouchard; trans. Donald F. Bouchard and Sherry Simon. Ithaca: Cornell University Press, 1977.

———, ed. *I, Pierre Riviere, Having Slaughtered My Mother, My Sister, and My Brother . . . : A Case of Parricide in the Nineteenth Century.* Trans. Frank Jellinek. Lincoln: University of Nebraska Press, 1982.

Fox-Genovese, Elizabeth, and Eugene D. Genovese. "The Ideological Bases of Domestic Economy: The Representation of Women and the Family in the Age of Expansion." In *Fruits of Merchant Capital: Slavery and Bourgeois Property in the Rise and Expansion of Capitalism*, pp. 299–336. Oxford: Oxford University Press, 1983.

Gallagher, Catherine. *The Industrial Reformation of English Fiction: Social Discourse and Narrative Form, 1832–1867*. Chicago: University of Chicago Press, 1985.

Gallop, Jane. *The Daughter's Seduction: Feminism and Psychoanalysis*. Ithaca: Cornell University Press, 1982.

Gamarnikow, Eva. "Sexual Division of Labour: The Case of Nursing." In Annette Kuhn and AnnMarie Wolpe, eds., *Feminism and Materialism: Women and Modes of Production*, pp. 96–213. London: Routledge and Kegan Paul, 1978.

Gasking, Elizabeth. *Investigations of Generation, 1651–1828*. London: Hutchinson, 1961.

Gay, Peter. "On the Bourgeoisie: A Psychological Interpretation." In John M. Merriman, ed., *Consciousness and Class Experience in Nineteenth-Century Europe*, pp. 187–203. New York: Holmes and Meier, 1979.

Geison, G. "Social and Institutional Factors in the Stagnancy of English Physiology, 1840–1870." *Bulletin of the History of Medicine* 46:1 (1972): 30–58.

Geldart, William. *Introduction to English Law*. 9th ed. Ed. D. C. M. Yardley. Oxford: Oxford University Press, 1984.

Gieryn, Thomas F. "Boundary-Work and the Demarcation of Science from Non-Science: Strains and Interests in Professional Ideologies of Scientists." *American Sociological Review* 48 (1983): 781–95.

Gilbert, Sandra M., and Susan Gubar. *The Madwoman in the Attic: The Woman Writer and the Nineteenth-Century Literary Imagination*. New Haven: Yale University Press, 1979.

Gilman, Charlotte Perkins. *Women and Economics*. Ed. Carl Degler. New York: Harper and Row, 1966.

Goldsmith, Margaret. *Florence Nightingale: The Woman and the Legend*. London: Hodder and Stoughton, 1937.

Gordon, A. K. "Puerperal Septic Disease." In R. W. Marsden, *A Practical Text-Book on Infectious Diseases*, pp. 263–87. Manchester, England: Manchester University Press, 1908.

Gordon, Laing. *Masters of Medicine: Sir James Simpson*. New York: Longmans, Green, 1897.

Gorham, Deborah. "A 'Maiden Tribute to Modern Babylon' Re-examined, Child Prostitution and the Idea of Childhood in Late Victorian England." *Victorian Studies* 21 (1978): 353–79.

———. *The Victorian Girl and the Feminine Ideal*. Bloomington: Indiana University Press, 1982.

Gorsley, Susan. "Old Maids and New Women: Alternatives to Marriage in

Englishwomen's Novels, 1847–1915." *Journal of Popular Culture* 8 (1973): 68–86.

Greenblatt, Stephen. *Renaissance Self-Fashioning: From More to Shakespeare.* Chicago: University of Chicago Press, 1980.

Gubar, Susan. "The Birth of the Artist as Heroine: (Re)production, the *Kunstlerroman* Tradition, and the Fiction of Katherine Mansfield." In Carolyn G. Heilbrun and Margaret R. Higonnet, eds., *The Representation of Women in Fiction: Selected Papers from the English Institute, 1981.* Baltimore: Johns Hopkins University Press, 1983.

Hall, Catherine. "The Early Formation of Victorian Domestic Ideology." In Sandra Burman, ed., *Fit Work for Women,* pp. 15–32. New York: St. Martin's Press, 1979.

Harrison, Brian. "Press and Pressure Group in Modern Britain." In Joanne Shattock and Michael Wolff, eds., *The Victorian Periodical Press: Samplings and Soundings,* pp. 261–96. Leicester and Toronto: Leicester University Press and University of Toronto Press, 1982.

————. "State Intervention and Moral Reform in Nineteenth-Century England." In Patricia Hollis, ed., *Pressure from Without in Early Victorian England,* pp. 289–322. New York: St. Martin's Press, 1974.

Harrison, Fraser. *The Dark Angel: Aspects of Victorian Sexuality.* London: Sheldon Press, 1977.

Harrison, J. F. C. *Early Victorian Britain, 1832–51.* London: Weidenfield and Nicolson, 1971. Reprint. London: Fontana/Collins, 1979.

Harrison, Rachel, and Frank Mort. "Patriarchal Aspects of Nineteenth-Century State Formation: Property Relations, Marriage and Divorce, and Sexuality." In Philip Corrigan, ed., *Capitalism, State Formation and Marxist Theory: Historical Investigations,* pp. 79–109. London: Quartet Books, 1980.

Hart, Jennifer. "Religion and Social Control in the Mid-Nineteenth Century." In A. P. Donajgrodzki, ed., *Social Control in Nineteenth Century Britain,* pp. 108–37. London: Croom Helm, 1977.

Hartmann, Heidi. "The Unhappy Marriage of Marxism and Feminism: Towards a More Progressive Union." In Lydia Sargent, ed., *Women and Revolution: A Discussion of the Unhappy Marriage of Marxism and Feminism,* pp. 1–42. Boston: South End Press, 1981.

Hayek, F. A., ed. *John Stuart Mill and Harriet Taylor: Their Correspondence and Subsequent Marriage.* Chicago: University of Chicago Press, 1951.

Heath, Stephen. *The Sexual Fix.* New York: Schocken Books, 1984.

Heaton, Claude Edwin. "The History of Anaesthesia and Analgesia in Obstetrics." *Journal of the History of Medicine and the Allied Sciences* 1 (1946): 567–72.

Helsinger, Elizabeth K., Robin Lauterbach Sheets, and William Veeder, eds., *The Woman Question: Society and Literature in Britain and America, 1837–1883.* 3 vols. New York: Garland Publishing, 1983.

Herstein, Sheila R. *A Mid-Victorian Feminist: Barbara Leigh Smith Bodichon.* New Haven: Yale University Press, 1985.

Hiller, Mary Ruth. "The Identification of Authors: The Great Victorian Enigma." In J. Don Vann and Rosemary T. Van Arsdel, eds., *Victorian Periodicals: A Guide to Research,* pp. 123–48. New York: Modern Language Association of America, 1978.

Hirst, Paul Q. "Introduction." In Bernard Edelman, *Ownership of the Image: Elements for a Marxist Theory of Law,* pp. 1–18. Trans. Elizabeth Kingdom. London: Routledge and Kegan Paul, 1979.

———. *On Law and Ideology.* London: Macmillan, 1979.

Holcombe, Lee. *Victorian Ladies at Work: Middle-Class Working Women in England and Wales, 1850–1914.* Hamden, Conn.: Shoe String Press, 1973.

———. *Wives and Property: Reform of the Married Women's Property Law in Nineteenth-Century England.* Toronto: University of Toronto Press, 1983.

Holdsworth, Sir William. *A History of English Law.* Vol 16. Ed. A. L. Goodhart and H. G. Hanbury. London: Methuen, 1966.

Hollis, Patricia. "Introduction." In Patricia Hollis, ed., *Pressure from Without in Early Victorian England,* pp. vii–xxvi. London: Edward Arnold, 1974.

Holloway, S. W. F. "Medical Education in England, 1830–1858: A Sociological Analysis." *History* 49 (1964): 299–324.

Holton, Sandra. "Feminine Authority and Social Order: Florence Nightingale's Conception of Nursing and Health Care." *Social Analysis* 15 (August 1984): 59–72.

Homans, Margaret. *Bearing the Word: Language and Female Experience in Nineteenth-Century Women's Writing.* Chicago: University of Chicago Press, 1986.

———. "Dreaming of Children: Literalization in *Jane Eyre* and *Wuthering Heights.*" In Juliann E. Fleenor, ed., *The Female Gothic,* pp. 257–79. Montreal: Eden Press, 1983.

Horine, Emmet F. "Episodes in the History of Anaesthesia." *Journal of the History of Medicine and the Allied Sciences* 1 (1946): 521–26.

Houghton, Walter E. "Periodical Literature and the Articulate Classes." In Joanne Shattock and Michael Wolff, eds., *The Victorian Periodical Press: Samplings and Soundings,* pp. 3–28. Leicester and Toronto: Leicester University Press and University of Toronto Press, 1982.

House, Humphrey. *The Dickens World.* London: Oxford University Press, 1941; 2d ed., 1942; paper ed., 1960.

Hughes, Winifred. *The Maniac in the Cellar: Sensation Novels of the 1860s.* Princeton: Princeton University Press, 1980.

Inkster, Ian. "Marginal Men: Aspects of the Social Role of the Medical Community in Sheffield, 1790–1850." In John Woodward and David Richards, eds., *Health Care and Popular Medicine,* pp. 128–63. New York: Holmes and Meier, 1977.

Jacobus, Mary. "Is There a Woman in This Text?" *New Literary History* (1982): 117–41.

Jameson, Fredric. *The Political Unconscious: Narrative as a Socially Symbolic Act.* Ithaca: Cornell University Press, 1981.

Janet, Pierre. *The Major Symptoms of Hysteria: Fifteen Lectures Given in the Medical School of Harvard University.* 2d ed. 1920. Reprint. New York: Hafner Publishing, 1965.

Johnson, Richard. "Educating the Educators: 'Experts' and the State, 1833–9." In A. P. Donajgrodzki, ed., *Social Control in Nineteenth Century Britain,* pp. 77–107. London: Croom Helm, 1977.

———. "Reading for the Best Marx: History-Writing and Historical Instruction." In Richard Johnson, Gregor McLennan, Bill Schwartz, and David Sutton, eds., *Making Histories: Studies in History-Writing and Politics,* pp. 153–201. London: Hutchinson, 1982.

Jordan, H. Donaldson. "The Reports of Parliamentary Debates, 1803–1908." *Economica* 11 (1931): 437–39.

Jordan, John O. "The Social Sub-Text of *David Copperfield.*" *Dickens Studies Annual: Essays on Victorian Fiction* 14 (1985): 81–92.

Jordanova, L. J. "Natural Facts: A Historical Perspective on Science and Sexuality." In Carol P. MacCormack and Marilyn Strathern, eds., *Nature, Culture and Gender,* pp. 42–69. Cambridge: Cambridge University Press, 1980.

Kamm, Josephine. *Rapiers and Battleaxes: The Women's Movement and Its Aftermath.* London: George Allen and Unwin, 1966.

Kanner, S. Barbara. "The Women of England in a Century of Social Change, 1815–1914: A Select Bibliography." In Martha Vicinus, ed., *Suffer and Be Still: Women in the Victorian Age,* pp. 173–206. Bloomington: Indiana University Press, 1972.

Knoepflmacher, U. C. "The Counterworld of Victorian Fiction and *The Woman in White.*" In Jerome H. Buckley, ed., *The Worlds of Victorian Fiction,* pp. 351–69. Cambridge: Harvard University Press, 1975.

Krafft-Ebbing, Richard von. *An Experimental Study in the Domain of Hypnotism.* 1893. Reprint. New York: Da Capo Press, 1982.

Kucich, John. *Excess and Restraint in the Novels of Charles Dickens.* Athens: University of Georgia Press, 1981.

Kuhn, Annette. *Women's Pictures: Feminism and Cinema.* London: Routledge and Kegan Paul, 1982.

Kuhn, Annette, and AnnMarie Wolpe. *Feminism and Materialism: Women and Modes of Production.* Boston: Routledge & Kegan Paul, 1978.

Laqueur, Thomas. "Orgasm, Generation, and the Politics of Reproductive Biology." *Representations* 14 (Spring 1986): 1–41.

Lasch, Christopher. *Haven in a Heartless World: The Family Besieged.* New York: Basic Books, 1977; paper ed. 1979.

Latey, William. *The Tide of Divorce.* London: Longman, 1970.

Leake, Chauncey D. "Historical Notes on the Pharmacology of Anaesthesia." *Journal of the History of Medicine and the Allied Sciences* 1 (1946): 573–82.

Leavitt, Judith Walzer. "Birthing and Anaesthesia: The Debate over Twilight Sleep." In Judith Walzer Leavitt, ed., *Women and Health in America: Historical Readings,* pp. 175–84. Madison: University of Wisconsin Press, 1984. Reprint from *Signs* 6 (1980): 147–64.

––––––, ed. *Women and Health in America: Historical Readings.* Madison: University of Wisconsin Press, 1984.

Leonard, Peter. *Personality and Ideology: Towards a Materialist Understanding of the Individual.* London: Macmillan, 1984.

L'Esperance, Jean. "Doctors and Women in Nineteenth-Century Society: Sexuality and Role." In John Woodward and David Richards, eds., *Health Care and Popular Medicine,* pp. 105–27. New York: Holmes and Meier, 1977.

London Feminist History Group. *The Sexual Dynamics of History: Men's Power, Women's Resistance.* London: Pluto Press, 1983.

Lutzker, Edythe. *Women Gain a Place in Medicine.* New York: McGraw-Hill, 1969.

Macherey, Pierre. *A Theory of Literary Production.* Trans. Geoffrey Wall. London: Routledge and Kegan Paul, 1978.

McBride, Theresa M. *The Domestic Revolution: The Modernization of Household Science in England and France, 1820–1920.* New York: Holmes and Meier, 1976.

McCandless, Peter. "Liberty and Lunacy: The Victorians and Wrongful Confinement." In Andrew Scull, ed., *Madhouses, Mad-Doctors, and Madmen,* pp. 339–62. Philadelphia: University of Pennsylvania Press, 1981.

McGregor, O. M. *Divorce in England: A Centenary Study.* London: Heinemann, 1957.

McIntosh, Mary. "The Welfare State and the Needs of the Dependent Family." In Sandra Burman, ed., *Fit Work for Women,* pp. 153–72. New York: St. Martin's Press, 1979.

Mackenzie, Charlotte. "Women and Psychiatric Professionalization, 1780–1914." In *The Sexual Dynamics of History: Men's Power, Women's Resistance,* pp. 107–19. London: Pluto Press, 1983.

McLaren, Angus. *Birth Control in Nineteenth-Century England.* New York: Holmes and Meier, 1978.

MacQuilty, Betty. *The Battle for Oblivion. The Discovery of Anaesthesia.* London: George G. Harrap, 1969.

Manton, Jo. *Sister Dora: The Life of Dorothy Pattison.* New York: Quartet Books, 1977.

Martin, Biddy. "Feminism, Criticism, and Foucault." *New German Critique* 27 (1982): 3–30.

Merskey, Harold, and F. G. Spear. *Pain: Psychological and Psychiatric Aspects.* London: Bailliere, Tindall and Cassell, 1967.

Metcalf, Thomas R. *The Aftermath of Revolt: India, 1857–1870.* Princeton: Princeton University Press, 1964.

Michaels, Walter Benn. *The Gold Standard and the Logic of Naturalism.* Berkeley: University of California Press, 1987.

Miller, John Hawkins. " 'Temple and Sewer': Childbirth, Prudery, and Victoria Regina." In Anthony S. Wohl, ed., *The Victorian Family: Structure and Stresses,* pp. 23–43. New York: St. Martin's Press, 1978.

Mintz, Steven. *A Prison of Expectations: The Family in Victorian Culture.* New York: New York University Press, 1983.

Mitchell, Juliet, and Ann Oakley, eds. *The Rights and Wrongs of Women.* Harmondsworth, England: Penguin Books, 1976.

Mitchell, Sally. *The Fallen Angel: Chastity, Class, and Women's Reading, 1835–1880.* Bowling Green, Ohio: Bowling Green University Popular Press, 1981.

Mueller, Hans-Eberhard. *Bureaucracy, Education, and Monopoly: Civil Service Reforms in Prussia and England.* Berkeley: University of California Press, 1984.

Musselwhite, David. "The Trial of Warren Hastings." In Frances Barker, Peter Hulme, Margaret Iversen, and Diana Loxley, eds., *Literature, Politics, and Theory: Papers from the Essex Conference, 1976–84.* London: Methuen, 1986.

Neale, R. S. *Class and Ideology in the Nineteenth Century.* London: Routledge and Kegan Paul, 1972.

Neff, Wanda F. *Victorian Working Women: An Historical and Literary Study of Women in British Industries and Professions, 1831–1850.* 1929. Reprint. New York: Humanities Press, 1966.

Newton, Judith Lowder. *Women, Power, and Subversion: Social Strategies in British Fiction, 1778–1860.* Athens: University of Georgia Press, 1981.

Nussbaum, Felicity A. *The Brink of All We Hate: English Satires on Women, 1660–1750.* Lexington: University of Kentucky Press, 1984.

Nutting, M. Adelaide, and Lavinia L. Dock. *A History of Nursing.* New York: G. P. Putnam's, 1907.

Oakley, Ann. *Sex, Gender, and Society.* London: Temple Smith; New York: Harper and Row, 1972.

———. *Women Confined: Towards a Sociology of Childbirth.* New York: Schocken Books, 1980.

Olney, Clarke. "Caroline Norton to Lord Melbourne." *Victorian Studies* 8 (1965): 255–62.

O'Neill, William L. *The Woman Movement: Feminism in the United States and England.* Chicago: Quadrangle Books, 1971.

Palmegiano, E. M. *Women and British Periodicals, 1832–1867: A Bibliography.* New York: Garland, 1976.

Parrinder, Patrick. *Authors and Authority: A Study of English Literary Criticism and Its Relation to Culture, 1750–1900.* London: Routledge and Kegan Paul, 1977.

Parris, Henry. *Constitutional Bureaucracy: The Development of British Central Administration since the Eighteenth Century.* New York: Augustus M. Kelley, 1969.

Parry, Noel, and José Parry. *The Rise of the Medical Profession: A Study of Collective Social Mobility.* London: Croom Helm, 1976.

Parry-Jones, William L. *The Trade in Lunacy: A Study of Private Madhouses in England in the Eighteenth and Nineteenth Centuries.* London: Routledge and Kegan Paul, 1972.

Patmore, Coventry. *The Poems of Coventry Patmore.* Ed. by Frederick Page. London: Oxford University Press, 1949.

Patten, Robert L. *Charles Dickens and His Publishers.* Oxford: Oxford University Press, 1978.

Pearsall, Ronald. *The Worm in the Bud: The World of Victorian Sexuality.* Toronto: Macmillan, 1969.

Peattie, Lisa, and Martin Rein. *Women's Claims: A Study in Political Economy.* Oxford: Oxford University Press, 1983.

Perkin, Harold. *The Origins of Modern English Society, 1780–1880.* London: Routledge and Kegan Paul, 1969.

Perkins, Jane Gray. *The Life of the Honourable Mrs. Norton.* New York: Henry Holt, 1909.

Perry, Ruth. *The Life and Times of Mary Astell (1666–1731): An Early English Feminist.* Chicago: University of Chicago Press, 1985.

————. "Mary Astell's Feminism: The Veil of Chastity." In Roseann Runte, ed., *Studies in Eighteenth Century Culture,* 9:25–43. Madison: University of Wisconsin Press, 1979.

Peterson, M. Jeanne. *The Medical Profession in Mid-Victorian London.* Berkeley: University of California Press, 1978.

————. "The Victorian Governess: Status Incongruence in Family and Society." In Martha Vicinus, ed., *Suffer and Be Still: Women in the Victorian Age.* Bloomington: Indiana University Press, 1972.

Phillips, Walter C. *Dickens, Reade, and Collins: Sensation Novelists.* New York: Columbia University Press, 1919. Reprint. New York: Garland Publishing, 1979.

Pinchbeck, Ivy. *Women Workers and the Industrial Revolution, 1750–1850.* 1930. Reprint. London: Virago Press, 1981.

Polikoff, Nancy D. "Why Are Mothers Losing: A Brief Analysis of Criteria Used in Child Custody Determinations." *Women's Rights Law Reporter* 7 (1982): 235–43.

Pollak, Ellen. *The Poetics of Sexual Myth: Gender and Ideology in the Verse of Swift and Pope.* Chicago: University of Chicago Press, 1985.

Poovey, Mary. *The Proper Lady and the Woman Writer: Ideology as Style in the Works of Mary Wollstonecraft, Mary Shelley, and Jane Austen.* Chicago: University of Chicago Press, 1984.

Reader, W. J. *Professional Men: The Rise of the Professional Classes in Nineteenth-Century England.* London: Weidenfield and Nicolson, 1966.

Reiser, Stanley Joel. *Medicine and the Reign of Technology.* Cambridge: Cambridge University Press, 1978; paper ed., 1981.

Rich, Adrienne. *Of Woman Born: Motherhood as Experience and Institution.* New York: Norton, 1976; Bantam Books, 1977.

Riemer, Eleanor S., and John C. Fout. *European Women: A Documentary History, 1789–1945.* New York: Schocken Books, 1980.

Riffaterre, Michael. "Interpretation and Descriptive Poetry: A Reading of Wordsworth's 'Yew-Trees.' " In Robert Young, ed., *Untying the Text: A Post-Structuralist Reader,* pp. 103–32. Boston: Routledge and Kegan Paul, 1981.

Roberts, David. *Paternalism in Early Victorian England.* New Brunswick, N.J.: Rutgers University Press, 1979.

Robertson, Priscilla. *An Experience of Women: Pattern and Change in Nineteenth-Century Europe.* Philadelphia: Temple University Press, 1982.

Rogers, Katherine M. *Feminism in Eighteenth-Century England.* Urbana: University of Illinois Press, 1982.

Rosen, George. *Madness in Society: Chapters in the Historical Sociology of Mental Illness.* New York: Harper and Row, 1968.

————. "Mesmerism and Surgery: A Strange Chapter in the History of Anaesthesia." *Journal of the History of Medicine and the Allied Sciences* 1 (1946): 527–50.

Rosenberg, Charles E. "Florence Nightingale on Contagion: The Hospital as Moral Universe." In Charles E. Rosenberg, ed., *Healing and History,* pp. 116–36. New York: Dawson, 1979.

Rover, Constance. *Women's Suffrage and Party Politics in Britain, 1866–1914.* London: Routledge and Kegan Paul, 1967.

Roy, Alec, ed. *Hysteria.* Chichester, England: John Wiley and Sons, 1982.

Rubin, Gayle. "The Traffic in Women." In Rayna Rapp Reiter, ed., *Toward an Anthropology of Women,* pp. 157–210. New York: Monthly Review Press, 1975.

Sachs, Albie, and Joan Hoff Wilson. *Sexism and the Law: A Study of Male Beliefs and Legal Bias in Britain and the United States.* Oxford: Martin Robertson, 1978.

Sandelowski, Margarete. *Pain, Pleasure, and American Childbirth: From the Twilight Sleep to the Reed Method, 1914–1960.* Westport, Conn.: Greenwood Press, 1984.

Sargent, Lydia. *Women and Revolution: A Discussion of the Unhappy Marriage of Marxism and Feminism.* Boston: South End Press, 1981.

Schafer, Roy. "Narration in the Psychoanalytic Dialogue." *Critical Inquiry* 7 (1980): 29–54.

Scull, Andrew. "A Brilliant Career? John Conolly and Victorian Psychiatry." *Victorian Studies* 27 (1984): 203–35.

————, ed. *Madhouses, Mad-Doctors, and Madmen.* Philadelphia: University of Pennsylvania Press, 1981.

Seymer, Lucy. *Florence Nightingale's Nurses: The Nightingale Training School, 1860–1960.* London: Pitman Medical Publishing, 1960.

Shanley, Mary. " 'One Must Ride Behind': Married Women's Rights and the Divorce Act of 1857." *Victorian Studies* 25 (1982): 355–76.

Shattock, Joanne, and Michael Wolff, eds. *The Victorian Periodical Press:*

Samplings and Soundings. Leicester and Toronto: Leicester University Press and University of Toronto Press, 1982.

Sheppard, Annamay T. "Unspoken Promises in Custody Litigation." *Women's Rights Law Reporter* 7 (1982): 229–34.

Showalter, Elaine. *A Literature of Their Own: British Women Novelists from Brontë to Lessing*. Princeton: Princeton University Press, 1977.

———. "Victorian Women and Insanity." In Andrew Scull, ed., *Madhouses, Mad-Doctors, and Madmen*, pp. 313–31. Philadelphia: University of Pennsylvania Press, 1981.

Silvio, Teri. "The Male Representing the Female Representing Herself: Wilkie Collins and Caroline Norton." Typescript. Bryn Mawr College, 1985.

Siskin, Clifford H. *The Historicity of Romantic Discourse*. New York: Oxford University Press, 1988.

Skultans, Vieda. *English Madness: Ideas on Insanity, 1580–1890*. London: Routledge and Kegan Paul, 1979.

———. *Madness and Morals: Ideas on Insanity in the Nineteenth Century*. London: Routledge and Kegan Paul, 1975.

Slater, Michael. *Dickens and Women*. Stanford: Stanford University Press, 1983.

Smart, Carol. *The Ties That Bind: Law, Marriage and the Reproduction of Patriarchal Relations*. London: Routledge and Kegan Paul, 1984.

Smith, F. B. *Florence Nightingale: Reputation and Power*. London: Croom Helm, 1982.

———. *The People's Health, 1830–1910*. New York: Holmes and Meier, 1979.

Smith, Graham. *Dickens, Money, and Society*. Berkeley: University of California Press, 1968.

Smith, Hilda L. *Reason's Disciple: Seventeenth-Century English Feminism*. Urbana: University of Illinois Press, 1982.

Smith, Karen W. *Constantin Guys: Crimean War Drawings, 1854–1856*. Cleveland: Cleveland Museum of Art, 1978.

Smith, Roger. "The Boundary between Insanity and Criminal Responsibility in Nineteenth-Century England." In Andrew Scull, ed., *Madhouses, Mad-Doctors, and Madmen*, pp. 363–84. Philadelphia: University of Pennsylvania Press, 1981.

———. *Trial by Medicine: Insanity and Responsibility in Victorian Trials*. Edinburgh: Edinburgh University Press, 1981.

Smith, W. D. A. *Under the Influence: A History of Nitrous Oxide and Oxygen Anaesthesia*. Park Ridge, Ill.: Wood Library Museum of Anaesthesiology, 1982.

Smith-Rosenberg, Carroll. "The Hysterical Women: Sex Roles and Role Conflict in Nineteenth Century America." *Social Research* 39 (1972): 652–78.

Smith-Rosenberg, Carroll, and Charles E. Rosenberg. "The Female Animal: Medical and Biological Views of Woman and Her Role in

Nineteenth-Century America." In Judith Walzer Leavitt, ed., *Women and Health in America: Historical Readings,* pp. 12–27. Madison: University of Wisconsin Press, 1984.

Sontag, Susan. *Illness as Metaphor.* New York: Farrar, Straus, and Giroux, 1977.

Spilka, Mark. "On the Enrichment of Poor Monkeys by Myth and Dream; or, How Dickens Rousseauisticized and Pre-Freudianized Victorian Views of Childhood." In Don Richard Cox, ed., *Sexuality and Victorian Literature,* pp. 161–79. Tennessee Studies in Literature, vol. 27. Knoxville: University of Tennessee Press, 1984.

Spivak, Gayatri Chakravorty. "Displacement and the Discourse of Woman." In Mark Krupnick, ed., *Displacement: Derrida and After,* pp. 169–95. Bloomington: Indiana University Press, 1983.

Spring, Eileen, and David Spring. "The Real Florence Nightingale?" *Bulletin of the History of Medicine* 57 (1983): 285–90.

Staves, Susan. "British Seduced Maidens." *Eighteenth-Century Studies* 14 (1980–81): 109–34.

———. "Money for Honor: Damages for Criminal Conversation." In Harry C. Payne, ed., *Studies in Eighteenth Century Culture,* 11: 179–97. Madison: University of Wisconsin Press, 1982.

———. *Players' Scepters: Fictions of Authority in the Restoration.* Lincoln: University of Nebraska Press, 1979.

———. "Where Is History but in Texts? Reading the History of Marriage." In John M. Wallace, ed., *The Golden and the Brazen World: Papers in Literature and History, 1650–1800,* pp. 125–49. Berkeley: University of California Press, 1985.

Stetson, Dorothy M. *A Woman's Issue: The Politics of Family Law Reform in England.* Westport, Conn.: Greenwood Press, 1982.

Stoehr, Taylor. *Dickens: The Dreamer's Stance.* Ithaca: Cornell University Press, 1965.

The Story of the Governesses' Benevolent Institution. Southwick, Sussex, England: Grange Press, 1962.

Strachey, Ray. *The Cause: A Short History of the Woman's Movement in Great Britain.* 1928. Reprint. London: Virago Press, 1978.

Summers, Anne. "A Home from Home: Women's Philanthropic Work in the Nineteenth Century." In Sandra Burman, ed., *Fit Work for Women,* pp. 33–63. New York: St. Martin's Press, 1979.

———. "Pride and Prejudice: Ladies and Nurses in the Crimean War." *History Workshop Journal* 16 (1982): 32–56.

Sutherland, John A. *Victorian Novelists and Publishers.* Chicago: University of Chicago Press, 1976.

Szasz, Thomas S. *The Myth of Mental Illness: Foundations of a Theory of Personal Conduct.* New York: Harper and Row, 1961.

Tanner, Tony. *Adultery in the Novel: Contract and Transgression.* Baltimore: Johns Hopkins University Press, 1979.

Taylor, Barbara. *Eve and the New Jerusalem: Socialism and Feminism in the Nineteenth Century.* New York: Pantheon, 1983.

Taylor, Ian. *Law and Order: Arguments for Socialism.* London: Macmillan, 1982.

Thomas, K. Bryn. *Development of Anaesthetic Apparatus.* Oxford: Blackwell Scientific Publications, 1975.

Thompson, Dorothy. "Women and Nineteenth-Century Radical Politics: A Lost Dimension." In Juliet Mitchell and Ann Oakley, eds., *The Rights and Wrongs of Women,* pp. 112–38. Harmondsworth, England: Penguin Books, 1976.

Thompson, E. P. *The Making of the English Working Class.* New York: Random House, 1966.

Tillotson, Kathleen. *Novels of the Eighteen-Forties.* Oxford: Clarendon Press, 1954.

Tilly, Louise A., and Joan W. Scott. *Women, Work, and Family.* New York: Holt, Rinehart, and Winston, 1978.

Todorov, Tzvetan. "How to Read?" In *The Poetics of Prose,* pp. 234–46. Trans. Richard Howard. Ithaca: Cornell University Press, 1977.

Tooley, Sarah A. *The History of Nursing in the British Empire.* London: S. H. Bousfield, 1906.

Travers, R. L. *Husband and Wife in English Law.* London: Gerald Duckworth, 1956.

Trent, Josiah Charles. "Surgical Anaesthesia, 1846–1946." *Journal of the History of Medicine and the Allied Sciences* 1 (1946): 505–14.

Trudgill, Eric. *Madonnas and Magdalens: The Origins and Development of Victorian Sexual Attitudes.* New York: Holmes and Meier, 1976.

Turner, Frank M. *Between Science and Religion: The Reaction to Scientific Naturalism in Late Victorian England.* New Haven: Yale University Press, 1974.

————. "The Victorian Conflict between Science and Religion: A Professional Dimension." *Isis* 69 (1978): 356–76.

Veith, Ilza. *Hysteria: The History of a Disease.* Chicago: University of Chicago Press, 1965.

Versluysen, Margaret. "Midwives, Medical Men and 'Poor Women Labouring of Child': Lying-in Hospitals in Eighteenth-Century London." In Helen Roberts, ed., *Women, Health and Reproduction,* pp. 18–49. London: Routledge and Kegan Paul, 1981.

Vicinus, Martha. *Independent Women: Work and Community for Single Women, 1850–1920.* Chicago: University of Chicago Press, 1985.

————, ed. *Suffer and Be Still: Women in the Victorian Age.* Bloomington: Indiana University Press, 1972.

————, ed. *A Widening Sphere: Changing Roles of Victorian Women.* Bloomington: Indiana University Press, 1977.

Waddington, Ivan. "General Practitioners and Consultants in Early Nineteenth-Century England: The Sociology of an Intra-Professional

Conflict." In John Woodward and David Richards, eds., *Health Care and Popular Medicine in Nineteenth Century England*. New York: Holmes and Meier, 1977.

―――. "The Role of the Hospital in the Development of Popular Medicine." *Sociology* 7 (1973): 211–25.

Walkowitz, Judith R. *Jack the Ripper's London*. Chicago: University of Chicago Press, forthcoming.

―――. *Prostitution and Victorian Society: Women, Class, and the State*. Cambridge: Cambridge University Press, 1980.

Webb, Igor. *From Custom to Capital: The English Novel and the Industrial Revolution*. Ithaca: Cornell University Press, 1981.

Weeks, Jeffrey. *Sex, Politics and Society: The Regulation of Sexuality since 1800*. New York: Longman, 1981.

―――. *Sexuality and Its Discontents: Meanings, Myths, and Modern Sexualities*. London: Routledge and Kegan Paul, 1985.

Welsh, Alexander. *The City of Dickens*. Oxford: Clarendon Press, 1971.

White, Hayden. "The Historical Text as Literary Artifact." In *Tropics of Discourse: Essays in Cultural Criticism*, pp. 81–100. Baltimore: Johns Hopkins University Press, 1978.

―――. "The Value of Narrativity in the Representation of Reality." *Critical Inquiry* 7 (1980): 5–27.

Whittaker, Elvi, and Virginia Oleson. "The Faces of Florence Nightingale: Functions of the Heroine Legend in an Occupational Sub-Culture." In Robert Dingwall and Jean McIntosh, eds., *Readings in the Sociology of Nursing*, pp. 19–35. Edinburgh and London: Churchill Livingston, 1978.

Wicke, Jennifer. *Advertising Fictions*. New York: Columbia University Press, forthcoming.

Wilding, Norman, and Philip Laundry. "Hansard." In *An Encyclopaedia of Parliament*, p. 255. London: Cassell, 1958.

Williams, Katherine. "Ideologies of Nursing: Their Meanings and Implications." In Robert Dingwall and Jean McIntosh, eds., *Readings in the Sociology of Nursing*, pp. 36–44. Edinburgh and London: Churchill Livingston, 1978.

Williams, Raymond. *Culture and Society, 1780–1950*. New York: Harper and Row, 1958.

―――. "Forms of English Fiction in 1848." In Frances Barker, Peter Hulme, Margaret Iversen, and Diana Loxley, eds., *Literature, Politics, and Theory. Papers from The Essex Conference, 1976–84*, pp. 1–16. New York: Methuen, 1986.

―――. *Keywords: A Vocabulary of Culture and Society*. New York: Oxford University Press, 1976.

―――. *Marxism and Literature*. Oxford: Oxford University Press, 1977.

Winnett, A. R. *The Church and Divorce*. London: A. R. Mowbray, 1968.

Wohl, Anthony S. *Endangered Lives: Public Health in Victorian Britain*. Cambridge: Harvard University Press, 1984.

————, ed. *The Victorian Family.* London: Croom Helm, 1978.

Woodham-Smith, Cecil. *Florence Nightingale, 1820–1910.* London: Constable, 1950.

Woodhouse, Margaret K. "The Marriage and Divorce Bill of 1857." *American Journal of Legal History* 3 (1959): 260–75.

Woodmansee, Martha. "The Genius and the Copyright: Economic and Legal Conditions of the Emergence of the 'Author.'" *Eighteenth-Century Studies* 17 (1983–84): 425–48.

Youngson, A. J. *The Scientific Revolution in Victorian Medicine.* New York: Holmes and Meier, 1979.

Index

Eastlake, Lady Elizabeth (née Rigby), 129–30, 132–36, 142, 145, 147, 148
Ellis, Havelock, 210 n. 26
English Woman's Journal, 124, 126, 150
Ether, 25, 26, 29, 30, 32, 38. *See also* Anesthesia; Chloroform

Falret, Jules, 46, 48
Farr, Dr. William, 180
Formalism, 16–17
Foucault, Michel, 17
Fowler, Orson S., 204 n. 12
Fraser's Magazine, 108, 158, 173. *See also* "Hints on the Modern Governess System"
Freud, Sigmund, 19, 172, 231 n. 39

Garrett, Elizabeth, 175
Gaskell, Peter: on female nature, 7; on home, 77; on woman's moral influence, 8
Germ theory, 180–81
Gilbert, Sandra M., 125
Gladstone, William Ewart, 61, 208 n. 11
Governess, 125, 126–49, 166, 177; and capitalism, 126, 132, 144; and class, 127, 128–29, 131, 132–35, 142, 146, 148, 159–60, 233 n. 9; and domestic ideal, 128, 131, 143–46, 148, 163; in *Jane Eyre,* 136–47; Lady Eastlake on, 132–36, 148; and lunatics, 14, 129–30, 131, 142, 143, 146; and the mother, 14, 127, 143–45, 235 n. 25; in novels, 126, 129, 136–47; plight of, 126–27, 129, 132, 144, 147, 159, 162–63; and prostitution, 14, 129, 131, 143, 145, 150; and sexuality, 12, 14, 128, 129–31, 135, 142, 145, 146, 163, 233 n. 13; and women's

work, 12, 126–27, 131, 144, 148–49, 150, 159, 162–63, 177
Governesses' Benevolent Institution, 126, 129, 132, 154, 163; activities of, 232 n. 2; history of, 232 n. 2
Gower, Dr. S., 210 n. 24
Gream, Dr. G. T., 33
Greenacre, James, 67, 86
Greg, W. R., 23; "Prostitution," 5–6; on sexual desire, 5–6, 224 n. 36; "Why Are Women Redundant?" 1–2, 4–5, 14, 15
Gregory, George, 39, 215 n. 56
Gregory, Samuel, 39
Gubar, Susan, 125

Hall, Catherine, 52
Herbert, Sidney, 167, 172
"Hints on the Modern Governess System," 129, 130, 131, 143, 147, 148–49
Holmes, Dr. Oliver Wendell, 46
Hysteria: and anesthesia, 30; and childbearing, 30, 37; and female physiology, 36, 37; and *Jane Eyre,* 141; problems posed by, 45–46; and sexual display, 30, 37, 46

Ideology, 1–23, 114, 141, 145, 149, 199–201; and the law, 65, 75–80; and literature, 123–24; and texts, 17–18. *See also* Domestic ideal; Symbolic economy; Women
Imperialism, 2; and the domestic ideal, 166, 186–97; and national character, 9, 197; and Nightingale, 186–97; and state formation, 195–96. *See also* India
India, 111, 165, 166, 200; and British imperialism, 194–97; and